Dan Dougherty

D0203269

Graph Drawing

Algorithms for the Visualization of Graphs

Giuseppe Di Battista
Dipartimento di Informatica e Automazione
Università degli Studi di Roma Tre

Peter Eades
Department of Computer Science
University of Newcastle

Roberto Tamassia
Department of Computer Science
Brown University

Ioannis G. Tollis
Department of Computer Science
The University of Texas at Dallas

An Alan R. Apt Book

PRENTICE HALL, *Upper Saddle River, New Jersey 07458*

Library of Congress Cataloging-in-Publication Data

Graph drawing: algorithms for the visualization of graphs /
    Giuseppe Di Battista . . . [et al.]
        p. cm.
    "An Alan R. Apt Book"
    Includes bibliographical references and index.
    ISBN: 0-13-301615-3 (alk. paper)
    1. Computer graphics. 2. Graph theory. I. Di Battista, Giuseppe.
T385.G6934   1999
511'.3—dc21   98-19177
                                                                 CIP

Publisher: Alan Apt
Editor: Laura Steele
Production Editor: Edward DeFelippis
Editor-In-Chief: Marcia Horton
Managing Editor: Eileen Clark
Assistant Vice President of Production and Manufacturing: David W. Riccardi
Art Director: Jayne Conte
Cover Designer: Anthony Gemmellaro
Copy Editor: Jerri Uzzo
Manufacturing Buyer: Pat Brown
Editorial Assistant: Kate Kaibni

©1999 by Prentice-Hall, Inc.
Simon & Schuster / A Viacom Company
Upper Saddle River, New Jersey 07458

All rights reserved. No part of this book may be
reproduced, in any form or by any means,
without permission in writing from the publisher.

The author and publisher of this book have used their best efforts in preparing this book. These efforts include the
development, research, and testing of the theories and programs to determine their effectiveness. The author and
publisher make no warranty of any kind, expressed or implied, with regard to these programs or the documentation
contained in this book. The author and publisher shall not be liable in any event for incidental or consequential
damages in connection with, or arising out of, the furnishing, performance, or use of these programs.

Printed in the United States of America

10 9 8 7 6 5 4 3 2 1

ISBN: 0-13-301615-3

Prentice-Hall International (UK) Limited, *London*
Prentice-Hall of Australia Pty. Limited, *Sydney*
Prentice-Hall Canada Inc., *Toronto*
Prentice-Hall Hispanoamericana, S.A., *Mexico*
Prentice-Hall of India Private Limited, *New Delhi*
Prentice-Hall of Japan, Inc., *Tokyo*
Simon & Schuster Asia Pte. Ltd., *Singapore*
Editora Prentice-Hall do Brasil, Ltda., *Rio de Janeiro*

Contents

iii

Preface

The visualization of complex conceptual structures is a key component of support tools for many applications in science and engineering. A graph is an abstract structure that is used to model information. Graphs are used to represent information that can be modeled as objects and connections between those objects. Hence, many information visualization systems require graphs to be drawn so that they are easy to read and understand. In this book, we describe algorithms for automatically generating clear and readable diagrams of complex conceptual structures.

Graph Drawing

Graph drawing addresses the problem of constructing geometric representations of graphs, networks, and related combinatorial structures. Geometric representations of graphs have been investigated by mathematicians for centuries, for visualization and intuition, as well as for the pure beauty of the interplay between graph theory and geometry. In the 1960s, computer scientists began to use graph drawings as diagrams to assist with the understanding of software. Knuth's 1963 paper on drawing flowcharts [Knu63] was perhaps the first paper to present an algorithm for drawing a graph for visualization purposes.

Today, the automatic generation of drawings of graphs finds many applications. Examples include software engineering (data flow diagrams, subroutine-call graphs, program nesting trees, object-oriented class hierarchies), databases (entity-relationship diagrams), information systems (organization charts), real-time systems (Petri nets, state-transition diagrams), decision support systems (PERT networks, activity trees), VLSI (circuit schematics), artificial intelligence (knowledge-representation diagrams), and logic programming (SLD-trees). Further applications can be found in other science and engineering disciplines, such as medical science (concept lattices), biology (evolutionary trees), chemistry (molecular drawings), civil engineering (floorplan maps), and cartography (map schematics).

Because of the combinatorial and geometric nature of the problems investigated, and the wide range of the application domains, research in graph drawing has been conducted within several diverse areas, including discrete mathematics (topological graph theory, geometric graph theory, order theory), algorithmics (graph algorithms, data structures, computational geometry, VLSI), and human-computer interaction (visual languages, graphical user interfaces, software visualization). A bibliography on graph drawing algorithms [DETT94] cites more than 300 papers. In addition, a large body of related nonalgorithmic literature exists on geometric graph theory, topological graph theory, and order theory.

Various graphic standards are used for drawing graphs. Usually, vertices are represented by symbols such as points or boxes, and edges are represented by simple open Jordan curves connecting the symbols that represent the associated vertices. However, the graphic standards may vary depending upon the application. For example, mathematicians seem to prefer straight-line drawings, where edges are straight-line segments, while circuit and database designers tend to use orthogonal drawings, where edges consist of horizontal and vertical segments. Within a graphic standard, a graph has infinitely many different drawings. The usefulness of a drawing of a graph depends on its readability, that is, the capability of conveying the meaning of the graph quickly and clearly. Readability issues can be expressed by means of aesthetic criteria, such as the minimization of crossings between edges, and the display of symmetries.

When drawing a graph, we would like to take into account a variety of aesthetic criteria. For example, planarity and the display of symmetries are often highly desirable in visualization applications. In general, in order to improve the readability of a drawing, it is important to keep the number of bends and crossings low. Also, to avoid wasting space on a page or a computer screen, it is important to keep the area of the drawing small, subject to resolution rules. In this scenario, many graph drawing problems can be formalized as multi-objective optimization problems (e.g., construct a drawing with minimum area and minimum number of bends and crossings). Trade-offs are often necessary in order to solve these problems.

The purpose of this book is to describe fundamental algorithmic techniques for constructing drawings of graphs.

Organization of the Book

This book is organized as follows:

In Chapter 1, we review the terminology of graphs and their drawings.

Chapter 2 presents general graph drawing methods which use the algorithms presented in the following chapters as building blocks. It provides guidelines for employing the technical material of the book in the design of graph drawing algorithms and systems.

Divide and conquer is an evergreen paradigm in computer science. In Chapter 3, we apply this technique to draw trees and series-parallel digraphs. Further, we show how to test the planarity of a graph using the divide and conquer paradigm.

Chapter 4 presents techniques for constructing various types of drawings of planar graphs. These techniques can also be used for drawing nonplanar graphs by means of a preliminary planarization step.

In Chapter 5, we present methods based on network flow. These methods construct a planar orthogonal drawing of an embedded planar graph, with the minimum number of bends.

Flow techniques are used again in Chapter 6 to address the upward planarity testing problem for digraphs. The study of upward planarity has fascinating connections with fundamental graph-theoretic and order-theoretic properties.

Incremental techniques are presented in Chapter 7. We apply these techniques to the graph planarization problem, and also use them to design algorithms suitable for interactive systems.

In Chapter 8, we focus on constructing orthogonal grid drawings of nonplanar graphs. The presented techniques are based first on orienting a given graph, and then drawing it one vertex at a time, following the order of the orientation.

Chapter 9 presents the hierarchical approach for creating polyline drawings of digraphs with vertices arranged in horizontal layers. This approach is highly intuitive and can be applied to any digraph.

Chapter 10 presents several techniques that take a graph as input and simulate a system of forces reflecting user preferences. A straight-line drawing results from an equilibrium configuration of the force system.

In Chapter 11, we present techniques for investigating the intrinsic limits of graph drawing algorithms, both in terms of the quality of the output and in terms of computational resources required.

In Appendix A, we tabulate upper and lower bounds on properties of drawings of graphs, and discuss trade-offs between such properties.

Use of the book

The reader is expected to be familiar with basic algorithms and data structures. This book is primarily written for three audiences.

- It can be used as a text in an advanced undergraduate or graduate course in graph drawing. It can also provide material for courses that devote part of their attention to graph drawing; these include computational geometry, graph algorithms, and information visualization.

- It provides researchers with techniques that cover the main themes of the graph drawing area. Also, the chapters are relatively self contained, allowing for independent reading.

- Engineers involved in creating user interfaces can use this book as a fundamental source for effective and practical graph drawing methods.

Most chapters end with several exercises and problems. Many of them are devoted simply to testing the level of knowledge of the material contained in the chapter. Some exercises require more thought, and some are suitable for advanced courses.

Acknowledgements

In 1987, when we started planning to write this book, we had no idea that research in graph drawing would grow as fast as we have seen in recent years. We also had no idea of the effort required to write a systematic description of such a dynamic field.

Many people gave us feedback on earlier versions of this book. Special thanks go to: Juergen Branke, Stina Bridgeman, Isabel Cruz, Walter Didimo, Joel Fenwick, Arne Frick, Tom Frisinger, Patrick Garvan, Mike Goodrich, Seokhee Hong, Konstantinos Kakoulis, Michael Kaufmann, Joseph LaViola, Xuemin Lin, Giuseppe Liotta, Brian Lucena, Kazuo Misue, Justin Monti, Petra Mutzel, Achilleas Papakostas, Maurizio Patrignani, Maurizio Pizzonia, Aaron Quigley, Galina Shubina, Janet Six, Robin Stacey, Jennifer Stewart, Chensu Sun, Jiankuan Sun, David Thomson, Francesco Vargiu, Luca Vismara, Paola Vocca, Sue Whitesides, and Weisheng Xu.

We acknowledge the support received from the Australian Research Council, the Esprit Project Alcom-IT, the National Institute of Standards and Technology, the National Science Foundation, the Texas Advanced Research

Program, the US Army Research Office, Fujitsu Laboratories, Brown University, the University of Newcastle, the University of Texas at Dallas, and the Third University of Rome.

Finally, this work would not have been possible without the encouragement and support of Alexandra, Caitriona, Cristina, Elvira, Isabel, Manfredo, Patrick, Pietro, Rossana, and Shelly.

Giuseppe Di Battista,
Peter Eades,
Roberto Tamassia,
Ioannis G. Tollis.

Chapter 1

Graphs and Their Drawings

Relational structures, consisting of a set of entities and relationships between those entities, are ubiquitous in computer science. Such structures are usually modeled as *graphs*: the entities are *vertices*, and the relationships are *edges*. For example, most tools in software engineering use graphs to model the dependency relationships between modules in a large program. A module is represented as a vertex in a graph, and the dependency of module *a* on module *b* is represented by an edge from *a* to *b*. These graphs are typically drawn as diagrams with text at the vertices and line segments joining the vertices as edges. The example in Figure 1.1 represents the dependencies between some of the modules in `Xwindows`. In the example in Figure 1.2, the vertices represent documents in a hypertext system and the edges represent hyperlinks between the documents.

Visualizations of relational structures are only useful to the degree that the associated diagrams effectively convey information to the people that use them. A good diagram helps the reader understand the system, but a poor diagram can be confusing and misleading.

For example, consider the two diagrams in Figure 1.3. Both diagrams represent a simple class hierarchy; vertices represent classes of geometric shapes, and edges describe the *is-a relation*. Here each vertex represents a class, and a directed edge between two vertices represents the class-subclass relationship. Figure 1.3.a is more difficult to follow than Figure 1.3.b. This book is about *graph drawing algorithms*, that is, methods to produce graph drawings which are easy to follow.

The main purpose of this introductory chapter is to define the basic concepts for graphs and graph drawings. Related material is available in many textbooks:

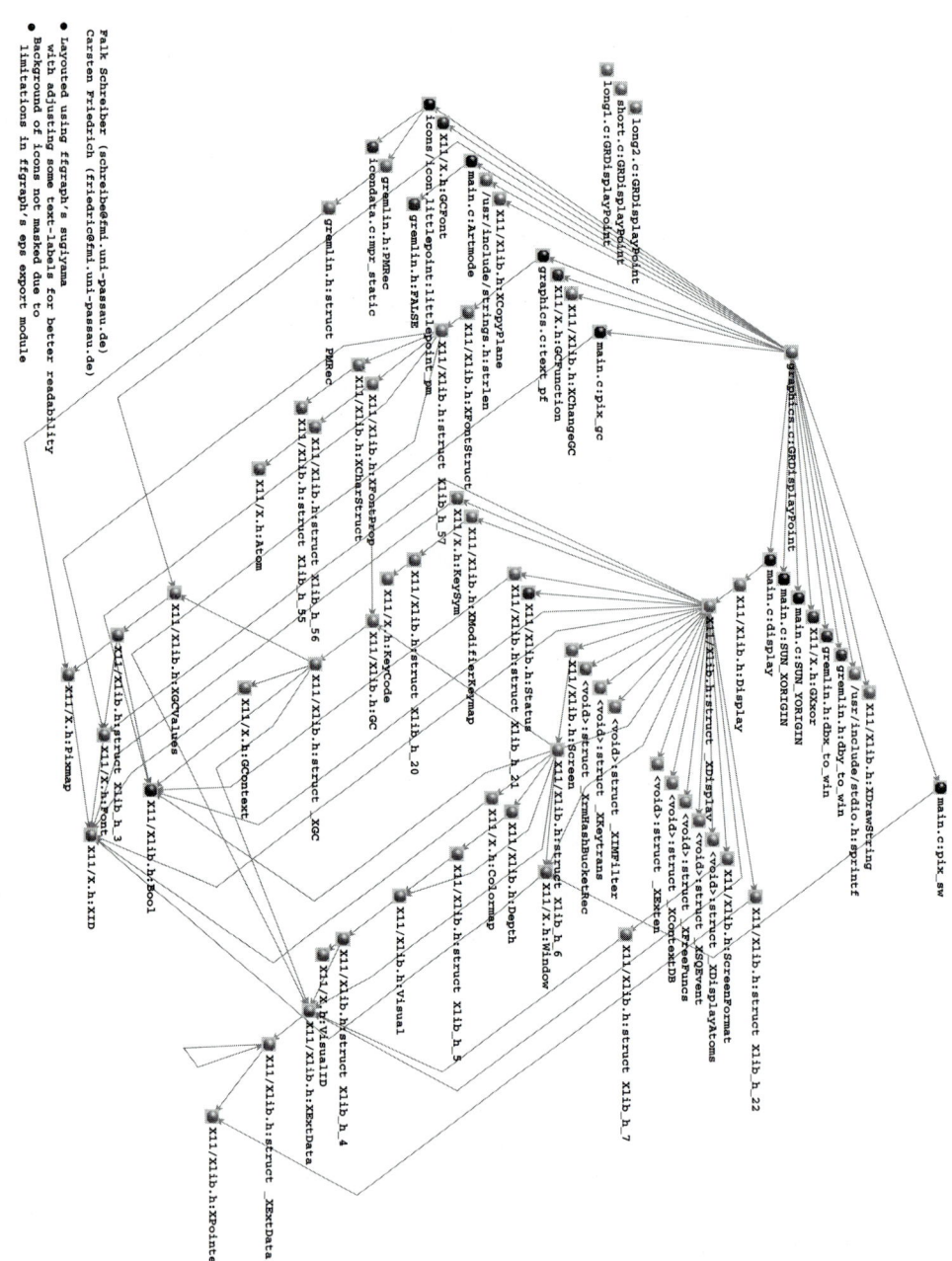

Figure 1.1: Dependency graph for some of the modules of Xwindows. (Courtesy of F. Schreiber and C. Friedrich.)

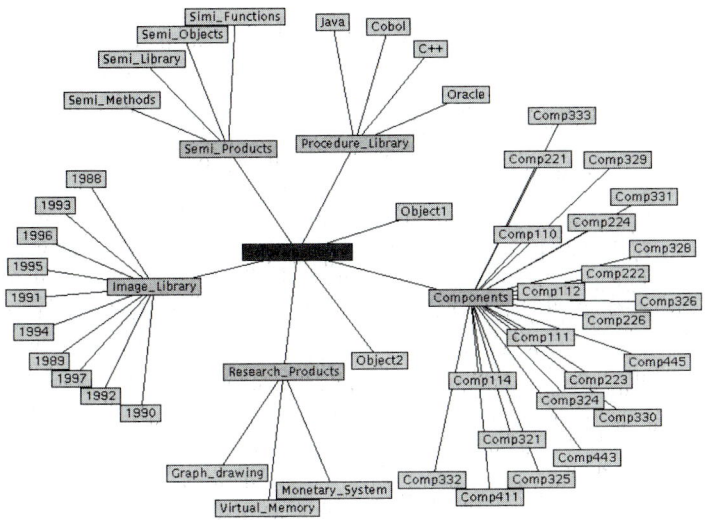

Figure 1.2: A graph representing hypertext documents and links between them. (Courtesy of M. Huang.)

- Graph theory is described in [BM76, Har72].

- Graph algorithms are illustrated in [Eve79, Gib80, Meh84, NC88, Tar83].

- There are many textbooks describing basic data structures and algorithms, for example, [CLR90, GT98]. Also, a reference book for computational complexity is [GJ79].

- Computational geometry provides a good background for many graph drawing methods (see [PS85]).

A *graph* $G = (V, E)$ consists of a finite set V of *vertices* and a finite multiset E of *edges*, that is, unordered pairs (u, v) of vertices. The vertices of a graph are sometimes called *nodes*; edges are sometimes called *links*, *arcs*, or *connections*.

An edge (u, v) with $u = v$ is a *self-loop*. An edge which occurs more than once in E is a *multiple edge*. A *simple graph* has no self-loops and no multiple edges. Most of this book deals with simple graphs, and unless otherwise specified, we assume that graphs are simple.

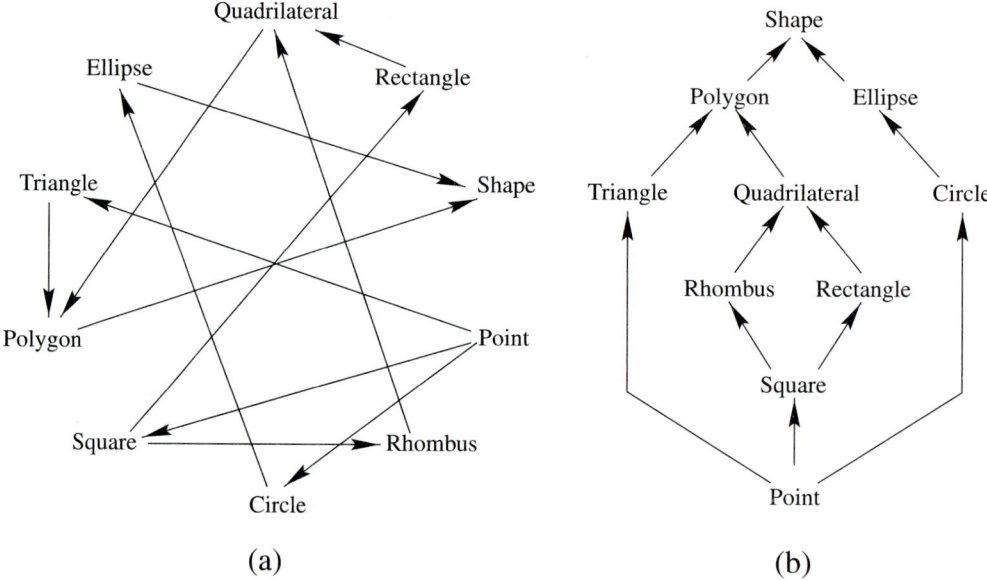

Figure 1.3: Two drawings of a class hierarchy.

The *end-vertices* of an edge $e = (u, v)$ are u and v; we say that u and v are *adjacent* to each other and e is *incident* to u and v. The *neighbors* of v are its adjacent vertices. The *degree* of v is the number of its neighbors.

A *directed graph* (or *digraph*) is defined similarly to a graph, except that the elements of E, called *directed edges*, are ordered pairs of vertices. The directed edge (u, v) is an *outgoing edge* of u and an *incoming edge* of v. Vertices without outgoing (resp. incoming) edges are called *sinks* (resp. *sources*). The *indegree* (resp. *outdegree*) of a vertex is the number of its incoming (resp. outgoing) edges.

A (directed) *path* in a (directed) graph $G = (V, E)$ is a sequence $(v_1, v_2, \ldots, v_h)$ of distinct vertices of G, such that $(v_i, v_{i+1}) \in E$ for $1 \leq i \leq h - 1$. A (directed) path is a (directed) *cycle* if $(v_h, v_1) \in E$. A directed graph is *acyclic* if it has no directed cycles.

An edge (u, v) of a digraph is *transitive* if there is a directed path from u to v that does not contain the edge (u, v). The *transitive closure* G' of a digraph G has an edge (u, v) for every path from u to v in G. In many applications, a digraph conveys the same information as its transitive closure. For example, since class inheritance is transitive, the class diagram in Figure 1.4 contains the same information as the one in Figure 1.3. However, as Figure 1.4 shows, transitive edges can clutter a graph drawing and cause confusion. In general, for many digraphs it is better to draw a *reduced digraph* (also called *transitive reduction*), that is, a digraph with no transitive edges. Figure 1.3 shows the reduced digraph of the digraph in Figure 1.4. Many of the algorithms in this book deal with reduced digraphs.

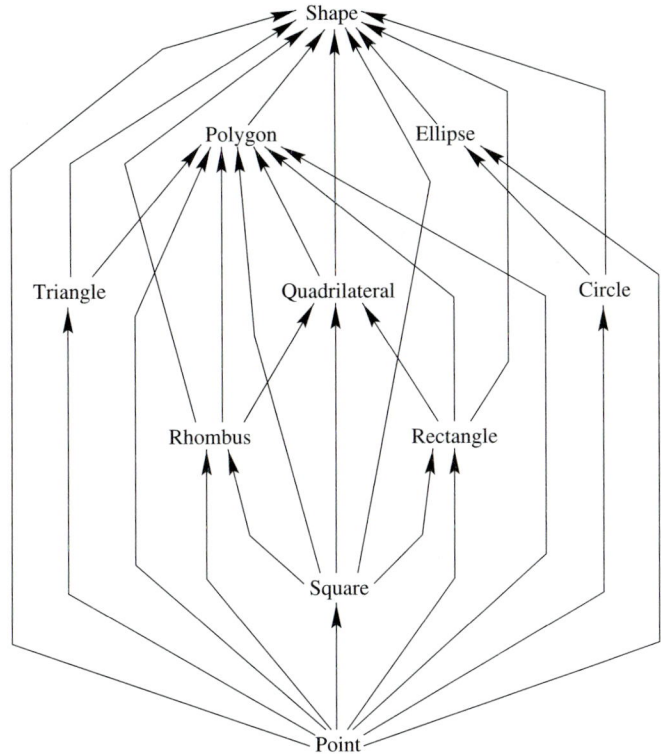

Figure 1.4: The transititive closure of the class hierarchy in Figure 1.3.

A graph $G' = (V', E')$, such that $V' \subseteq V$ and $E' \subseteq E \cap (V' \times V')$, is a *subgraph* of graph $G = (V, E)$. If $E' = E \cap (V' \times V')$ then G' is *induced* by V'.

A graph $G = (V, E)$ with n vertices may be described by a $n \times n$ *adjacency matrix* A whose rows and columns correspond to vertices, with $A_{uv} = 1$ if $(u, v) \in E$ and $A_{uv} = 0$ otherwise. Table 1.1 gives a description of a graph (let us call it G_1) as an adjacency matrix.

Another way to describe a graph is by giving a list L_u of edges incident to vertex u for each $u \in V$. A description of a directed graph (let us call it G_2) in this format appears in Table 1.2.

	1	2	3	4	5
1	0	1	1	1	1
2	1	0	1	1	0
3	1	1	0	1	0
4	1	1	1	0	1
5	1	0	0	1	0

Table 1.1: An adjacency matrix for graph G_1 shown in Figure 1.5.a.

L_1	$(1,2)$, $(1,5)$
L_2	$(2,3)$
L_3	$(3,4)$
L_4	$(4,5)$, $(4,6)$
L_5	$(5,2)$
L_6	$(6,3)$

Table 1.2: Adjacency lists for digraph G_2 shown in Figure 1.5.b.

In its simplest form, a *drawing* Γ of a graph (digraph) G is a function which maps each vertex v to a distinct point $\Gamma(v)$ and each edge (u,v) to a simple open Jordan curve $\Gamma(u,v)$, with endpoints $\Gamma(u)$ and $\Gamma(v)$. A directed edge is usually drawn as an arrow. Figure 1.5 contains a drawing of graph G_1 whose adjacency matrix is in Table 1.1, and a drawing of digraph G_2 whose adjacency lists are in Table 1.2.

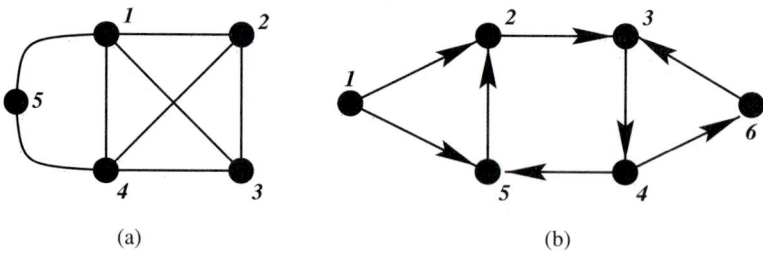

(a)   (b)

Figure 1.5: (a) A drawing of graph G_1. (b) A drawing of directed graph G_2.

At this stage, it is important to note that a graph and its drawing are quite different objects. In general, a graph has many different drawings: for example, Figure 1.6 contains four drawings of the same graph. Nevertheless, it is common to use the same terminology for an edge (u,v) and the drawing

$\Gamma(u, v)$ of the edge. The statement "the edge (u, v) is a straight line" is usually interpreted as "the image $\Gamma(u, v)$ of the edge (u, v) is a straight line."

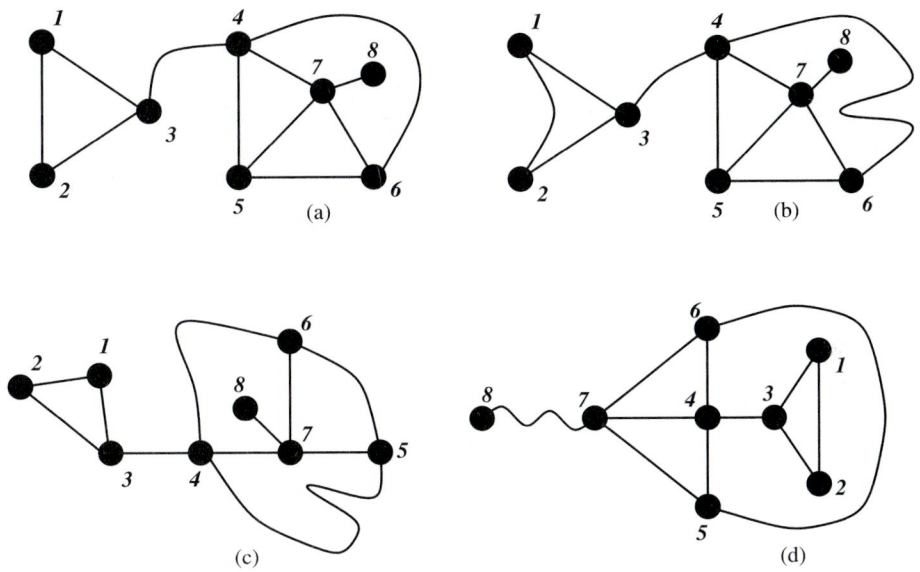

Figure 1.6: Four planar drawings of the same graph.

A drawing Γ is *planar* if no two distinct edges intersect. A graph is *planar* if it admits a planar drawing. All the drawings in Figure 1.6 are planar.

Planar graphs play an important role in graph drawing for three reasons. First, edge crossings reduce readability (see [BPCJ95, PCJ96, Pur97]). Second, the theory of planar graphs has a long history in graph theory (see, for example, [NC88]). This well-developed theory can be used to greatly simplify topological concepts that otherwise would prove cumbersome. Third, planar graphs are "sparse": Euler's formula [BM76] implies that a simple planar graph with n vertices has at most $3n - 6$ edges.

A planar drawing partitions the plane into topologically connected regions called *faces*. The unbounded face is usually called the *external face*. A planar drawing determines a circular ordering on the neighbors of each vertex v according to the clockwise sequence of the incident edges around v. Two planar drawings of the same graph G are *equivalent* if they determine the same circular orderings of the neighbor sets. A (*planar*) *embedding* is an equivalence class of planar drawings and is described by the circular order of the neighbors of each vertex. An *embedded graph* is a graph with a specified embedding. Note that a planar graph may have an exponential number of embeddings.

As an example, the graph drawings in Figure 1.6.a, 1.6.b, and 1.6.c, all have the same embedding. However, Figure 1.6.d has a different embedding.

The *dual graph* G^* of an embedding of a planar graph G has a vertex for each face of G, and an edge (f, g) between two faces f and g for each edge that is shared by f and g. A planar graph and its dual graph are shown in Figure 1.7. In a sense, the dual graph G^* captures the combinatorial information in the embedding. If two drawings have the same embedding then they have the same dual graph. Note that a dual graph may have self-loops and multiple edges.

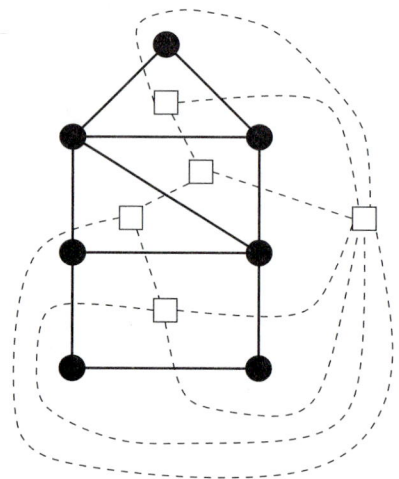

Figure 1.7: Dual graph (shown with boxes for vertices and dashed lines for edges) of an embedding of a planar graph.

A graph is *connected* if there is a path between u and v for each pair (u, v) of vertices. A maximal connected subgraph of a graph G is a *connected component* of G.

The notions of planarity and connectivity have an interesting interplay in graph drawing, and we now review some stronger notions of connectivity.

A *cutvertex* in a graph G is a vertex whose removal disconnects G. A connected graph with no cutvertices is *biconnected*. The maximal biconnected subgraphs of a graph are its *blocks* (sometimes called *biconnected components*). Many algorithms in graph drawing assume that the input graph is biconnected. This is seldom a serious restriction because it is relatively easy to decompose a graph into its blocks (see [Eve79]). For example, a graph is planar if and only if its blocks are planar. Biconnectivity notions are illustrated in Figure 1.8.

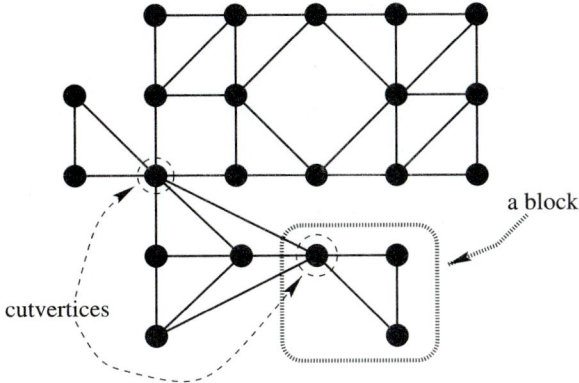

Figure 1.8: Cutvertices and blocks.

A pair (u, v) of vertices in a biconnected graph G is a *separating pair* if the removal of u and v disconnects G. A separating pair is illustrated in Figure 1.9. A biconnected graph without separating pairs is *triconnected*. Triconnectivity is an important concept for geometry and topology. The interplay between connectivity, geometry, topology, and planarity is illustrated by two important examples:

- The skeleton of a convex polyhedron is a planar triconnected graph.

- A planar triconnected graph has a unique embedding, up to a reversal of the circular ordering of the neighbors of each vertex.

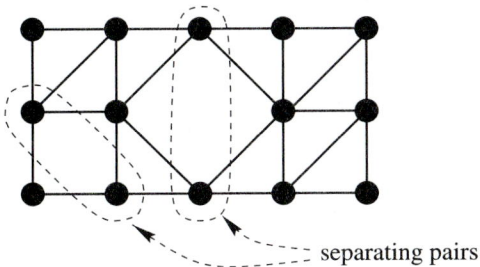

Figure 1.9: Separating pairs.

Finally, note that for each directed graph, we can construct the *underlying undirected graph* by forgetting the directions of the edges. This allows the terminology of graphs to be applied to digraphs.

Chapter 2

Paradigms for Graph Drawing

This chapter overviews general techniques for graph drawing, which use the algorithms presented in the following chapters as building blocks, and provides guidelines for employing the technical material of this book in the design of graph drawing algorithms and systems.

In Section 2.1, we begin by defining fundamental issues in graph drawing: the conventions used when drawing a graph, the æsthetic criteria for a readable drawing, and the constraints that a drawing may be required to satisfy. Section 2.2 shows how graph drawing algorithms have to consider a priority among the desired features of a drawing. Sections 2.3–2.8 describe several approaches to the design of graph drawing algorithms. Each approach is characterized by a sequence of elementary algorithmic steps. Finally, Section 2.9 describes a general framework for graph drawing, where each approach can be seen as a path in an inheritance hierarchy of graph classes. This framework can be used as a model for a general graph drawing system (see [BDL95, DLV95, DGST90, BBDL91]).

2.1 Parameters of Graph Drawing Methods

The obvious input to a graph drawing algorithm is a graph G that needs to be drawn. Quite often, to draw G, it is important to take some combinatorial properties of G into account. For example, we may know that G is directed and acyclic, or that it is a tree, or that it is planar. More generally, we often know the *class of graphs* to which G belongs. This knowledge is important for at least two reasons.

- Several graph drawing algorithms work only (or work better) on graphs belonging to specific classes.

- The user often wants the drawing of G to illustrate the combinatorial properties of G. For example, if G is an acyclic digraph, then it may be important to draw all the edges following the same direction, to emphasize the absence of cycles.

Thus the class of the input graph is an essential parameter of a graph drawing methodology.

The need for another kind of parameter arises from observing that "the best" drawing of a graph may not exist. Human perception of the same drawing changes from individual to individual, and different application domains require different kinds of drawings. Therefore another essential parameter of a graph drawing methodology is the particular environment in which it will be used. Actually, words like "application domain" or "environment" are too abstract to be effectively used in our algorithmic framework. Thus we need more specific concepts to describe the requirements of a nice drawing. For this purpose, we introduce three important graph drawing concepts. Namely, we describe the concept of *drawing convention*, the concept of *aesthetic*, and the concept of *constraint*.

2.1.1   Drawing Conventions

A *drawing convention* is a basic rule that the drawing *must* satisfy to be admissible. For example, in drawing data flow diagrams for a software engineering application, we can adopt the convention of representing all the vertices as boxes and all the edges as polygonal chains consisting of horizontal and vertical segments. A drawing convention of a real-life application can be very complex and can involve many details of the drawing. A list of widely used drawing conventions is given below (see Figures 2.1 and 2.2):

Polyline Drawing: Each edge is drawn as a polygonal chain (Figure 2.1.a).

Straight-line Drawing: Each edge is drawn as a straight line segment (Figure 2.1.b).

Orthogonal Drawing: Each edge is drawn as a polygonal chain of alternating horizontal and vertical segments (Figure 2.1.c).

Grid Drawing: Vertices, crossings, and edge bends have integer coordinates (Figure 2.1.d).

Planar Drawing: No two edges cross (Figure 2.2.a).

Upward (resp. downward) Drawing: For acyclic digraphs, each edge is
drawn as a curve monotonically nondecreasing (resp. nonincreasing)
in the vertical direction (Figure 2.2.b). In particular, a drawing is
strictly upward (*strictly downward*) if each edge is drawn as a curve
strictly increasing (strictly decreasing) in the vertical direction.

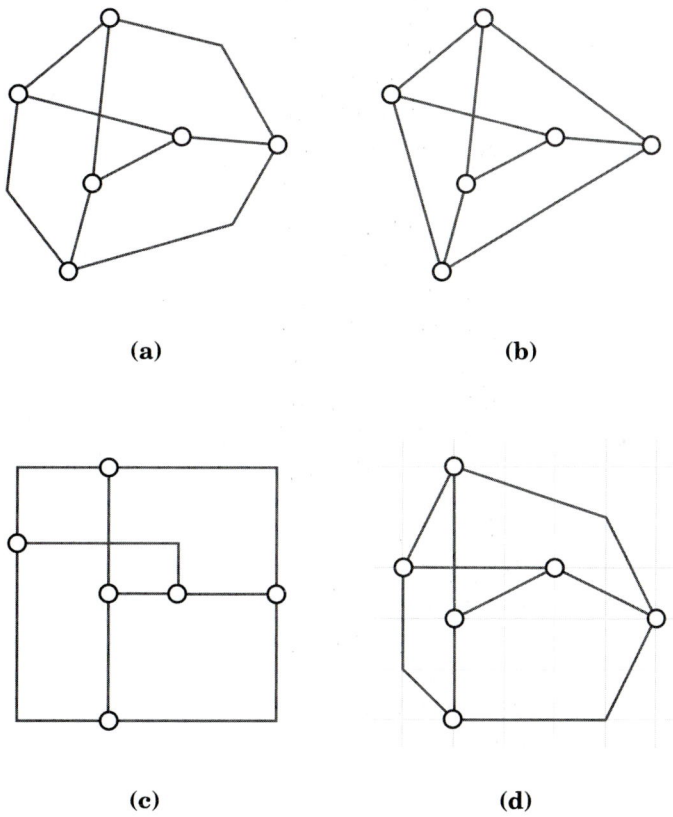

(a)   (b)

(c)   (d)

Figure 2.1: Drawings of the same graph: (a) polyline; (b) straight-line;
(c) orthogonal; (d) polyline grid.

Straight-line and orthogonal drawings are special cases of polyline drawings. Polyline drawings provide great flexibility since they can approximate
drawings with curved edges. However, edges with more than two or three
bends may be difficult to follow by eye. Straight-line drawings are common
in graph theory books and papers. Orthogonal drawings are widely used

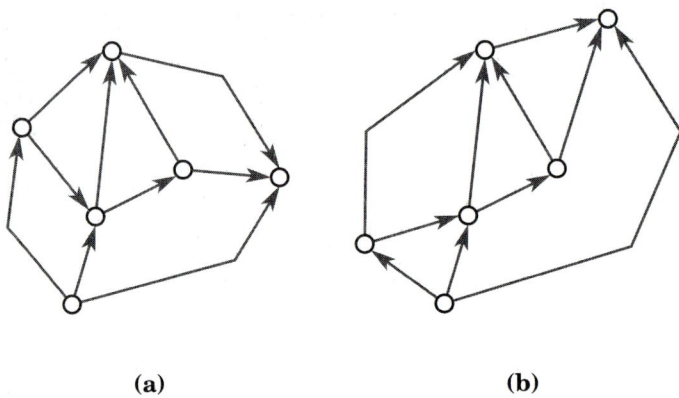

(a)   **(b)**

Figure 2.2: Drawings of the same digraph: (a) planar polyline; (b) strictly upward planar polyline.

in circuit schematics and software engineering diagrams (see Figure 2.3). Planar drawings are aesthetically appealing (see Section 2.1.2) although not every graph admits such a drawing. Acyclic digraphs representing hierarchical structures (e.g., PERT diagrams and class inheritance diagrams) are frequently drawn upward.

2.1.2   Aesthetics

Aesthetics specify graphic properties of the drawing that we would like to apply, *as much as possible*, to achieve readability. Commonly adopted aesthetics (see, e.g., the studies in [BFN85, PCJ96, STT81]) include:

***Crossings*:** Minimization of the total number of crossings between edges. Ideally, we would like to have a planar drawing, but not every graph admits one.

***Area*:** Minimization of the area of the drawing. The ability to construct area-efficient drawings is essential in practical visualization applications, where saving screen space is of utmost importance. This aesthetic is meaningful only if the drawing convention adopted prevents drawings from being arbitrarily scaled down (e.g., grid drawing, or straight-line drawing where any two vertices have distance at least one). The area of a drawing can be formally defined in different ways. For example, we can define it as the area of the smallest convex poly-

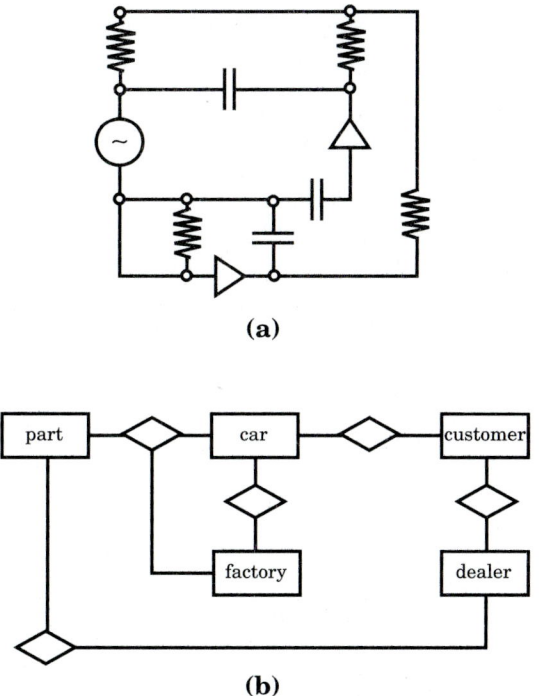

(a)

(b)

Figure 2.3: Examples of planar orthogonal drawings: (a) circuit schematics; (b) entity-relationship diagram.

gon covering the drawing (convex hull), or as the area of the smallest rectangle with horizontal and vertical sides covering the drawing.

Total Edge Length: Minimization of the sum of the lengths of the edges. This aesthetic is meaningful only if the drawing convention adopted prevents drawings from being arbitrarily scaled down.

Maximum Edge Length: Minimization of the maximum length of an edge. This aesthetic is meaningful only if the drawing convention adopted prevents drawings from being arbitrarily scaled down.

Uniform Edge Length: Minimization of the variance of the lengths of the edges.

Total Bends: Minimization of the total number of bends along the edges. This aesthetic is especially important for orthogonal drawings, while it is trivially satisfied by straight-line drawings.

Maximum Bends: Minimization of the maximum number of bends on an edge.

Uniform Bends: Minimization of the variance of the number of bends on the edges.

Angular Resolution: Maximization of the smallest angle between two edges incident on the same vertex. This aesthetic is especially relevant for straight-line drawings.

Aspect Ratio: Minimization of the aspect ratio of the drawing, which is defined as the ratio of the length of the longest side to the length of the shortest side of the smallest rectangle with horizontal and vertical sides covering the drawing. A drawing with high aspect-ratio may not be conveniently placed on a workstation screen, even if it has modest area. Hence it is important to keep the aspect-ratio small. Ideally, we would like to obtain small area for any aspect-ratio in a given range. This would provide the flexibility of fitting drawings in arbitrarily shaped windows.

Symmetry: Display the symmetries of the graph in the drawing. This aesthetic can be further formalized by introducing a mathematical model of symmetries in graphs and drawings (see, e.g., [Ead88, LNS85, MAC+95]).

The above aesthetics are naturally associated with optimization problems. However, most of these problems are computationally hard (see Section A.6). Thus many approximation strategies and heuristics have been devised.

2.1.3 Constraints

While drawing conventions and aesthetics are general rules and criteria that refer to the entire graph and to the entire drawing, *constraints* refer to specific subgraphs and subdrawings. For example, we may want to draw a PERT diagram such that the edges representing the activities of a given critical path are aligned, or we may want to draw a data flow diagram such that the vertices representing interfaces are placed on the outer boundary of the drawing.

Constraints commonly used in visualization applications include (see also [KMS94, TDB88]):

Center: Place a given vertex close to the center of the drawing.

External: Place a given vertex on the outer boundary of the drawing.

Cluster: Place a given subset of vertices close together.

Left-right (top-bottom) Sequence: Draw a given path horizontally aligned from left to right (vertically aligned from top to bottom).

Shape: Draw a given subgraph with a predefined "shape."

The graph drawing requirements of an application domain can be modeled in terms of a drawing convention, a set of aesthetics, and a set of constraints. These are fundamental parameters for graph drawing methodologies.

2.1.4 Efficiency

Finally, an important parameter of a graph drawing algorithm is its computational *efficiency*. Interactive applications require real-time response, even for large drawings. Hence efficiency is a crucial issue for any practical graph drawing technique.

2.2 Precedence Among Aesthetics

Most graph drawing methodologies are based on the following two simple observations:

- Aesthetics often conflict with each other. Thus tradeoffs are unavoidable.

- Even if the adopted aesthetics do not conflict, it is often algorithmically difficult to deal with all of them at the same time.

For example, suppose that the orthogonal grid drawing convention is adopted. Figure 2.4 shows two drawings of the same graph, one minimizing the number of bends and the other minimizing the number of crossings. For this graph, there is no orthogonal grid drawing that minimizes both.

Figure 2.5 shows six different straight-line drawings of the cube graph. Drawings (a) and (b) are planar, while the others are nonplanar. Depending on the specific definition of area adopted (area of convex hull or area of covering rectangle), the area of drawing (a) is larger than or equal to the

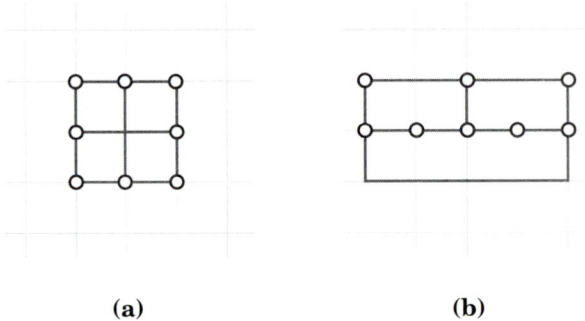

(a)   **(b)**

Figure 2.4: Two orthogonal grid drawings of the same graph: (a) with the minimum number of bends; (b) with the minimum number of crossings.

area of drawing (b). Drawing (a) is "more symmetric" than drawing (b). Among the nonplanar drawings (c)–(f), only drawings (c) and (d) are grid drawings, since the crossings in drawings (e) and (f) do not have integer coordinates. Drawing (f) minimizes the area of the convex hull over all straight-line drawings with vertices placed at integer coordinates. However, this drawing is clearly aesthetically unpleasing. Drawings (c) and (e) satisfy external constraints for all the vertices and visually depict the existence of a Hamiltonian cycle (simple cycle traversing all the vertices). Perhaps the most satisfying drawing is (d) because it looks like the projection of a three-dimensional cube.

From the above discussion, it follows that most graph drawing methodologies establish a precedence relation among aesthetics. Such a precedence relation is suitable for certain applications and less suitable for others. The approaches presented in the literature usually divide the graph drawing process into a sequence of algorithmic steps, each one targeted to satisfy a certain subclass of aesthetics. The remainder of this chapter describes the most popular of these methodologies.

2.3   The Topology-Shape-Metrics Approach

Orthogonal drawings are extensively used in real-life applications. For example, entity-relationship and data flow diagrams, well known in information systems, databases, and software engineering areas, are quite often represented by orthogonal drawings. The topology-shape-metrics approach (originally proposed in [BNT86, Tam87, TDB88]) has been devised to con-

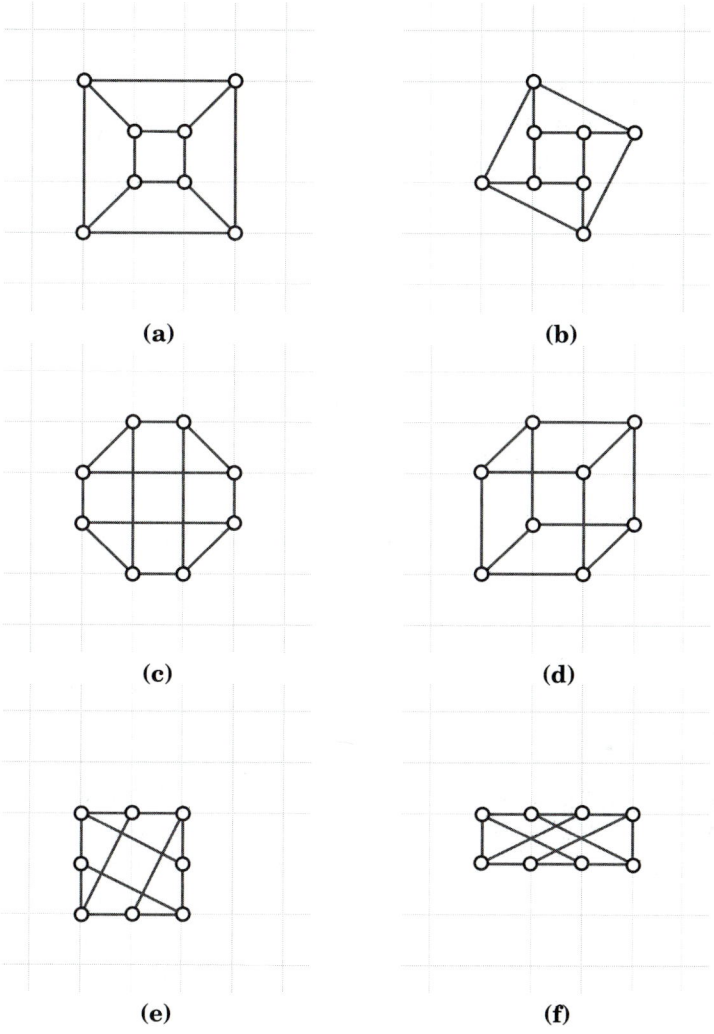

Figure 2.5: Six straight-line grid drawings of the cube graph.

struct orthogonal grid drawings, and allows homogeneous treatment of a wide range of aesthetics and constraints.

The basic idea of the approach is that an orthogonal drawing is characterized by three fundamental properties, defined in terms of the equivalence classes they establish among orthogonal drawings of the same graph:

- *Topology*: Two orthogonal drawings have the same topology if one can be obtained from the other by means of a continuous deformation that does not alter the sequences of edges contouring the faces of the drawing.

- *Shape*: Two orthogonal drawings have the same shape if they have the same topology, and one can be obtained from the other by modifying only the lengths of the segments that compose the orthogonal chains representing the edges, without changing the angles formed by them.

- *Metrics*: Two orthogonal drawings have the same metrics if they are congruent, up to a translation and/or a rotation.

Each one of the above properties provides a description of the drawing that is a refinement of the previous one. Namely, two drawings with the same metrics also have the same shape, and two drawings with the same shape also have the same topology. Note that the above concepts can be used to characterize not only orthogonal drawings, but more generally polyline drawings.

The hierarchical relationship between topology, shape, and metrics suggests a stepwise generation of the drawing, where at each step an intermediate representation is produced. Such a general strategy is depicted in Figure 2.6.

- The *planarization step* determines the topology of the drawing, which is described by a planar embedding. In this phase, the problem is to reduce the number of edge crossings as much as possible. This problem has been intensively investigated in the literature [CNS79, JLM97, JM96, JTS86, Kan92b, NT84]. An example of a technique that is used in practice is the following: a maximal planar subgraph of the given graph is extracted; the "nonplanar" edges are successively reinserted one by one, minimizing the number of crossings caused at each insertion. Each crossing is represented by a dummy vertex so that the final topology is planar.

- Given a topology, the *orthogonalization step* determines the shape of the drawing. It outputs an orthogonal representation of the graph. In an orthogonal representation, vertices do not have coordinates and each edge (u, v) is equipped with a list of angles. Such a list describes the bends that the orthogonal line representing (u, v) will have in the final drawing. In the following chapters, we will see how an orthogonal representation can be computed with a trade-off between number of bends and time complexity.

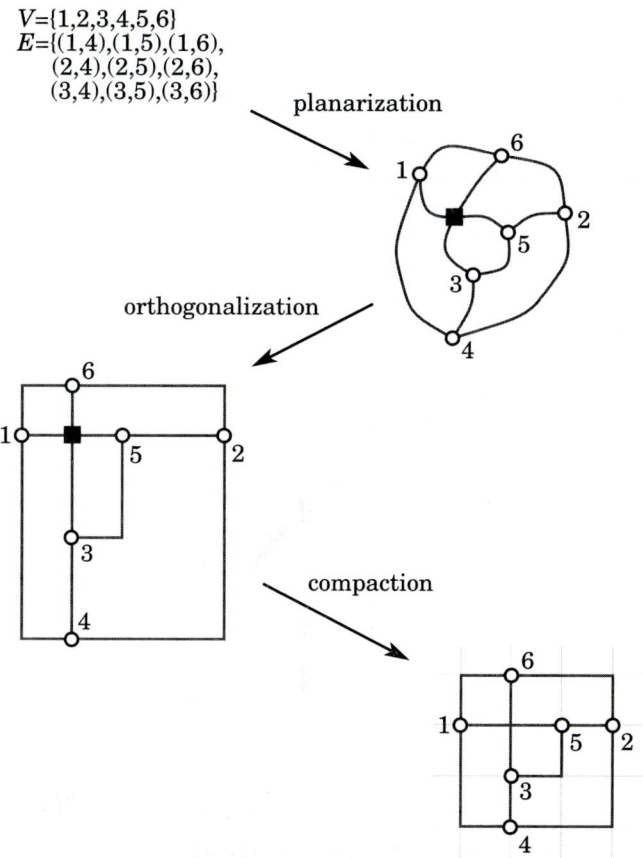

Figure 2.6: The topology-shape-metrics approach for orthogonal grid drawings. The dummy vertex introduced by the planarization step is represented by a square.

- Given an orthogonal representation, the *compaction step* determines the final coordinates of the vertices and of the edge bends. In this phase, the problem is usually one of producing a drawing with the minimum possible area. Also, dummy vertices introduced in the planarization step are removed.

Observe that the above strategy determines an implicit order of importance among the aesthetics. Namely, the number of bends of the shape is affected by the topology, and different choices of topology can lead to shapes with a different number of bends (see Figure 2.4). However, the topology-shape-metrics approach gives higher priority to the minimization of crossings than to the minimization of bends, since it performs the planarization step before the orthogonalization step. Also, the shape and the topology affect the area of the drawing, but the problem of minimizing the area is viewed by the topology-shape-metrics approach as less important than the other two aesthetics mentioned above. In the compaction step, other aesthetics besides the area can be taken into account, such as the minimization of the sum of the lengths of the edges or the minimization of the length of the longest edge.

Several types of constraints can be taken into account within the topology-shape-metrics approach. They can be subdivided into topological, shape, and metrics constraints. In the planarization step we can, for example, constrain certain vertices to stay on the external face of the drawing or prevent edges from crossing a certain path. In the orthogonalization step, we can require that a given path does not contain bends. We can also impose specific sequences of bends on specific edges. In the compaction step, we can constrain certain vertices to have larger or smaller coordinates than other vertices. Of course, because of the order of the steps, the approach assigns higher priority to the satisfaction of topological constraints than shape constraints, and higher priority to the satisfaction of shape constraints than metrics constraints.

2.4   The Hierarchical Approach

Digraphs are widely used in applications to model dependency relationships. Examples include PERT diagrams, *is-a* hierarchies, and subroutine-call graphs. Acyclic digraphs are usually represented with the polyline downward (or upward) drawing convention. The hierarchical approach, originally proposed in [STT81, Car80, War77a], is intuitive and is depicted in Figure 2.7.

- The *layer assignment* step receives an acyclic digraph as input and first produces a *layered digraph*, where the vertices of G are assigned to layers $L_1, L_2, \ldots, L_h$, such that, if (u, v) is an an edge with $u \in L_i$ and $v \in L_j$, then $i > j$. In the final drawing, each vertex in layer L_i will have y coordinate equal to i. Next, the layered digraph is transformed into a *proper layered digraph*, that is, a layered digraph such that, if (u, v) is an an edge with $u \in L_i$ and $v \in L_j$, then $i = j+1$. This is done by inserting dummy vertices along the edges that span more than two layers.

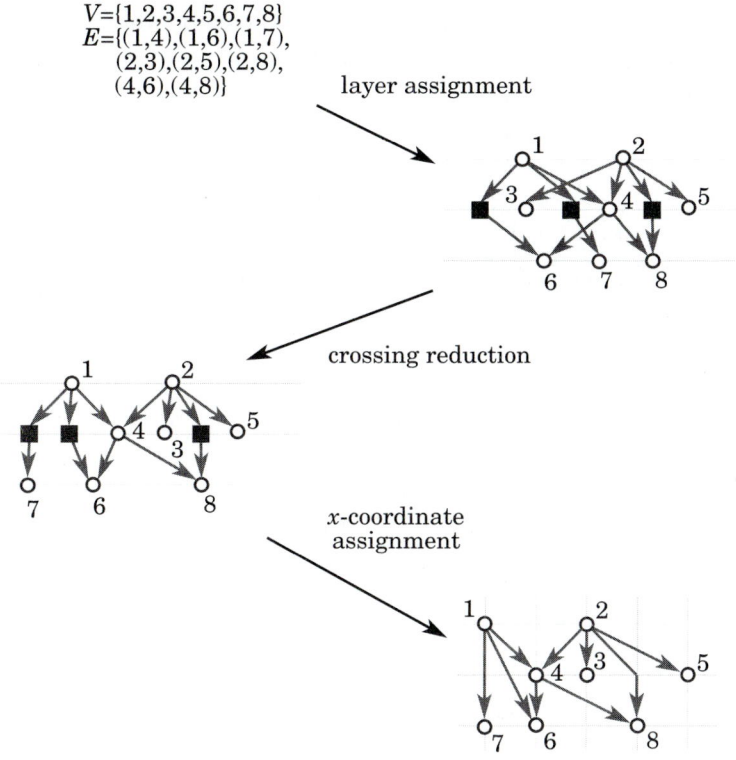

Figure 2.7: The hierarchical approach. The dummy vertices introduced in the layer assignment step are represented by squares.

- The *crossing reduction* step receives a proper layered digraph as input and produces a new proper layered digraph in which an order is specified for the vertices on each layer. The orders of the vertices on the layers determine the topology of the final drawing and are chosen in such a way that the number of crossings is kept as small as possible.

- The *x-coordinate assignment* step receives a proper layered digraph as input and produces final x coordinates for the vertices preserving the ordering computed in the crossings reduction step. At the end of this step, the final drawing is obtained by first representing each edge with a straight-line segment and then by removing dummy vertices. (In this way, long edges may be represented by polygonal lines.)

  Observe that several aesthetics can be taken into account during the x-coordinate assignment step; for example, the dummy vertices introduced in the long edges replacement step can be aligned to reduce the number of bends in the final drawing, or vertices can be horizontally displaced to emphasize symmetries of the digraph. Vertices can also be packed to reduce the area of the drawing.

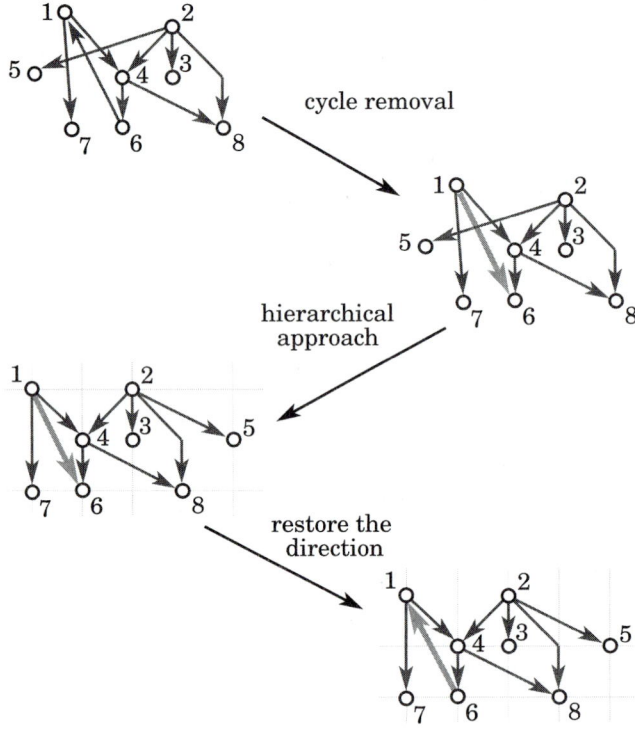

Figure 2.8: The hierarchical approach for general digraphs.

As was the case with the topology-shape-metrics approach, the hierarchical approach implicitly establishes an ordering among aesthetics through the ordering of the steps.

The hierarchical approach can also be used when the input digraph is not acyclic. Here, it is impossible to use the downward convention, but we can try to minimize the number of edges that do not point downward. Observe that in this case, downwardness is not satisfied everywhere and thus it is no longer a drawing convention but rather an aesthetic. We can use the following strategy (see Figure 2.8):

- Force the graph to be acyclic by temporarily reversing a subset of its edges. The set of reversed edges should be kept as small as possible to obtain a drawing in which most of the edges follow the downward direction.

- Apply the hierarchical approach to the acyclic digraph computed in the previous step.

- Restore the original direction of the edges that were reversed.

The method can also be extended to undirected graphs by preprocessing the graph to give it an artificial acyclic orientation. In this case, the layer assignment step effectively simplifies the drawing problem by reducing the size of its solution space.

The hierarchical approach supports several kinds of constraints. For example, two given vertices on the same layer can be constrained to stay close to each other in the crossing reduction step. Further, vertices on different layers can be vertically aligned during the x-coordinate assignment step.

2.5 The Visibility Approach

The visibility approach, originally proposed in [DT88, DTT92b], is a general purpose methodology for drawing graphs with the polyline drawing convention. It consists of the following three steps, illustrated in Figure 2.9.

- The *planarization* step. This is the same as in the topology-shape-metrics approach presented in Section 2.3.

- The *visibility* step constructs a *visibility representation* of the graph. In a visibility representation, each vertex is mapped to a horizontal segment and each edge to a vertical segment. The vertical segment representing the edge (u, v) has its endpoints on the horizontal segments representing vertices u and v, and does not intersect with any other horizontal segment. Roughly speaking, a visibility representation can be considered a skeleton or a sketch of the final drawing.

- The *replacement* step constructs the final polyline drawing by replacing the horizontal and vertical segments of the visibility representation as follows. Each horizontal segment is replaced by a point representing the corresponding vertex and each vertical segment is replaced by a polygonal line representing the corresponding edge, roughly following

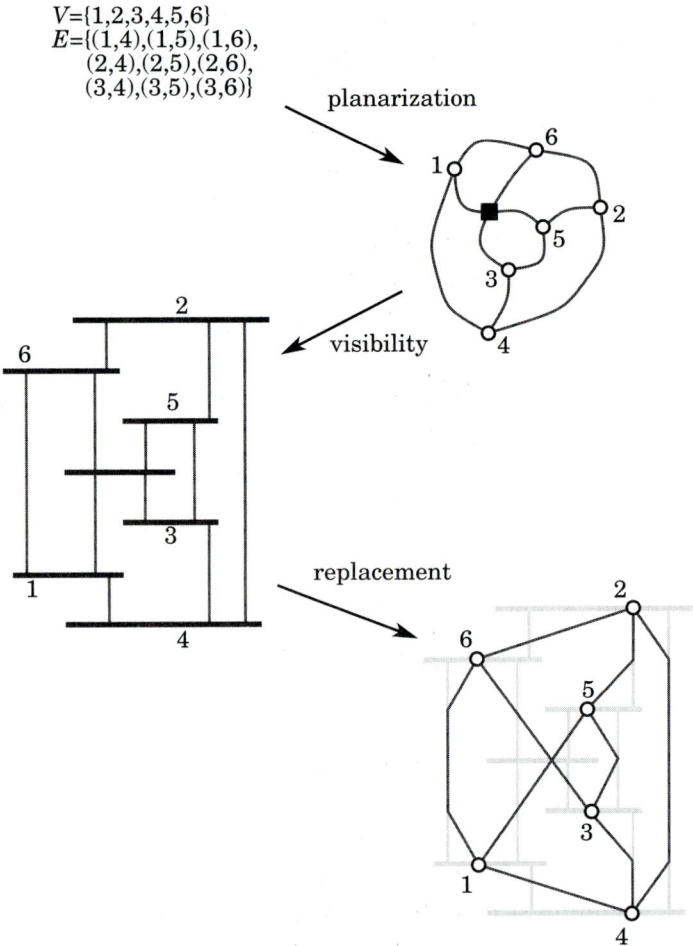

Figure 2.9: The visibility approach.

the original vertical segment. There are several replacement strategies that allow the construction of a planar polyline drawing from a visibility representation.

The planarization step performed at the beginning makes the visibility approach similar to the topology-shape-metrics approach in managing the topology of the drawing. On the other hand, the visibility step is similar to the layer assignment step of the hierarchical approach. In this sense, the visibility approach can be considered as a meeting point of the previous two approaches.

The planarization step makes the crossing reduction the primary aesthetic of this approach. In the visibility step, it is desirable to minimize the area of the visibility representation. In the replacement step, several aesthetics can be taken into account. For example, there are replacement strategies that attempt to minimize the number of bends, strategies that emphasize symmetries of the graph, and strategies that balance, as much as possible, the distribution of the vertices in the drawing. In Figure 2.10, we show how different replacement strategies lead to different numbers of bends or to more or less balanced drawings.

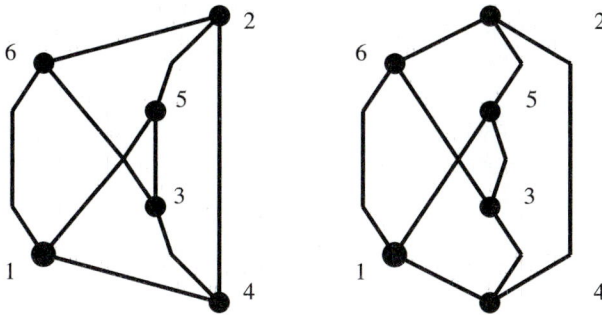

Figure 2.10: Different replacement strategies in the visibility approach.

Constraints can be imposed in each of the three steps. Topological constraints are identical to the ones of the topology-shape-metrics approach. In the visibility and replacement steps, it is possible to impose constraints on the vertical alignment of the vertices of selected paths, constraints on the relative horizontal and vertical position of pairs of vertices, and constraints on the shape of selected edges.

2.6 The Augmentation Approach

The augmentation approach is a further general purpose methodology for drawing graphs in the polyline drawing convention. The basic idea is to add edges and/or vertices to the graph to obtain a new graph with a stronger structure and hence better drawability properties. The method consists of the following three steps, illustrated in Figure 2.11.

- The *planarization* step. This is the same as in the topology-shape-metrics approach presented in Section 2.3.

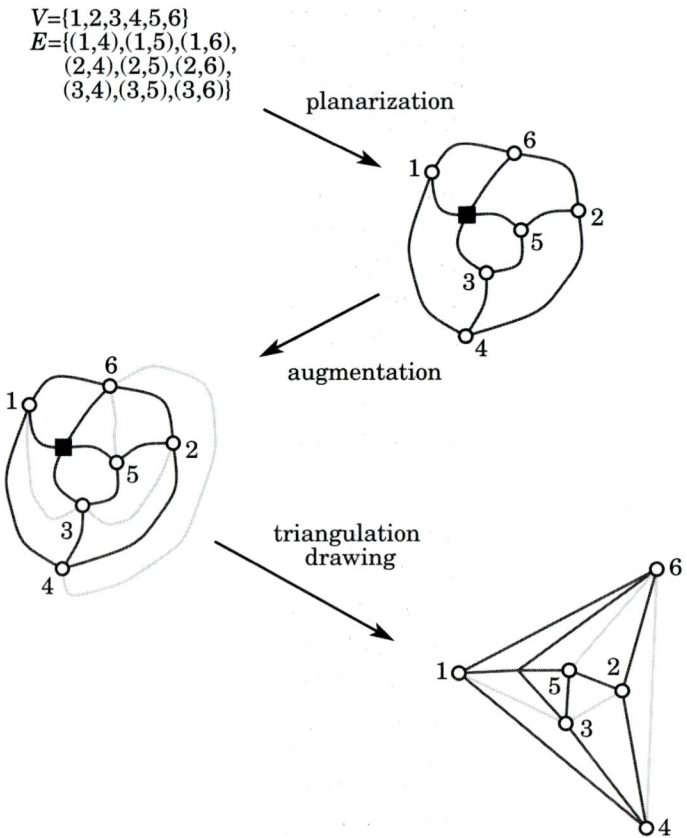

V={1,2,3,4,5,6}
E={(1,4),(1,5),(1,6),
(2,4),(2,5),(2,6),
(3,4),(3,5),(3,6)}

planarization

augmentation

triangulation
drawing

Figure 2.11: The augmentation approach.

- The *augmentation* step adds a suitable set of edges (sometimes vertices as well) to the planar embedding constructed in the previous step, to obtain a maximal planar graph, that is, a planar graph whose faces have three edges.

  Since the quality of the drawing of a maximal planar graph, in terms of area requirement and angular resolution, is usually affected by the degrees of the vertices, it is typical to use augmentation techniques that attempt to keep the degrees of the vertices as small as possible.

- The *triangulation drawing* step constructs the final drawing by representing each face as a triangle. Dummy edges and vertices are removed. There are several algorithms for this step. They all exploit the special properties of triangulations, in that they are either based on the construction of interleaved spanning trees of the triangulation or on a canonical vertex numbering scheme.

Of course, if the graph is planar, then the resulting drawing is straight-line. Otherwise, the dummy vertices that represent crossings become bends. As with other strategies, the initial execution of the planarization step makes crossing reduction the most important aesthetic.

During the augmentation and the triangulation drawing steps, strategies can be used to minimize the area, to maximize the angular resolution, and to distribute the vertices uniformly. The augmentation approach is less suitable than others for supporting constraints.

Since there are several algorithms for straight-line drawings of triconnected or even of biconnected planar graphs, there are variations of the augmentation step that do not produce a maximal planar graph, but rather a planar graph with a certain level of connectivity.

2.7   The Force-Directed Approach

Force directed algorithms are intuitive methods for creating straight-line drawings of undirected graphs. They are quite popular because their basic versions are easy to understand and to code.

Roughly speaking, a force directed algorithm simulates a system of forces defined on an input graph, and outputs a locally minimum energy configuration. There are two ingredients of this approach:

- A force model. For example, we can assign a "spring" of "natural length" ℓ_{uv} to each pair (u, v) of vertices. We can choose ℓ_{uv} to be the number of edges on the shortest path between u and v. The spring follows Hooke's law, that is, it induces a force of magnitude $d_{uv} - \ell_{uv}$ on u, where d_{uv} is proportional to the Euclidean distance between u and v.

- A technique for finding a locally minimum energy configuration. Such techniques are usually the product of numerical analysis rather than combinatorial algorithms. Simple iterative methods are commonly used.

Experience with force directed methods shows that they can produce beautiful pictures of some of the well known graphs in Graph Theory (such as the skeletons of the Platonic solids). They often give highly symmetric drawings, and tend to distribute vertices evenly. Further, a variety of constraints can be used. For example, special forces can be used to constrain a set of vertices to lie within a given region, or on a given curve.

2.8   The Divide and Conquer Approach

The divide and conquer approach is widely adopted in graph drawing. The basic idea is the following. First, the graph is split into subgraphs; second, subgraphs are recursively drawn; and third, the drawing of the whole graph is obtained by suitably gluing the drawings of the subgraphs. Of course, the best results have been obtained for drawing graphs that can be easily decomposed into subgraphs, such as trees or series-parallel digraphs.

In order to provide intuition into how divide and conquer can be used in graph drawing, we outline an algorithm for drawing binary trees, originally proposed in [RT81]. The algorithm consists of two main steps:

- The *layer assignment* step is analogous to the one of the hierarchical approach. The vertices of the tree are assigned to layers in a way that minimizes the distance from the root.

- The *divide and conquer* step is as follows:

  If the tree consists of a single vertex, then trivially construct its drawing on the assigned layer. If the tree is empty, then nothing has to be done.

  Else, (*divide*) recursively draw the left and right subtrees and (*conquer*) place the two subdrawings obtained close to one another, so that the horizontal distance between them is 2, where the root is positioned halfway between the roots of the subtrees. (If one of the subtrees is empty, the root is placed at distance 1 from the root of the other subtree.)

The algorithm works with the planar straight-line grid drawing convention and takes into account several aesthetics. For example, the width of the drawing is kept small, isomorphic subtrees have the same drawing, and symmetric subtrees have mirror image drawings.

2.9   A General Framework for Graph Drawing

The graph drawing techniques we have surveyed in the previous sections are representative of the large amount of existing methods, algorithms, and rules of thumb that have been developed in the graph drawing literature. Furthermore, the main steps of such techniques can be mixed together in several ways, giving rise to many possible methods and approaches. Hence, in order to describe graph drawing algorithms in a more systematic way, we use the framework originally proposed in [BDL95], which is based on a taxonomy of classes of graphs and algorithms involved in graph drawing. Such a taxonomy is justified in the following two simple observations.

- Let C be a class of graphs and let C' be a subclass of C. An algorithm that can be applied to the graphs of C can also be applied to the graphs of C'. For example, an algorithm that can construct a visibility representation of a biconnected graph works even if the graph is triconnected; an algorithm that can draw an acyclic digraph can also draw an acyclic bipartite digraph. Using object-oriented terminology, we say that a graph drawing algorithm devised for C is *inherited* by C'.

- In the previous subsections, we have seen how a graph drawing methodology is a pipeline process of relatively independent functional steps. Each step executes a single task and provides an input to the next one. Inputs and outputs of the steps are always graphs, enriched more and more with drawing features. Furthermore, it is possible to synthesize new methodologies by concatenating functional steps from other methodologies.

The above observations lead to a taxonomy consisting of:

- An *inheritance hierarchy* of classes of graphs extensively studied in graph drawing. The hierarchy also includes drawings and other intermediate representations, such as planar embeddings and orthogonal representations.

- A set of *methods* with the following characteristics.

  - Each method is associated with a class of graphs and maps a graph of that class into a graph of another class.
  - A method associated with a class of graphs C is also associated with all the descendant classes of C in the hierarchy.

A hierarchy including some of the most interesting classes of graphs for graph drawing is depicted in Figure 2.12.

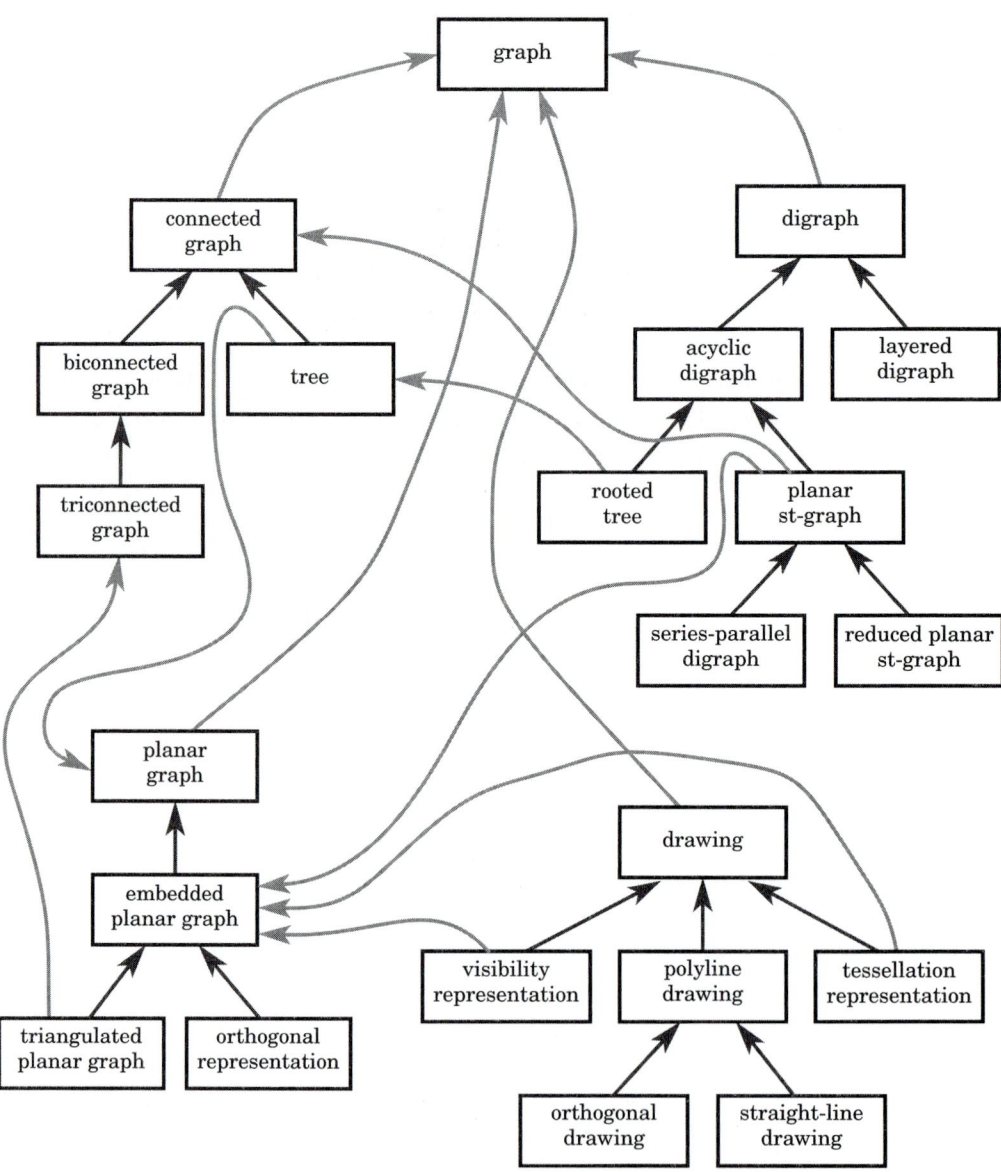

Figure 2.12: Inheritance hierarchy of classes of graphs, drawings, and related representations.

The most general class is Graph. The hierarchy is then structured according to four main properties, connectivity, planarity, orientation, and geometry, which are associated with classes Connected Graph, Planar Graph, Digraph, and Drawing.

A graph drawing algorithm can be viewed as a path whose vertices are classes of the hierarchy and whose edges are methods transforming an instance of a class into an instance of another class. The topology-shape-metrics approach, illustrated in Figure 2.6, can be represented as shown in Figure 2.13. Figures 2.14, 2.15, and 2.16 illustrate the hierarchical, visibility, and augmentation approaches. Note that the force-directed approach does not consist of functional steps which produce graphs as intermediate products. It can be thought of as a unique method connecting class *Graph* and class *Straight-Line Drawing*.

Selected graph drawing methods presented in this book are summarized in Table 2.1. For each method, we give the input class, the output class, and the chapter where the method is described. Table 2.1 can be used as a key to reading this book.

2.10 Beyond this Book

There are a number of subjects relevant to graph drawing that have not been covered in this book. We list some of them and provide sample references.

Topological Graph Theory studies embeddings of graphs on surfaces. An introduction to this subject can be found in [GT87]. A survey on algorithms and lower bounds techniques for the crossing number problem appears in [SSV95].

Geometric Graph Theory studies the combinatorial and geometric properties of straight-line drawings. See, for example, [KPTV97, PSS96].

Proximity Drawings represent graphs by means of a geometric proximity relation (e.g., a tree is drawn as the Euclidean minimum spanning tree of a set of points). A survey of this area appears in [DLL95]. Recent work includes [BLL96, ELL$^+$95, EW96b, LTTV97, LL97].

Intersection and Contact Drawings represent graphs by the intersection or contact relation among geometric figures. Relevant work includes [BK98, KM94, Moh93].

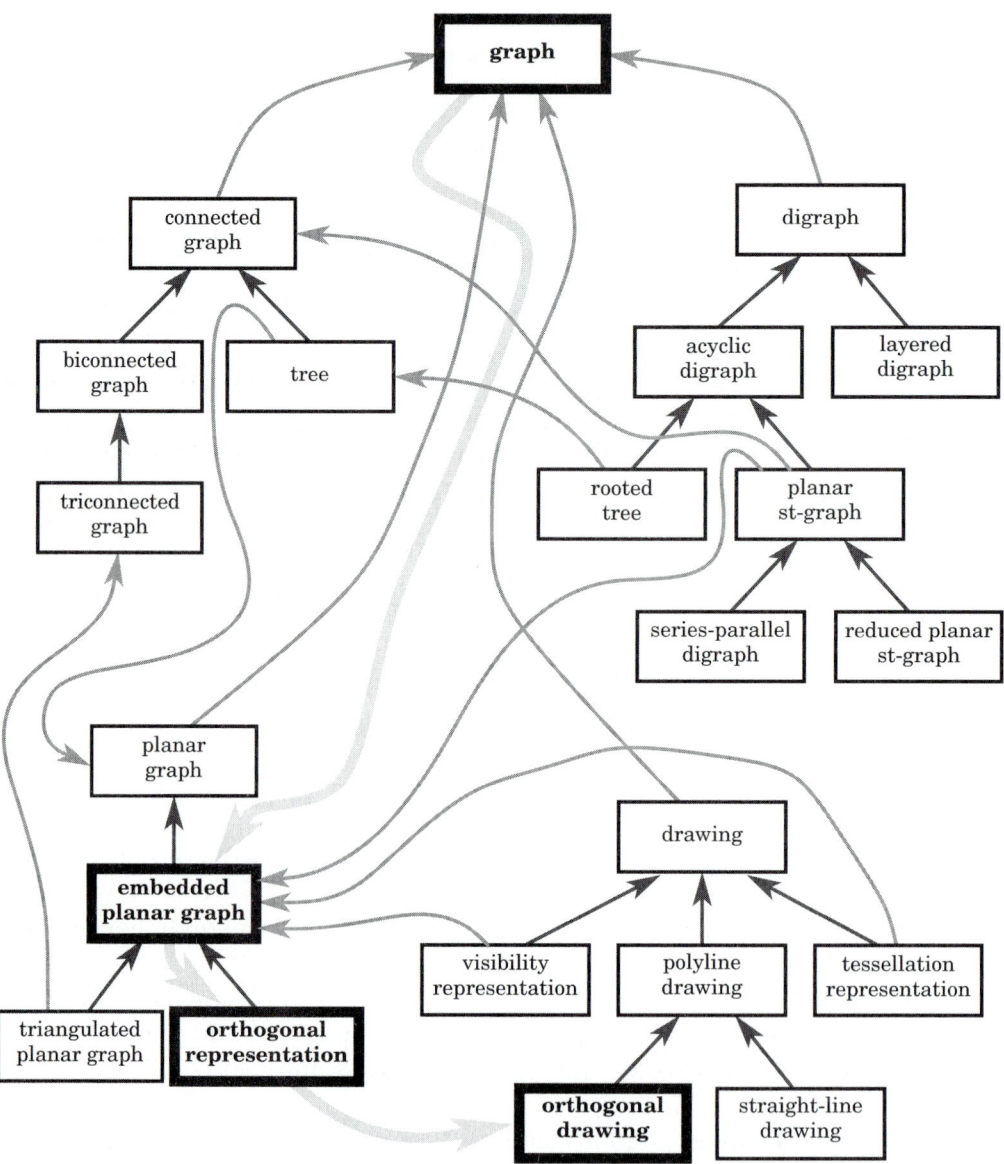

Figure 2.13: The topology-shape-metrics approach. Thick edges represent the methods. For example, the thick edge connecting the classes Embedded Planar Graph and Orthogonal Representation denotes the orthogonalization step.

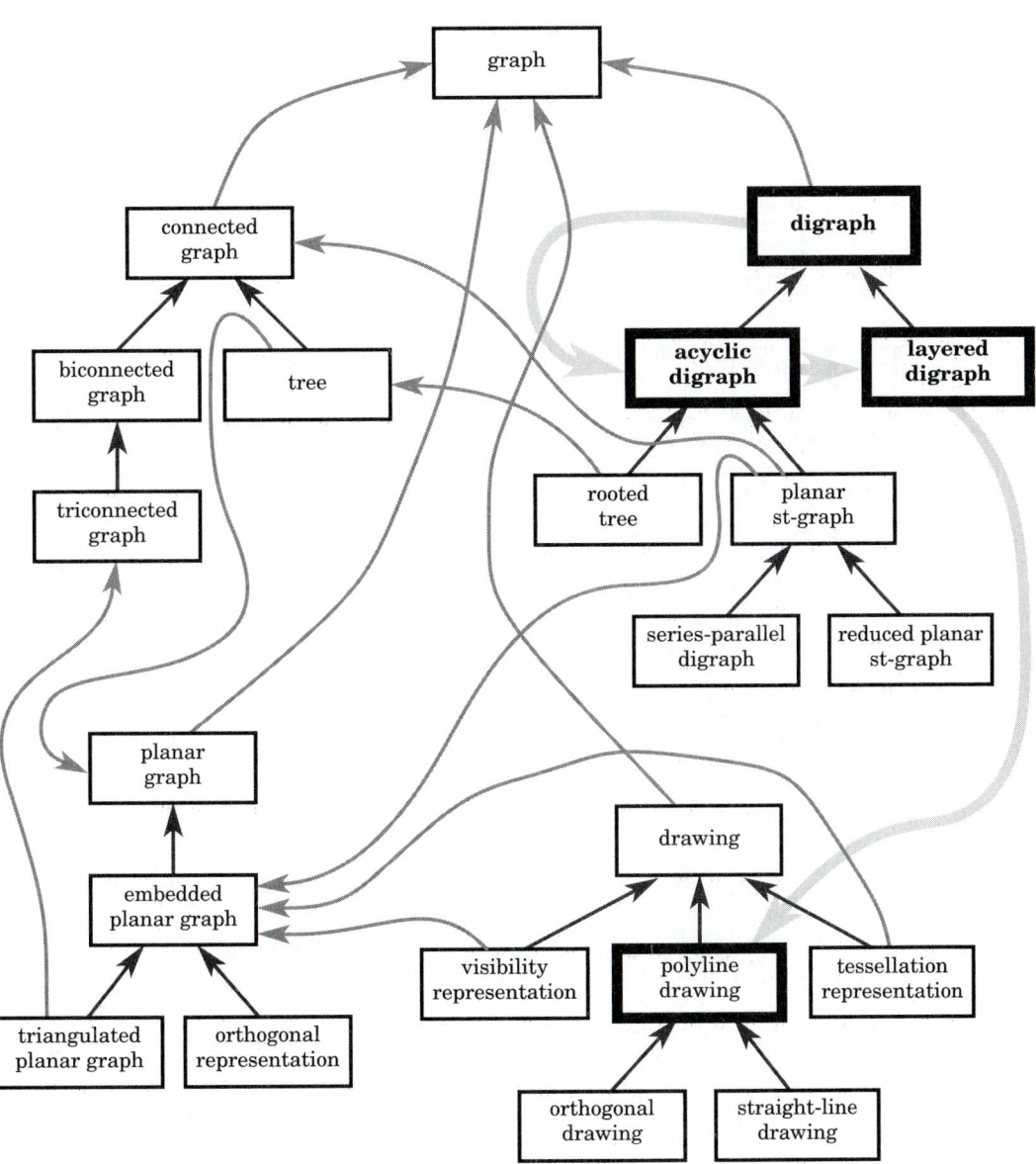

Figure 2.14: The hierarchical approach.

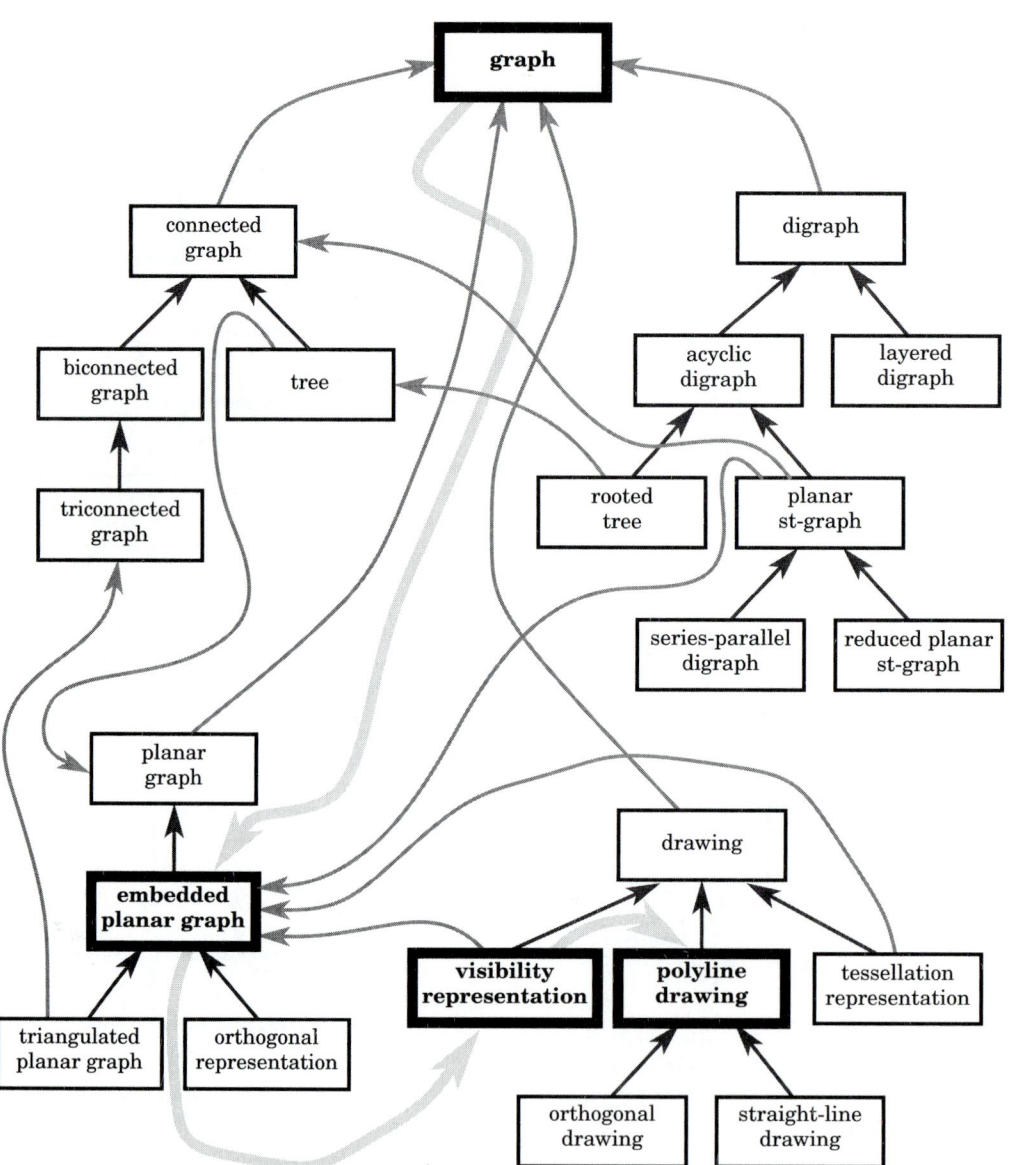

Figure 2.15: The visibility approach.

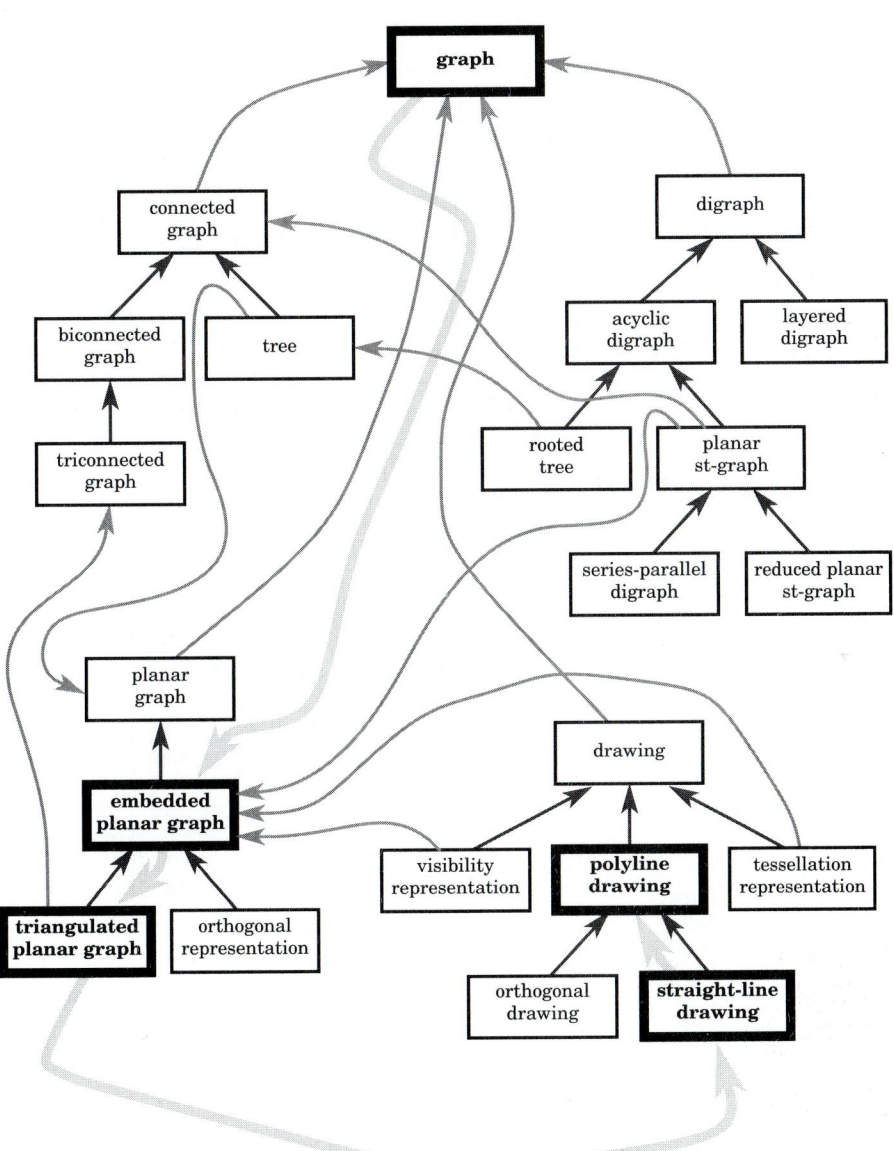

Figure 2.16: The augmentation approach.

Method	Input Class	Output Class	Chapter
Planarization	graph	embedded planar graph	3, 7
Layered Tree Drawing	tree	straight-line drawing	3
Δ-drawing	series-parallel digraph	straight-line drawing	3
Cycle Removal	digraph	acyclic digraph	9
Layer Assignment	acyclic digraph	layered digraph	9
Augmentation	layered digraph	proper layered digraph	9
Crossing Reduction	proper layered digraph	proper layered digraph	9
x-coordinate Assignment	proper layered digraph	polyline drawing	9
Augmentation	planar graph	planar st-graph	4
Tessellation	planar st-graph	tessellation representation	4
Visibility	tessellation representation	visibility representation	4
Vertex-Segment Replacement	visibility representation	polyline drawing	4
Vertex-Segment Replacement	visibility representation	orthogonal drawing	4
Augmentation	planar st-graph	reduced planar st-graph	4
Dominance	reduced planar st-graph	straight-line drawing	4
Orthogonalization	planar graph	orthogonal representation	4, 5
Compaction	orthogonal representation	orthogonal drawing	5
Augmentation	digraph	planar st-graph	6
Orientation and Pairing	graph	orthogonal drawing	8
Interactive	graph	orthogonal drawing	7
Force Directed	graph	straight-line drawing	10

Table 2.1: Selected graph drawing techniques presented in this book.

3D Drawings are becoming popular due to the availability of inexpensive graphics hardware and software. Work on 3D graph drawing includes [CELR95, CGT96, ESW96, ESW97, GT97a, GTV96, HR94, JJ95, LD95, PT97a, PV97, Rei95, RMC91].

Experimental Comparative Studies are important in order to evaluate the practical performance of a graph drawing algorithm in visualization applications. Examples include [BHR96, DGL+97a, DGL+97b, Him95a, JEM+91, JM97, PST97].

Labeling the vertices and edges of a drawing is a difficult problem akin to the classic problem of labeling cartographic maps. Specific work includes [CMS95, KT97, KT98].

Declarative Approaches to graph drawing focus on constraint satisfaction. Relevant work includes [Bra95, CG95, DFM93, HM97, Kam89b, KMS94, KKR96, LE95, LES95, Mar91, RMS97].

Systems for constructing drawings of graphs include [BDL95, BGT97, DLV95, EFK88, FLM95, FW95, Him95b, KN95, MAC+95, MSG95, San95, SM95a, VW95].

Chapter 3

Divide and Conquer

Some classes of graphs can be described recursively. For example, a rooted binary tree is either empty or consists of a root and two rooted binary trees. For such classes, elegant drawing algorithms that follow the divide-and-conquer paradigm (see Section 2.8) have been devised.

In Section 3.1, we present divide-and-conquer techniques for drawing trees. In Section 3.1.2, we describe the pioneering algorithm by Reingold and Tilford [RT81], where vertices are placed on horizontal layers. Radial drawings, where the layers are mapped to concentric circles, are discussed in Section 3.1.3. They are studied in [Ead92, Ber81, Esp88, Kam88, MA88]. In Section 3.1.4, we study hv-drawings, where the edges are drawn as rightward horizontal or downward vertical segments. Such drawings were introduced by Shiloach [Shi76] and are further investigated in [CDP92, CP95b, ELL92, ELL93, Kim95, Kim96, Tre96]. By allowing leftward horizontal edges in hv-drawings, we can obtain drawings with constant aspect ratio and small area [CGKT97], as shown in Section 3.1.5. Other results on drawing trees are discussed in Sections A.1 and A.4. In Section 3.2, we present the algorithm of [BCD$^+$94] for constructing straight-line upward drawings of series-parallel digraphs.

A divide-and-conquer strategy can also be used to test whether a graph is planar, as shown in Section 3.3, where we present the simple planarity testing algorithm of [AP61, Shi69].

3.1 Rooted Trees

The importance of rooted trees as data structures and as representations of simple hierarchies (such as organization charts, family trees, and parse trees) has ensured that a variety of specialized algorithms are available for drawing rooted trees.

Since rooted trees can be viewed as directed acyclic graphs with all edges directed away from the root, any technique for drawing directed acyclic graphs, as described in later chapters, can be used to draw rooted trees. However, the relatively simple structure of trees invites other approaches.

A natural way of representing rooted trees is to use a downward planar drawing, that is, a planar drawing in which a child vertex is placed no higher than its parent (see Section 2.1). In this section, we present four divide-and-conquer techniques for constructing downward planar drawings:

- Layering (see Section 3.1.2)

- Radial drawing (see Section 3.1.3)

- hv-drawing (see Section 3.1.4)

- Recursive winding (see Section 3.1.5).

Firstly, however, we review the terminology of rooted trees.

3.1.1   Terminology for Trees

A *tree* is a connected acyclic graph. A *rooted tree* consists of a tree T and a distinguished vertex r of T. The vertex r is called the *root* of T.

Suppose that T is a rooted tree with root r. It is common to regard T as a directed graph, with all edges oriented away from the root. Thus we apply the terminology of digraphs to rooted trees. If (u, v) is a directed edge in T, then u is the *parent* of v and v is a *child* of u. A *leaf* is a vertex with no children.

An *ordered tree* consists of a rooted tree and, for each vertex v, an ordering of the children of v. A *binary tree* is a rooted tree where each vertex has at most two children. In most applications, binary trees are ordered, and unless otherwise specified, we assume that a binary tree is ordered. If vertex v in a binary tree has two children, then the first child of a vertex is the *left* child, and the second child is the *right* child. If v has one child, then it is either *left* or *right*.

If v is a vertex of T, then the *subtree* rooted at v consists of the subgraph induced by all vertices on paths originating from v; and of course it has root v. If T is binary and v has two children, then the subtree rooted at the left (right) child of v is called *left subtree* (*right subtree*) of v.

The *depth* of a vertex v of T is the number of edges of the path of T between v and the root. The *height* of T is the maximum depth of a vertex of T.

3.1.2 Layering

A simple and effective method for constructing a downward planar drawing of a rooted tree T is to use the layering approach described in Section 2.4. We can transform T into a proper layered digraph by placing each vertex with depth i into layer L_i. In particular, the root of T is placed into layer L_0. A *layered drawing* of a tree T is a drawing of T such that a vertex v of depth i has y-coordinate $y(v) = -i$. Note that a layered drawing is strictly downward. Avoiding crossings in a layered drawing of T is merely a matter of ensuring that if two vertices v' and v'' are on the same layer L_i, then their left-to-right relative order is the same as the one of their parents u' and u'' in layer L_{i-1}, that is, $x(v'') - x(v')$ has the same sign as $x(u'') - x(u')$.

Since the definition of a layered drawing prescribes the y-coordinates of the vertices, an algorithm for constructing such a drawing has to compute only the x-coordinates. An obvious requirement is that a parent be placed within the horizontal span of its children, possibly in a central position. Note that in many applications, the ordering of the children of a vertex is semantically significant (for example, in binary search trees), and hence the left-to-right order of vertices for a specific layer may be fixed.

A simple method for assigning x-coordinates in a layered drawing of a binary tree T is to set $x(v)$ equal to the rank of v in the inorder traversal of T, that is, if vertex v is the i-th vertex encountered in the inorder traversal of T, then $x(v) = i$. An example of a drawing obtained with this method is shown in Figure 3.1.a. This method does not typically yield aesthetically pleasing drawings. In particular, two flaws are apparent:

- The drawing is usually much wider than necessary

- A parent vertex is not necessarily centered with respect to its children.

We give an informal description of Algorithm *Layered-Tree-Draw* for constructing a layered drawing of a binary tree T below. This algorithm is based on a divide-and-conquer strategy that uses a local optimization heuristic at each conquer step to reduce the width, and horizontally centers a parent vertex with respect to its children.

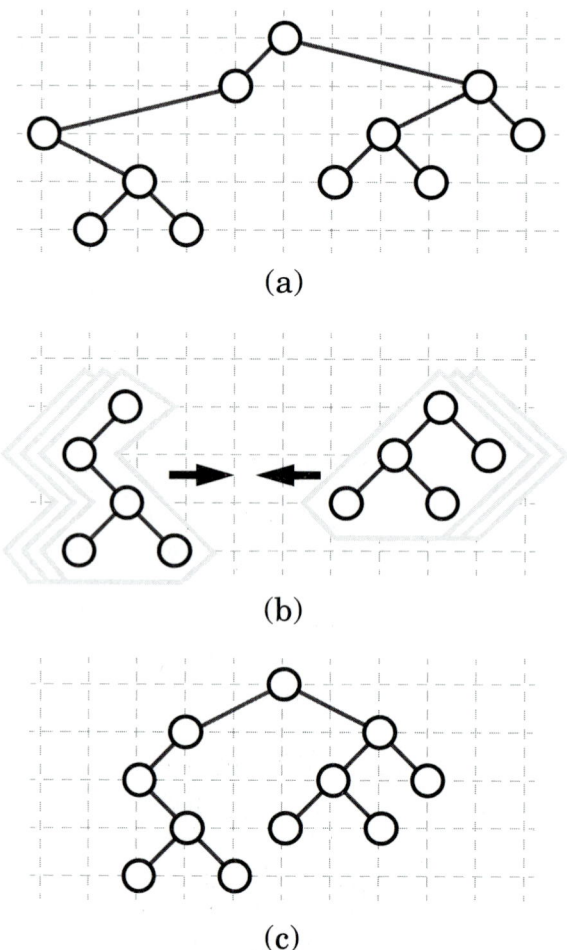

Figure 3.1: Layered drawings of a binary tree T: (a) x-coordinates assigned with an inorder traversal; (b) conquer step of Algorithm 3.1 *Layered-Tree-Draw*; (c) x-coordinates assigned by Algorithm *Layered-Tree-Draw*.

An example of a drawing constructed by Algorithm 3.1 *Layered-Tree-Draw* is shown in Figure 3.1.c. This algorithm yields aesthetically pleasing drawings and has been widely used in visualization applications.

We say that two binary trees T' and T'' are *simply isomorphic* if they meet either one of two conditions:

- Both T' and T'' are empty

Algorithm 3.1 *Layered-Tree-Draw*
    Input: a binary tree T
    Output: a layered drawing of T

1. *Base Case:* If T consists of a single vertex, its drawing is trivially defined.

2. *Divide:* Recursively apply the algorithm to draw the left and right subtrees of T.

3. *Conquer:* Imagine that each subtree is drawn on a separate sheet of paper. Move the drawings of the subtrees towards each other until their horizontal distance becomes equal to 2 (see Figure 3.1.b). Finally, place the root r of T vertically one unit above and horizontally half way between its children. If r has only one subtree, say the left one, then place r at horizontal distance 1 to the right of its left child.

$\square$

- The left subtrees of T' and T'' are simply isomorphic and the right subtrees of T' and T'' are simply isomorphic.

Also, we say that two binary trees T' and T'' are *axially isomorphic* if the binary trees obtained from T' and T'', by exchanging the left and right subtrees of each vertex, are simply isomorphic.

Because of its recursive formulation, Algorithm 3.1 *Layered-Tree-Draw* draws a subtree of T independently from the rest of the tree. Thus, it constructs drawings that have the following symmetry properties (see Figure 3.2):

- Simply isomorphic subtrees have congruent drawings, up to a translation

- Axially isomorphic subtrees have congruent drawings, up to a translation and a reflection around the y-axis.

As described above, Algorithm 3.1 *Layered-Tree-Draw* may not yield a grid drawing, since the x-coordinates are in general rational numbers. If a grid drawing is required, the conquer step can be modified by placing the subtrees at horizontal distance either 2 or 3, such that the distance between the roots of the subtrees is even.

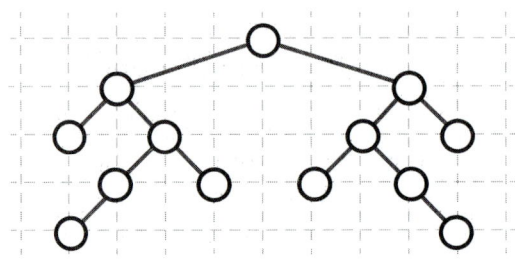

Figure 3.2: Isomorphisms and symmetries displayed by Algorithm 3.1 *Layered-Tree-Draw*.

Algorithm 3.1 *Layered-Tree-Draw* can be implemented by means of two traversals of the input binary tree T. A first postorder traversal recursively computes for each vertex v, the horizontal displacement of the left and right children of v with respect to v. A second preorder traversal computes the x-coordinates of the vertices by accumulating the displacements on the path from each vertex to the root, and the y-coordinates of the vertices by determining the depth of each vertex.

Special care is needed in order to implement the postorder traversal so that it runs in linear time. The *left contour* of a binary tree T with height h is the sequence of vertices $v_0, \ldots, v_h$ such that v_i is the leftmost vertex of T with depth i. The *right contour* is defined similarly. In the conquer step, we need to follow the right contour of the left subtree and the left contour of the right subtree.

In the postorder traversal, we maintain the invariant that after completing the processing of a vertex v, the left and right contours of the subtree rooted at v are stored in linked lists.

Thus, processing vertex v in the postorder traversal can be done by scanning the right contour of the left subtree of v (following the recursively computed right contour list) and the left contour of the right subtree of v (following the recursively computed left contour list). During the scan, we accumulate the displacements of the vertices encountered on the left and right contour and we keep track of the maximum cumulative displacement at any depth.

Let $T(v)$ be the subtree rooted at v, and T' and T'' be the left and right subtrees of v, respectively. The left and right contour lists of $T(v)$ can be constructed as follows (see Figure 3.3):

- If T' and T'' have the same height, then the left contour list of $T(v)$

is the same as the left contour list of T' plus vertex v, and the right contour list of $T(v)$ is the same as the right contour list of T'' plus v.

- If the height of T' is less than the height of T'', the right contour list of $T(v)$ is the same as the right contour list of T''. Let h' be the height of T' and let u be the bottommost vertex on the left contour of T'. Let w be the vertex of the left contour of T'' such that w has depth $h'+1$ in T''. The left contour list of $T(v)$ consists of the concatenation of vertex v, the left contour list of T', and the portion of the left contour list of T'' beginning at vertex w. This case is illustrated in Figure 3.3.

- The case in which the height of T' is greater than the height of T'' is analogous to the previous one, and can be illustrated with a mirror image of Figure 3.3.

A crucial observation that proves the efficiency of the algorithm is that it is necessary to travel down the contours of T' and T'' only as far as the height of the subtree of lesser height. Thus, the time spent processing vertex v in the postorder traversal is proportional to the minimum of the heights of T' and T''. The running time of the postorder traversal of tree T is given by the following formula, where for a vertex v of T, we denote the height of the left subtree of v by $h'(v)$ and the height of the right subtree of v by $h''(v)$

$$\sum_{v \in T} (1 + \min\{h'(v), h''(v)\}) = n + \sum_{v \in T} \min\{h'(v), h''(v)\}.$$

We can visualize the sum

$$\sum_{v \in T} \min\{h'(v), h''(v)\}$$

by connecting with new edges pairs of consecutive vertices with the same depth (see Figure 3.4). The sum over all vertices v of the minimum height of the subtrees of v is equal to the number of new edges added to the tree. Each vertex is incident to at most one new edge on its right. Thus, the number of new edges, and therefore the above sum, is no more than the number of vertices of the tree.

Further details on Algorithm 3.1 *Layered-Tree-Draw* can be found in [RT81]. We summarize the properties of Algorithm *Layered-Tree-Draw* in the following theorem.

Theorem 3.1 *Let T be a binary tree with n vertices. Algorithm 3.1 Layered-Tree-Draw constructs a drawing Γ of T in $O(n)$ time, such that:*

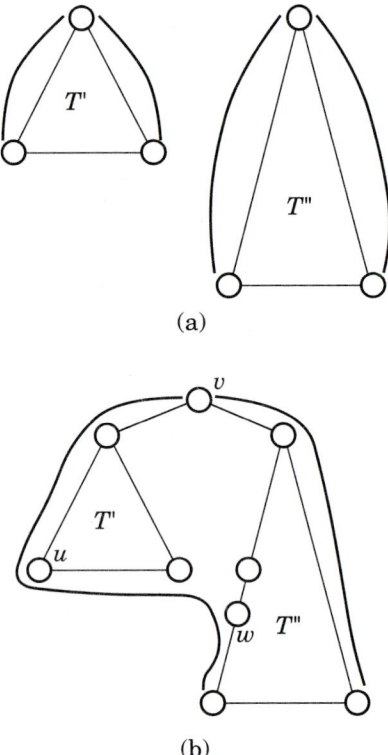

(a)

(b)

Figure 3.3: Construction of the contour lists of subtree $T(v)$, from those of the subtrees of v in the conquer step of Algorithm 3.1 *Layered-Tree-Draw*, for the case when the left subtree T' of v is shorter than the right subtree T'' of v: (a) contour lists of T' and T''; (b) contour lists of $T(v)$.

- Γ *is layered, that is, the y-coordinate of each vertex is equal to minus the depth of the vertex*

- Γ *is planar, straight-line, and strictly downward*

- Γ *is embedding-preserving, that is, the left-to-right order of the children of each vertex is preserved*

- *Any two vertices of* Γ *are at horizontal and vertical distance at least 1*

- *The area of* Γ *is* $O(n^2)$

- *The x-coordinate of a parent with two children is the average of the x-coordinates of its children*

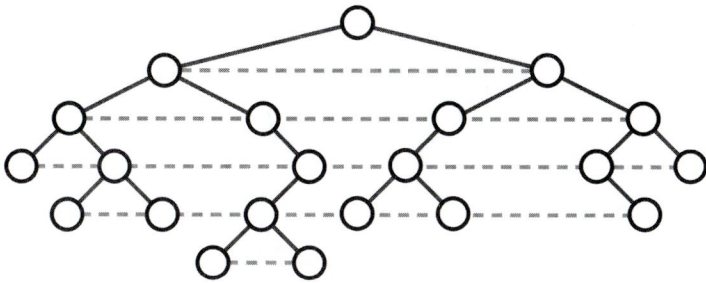

Figure 3.4: Connecting, with new (dashed) edges, pairs of consecutive vertices with the same depth in the analysis of the running time of Algorithm 3.1 *Layered-Tree-Draw*.

- *Simply isomorphic subtrees have congruent drawings, up to a translation*

- *Axially isomorphic subtrees have congruent drawings, up to a translation and a reflection around the y-axis.*

While Algorithm 3.1 *Layered-Tree-Draw* tries to reduce the width of the drawing by performing a local horizontal compaction at each conquer step, it does not always compute a drawing of minimal width. In Figure 3.5, we show two drawings of the same binary tree that satisfy the properties listed in Theorem 3.1. The drawing in Figure 3.5.a, constructed by Algorithm *Layered-Tree-Draw*, is wider than the drawing in Figure 3.5.b, where constructing a suboptimal drawing of a subtree has the effect of reducing the overall width of the drawing. This example shows that any divide-and-conquer strategy for layered drawings of binary trees that does not modify the recursively computed drawing of a subtree cannot in general achieve optimal width or area.

In fact, the problem of constructing a drawing of a binary tree that satisfies the properties listed in Theorem 3.1 and has minimum width can be solved in polynomial time by means of linear programming (see [SR83]). However, if a grid drawing is also required, then the problem becomes NP-hard [SR83].

Algorithm 3.1 *Layered-Tree-Draw*, as described above, works efficiently and effectively for binary trees. It has a straightforward generalization to rooted trees, as follows. Suppose that tree T has subtrees $T_1, T_2, \ldots, T_m$.

Divide: Draw each subtree T_i recursively.

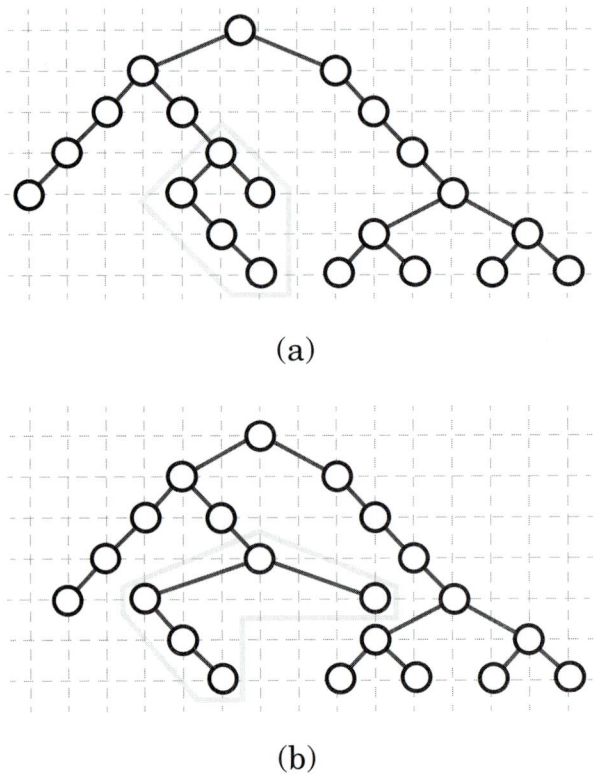

(a)

(b)

Figure 3.5: Example of nonoptimality of Algorithm 3.1 *Layered-Tree-Draw*:
(a) drawing constructed by the algorithm, where the shaded subtree is drawn
optimally; (b) a narrower drawing, where the shaded subtree is drawn non-
optimally.

Conquer: For $i = 2,\ldots,m$, place the drawing of T_i to the right of the
drawing of T_{i-1}, and at horizontal distance 2 from it. Finally, position
the root half-way between the root of T_1 and the root of T_m.

The definition of simply and axially isomorphic can be extended in a
straightforward manner to rooted ordered trees. We have:

Theorem 3.2 *Let T be a rooted tree with n vertices. There exists an algorithm that constructs a drawing Γ of T in $O(n)$ time, such that:*

- *Γ is layered, that is, the y-coordinate of each vertex is equal to minus
  the depth of the vertex*

- Γ *is planar, straight-line, and strictly downward*

- Γ *is embedding-preserving, that is, the left-to-right order of the children of each vertex is preserved*

- *Any two vertices of* Γ *are at horizontal and vertical distance at least* 1

- *The area of the drawing is* $O(n^2)$

- *Simply isomorphic subtrees have congruent drawings, up to a translation.*

The above algorithm for layered drawings of rooted trees gives reasonable drawings in most cases. However, it suffers from a small imbalance problem, as shown in the following example. Suppose that T has subtrees T_1, T_2, T_3, and T_4, and that T_1 and T_4 are much larger than T_2 and T_3. Because the algorithm works from left to right, it will place T_2 and T_3 much closer to T_1 than to T_4 in the conquer step (see Figure 3.6).

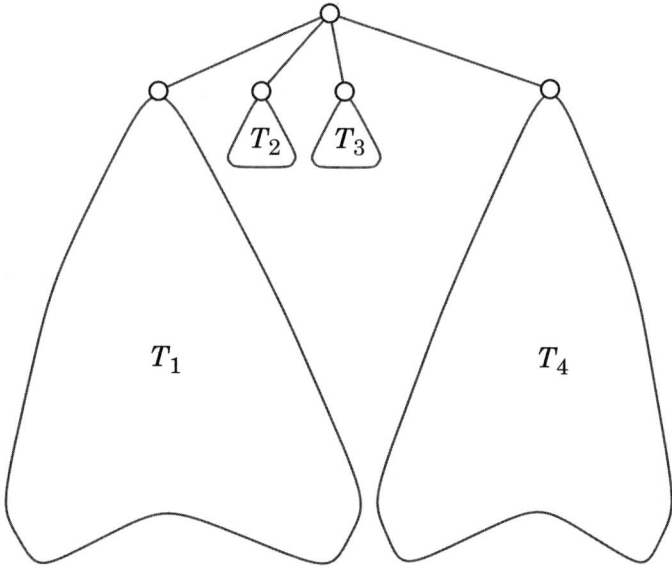

Figure 3.6: Imbalanced layered drawing of a tree.

In order to solve the imbalance problem, we should space the drawings of the subtrees of each vertex uniformly. For this purpose, we can either modify the conquer step or perform a postprocessing [Til81, Wal90].

3.1.3   Radial Drawing

In this section, we consider radial drawings of trees. A *radial drawing* is a variation of a layered drawing where the root of the tree is placed at the origin and layers are concentric circles centered at the origin. An example of such a drawing is shown in Figure 3.7.

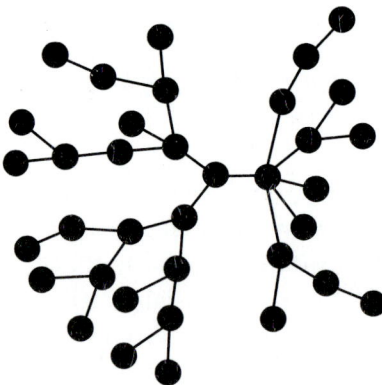

Figure 3.7: A radial drawing of a tree.

Simple algorithms for constructing radial drawings can be derived from the algorithms for constructing layered drawings illustrated in Section 3.1.2.

In radial drawings, a subtree is usually drawn within an *annulus wedge*. The layers $C_1, C_2, \ldots, C_k$ (where k is the height of the tree) of a radial drawing and an annulus wedge are illustrated in Figure 3.8. Observe that vertices of depth i are placed on circle C_i and the radius of C_i is given by an increasing function $\rho(i)$.

The subtree rooted at a vertex v is drawn in annulus wedge W_v. It may seem reasonable to choose the angle of W_v to be proportional to the number $\ell(v)$ of leaves in the subtree rooted at v; however, this strategy can lead to edge crossings, because an edge with endpoints within W_v can extend outside W_v and intersect other edges, as in Figure 3.9. To guarantee planarity, we must restrict the vertices to a convex subset of the wedge.

Suppose that v lies on C_i, and that the tangent to C_i through v meets C_{i+1} at a and b as in Figure 3.10. The unbounded region F_v in Figure 3.10, formed by the line segment ab and the rays from the origin through a and b, is convex. We restrict the subtree rooted at v to lie within the region F_v. The children of v are arranged on C_{i+1} according to the number of leaves in their respective subtrees. More precisely, for each child u of v, the angle β_u

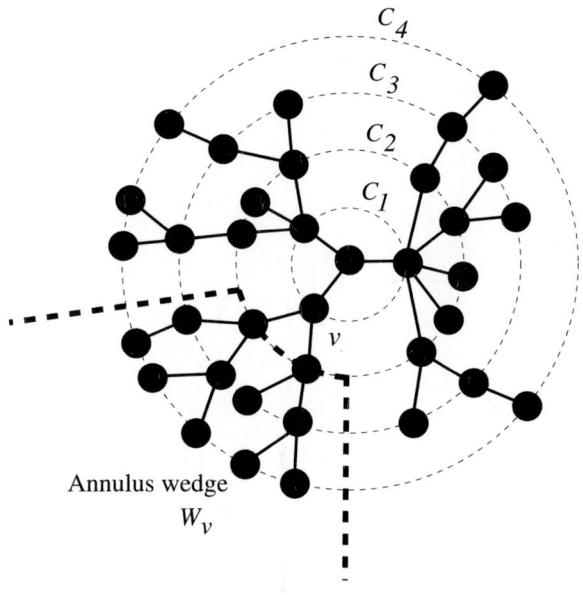

Figure 3.8: Parameters for radial drawings of trees.

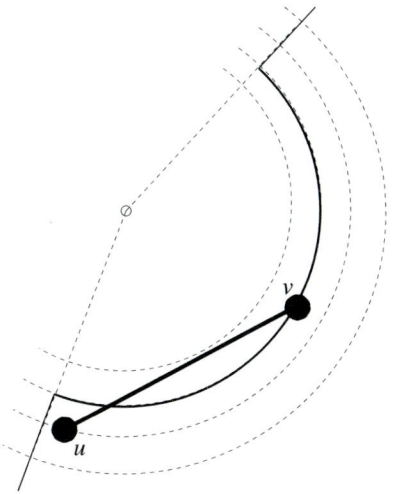

Figure 3.9: Edge escaping from an annulus wedge.

of W_u is

$$\beta_u = \min\left(\frac{\ell(u)\beta_v}{\ell(v)}, \tau\right)$$

where β_v is the angle of W_v and τ is the angle formed by the region F_u. The child u is placed on C_i at the center of W_u. Note that $\cos(\tau/2) = \frac{\rho(i)}{\rho(i+1)}$.

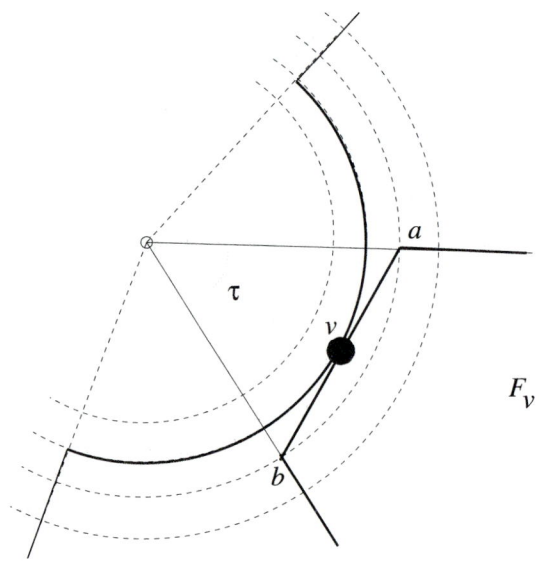

Figure 3.10: Convex subset of the wedge.

From the previous description and from the algorithms illustrated in Section 3.1.2, it is easy to derive an algorithm that runs in linear time and gives a planar radial drawing. Further, the area of the drawings is polynomial in the number of vertices of the tree, in the following sense. Suppose that the minimum distance between two vertices is 1, the tree has height h, and the maximum number of children of a vertex is d_M. If we assume that $\rho(i)$ is defined in such a way that the distance between any two consecutive circles and the distance between the center and the first circle is the same, then it is not difficult to show that the drawing occupies area $O(h^2 d_M{}^2)$. A tree which achieves this bound is illustrated in Figure 3.11. Observe that circle C_1 has perimeter at least d_M. It follows that its radius is $O(d_M)$. Because of the definition of $\rho(i)$, the radius of the final circle C_k is $O(hd_M)$.

To make it easy to follow paths in the drawing, it is sometimes desirable that specific paths follow a straight line. Although paths of vertices of degree two are not always straight in radial drawings, long paths are mostly

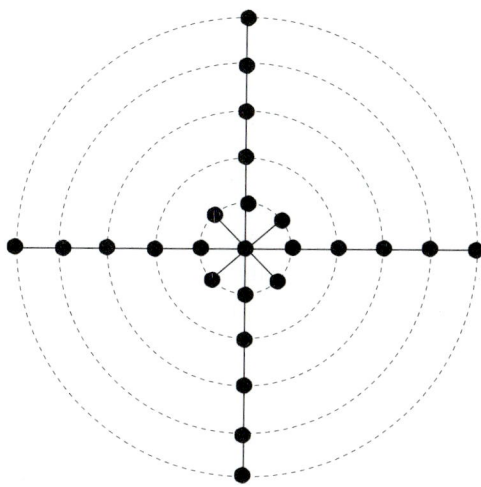

Figure 3.11: A radial drawing with large area.

straight: the only bends are at the second vertex and the the second to last vertex in the path.

Radial drawings are frequently used for representing *free trees*, that is trees without a prespecified root. For a free tree, a fictitious root is usually selected to be a *center* of the tree, that is, a root such that the height of the resulting rooted tree is minimized. A tree has either a unique center or two adjacent centers. The center(s) can be found in linear time using a simple recursive leaf pruning algorithm: if the tree has at most two vertices, then we have found the center(s); if not, then we remove all the leaves. This step is done recursively until we find the center(s). If the center is unique, then it is placed at the origin. If there are two centers, then the edge which joins them is drawn as a horizontal line of length one with midpoint at the origin.

There are many other radial algorithms for free trees, depending on the choice of root, the radii of the circles, and the method for determining the size of the annulus wedge (see [Ead92, Ber81, Esp88]). Bernard [Ber81] has noted that a radial layout can be used to draw trees symmetrically. It is comparatively easy to find automorphisms of trees (see, for example, [AHU74]), and all automorphisms preserve the center and the depth of vertices. Symmetry oriented radial algorithms are presented in [Kam88, MA88]. Further, a free tree can be drawn using any algorithm for rooted trees described in this chapter, by arbitrarily selecting a root as described above.

3.1.4   HV-Drawing

We define an *hv-drawing* (where "hv" stands for horizontal-vertical) of a binary tree as a straight-line grid drawing such that, for every vertex u:

- A child of u is either horizontally aligned with and to the right of u, or vertically aligned with and below u

- The bounding rectangles (smallest rectangles with horizontal and vertical sides covering the drawings) of the subtrees of u do not intersect.

An example of an hv-drawing is shown in Figure 3.12. Is is easy to see that an hv-drawing is planar, straight-line, orthogonal, and downward, but not strictly downward (due to the presence of horizontal edges). Lisp programs can be visualized with hv-drawings [Kam89b].

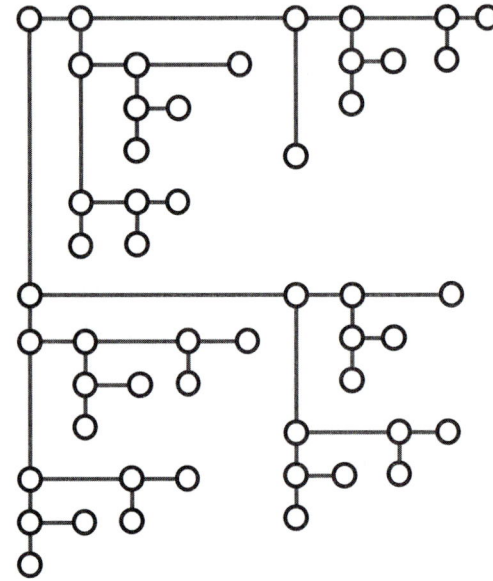

Figure 3.12: Example of an hv-drawing of a binary tree.

A general divide-and-conquer scheme for constructing hv-drawings works as follows:

Divide: Recursively construct hv-drawings for the left and right subtrees.

Conquer: Perform either a *horizontal combination* or a *vertical combination*, as shown in Figure 3.13.

Note that within this scheme, the embedding (order of the children) is preserved only if the left subtree is placed to the left in a horizontal combination and below in a vertical combination. Also, it is easy to verify that because there are no rows or columns without vertices in a drawing constructed with this scheme, the height and width are each at most $n - 1$, where n is the number of vertices of the tree.

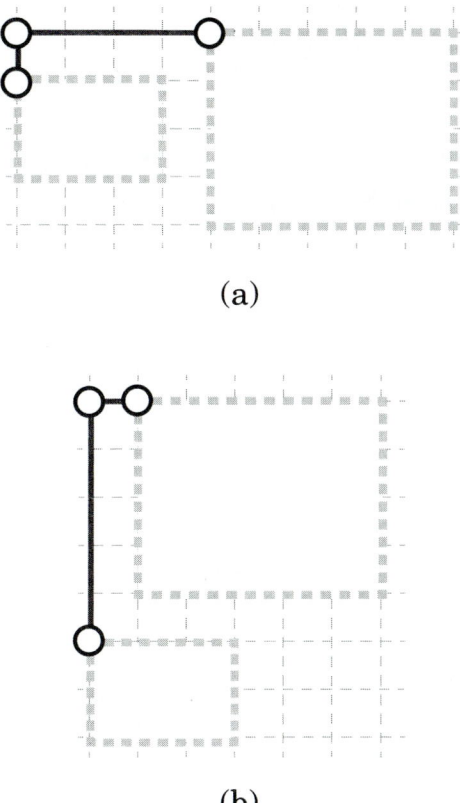

(a)

(b)

Figure 3.13: A general divide-and-conquer scheme for constructing hv-drawings: (a) horizontal combination; (b) vertical combination.

A simple specialization of the above scheme, called Algorithm 3.2 *Right-Heavy-HV-Tree-Draw*, uses only horizontal combinations and places the largest (in terms of number of vertices) subtree to the right of the smallest subtree (see Figure 3.14). Note that Algorithm *Right-Heavy-HV-Tree-Draw* is not embedding-preserving.

Algorithm 3.2 *Right-Heavy-HV-Tree-Draw*

    Input: a binary tree T

  Output: an hv-drawing of T

1. Recursively construct drawings of the left and right subtrees of T.

2. Using a horizontal combination, place the subtree with the largest number of vertices to the right of the other one.

                    □

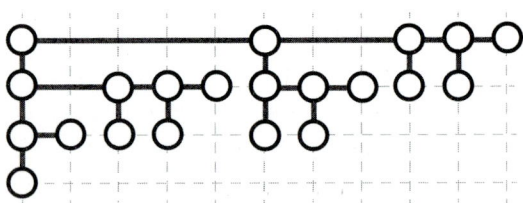

Figure 3.14: Example of an hv-drawing constructed by Algorithm 3.2 *Right-Heavy-HV-Tree-Draw*.

Lemma 3.1 *Let T be a binary tree with n vertices. The height of the drawing of T constructed by Algorithm 3.2* Right-Heavy-HV-Tree-Draw *is at most* $\log n$.

Proof: Let w be the lowest vertex in the drawing of T. Since only horizontal combinations are used to construct the drawing, each vertical edge has unit length. Hence, the height of the drawing is equal to the number of vertical edges encountered when traversing the path from w to the root. Since the largest subtree is always placed to the right of the smallest one, each vertical edge (u, v) traversed going from w to the root is such that the subtree rooted at the parent vertex u is at least twice the size of the subtree rooted at the child vertex v. Hence, the number of vertical edges traversed is at most $\log n$.   □

It is easy to implement Algorithm 3.2 *Right-Heavy-HV-Tree-Draw* to run in linear time. Hence, we have:

Theorem 3.3 *Let T be a binary tree with n vertices. Algorithm 3.2* Right-Heavy-HV-Tree-Draw *constructs a drawing Γ of T in $O(n)$ time, such that:*

- Γ *is an hv-drawing (and thus it is downward, planar, grid, straight-line, and orthogonal)*

- *The area of Γ is $O(n \log n)$*

- *The width of Γ is at most $n - 1$*

- *The height of Γ is at most $\log n$*

- *Simply and axially isomorphic subtrees have congruent drawings, up to a translation.*

While the drawings constructed by Algorithm 3.2 *Right-Heavy-HV-Tree-Draw* have a good area bound, they are penalized by a poor aspect ratio ($\Omega(n/\log n)$). Clearly, in order to get a better aspect ratio, we should use both horizontal and vertical combinations. For example, given a complete binary tree T, we can use horizontal combinations for subtrees rooted at vertices of odd depth, and vertical combinations for subtrees rooted at vertices of even depth. It can be shown that the resulting drawing, shown in Figure 3.15, has $O(n)$ area and constant aspect ratio. The proof is left as an exercise.

For a general binary tree, it is possible to construct an hv-drawing that is optimal with respect to one of several cost measures, including area and perimeter, in $O(n^2)$ time (see [ELL92, ELL93]).

Algorithm 3.2 *Right-Heavy-HV-Tree-Draw* can be extended to general rooted trees as shown in Figure 3.16. We have:

Theorem 3.4 *Let T be a rooted tree with n vertices. There exists an algorithm that constructs a drawing Γ of T in $O(n)$ time, such that:*

- Γ *is downward, planar, grid, and straight-line*

- *The area of Γ is $O(n \log n)$*

- *The width of Γ is at most $n - 1$*

- *The height of Γ is at most $\log n$*

- *Simply and axially isomorphic subtrees have congruent drawings, up to a translation.*

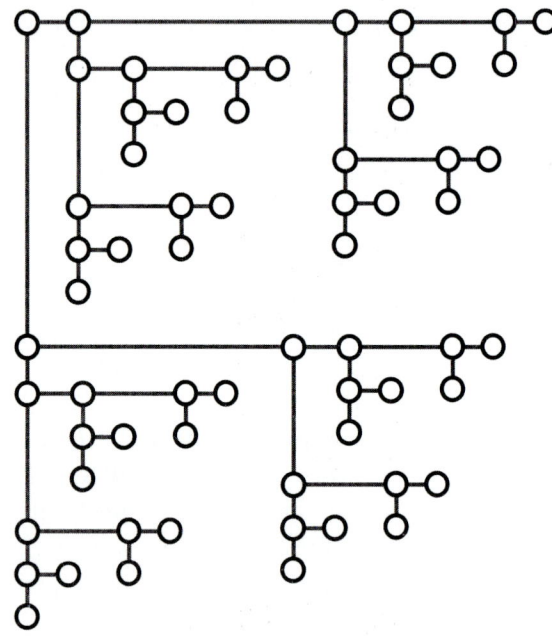

Figure 3.15: An hv-drawing of a complete binary tree with linear area and constant aspect ratio.

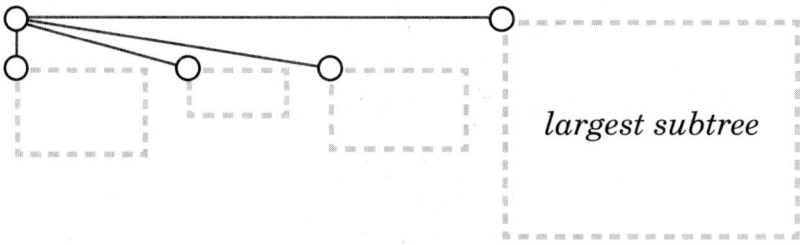

Figure 3.16: Extension of Algorithm 3.2 *Right-Heavy-HV-Tree-Draw* to general rooted trees.

3.1.5   Recursive Winding

In this section, we present an algorithm called Algorithm *Recursive-Wind-Tree-Draw*, which constructs planar downward straight-line grid drawings of binary trees with constant aspect ratio and almost linear area.

Let T be a binary tree with n vertices and ℓ leaves, and assume, without loss of generality, that each internal vertex has two children; thus, $n = 2\ell - 1$. Given an internal vertex v, let $left(v)$ and $right(v)$ denote the left child and the right child of v respectively. Let $T(v)$ denote the subtree of T rooted at v, and let $\ell(v)$ be the number of leaves in $T(v)$. Arrange the tree so that $\ell(left(v)) \leq \ell(right(v))$ at every vertex v. This preprocessing requires only linear time.

Let $H(\ell)$ and $W(\ell)$ denote the height and width of the drawing of a binary tree T with ℓ leaves constructed by Algorithm *Recursive-Wind-Tree-Draw*. Also, let $t(\ell)$ be the running time of the algorithm. Fix a parameter $A > 1$ to be determined later. If $\ell \leq A$, then we draw the tree using Algorithm *Right-Heavy-HV-Tree-Draw*. This provides the base case

$$H(\ell) \leq \log_2 \ell, \ W(\ell) \leq A, \ \text{and} \ t(\ell) = O(A) \ \text{if} \ \ell \leq A.$$

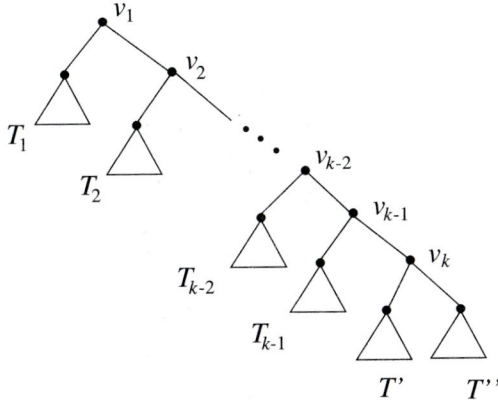

Figure 3.17: Structure of binary tree T.

Suppose that $\ell > A$. Define a sequence $\{v_i\}$ of vertices as follows: v_1 is the root and $v_{i+1} = right(v_i)$ for $i = 1, 2 \ldots$. Let $k \geq 1$ be an index with $\ell(v_k) > \ell - A$ and $\ell(v_{k+1}) \leq \ell - A$. Such an index can be found in $O(k)$ time, since $\ell(v_1), \ell(v_2), \ldots$ is a strictly decreasing sequence of integers. Let $T_i = T(left(v_i))$ and $\ell_i = \ell(left(v_i))$ for $i = 1, \ldots, k-1$. Let $T' = T(left(v_k))$, $T'' = T(right(v_k))$, $\ell' = \ell(left(v_k))$, and $\ell'' = \ell(right(v_k))$. Note that $\ell' \leq \ell''$, since T is right heavy. (See Figure 3.17.) Note also the following properties:

1. $\ell_1 + \cdots + \ell_{k-1} = \ell - \ell(v_k) < A$

2. $\max\{\ell', \ell''\} = \ell(v_{k+1}) \leq \ell - A$.

We distinguish three cases:

- If $k = 1$ (see Figure 3.18.a), the subtrees T' and T'' are drawn recursively below v_1.

- If $k = 2$ (see Figure 3.18.b), the subtree T_1 is drawn with Algorithm *Right-Heavy-HV-Tree-Draw*, while the subtrees T' and T'' are drawn recursively.

- If $k > 2$ (see Figure 3.18.c), the subtrees $T_1, \ldots, T_{k-2}$ are drawn from left to right with Algorithm *Right-Heavy-HV-Tree-Draw*. The subtree T_{k-1} is drawn according to Algorithm *Right-Heavy-HV-Tree-Draw* and then reflected around the y-axis and rotated by $\pi/2$ clockwise. The subtrees T' and T'' are drawn recursively below $T_1, \ldots, T_{k-2}$ and then reflected around the y-axis so that their roots are placed at upper right-hand corners. (This is the "recursive winding.")

In any case, the following bounds hold on the height and width of the drawing and on the running time of the algorithm

$$
\begin{aligned}
H(\ell) &\leq \max\{H(\ell') + H(\ell'') + \log_2 A + 3, \; \ell_{k-1} - 1\} \\
W(\ell) &\leq \max\{W(\ell') + 1, \; W(\ell''), \; \ell_1 + \cdots + \ell_{k-2}\} + \log_2 \ell_{k-1} + 1 \\
t(\ell) &\leq t(\ell') + t(\ell'') + O(\ell_1 + \cdots + \ell_{k-1} + 1).
\end{aligned}
$$

By property 1, we can write the recurrences as

$$
\begin{aligned}
H(\ell) &\leq \max\{H(\ell') + H(\ell'') + O(\log A), \; A\} \\
W(\ell) &\leq \max\{W(\ell'), \; W(\ell''), \; A\} + O(\log A) \\
t(\ell) &\leq t(\ell') + t(\ell'') + O(A).
\end{aligned}
$$

By property 2, we can see that $W(\ell) = O(\lceil \ell/A \rceil \log A + A)$.

Lemma 3.2 *Suppose $A > 1$ and f is a function such that*

- *if $\ell \leq A$, then $f(\ell) \leq 1$*

- *if $\ell > A$, then $f(\ell) \leq f(\ell') + f(\ell'') + 1$ for some $\ell', \ell'' \leq \ell - A$ with $\ell' + \ell'' \leq \ell$.*

Then $f(\ell) < 4\ell/A - 1$ for all $\ell > A$.

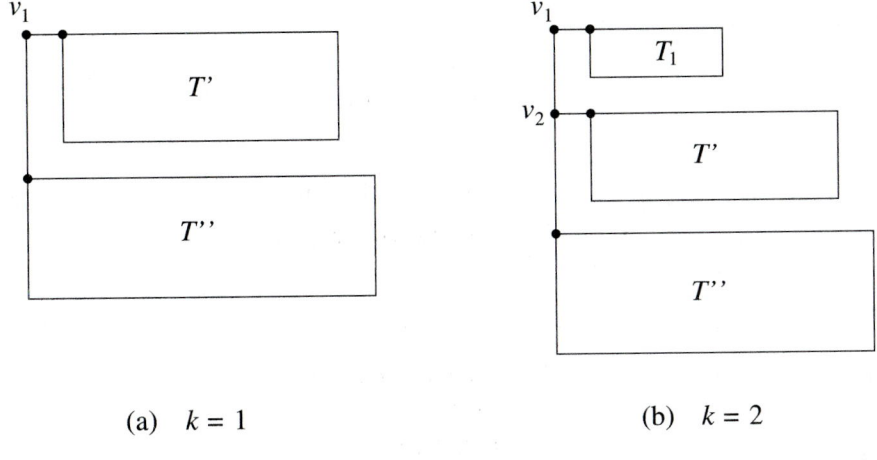

(a) $k = 1$ (b) $k = 2$

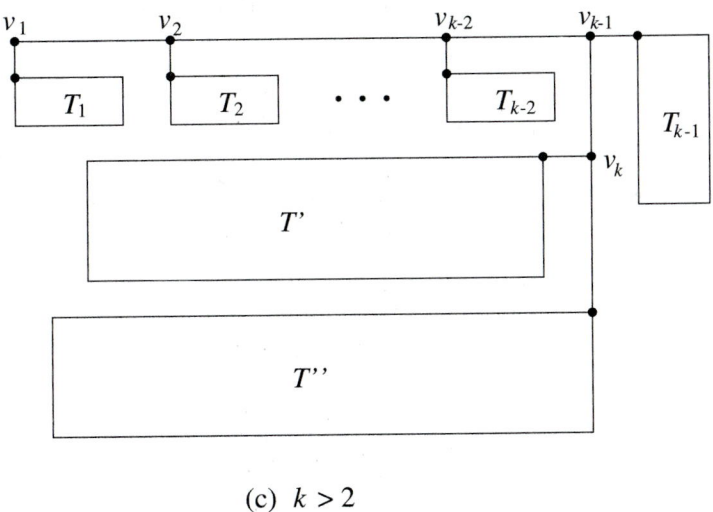

(c) $k > 2$

Figure 3.18: Three cases in the recursive winding drawing method depending on the value of index k: (a) $k = 1$; (b) $k = 2$; (c) $k > 2$.

Proof: The proof is by induction. Suppose the theorem is true for ℓ' and ℓ''. If both $\ell', \ell'' \leq A$, then $f(\ell) \leq 3 < 4\ell/A - 1$. If $\ell' \leq A$ and $\ell'' > A$, then

$$f(\ell) \; \leq \; f(\ell'') + 2 \; < \; 4\ell''/A + 1 \; \leq \; 4(\ell - A)/A + 1 \; < \; 4\ell/A - 1.$$

Finally, if both $\ell', \ell'' > A$, then

$$f(\ell) \;\leq\; f(\ell') + f(\ell'') + 1 \;<\; 4\ell'/A + 4\ell''/A - 1 \;\leq\; 4\ell/A - 1.$$

$\square$

Using the fact that $\ell' + \ell'' \leq \ell$, we obtain that $H(\ell) = O(\lceil \ell/A \rceil \log A + A)$ and $t(\ell) = O(\lceil \ell/A \rceil A)$ by a direct application of Lemma 3.2. By setting parameter A as $A = \sqrt{\ell \log_2 \ell}$, we obtain the following theorem:

Theorem 3.5 *Given a binary tree T with n vertices, Algorithm* Recursive-Wind-Tree-Draw *constructs a drawing Γ of T in $O(n)$ time, such that:*

- *Γ is planar, downward, grid, straight-line, and orthogonal*

- *The area of Γ is $O(n \log n)$*

- *The height and width of Γ are $O(\sqrt{n \log n})$ and thus the aspect ratio of Γ is $O(1)$.*

An example of a drawing constructed by Algorithm *Recursive-Wind-Tree-Draw* is shown in Figure 3.19.

3.2   Series-Parallel Digraphs

In this section, we illustrate how the divide and conquer drawing paradigm can be used to construct straight-line upward drawings of series-parallel digraphs. Such digraphs arise in a variety of problems such as scheduling, electrical networks, data-flow analysis, database logic programs, and circuit layout.

A *series-parallel digraph* is recursively defined as follows (see Figure 3.20): An edge joining two vertices is a series-parallel digraph (see Figure 3.20.a). Let G' and G'' be two series-parallel digraphs. Their series and parallel compositions, defined below, are also series-parallel digraphs.

- The series composition of G' and G'' is the digraph obtained identifying the sink of G' with the source of G'' (see Figure 3.20.b).

- The parallel composition of G' and G'' is the digraph obtained by identifying the source of G' with the source of G'' and the sink of G' with the sink of G'' (see Figure 3.20.c).

This defines the digraphs that are sometimes called *two terminal series-parallel digraphs* [VTL82]. A series-parallel digraph has one source and one sink that are called its *poles*. In the following, we deal with series-parallel digraphs not containing multiple edges.

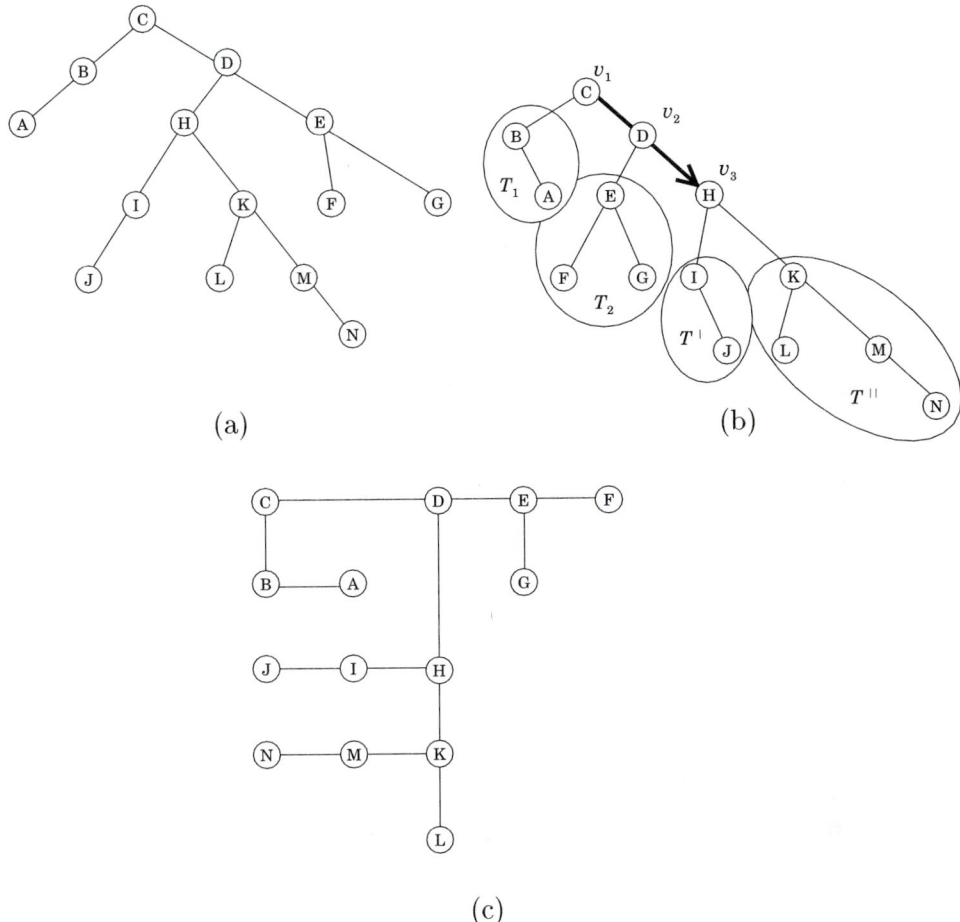

(a)

(b)

(c)

Figure 3.19: Drawing of a binary tree T constructed with the recursive winding technique: (a) input binary tree T; (b) subtrees T_1, T_2, T', and T'' of T; (c) drawing constructed by the algorithm. (Courtesy of J. Stewart.)

3.2.1 Decomposition of Series-Parallel Digraphs

A series-parallel digraph G is naturally associated with a binary tree T, which is called *decomposition tree* of G (also known as *parse tree*). The nodes of T are of three types, S-nodes, P-nodes, and Q-nodes. Tree T is defined recursively as follows: If G is a single edge, then T consists of a single *Q-node*. If G is created by the parallel composition of series-parallel digraphs G' and G'', where G' is to the left of G'' in the embedding, let T'

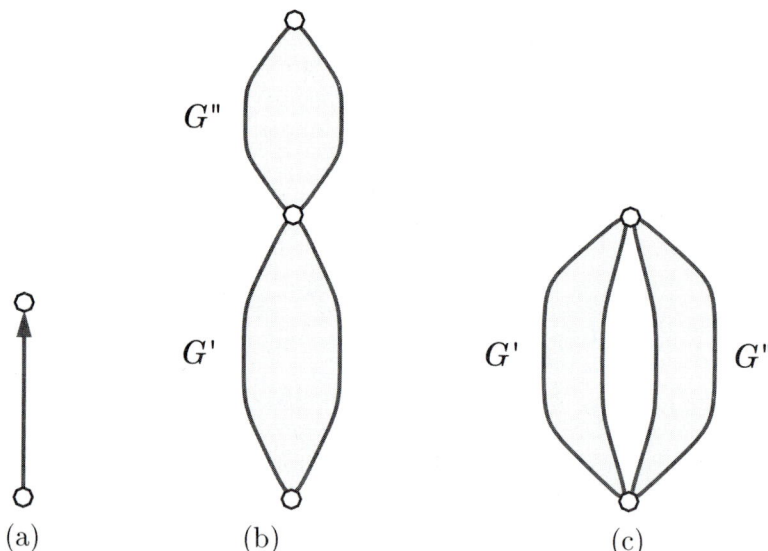

Figure 3.20: Recursive definition of a series-parallel digraph: (a) base case; (b) series composition; (c) parallel composition.

and T'' be the decomposition trees of G' and G'', respectively. The root of T is a *P-node* and has left subtree T' and right subtree T''. If G is created by the series composition of series-parallel digraphs G' and G'', where the sink of G' is identified with the source of G'', let T' and T'' be the decomposition trees of G' and G'', respectively. The root of T is an *S-node* and has left subtree T' and right subtree T''.

The leaves of T are Q-nodes. The internal nodes of T are either P-nodes or S-nodes. We further require that if a node μ and its parent ν have the same type, then μ is a right child of ν. Note that T is unique and that the order of the children of the P-nodes of T defines the embedding of G. If G has n vertices, then T has $O(n)$ leaves and hence $O(n)$ nodes. Recall that unless otherwise specified, we assume that graphs are simple, that is, with no self-loops and no multiple edges.

In the following, we assume that the decomposition tree T of the series-parallel digraph G currently being considered is given as part of the input. If not, it can be constructed in $O(n)$ time using the algorithm of [VTL82].

We now define the components of series-parallel digraphs (see Figure 3.21). Let C be a maximal path of nodes of T of the same type, and let $\mu_1, \cdots, \mu_k$ be the children of the nodes of C that are not on C, from left to right. A *closed component* of G is either G or the composition of the series-parallel digraphs associated with a subsequence $\mu_i, \ldots, \mu_j$, where $1 < i \leq j < k$ and C consists of S-nodes. An *open component* of G is either G or the composition of the series-parallel digraphs associated with a subsequence $\mu_i, \ldots, \mu_j$, minus its poles, where $1 \leq i \leq j \leq k$. A *component* is either an open or a closed component.

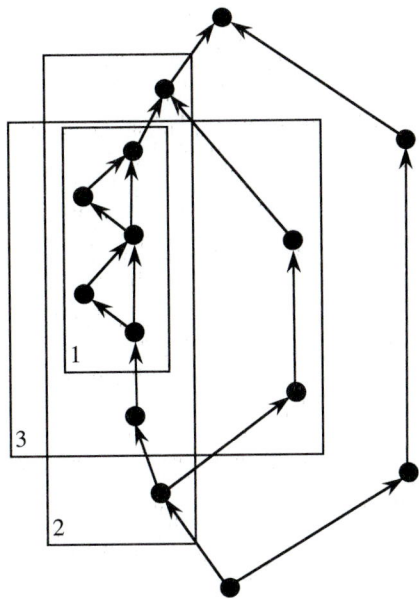

Figure 3.21: The digraph induced by vertices in box 1 is a closed component, the digraph induced by vertices in box 2 is not a closed component, and the digraph induced by vertices in box 3 is an open component.

3.2.2   An Algorithm for Drawing Series-Parallel Digraphs

It can be shown that there exist embedded series-parallel digraphs such that any of their upward straight-line drawings that preserves the embedding requires exponential area (see Table A.4). Thus, to have drawings with polynomial area it is (in general) necessary to change the given embedding.

We recall that an edge (u, v) of a digraph is transitive if there is directed path from vertex u to vertex v distinct from (u, v). Now we show how to construct an upward drawing of a series-parallel digraph G with n vertices. We present an algorithm that modifies the embedding of a given series-parallel digraph so that each transitive edge (u, v) is embedded on the right side of all the components whose poles are u and v. We call such embedding right-pushed. A variation of this algorithm constructs upward grid drawings with $O(n^2)$ area.

Algorithm 3.3 Δ-SP-Draw recursively produces a drawing Γ of G inside a bounding triangle $\Delta(\Gamma)$ that is isosceles and right-angled (see Figure 3.22). Hereafter we denote the sides of $\Delta(\Gamma)$ with base (hypotenuse), top side, and bottom side. In a series composition, the subdrawings are placed one above the other. In a parallel composition, the subdrawings are placed one to the right of the other and are deformed in order to identify the end vertices, guaranteeing that their edges do not cross. The algorithm is described here at a level of detail that allows to deal with its correctness. In Subsection 3.2.3, it will be detailed further for the time complexity analysis.

Note that in the parallel composition of G' with G'', the rightmost edges (s', u) and (v, t') incident on the source and sink of G', respectively, are drawn as vertical segments (see Figure 3.22.c), as can be shown by a simple inductive argument. Also, in the parallel composition of G' with a single edge (the transitive edge (s, t) from the source to the sink of G), we move the source and sink of G' to the intersection of a vertical line (at least one unit) to the right of $\Delta(G')$, and the lines extending the top and bottom sides of $\Delta(G')$, respectively (see Figure 3.22.d).

The correctness of Algorithm 3.3 Δ-SP-Draw can be shown with an inductive argument based on maintaining the following invariants:

1. The drawing is contained inside an isosceles right-angled triangle $\Delta(\Gamma)$, such that the base is vertical, and the other sides are to the left of the base.

2. The source and sink are placed at the bottom and top corner of $\Delta(\Gamma)$, respectively. The left corner of $\Delta(\Gamma)$ is not occupied by any vertex of G.

3. For any vertex u adjacent to the source s of G, the wedge formed at u by the rays with slopes $-\pi/2$ and $-\pi/4$ does not contain any vertex of G except s.

4. For any vertex v adjacent to the sink t of G, the wedge formed at v by the rays with slopes $\pi/2$ and $\pi/4$ does not contain any vertex of G except t.

Clearly, by the construction of the algorithm, Invariants 1 and 2 are always satisfied. Invariant 3 is immediately satisfied after a series composition

---

Algorithm 3.3 Δ-*SP-Draw*

    Input: a series-parallel digraph G

    Output: a strictly upward planar straight-line grid drawing Γ of G

1. Compute a decomposition tree of G.

2. Modify the embedding of G into a right-pushed embedding and perform the corresponding modifications on T.

3. If G consists of a single edge, it is drawn as a vertical segment of length 2, with bounding triangle having width 1 (see Figure 3.22.a).

4. If G is the series composition of G' and G'', the two drawings Γ' and Γ'' of G' and G'' are first recursively produced (*divide*). Then (*conquer*), Γ is drawn by translating Γ'' so that the sink of G' is identified with the source of G'' (see Figure 3.22.b). The bounding triangle $\Delta(\Gamma)$ is obtained by extending the bottom side of $\Delta(\Gamma')$ and the top side of $\Delta(\Gamma'')$.

5. If G is the parallel composition of G' and G''. The two drawings Γ' and Γ'' of G' and G'' are first recursively produced (*divide*). Then (*conquer*), we consider the rightmost edges (s', u) and (v, t') incident on the source and sink of G', respectively (see Figure 3.22.c). Let λ_u be the line through u that is parallel to the bottom side of the bounding triangle of G', and λ_v be the line through v that is parallel to the top side of the triangle of G. Also, let κ be the vertical line extending the base of the triangle of G'. The *prescribed-region* of Γ' is the region to the right of κ, λ_u, and λ_v. First, we translate Γ'' so that its triangle is anywhere inside the prescribed-region of Γ'. Then, we identify the sources and sinks of G' and G'' by moving them to the intersections s and t of the base of $\Delta(G'')$ with the lines extending the top and bottom sides of $\Delta(G')$, respectively.

                                                                        □

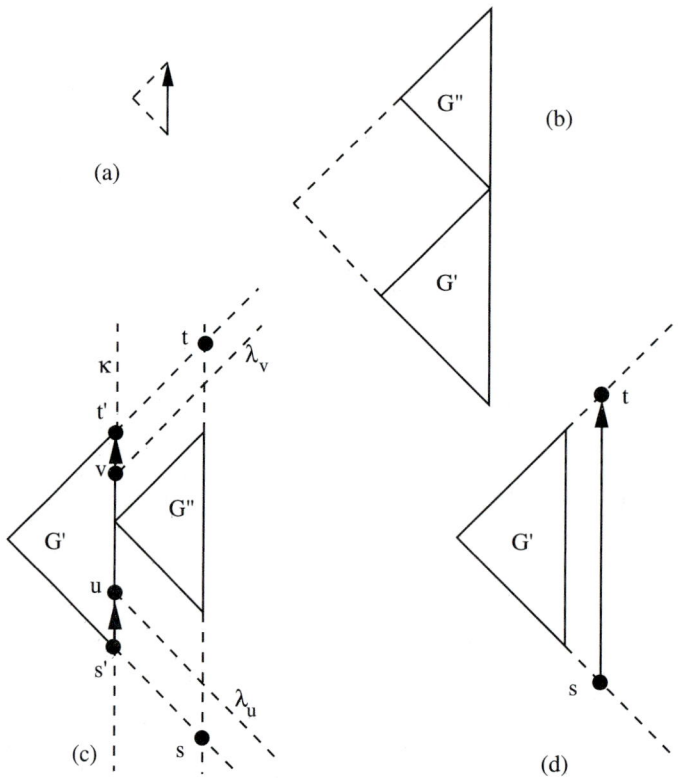

Figure 3.22: Illustration of Algorithm 3.3 Δ-SP-Draw: (a) a series-parallel digraph consisting of a single edge; (b) a series composition; (c) a parallel composition; (d) a parallel composition with a transitive edge.

since the relative position of the vertices of G' remains unchanged, and all the vertices of G'' are placed above the sink of G'.

Lemma 3.3 *Let u' and u'' be neighbors of the source vertex s, such that edge (s, u') is to the left of edge (s, u''), and let $\lambda_{u'}$ and $\lambda_{u''}$ be the rays of slope $-\pi/4$ originating at u' and u'', respectively. If Invariant 3 holds, then $\lambda_{u'}$ is below $\lambda_{u''}$ (see Figure 3.23).*

Proof: By Invariant 1, all the outgoing edges of the source have slope greater than $\pi/2$. Therefore, if $\lambda_{u'}$ were above $\lambda_{u''}$, then u'' would be contained in the angle formed at u' by $\lambda_{u'}$ and the upward ray, which contradicts Invariant 3 for vertex u'. □

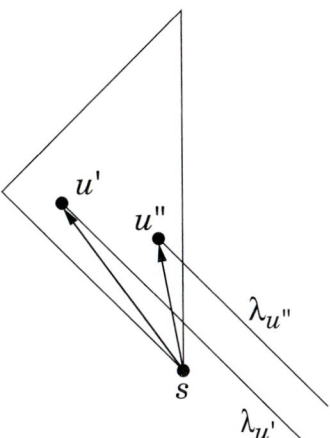

Figure 3.23: Illustration of Lemma 3.3.

In a parallel composition, G'' is placed to the right of G' and above line λ_u, where (s, u) is the rightmost edge incident on the source s. By Lemma 3.3, no vertex of G'' is inside the wedges associated with the neighbors of s. Hence, Invariant 3 is satisfied for G if it was satisfied for G' and G''. Invariant 4 can be proved in a similar manner as Invariant 3.

Invariants 3 and 4 guarantee that s and t can be moved as described in the algorithm without creating crossings. Thus, every composition step yields a correct drawing provided the components are correctly drawn.

As described in the algorithm, the series composition of two components exactly determines the relative positions of Γ' and Γ'' by identifying the source of G'' with the sink of G'. However, we have not described how to exactly place Γ'' with respect to Γ' in the parallel composition. We simply said that Γ'' has to be placed inside the prescribed-region of Γ'.

A possible placement consists of translating Γ'' in the prescribed region so that the left corner of $\Delta(\Gamma'')$ is placed on the base of $\Delta(\Gamma')$. By Invariant 2, there is no vertex of G'' on this corner. This placement yields drawings with $O(n^2)$ area. In order to prove this bound, we observe that the base of the resulting triangle is always equal to the sum of the bases of the triangles of Γ' and Γ''. Therefore, the length of the base of $\Delta(\Gamma)$ is equal to $2m$, where m is the number of edges of G. Hence, the area of Γ is proportional to m^2.

Since Algorithm 3.3 Δ-*SP-Draw* operates recursively on the decomposition tree T of G, isomorphic components are drawn in the same way. Hence, we conclude:

Theorem 3.6 *Let G be a series-parallel digraph with n vertices. Algorithm 3.3 Δ-SP-Draw produces a strictly upward planar straight-line grid drawing of G with $O(n^2)$ area such that isomporphic components of G have drawings congruent up to a translation.*

3.2.3 Detailed Description of Algorithm Δ-*SP-Draw*

Let Γ be a drawing produced by Algorithm 3.3 Δ-*SP-Draw*. We describe the bounding triangle $\Delta(\Gamma)$ by means of the length b of its base. Further, we describe the prescribed region of Γ by means of parameters b' and b'', where b' is the vertical distance between λ_u and the bottom corner of $\Delta(\Gamma)$, and b'' is the vertical distance between λ_v and the top corner of $\Delta(\Gamma)$ (see Figure 3.24.a).

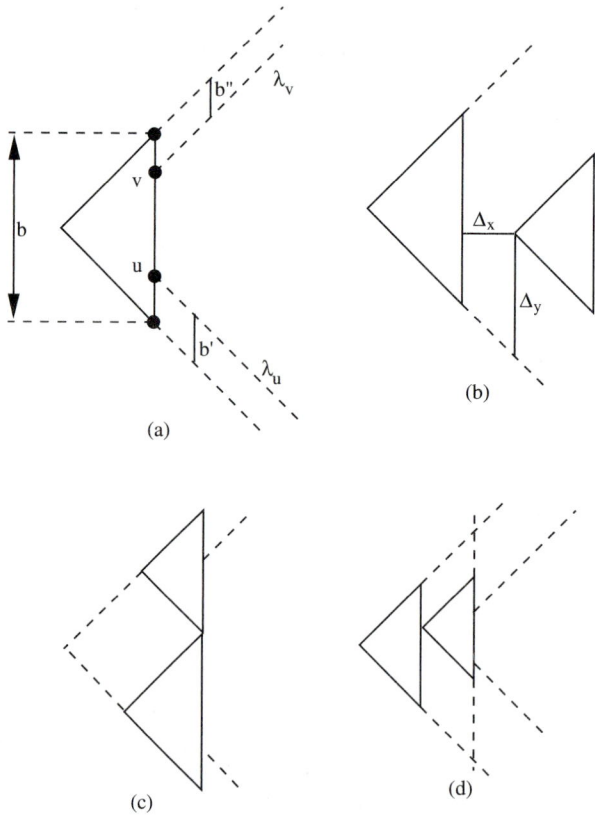

Figure 3.24: b, b', b'', Δ_x, and Δ_y.

The root of each subtree T of the decomposition tree of G is labeled
by Algorithm 3.4 Δ-SP-$Label$ with the values of $b(T)$, $b'(T)$, and $b''(T)$
that describe the bounding triangle and the prescribed region of the upward
drawing of the digraph whose decomposition tree is T.

Algorithm 3.4 Δ-SP-$Label$

      Input: decomposition tree T of a series-parallel di-
               graph G

    Output: labeling of each subtrees of T with values b,
               b', and b''

if the root of T is a Q-node
then
    $b(T) = b''(T) = b'(T) = 2$
else
    let T_1 and T_2 be the left and right subtrees of T, respectively
    for each $i = 1, 2$ **do**
        Δ-SP-$Label(T_i)$
    if the root of T is an S-node
    then (see Figure 3.24.c)
        $b(T) = b(T_1) + b(T_2)$
        $b'(T) = b'(T_1)$
        $b''(T) = b''(T_2)$
    else (the root of T is a P-node, see Figure 3.24.d)
        $b(T) = b(T_1) + b(T_2) + 2\Delta_x$
        if T_2 is a Q-node (transitive edge)
        then
            $b''(T) = b'(T) = b(T)$
        else
            $b''(T) = b(T_1) + 2\Delta_x - \Delta_y + b''(T_2)$
            $b'(T) = b'(T_2) + \Delta_y$

                                             $\square$

In Algorithm 3.4 Δ-SP-$Label$, we assume that in each parallel composition the displacement of $\Delta(\Gamma_2)$ with respect to the base of $\Delta(\Gamma_1)$ is denoted
by means of Δ_x and Δ_y, where Δ_x is the horizontal distance between $\Delta(\Gamma_1)$
and $\Delta(\Gamma_2)$, and Δ_y is the vertical distance between the line extending the
bottom side of $\Delta(\Gamma_1)$ and the left corner of $\Delta(\Gamma_2)$ (see Figure 3.24.b).

In order to place $\Delta(\Gamma_2)$ into the prescribed region of Γ_1, we must have

$\Delta_x \geq 0$ and $b'(T_1) \leq \Delta_y \leq b(T_1) - b''(T_1)$, where T_1 is the decomposition tree of G_1. Observe that in the variation of Algorithm Δ-SP-$Draw$ of Theorem 3.6, $\Delta_x = 0$ and Δ_y can be set equal to $b'(T_1)$.

The labeled decomposition tree obtained in this way is an implicit representation of the drawing. In fact, it is easy to obtain a drawing of the nested triangles by traversing the tree in preorder. Finally, it is immediate to compute the coordinates of the vertices from the drawing of the nested triangles.

Theorem 3.7 *Algorithm 3.4* Δ-SP-Draw *can be implemented to run in* $O(n)$ *time and space on a series-parallel digraph with* n *vertices.*

3.3   Planarity Testing

In this section, we present a simple planarity testing algorithm due to [AP61, Gol63, Shi69], which is based on the divide and conquer paradigm, and we show how it can be implemented to run in $O(n^3)$ time. A sophisticated algorithm inspired by this method, due to Hopcroft and Tarjan [HT74], tests planarity in optimal $O(n)$ time. Linear-time planarity testing methods based on different techniques are given in [BL76, ET76, dFR82, LEC67]. Planarity testing algorithms can also be modified to compute a planar embedding if the graph is found to be planar. (See, e.g., [CNAO85, HT74].) A detailed description of the Hopcroft-Tarjan planarity testing algorithm [HT74] that covers important implementation issues is given in [MM96].

As a first application of the divide and conquer principle, we observe that:

- A graph is planar if and only if all its connected components are planar

- A connected graph is planar if and only if all its biconnected components are planar.

Thus, via a preliminary decomposition into connected and biconnected components, we can restrict our attention to the problem of testing the planarity of a biconnected graph.

As a further application of the divide-and-conquer paradigm to planarity testing, we use a cycle to decompose a biconnected graph into "pieces." Let G be a biconnected graph. Given a cycle C of G, we partition the edges of G not in C into classes as follows: two edges are in the same class if there is a path between them that does not contain any vertex of C. The subgraph induced by the edges in a class is called a *piece* of G with respect to C. In Figure 2.2, we show a graph G and a cycle C. The pieces of G with respect to C are shown in Figure 3.26.

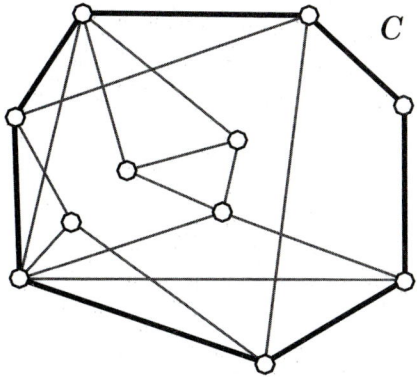

Figure 3.25: A biconnected graph G and a cycle C.

There are two types of pieces:

- Pieces consisting of a single edge between two vertices of C (for example, pieces P_3, P_4, P_5, and P_6 in Figure 3.26)

- Pieces consisting of a connected graph with at least one vertex not in C (for example, pieces P_1 and P_2 in Figure 3.26).

The vertices of a piece P that are in C are called the *attachments* of P. Cycle C induces a circular ordering on the attachments of P. Since G is biconnected, a piece has at least two attachments.

A cycle C of G is said to be *separating* if it has at least two pieces, and is called *nonseparating* if it has one piece. Of course, if $G = C$, then C has no pieces. In the example of Figure 3.25, cycle C is separating since it has six pieces, while in the example of Figure 3.27.a, cycle C is nonseparating.

Lemma 3.4 *Let G be a biconnected graph and let C be a nonseparating cycle of G with piece P. If P is not a path, then G has a separating cycle C' consisting of a subpath of C plus a path of P between two attachments.*

Proof: Let u and v be two attachments of P that are consecutive in the circular ordering, and let γ be a subpath of C between u and v that does not contain any attachment of C. Since P is connected, there is a path π

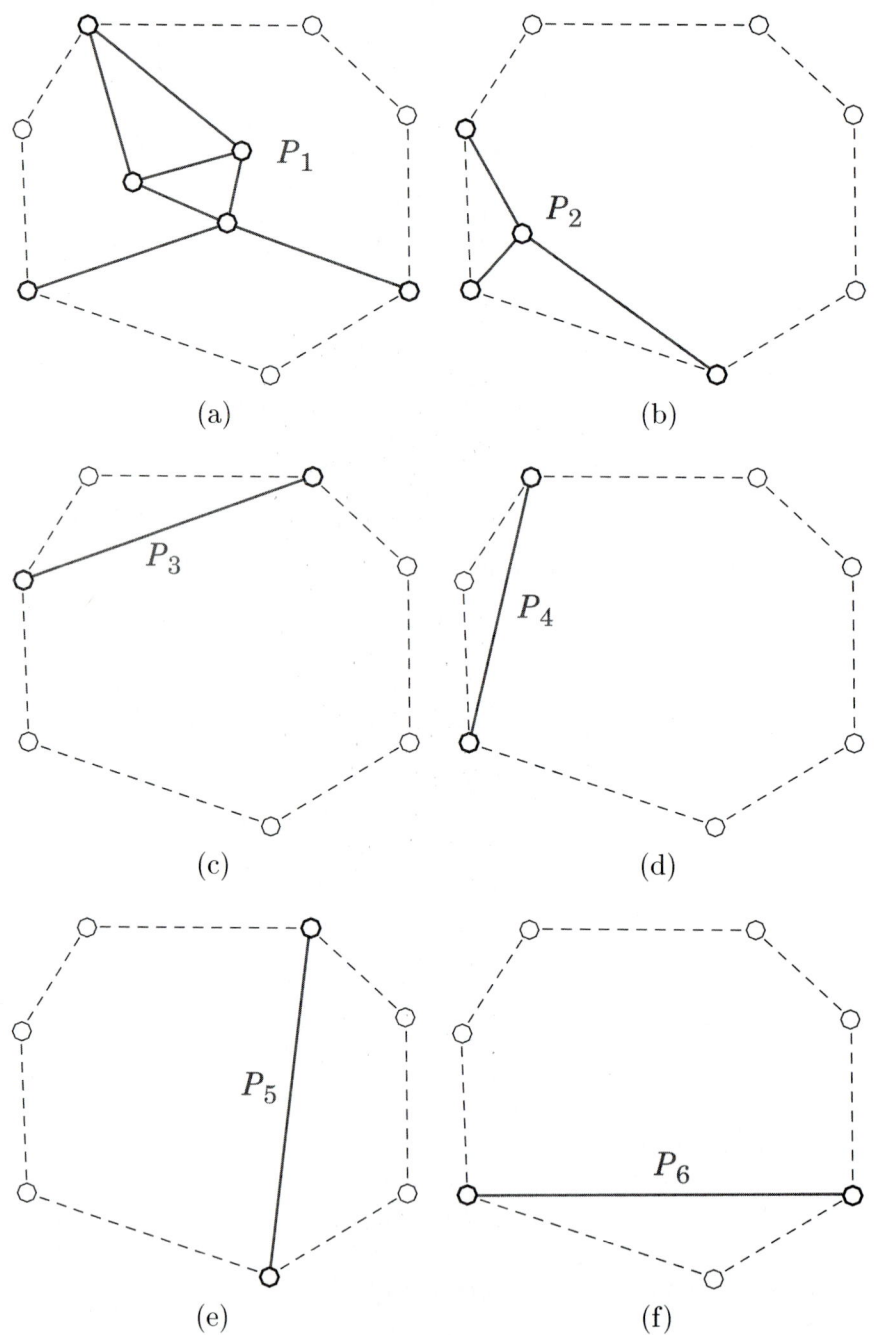

Figure 3.26: Pieces of the graph G of Figure 3.25 with respect to cycle C.

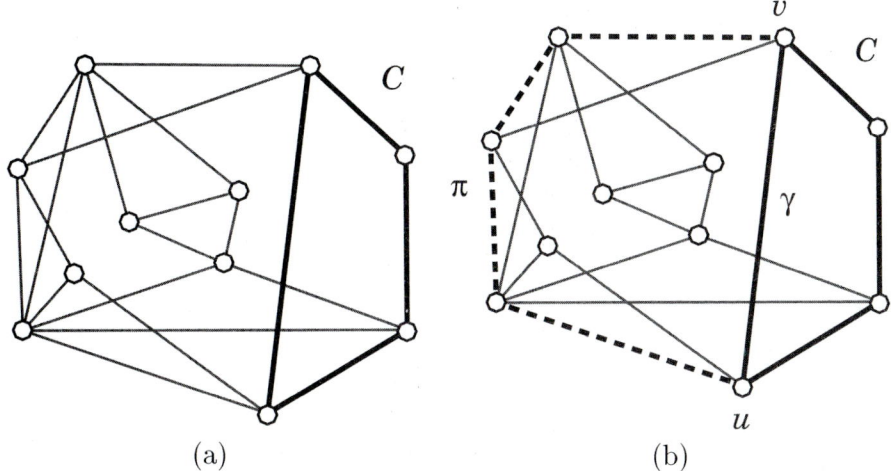

Figure 3.27: (a) Nonseparating cycle C. (b) Separating cycle C' obtained from C as shown in the proof of Lemma 3.4.

in P between u and v. Let C' be the cycle obtained from C by replacing γ with π. We have that γ is a piece of G with respect to C'. If P is not a path, let e be an edge of P not in π. There is a piece of C' distinct from γ containing e. Thus, if P is not a path, then C' has at least two pieces and is thus a separating cycle of G. □

If the graph G is planar, then in any planar drawing of G each piece is drawn either entirely inside C or entirely outside C. We say that two pieces of G, with respect to C, *interlace* if they cannot be drawn on the same side of C without violating planarity. In the example of Figure 3.26, pieces P_1 and P_2 interlace, while P_1 and P_4 do not interlace.

The *interlacement graph* of the pieces of G, with respect to C, is the graph whose vertices are the pieces of G and whose edges are the pairs of pieces that interlace. In Figure 3.28.b, the interlacement graph I of the pieces of the graph G of Figure 3.25, with respect to cycle C, is shown. Clearly, if G is planar, then the interlacement graph of the pieces of G, with respect to C, must be bipartite, since two pieces that interlace must be drawn on opposite sides of C. For example, since the graph G of Figure 3.25 is planar (as shown in Figure 3.28.a), the graph I interlacement graph of the pieces of G with respect to C is bipartite. Now let G be the graph shown in Figure 3.29.a with a separating cycle C. The interlacement graph I of the pieces of G, shown in Figure 3.29.b, is not bipartite. Thus, we conclude that G is nonplanar.

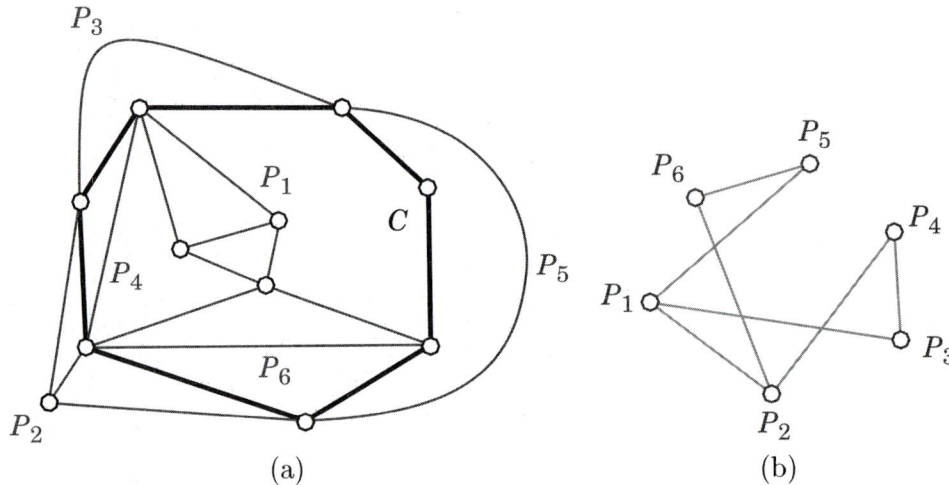

Figure 3.28: (a) A planar drawing of the graph G of Figure 3.25, where pieces P_1, P_4, and P_6 are drawn inside cycle C and the other pieces are drawn outside. (b) The interlacement graph I of the pieces of G with respect to cycle C. Graph I is bipartite, with P_1, P_4, and P_6 on one side, and the other pieces on the other side.

The following recursive characterization of planarity for biconnected graphs is intuitive. We leave its proof as an exercise.

Theorem 3.8 *A biconnected graph G with a cycle C is planar if and only if the following two conditions hold:*

- *For each piece P of G with respect to C, the graph obtained by adding P to C is planar.*

- *The interlacement graph of the pieces of G, with respect to C, is bipartite.*

Algorithm 3.5 *Planarity-Testing* is based on Theorem 3.8 and uses a divide-and-conquer strategy that decomposes a graph into pieces with a separating cycle. Since by Euler's formula a planar graph with n vertices has at most $3n - 6$ edges, we can assume that the input to the algorithm is a graph with at most $3n - 6$ edges. Otherwise, a simple preprocessing based on counting the edges will detect that the graph is nonplanar. Also, we assume that a separating cycle C of G is given. Otherwise, by Lemma 3.4, we can conclude that G is planar.

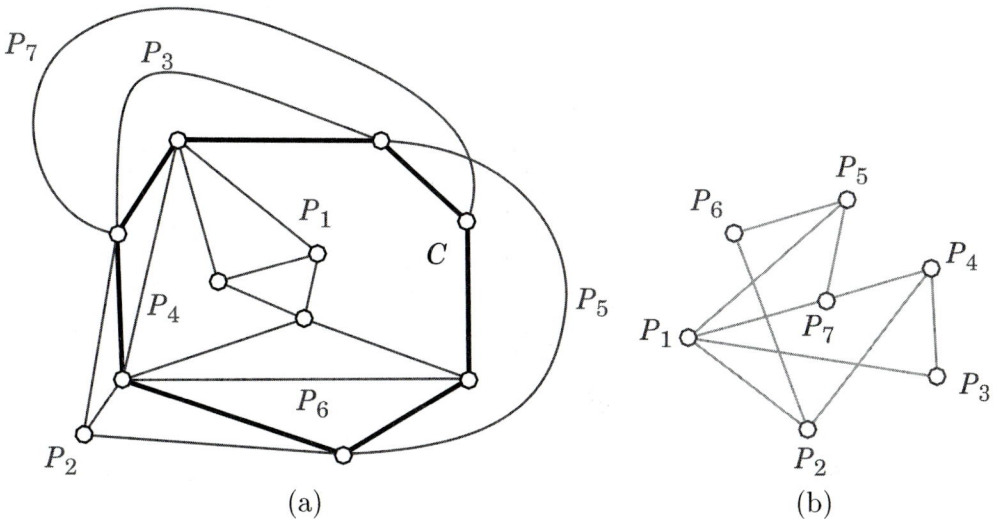

Figure 3.29: (a) A graph G and a cycle C with seven pieces. (b) The interlacement graph I of the pieces of graph G with respect to C. Graph I is not bipartite, which implies that G is not planar.

The correctness of Algorithm 3.5 *Planarity-Testing* is based on Lemma 3.4, Theorem 3.8, and on the fact that the graph P', obtained by adding a piece P to cycle C, is biconnected.

As an example, consider a run of Algorithm 3.5 *Planarity-Testing* on the graph G of Figure 3.25 and on the cycle C shown in Figure 3.25. The pieces computed in Step 1 are shown in Figure 3.26. The graph obtained by adding cycle C to piece P_1, and its separating cycle to be used in the recursive invocation of the algorithm is shown in Figure 3.30. It is straightforward to verify that all the graphs recursively tested for planarity in Step 2 are planar. The interlacement graph I computed in Step 3 is shown in Figure 3.28.a. This graph is bipartite. Thus, the algorithm returns "planar" in Step 5.

We now analyze the running time of Algorithm 3.5 *Planarity-Testing*. In Step 1, we determine the pieces of G with respect to C by computing the connected components of the graph obtained from G by removing C. This step takes $O(n)$ time. In Step 2, computing the cycle C' of P' can be done in time proportional to the number of edges of P'. Note that by Lemma 3.4, C' is a separating cycle of P'.

In Step 3, the interlacement graph I of the pieces can be computed in $O(n^2)$ time as follows. Given a piece P with attachments $v_0, \ldots, v_{k-1}$, in

---

Algorithm 3.5 *Planarity-Testing*

   Input: a biconnected graph G with n vertices and at
               most $3n - 6$ edges, and a separating cycle C
               of G
 Output: an indication of whether G is planar

1. Compute the pieces of G with respect to C.

2. For each piece P of G that is not a path (of one or more edges):

   (a) let P' be the graph obtained by adding P to C

   (b) let C' be the cycle of P' obtained from C by replacing the por-
       tion of C between two consecutive attachments with a path of P
       between them

   (c) apply the algorithm recursively to graph P' and cycle C'. If P'
       is nonplanar, return "nonplanar".

3. Compute the interlacement graph I of the pieces.

4. Test whether I is bipartite. If I is not bipartite, return "nonplanar".

5. Return "planar".

   $\square$

---

this order around C, we label the vertices of v with integers in the range
$[0, 2n - 1]$, where vertex v_i is labeled with $2i$, and the vertices between v_i
and $v_{i+1 \bmod k}$ are all labeled with $2i + 1$. This labeling can be done in $O(n)$
time. Note that a piece Q does not interlace with P, if and only if, all its
attachments have labels in a range of the type $[2i, 2i + 2 \bmod 2n]$. Hence,
testing whether Q interlaces with P takes time proportional to the number
of attachments of Q. Since the number of attachments of a piece is no more
than one plus the number of its edges, and all the pieces are edge disjoint, we
conclude that determining the pieces that interlace with a given piece takes
$O(n)$ time. Therefore, computing the interlacement graph I takes $O(n^2)$
time. The interlacement graph I has $O(n)$ vertices and $O(n^2)$ edges. Hence,
testing whether it is bipartite in Step 4 takes $O(n^2)$ time.

   The above analysis indicates that a recursive invocation of Algorithm 3.5
Planarity-Testing takes $O(n^2)$ time. In order to determine the overall running time, we observe that the number of recursive invocations of the al-

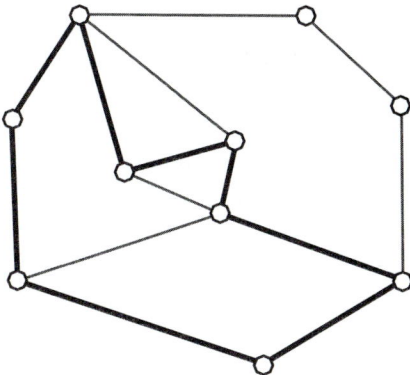

Figure 3.30: Graph obtained by adding cycle C to piece P_1 of Figure 3.26.a, and its separating cycle C' to be used in the recursive invocation of Algorithm 3.5 *Planarity-Testing*.

gorithm is $O(n)$ by associating with each invocation a distinct edge of G. Namely, for a given invocation of the algorithm on a graph P' and a cycle C', we select an edge e of C' that is not in the cycle C of the parent invocation. Such an edge always exists because of the way C' is constructed from C in Step 2. We conclude that the running time of Algorithm 3.5 *Planarity-Testing* is $O(n^3)$.

3.4 Exercises

1. Let T be a binary tree. Consider the algorithm that assigns x-coordinates to the vertices of T, using the rank of each vertex in a postorder traversal of T, and y-coordinates according to the depth of each vertex. Show that the resulting straight-line drawing is planar. What is the area of the drawing? What happens if instead of a postorder traversal we use a preorder traversal? Can the algorithm be extended to rooted ordered trees?

2. Let T be a binary tree. For each vertex v of T, we set $x(v)$ equal to the rank of v in a preorder traversal of T, and $y(v)$ equal to the rank of v in a postorder traversal of T. Show that the resulting straight-line drawing is planar and strictly downward. Show that a vertex v is in the subtree rooted at vertex u if and only if $x(v) > x(u)$ and $y(v) < y(u)$. Does the drawing display isomorphisms of subtrees? What is the area

of the drawing? Modify the assignment of coordinates to produce a
more compact drawing.

3. Prove that the area of drawings constructed by Algorithm *Layered-
   Tree-Draw* is $O(n^2)$. Are there trees that require that much area?

4. Let T be a binary tree with n vertices. For a vertex u of T, we denote
   the height of the left subtree of u by $h'(u)$ and the height of the right
   subtree of u by $h''(u)$. Prove by induction that

$$\sum_{u \in T} (1 + \min\{h'(u), h''(u)\})$$

   is $O(n)$.

5. Write the details of Algorithm *Layered-Tree-Draw* to show that it runs
   in $O(n)$ time.

6. Give a formal proof that the area of radial drawings, constructed as
   shown in Section 3.1.3, is $O(h^2 d_M{}^2)$, where h is the height of the tree
   and d_M is the maximum degree.

7. Consider the hv-drawing Γ of a complete binary tree T with n vertices
   obtained by using horizontal combinations for subtrees rooted at vertices of odd depth, and vertical combinations for subtrees rooted at
   vertices of even depth (see Figure 3.15). Prove that Γ has height and
   width at most $\sqrt{n}$.

8. Give a complete proof of Theorem 3.4.

9. Draw the series-parallel digraph of Figure 3.21 using Algorithm Δ-SP-
   Draw.

10. Show how to modify Algorithm Δ-SP-Draw so that for any two vertices
    v and w, there is a directed path from v to w if and only if $x(v) < x(w)$
    and $y(v) < y(w)$. What is the area of the resulting drawing?

11. Give a proof of Theorem 3.8.

12. Show that a biconnected graph that has no separating cycle is planar.
    What does such a graph look like?

13. Let P be a piece of a biconnected graph with respect to a cycle C:

(a) Show that if P has at least one vertex, the number of edges of P is greater than or equal to the number of attachments of P.

(b) Show that the graph obtained by adding P to C is biconnected.

14. Give a detailed proof of the correctness of Algorithm 3.5 *Planarity-Testing*.

15. Write the details of the complexity analysis of Algorithm 3.5 *Planarity-Testing*.

16. Show how to modify Algorithm 3.5 *Planarity-Testing* so that it also computes an embedding when the graph is found to be planar.

Chapter 4

Planar Orientations

Several algorithms for drawing planar graphs are based on numbering the vertices and then orienting the edges from low numbered vertices to high numbered vertices, such that the resulting digraph, called a planar st-graph, has certain special properties. In this chapter, we present techniques for constructing various types of drawings of planar st-graphs, and then show how to apply them to general planar graphs. These techniques can also be used for drawing general nonplanar graphs by means of a preliminary planarization step (see Section 7.1).

In addition to previously defined straight-line, orthogonal, and polyline drawings, this chapter also considers two geometric representations of planar graphs, called visibility representation and tessellation representation.

We say that two horizontal segments of a given set are *visible* if they can be joined by a vertical segment that does not intersect any other horizontal segment. A *visibility representation* (see Figure 4.1.a and Figure 4.1.b) of a graph draws vertices as nonoverlapping horizontal segments, and edges as vertical segments drawn between visible vertex-segments. It is easy to see that a graph that admits such a representation must be planar.

A *tessellation representation* of an embedded planar graph draws each vertex, edge, and face as a rectangular tile with horizontal and vertical sides, such that:

- There is no intersection between the interiors of any two tiles

- The boundaries of two tiles intersect if and only if the corresponding objects in the graph are incident

- The union of all the tiles is a rectangle.

85

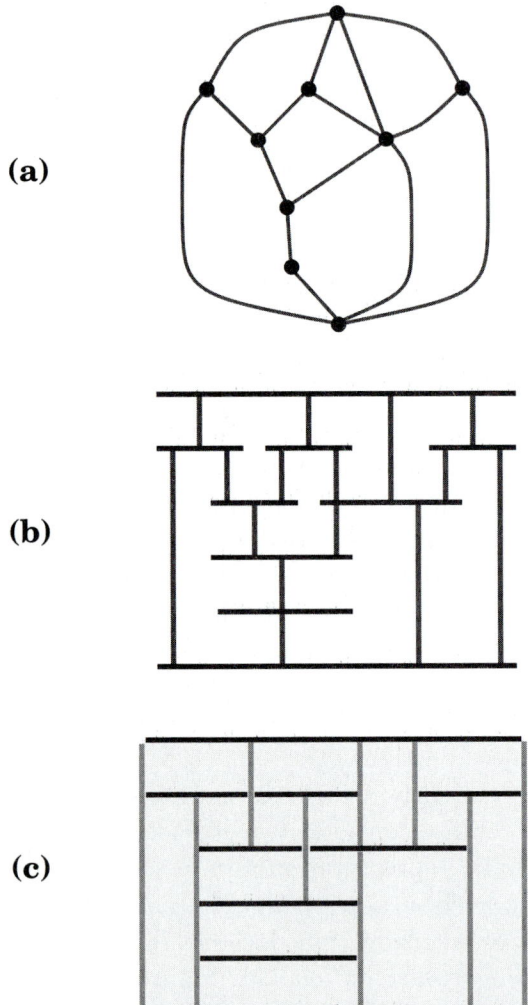

Figure 4.1: (a) A graph G, (b) a visibility representation of G, and (c) a tessellation representation of G where the vertex- and face-tiles are (degenerate) line segments.

Figure 4.1.c depicts a tessellation representation such that the vertex- and face-tiles are (degenerate) line segments.

This chapter is organized as follows.

In Section 4.1, we review preliminary concepts on numberings of acyclic digraphs, related to topological sorting and longest paths. Detailed coverage can be found in any book on graph algorithms.

Section 4.2 introduces planar st-graphs and presents several of their basic properties. Planar st-graphs were introduced in conjunction with an early planarity testing algorithm [LEC67]. Also, they are closely related to the covering digraphs of planar lattices [KR75]. Their properties are further explored in [RT86, TP90, TT86].

The construction of tessellation representations is described in Section 4.3 [TT89b]. A tessellation representation provides a floorplan for other types of drawings. Extensions of tessellation representations to other surfaces are studied in [MR95].

Algorithms for visibility representations are described in Sections 4.4 and 4.5. The study of visibility representations was originally motivated by VLSI layout and compaction problems [OvW78, SLM+84]. Visibility representations are studied in [DT88, DHVM83, KW89, LMW87, RT86, TT86, TT91, Tho84, Wis85]. Algorithms that construct visibility representations in linear time are given in [DT88, Kan93, RT86, TT86]. A complete combinatorial characterization of three classes of visibility representations and linear time drawing algorithms are presented in [TT86]. An algorithm for constructing constrained visibility representations, that is, representations where the edges of given paths are aligned, is presented in [DTT92b].

Polyline drawings derived from visibility representations are covered in Section 4.6 [DT88, DTT92b]. Related work on planar polyline drawings appears in [Kan96, Kan92a].

In Section 4.7, we consider dominance drawings of planar st-graphs, which display the transitive closure by means of the geometric dominance relation among points in the plane [DTT92a]. The combinatorial underpinnings of dominance drawings are in the two-dimensionality of planar lattices [KR75]. Dominance drawings can be used to construct planar polyline drawings with fewer bends than those derived from visibility representations. Related work appears in [EGHL+93].

In Section 4.8, we show how to extend the drawing methods above for planar st-graphs to undirected planar graphs by means of preliminary orientation and augmentation steps.

Planar orthogonal drawings derived from visibility representations are covered in Section 4.9 [TT89b]. Other linear-time algorithms for constructing planar orthogonal drawings are presented in [BK94, Kan96]. A quadratic-time algorithm for minimizing bends in orthogonal drawings is presented in Chapter 5 (see [Tam87]).

Results on planar straight-line drawings are briefly reviewed in Section 4.10.

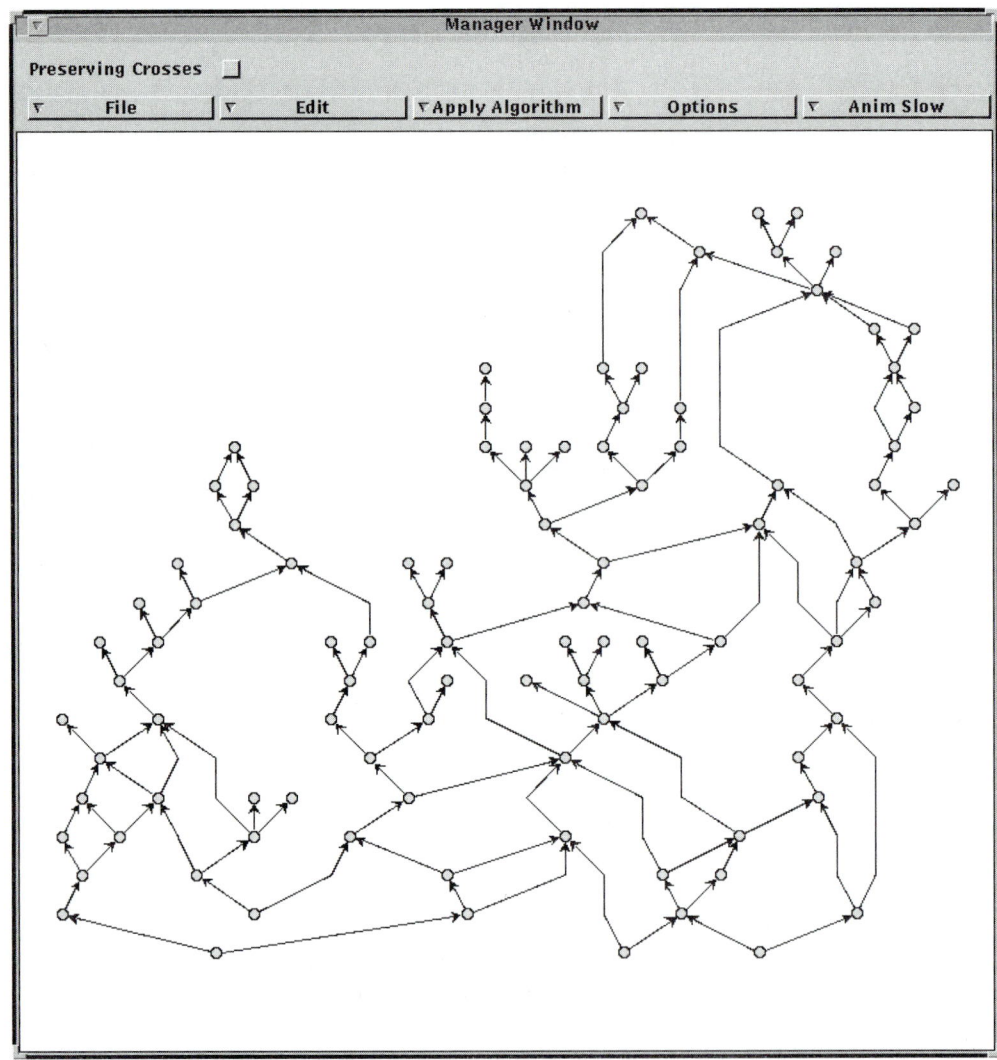

Figure 4.2: A polyline drawing created by the GDToolkit software. (Courtesy of W. Didimo, A. Leonforte, and M. Patrignani.)

A drawing of a 100 vertices digraph, constructed with a variation of the techniques presented in this chapter, is shown in Figure 4.2. It is a polyline drawing derived from a visibility representation.

4.1 Numberings of Digraphs

Let G be a digraph with n vertices and m edges. A *topological numbering* of G is an assignment of numbers to the vertices of G, such that, for every edge (u, v) of G, the number assigned to v is greater than the one assigned to u (i.e., $number(v) > number(u)$). A *topological sorting* is a topological numbering of G, such that every vertex is assigned a distinct integer between 1 and n. A topological sorting is not unique unless G has a directed path that visits every vertex. It is easy to show that the following statements are equivalent:

- G is acyclic

- G admits a topological numbering

- G admits a topological sorting.

If the edges of digraph G have nonnegative weights associated with them, a *weighted topological numbering* is a topological numbering of G, such that, for every edge (u, v) of G, the number assigned to v is greater than or equal to the number assigned to u plus the weight of (u, v) (i.e., $number(v) \geq number(u) + weight(u, v)$). The numbering is *optimal* if the range of numbers assigned to the vertices is minimized (i.e., $\max_v number(v) - \min_u number(u)$ is minimum). An example of an optimal weighted topological numbering is shown in Figure 4.3.

There are simple algorithms for computing a (weighted) topological numbering or sorting that run in $O(n + m)$ time. For example, an optimal weighted topological numbering can be obtained by assigning, to each vertex, a number equal to the number of edges on a longest directed path terminating at that vertex. Note that all source vertices of G are assigned number 0.

The definitions of topological numbering and sorting adopted in this chapter are related to the concept of layering used in Chapter 9.

4.2 Properties of Planar Acyclic Digraphs

An acyclic digraph with a single source s and a single sink t is called an *st-graph*. Let G be an *st*-graph. The following simple properties hold:

- Given a topological numbering of G, every directed path of G visits vertices with increasing numbers.

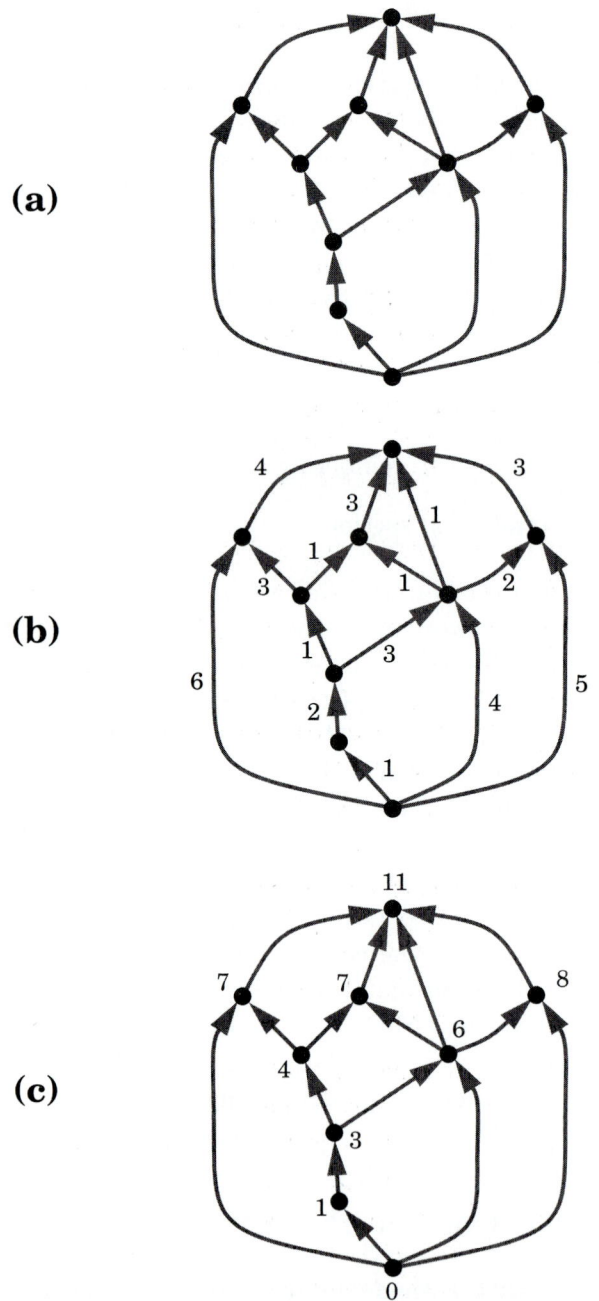

Figure 4.3: (a) Example of a planar st-graph G; (b) weights on the edges of G; (c) optimal weighted topological numbering of G.

- For every vertex v of G, there exists a simple directed path P from s to t that contains v.

The first property holds because of the way the numbers correspond with the direction of the edges. If the second property is not true, then it is easy to see that either there is no path from s to v or there is no path from v to t. This implies that either s is not the only source, or t is not the only sink.

A *planar st-graph* is an *st*-graph that is planar and embedded with vertices s and t on the boundary of the external face. It is customary to visualize a planar *st*-graph as drawn upward in the plane (with s at the bottom and t at the top), as shown in Figure 4.3.a. Since a planar *st*-graph is acyclic, it admits a topological ordering (numbering). Note that a planar *st*-graph with n vertices without multiple edges has at most $3n - 6$ edges, since it is a planar graph (see Chapter 1).

Let G be a planar *st*-graph and F be its set of faces (recall that G is embedded). We conventionally assume that F contains two representatives for the external face: the "left external face" s^*, which is incident with the edges on the left boundary of G, and the "right external face" t^*, which is incident with the edges on the right boundary of G. For each edge $e = (u, v)$, we define $orig(e) = u$ and $dest(e) = v$. Also, we define $left(e)$ (resp. $right(e)$) to be the face to the left (resp. right) of e.

We define a digraph G^*, associated with planar *st*-graph G, as follows (see Figure 4.4):

- The vertex set of G^* is the set F of faces of G (recall that F has two representatives, s^* and t^*, of the external face)

- For every edge $e \neq (s, t)$ of G, G^* has an edge $e^* = (f, g)$ where $f = left(e)$ and $g = right(e)$.

Note that digraph G^* may have multiple edges (as in the example of Figure 4.4). Also, G^* is an orientation of the dual graph of G, except that the dual vertex associated with the external face is duplicated, such that the left (resp. right) external face inherits the outgoing (resp. incoming) edges. It is customary to visualize G^* with a rightward drawing. It is easy to see that digraph G^* is a planar *st*-graph.

As we will show next, each face of G consists of two directed paths with common origin and destination, and the incoming (outgoing) edges of each vertex of G appear consecutively (see Figure 4.5). The face separating the incoming from the outgoing edges in the clockwise direction is called $left(v)$ and the other separating face is called $right(v)$ (see Fig. 4.5).

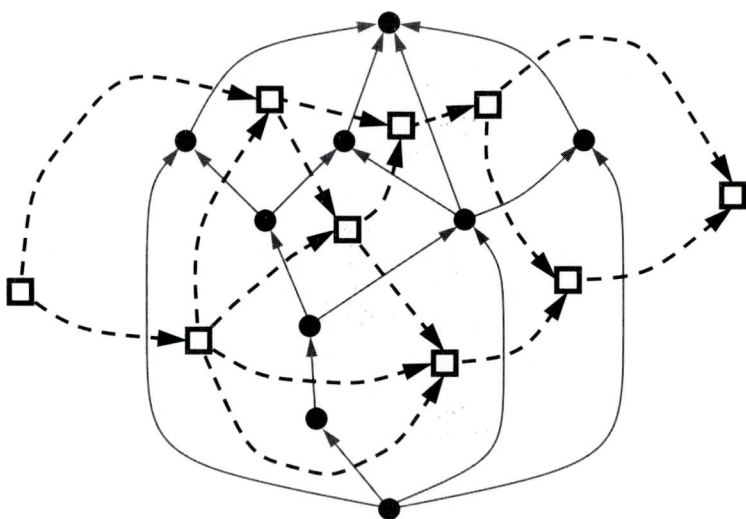

Figure 4.4: Digraph G^* (represented with dashed lines) associated with the planar st-graph G (drawn with solid lines) of Figure 4.3.a.

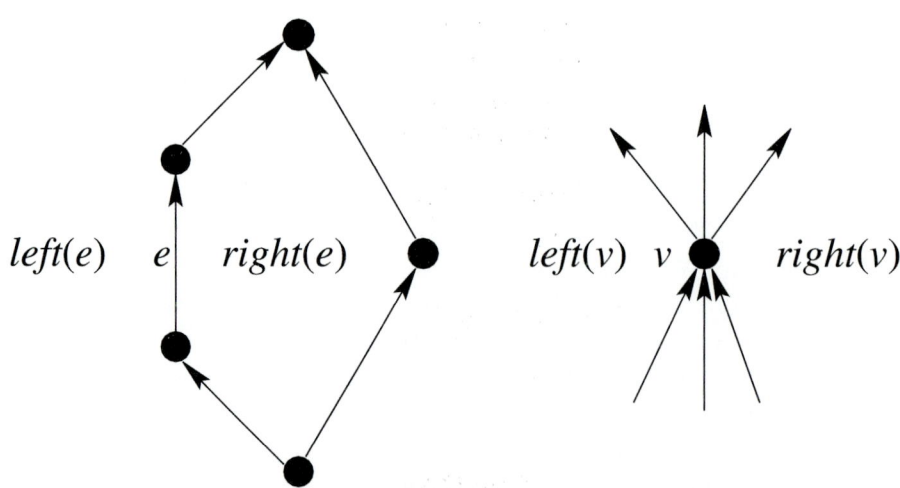

Figure 4.5: Properties of planar st-graphs.

Lemma 4.1 *Each face f of G consists of two directed paths with common origin, called orig(f), and common destination, called dest(f).*

Proof: Let f be a face of G for which the lemma is not true. Then there exists a (directed) edge (w, u) on the boundary of f directed from $dest(f)$ to $orig(f)$. Using the above facts, there are directed paths P_1 from u to t and P_2 from s to w (see Figure 4.6). Additionally, since G is planar, these two paths must intersect at a common vertex x. But then G has a cycle that consists of: the edge (w, u), the subpath of P_1 from u to x, and the subpath of P_2 from x to w. This contradicts the fact that G is a planar st-graph. $\square$

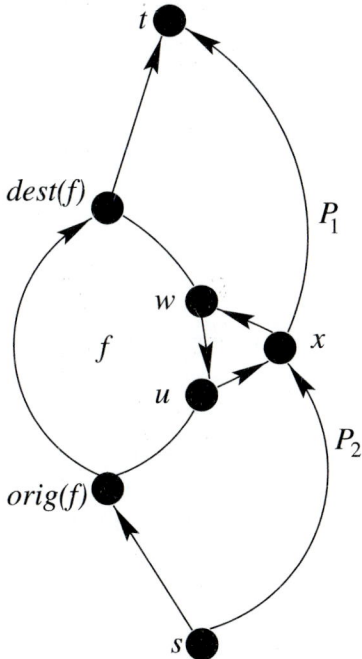

Figure 4.6: Directed paths in the proof of Lemma 4.1.

A planar st-graph has another important property.

Lemma 4.2 *The incoming edges for each vertex v of G appear consecutively around v, and so do the outgoing edges.*

Proof: The lemma holds trivially for the vertices s and t. Let v be any other vertex, and suppose, for a contradiction, that there are edges (v, w_0), (w_1, v),

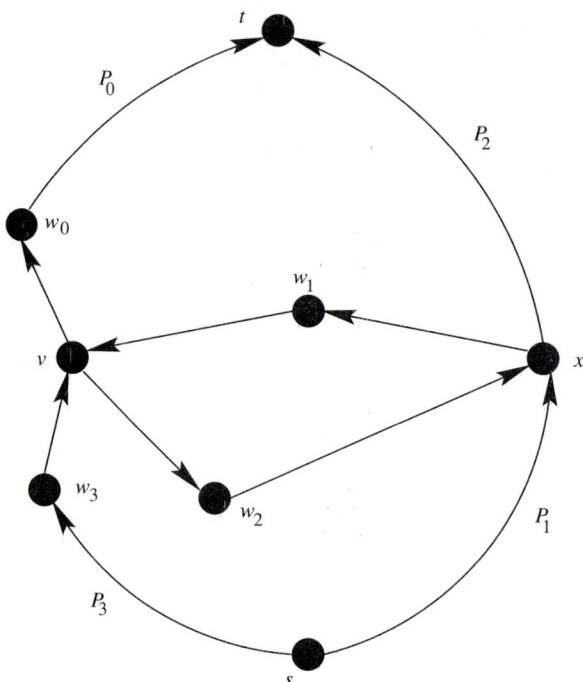

Figure 4.7: Directed paths in the proof of Lemma 4.2.

(v, w_2), and (w_3, v), appearing in clockwise order around v (see Figure 4.7). By the facts above, there are directed paths P_0 and P_2 from w_0 and w_2 to t, respectively. Similarly, there are directed paths P_1 and P_3 from s to w_1 and w_3, respectively. But then one of P_2 and P_0 must intersect either P_1 or P_3 at a common vertex x. This implies that G has a cycle, which contradicts the fact that G is a planar st-graph.   □

This property is in a sense dual to the property described in Lemma 4.1. If we imagine a vertex in the middle of a face f and the dual edges that cross the edges of graph G, then all the incoming edges of f appear consecutively around f, and so do all the outgoing edges.

There is an interesting interplay between the paths of digraphs G and G^*, as expressed by the following lemma.

Lemma 4.3 *For any two faces f and g of a planar st-graph G, exactly one of the following holds:*

- *G has a directed path from $dest(f)$ to $orig(g)$*

- G has a directed path from $dest(g)$ to $orig(f)$

- G^* has a directed path from f to g

- G^* has a directed path from g to f.

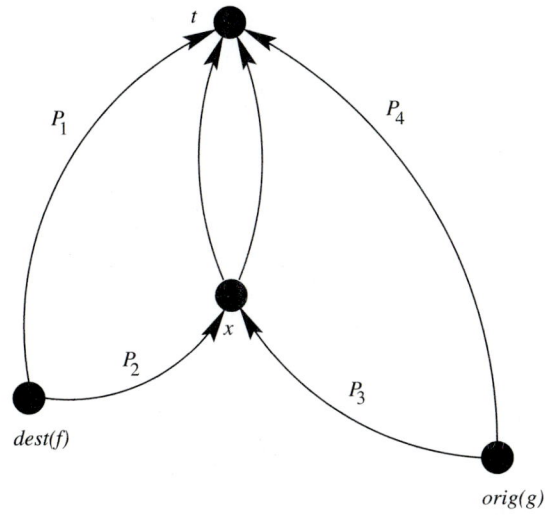

Figure 4.8: Directed paths in the proof of Lemma 4.3.

Proof: Consider a topological sorting of G and, without loss of generality, assume that the number of $dest(f)$ is less than the number of $orig(g)$. The path from a vertex v of G that always takes the leftmost outgoing edge is called the *leftmost path* from v. The *rightmost path* is similarly defined. Consider the leftmost and rightmost paths of G from $dest(f)$ to t, and call them P_1 and P_2, respectively. Similarly, let P_3 and P_4 be the leftmost and rightmost paths of G from $orig(g)$ to t. If there is a directed path of G from $dest(f)$ to $orig(g)$, the lemma holds. Otherwise, either P_2 crosses P_3 (at a common vertex), or P_1 crosses P_4. For simplicity, we consider only the first case. Let x be the first vertex at which P_2 and P_3 intersect (see Figure 4.8). Clearly, from Lemma 4.2, every edge incident to any vertex in path P_2, from the right side of P_2, is incoming. The same happens for the edges incident to P_3 from the left. Because of the construction of G^*, there is a directed path in G^* from f to g. □

It turns out that the above lemma is a special case of a more general property of planar st-graphs, which establishes a total order on the vertices, edges, and faces. An element of $V \cup E \cup F$ is called an *object* of planar *st*-graph G. We extend the above definitions of $orig(\cdot)$, $dest(\cdot)$, $left(\cdot)$, and $right(\cdot)$ to all the objects of G, as follows. For a vertex v, we define $orig(v) = dest(v) = v$. For a face f, we define $left(f) = right(f) = f$.

Lemma 4.4 *For any two objects o_1 and o_2 of a planar st-graph G, exactly one of the following holds:*

- *G has a directed path from $dest(o_1)$ to $orig(o_2)$*

- *G has a directed path from $dest(o_2)$ to $orig(o_1)$*

- *G^* has a directed path from $right(o_1)$ to $left(o_2)$*

- *G^* has a directed path from $right(o_2)$ to $left(o_1)$.*

4.3   Tessellation Representations

A *tile* is a rectangle with sides parallel to the coordinate axes. A tile can be unbounded or can degenerate to a segment or a point. Two tiles are *horizontally (vertically) adjacent* if they share a portion of a vertical (horizontal) side. The coordinates of a tile θ will be denoted by $x_L(\theta)$, $x_R(\theta)$, $y_B(\theta)$, and $y_T(\theta)$.

Let G be a planar *st*-graph. As usual, we denote the sets of vertices, edges, and faces of G by V, E, and F, respectively. (Recall that F has two "external faces", s^* and t^*.) A *tessellation representation* Θ for G maps each object (vertex, edge, or face) o of G into a tile $\Theta(o)$, such that (see Figure 4.9.b):

- The interiors of tiles $\Theta(o_1)$ and $\Theta(o_2)$ are disjoint whenever $o_1 \neq o_2$.

- The union of all tiles $\Theta(o)$, $o \in V \cup E \cup F$, is a rectangle.

- Tiles $\Theta(o_1)$ and $\Theta(o_2)$ are horizontally adjacent if and only if

$$o_1 = left(o_2) \textbf{ or } o_1 = right(o_2) \textbf{ or } o_2 = left(o_1) \textbf{ or } o_2 = right(o_1).$$

- Tiles $\Theta(o_1)$ and $\Theta(o_2)$ are vertically adjacent if and only if

$$o_1 = orig(o_2) \textbf{ or } o_1 = dest(o_2) \textbf{ or } o_2 = orig(o_1) \textbf{ or } o_2 = dest(o_1).$$

Algorithm 4.1 *Tessellation*
      Input: a planar *st*-graph G
     Output: a tessellation representation Θ for G such that
                 each vertex- and face-tile is a segment

1. Construct planar *st*-graph G^*.

2. Compute a topological numbering Y of G.

3. Compute a topological numbering X of G^*.

4. For each object $o \in V \cup E \cup F$, let the coordinates of tile $\Theta(o)$ be

$$
\begin{aligned}
x_L(o) &= X(\mathit{left}(o)); \\
x_R(o) &= X(\mathit{right}(o)); \\
y_B(o) &= Y(\mathit{orig}(o)); \\
y_T(o) &= Y(\mathit{dest}(o)).
\end{aligned}
$$

$\square$

Algorithm 4.1 *Tessellation* constructs a tessellation representation Θ for a planar *st*-graph G. An example of a run of algorithm *Tessellation* is shown in Figure 4.9. The correctness of algorithm *Tessellation* is based on the fact that, by Lemma 4.4, the tiles of any two distinct objects are separated either by a vertical or by a horizontal line. Clearly, each step of the algorithm takes linear time. Hence, we have:

Theorem 4.1 *Let G be a planar st-graph with n vertices. Algorithm 4.1 Tessellation constructs a tessellation representation Θ of G in $O(n)$ time.*

We can modify Algorithm 4.1 *Tessellation* to support user-defined constraints on the size of the edge-tiles. Namely, let $h(e)$ and $w(e)$ be nonnegative numbers associated with each edge e of G. By replacing the first two steps of Algorithm 4.1 *Tessellation* with the following ones, we obtain a tessellation representation of G, such that the tile of each edge e has height at least $h(e)$ and width at least $w(e)$:

1. Assign weight $h(e)$ to each edge e of G and compute an optimal weighted topological numbering Y of G.

2. Assign weight $w(e)$ to each edge e^* of G^* and compute an optimal weighted topological numbering X of G^*.

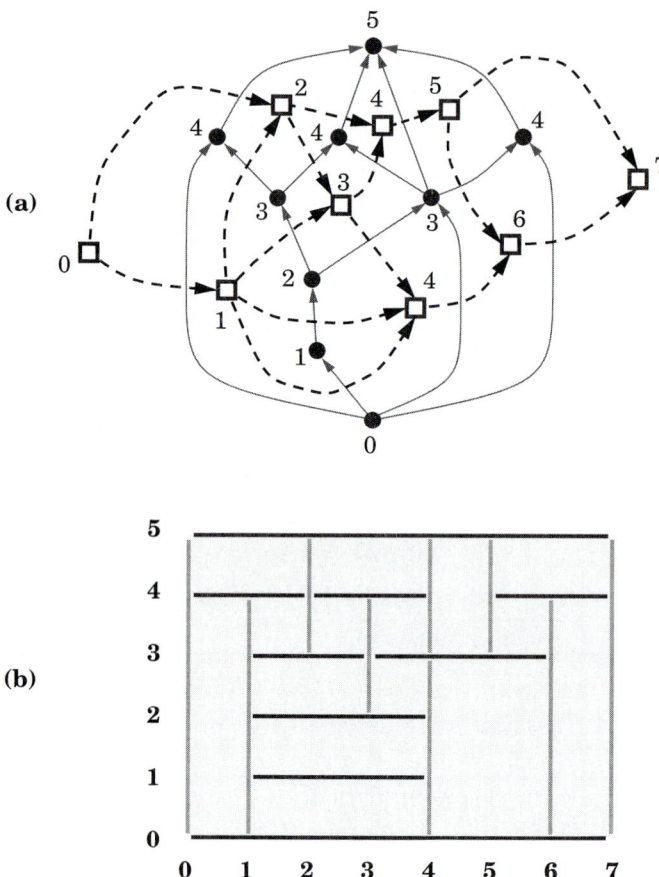

Figure 4.9: Example of a run of Algorithm 4.1 *Tessellation*: (a) planar *st*-graphs G and G^* labeled by topological numberings Y and X, respectively; (b) tessellation representation Θ of G constructed by Algorithm 4.1 *Tessellation*.

Algorithm 4.1 *Tessellation* can also be further modified to support user-defined constraints on the size of the vertex- and face-tiles. Namely, we construct from G a new planar *st*-graph G' as follows:

- Let $G' = G$.

- For each vertex v of G', we expand v into vertices v' and v'', joined by an edge e_v from v' to v'', such that v' inherits the incoming edges of v and v'' inherits the outgoing edges of v.

- For each face f of G', we add an edge e_f into face f from $orig(f)$ to $dest(f)$.

Note that every object of G is associated with an edge of G'. We then simply apply Algorithm 4.1 *Tessellation* to G', and represent each object of G with the tile of the associated edge of G'. We conclude:

Theorem 4.2 *Given a planar st-graph G with n vertices and nonnegative numbers $h(o)$ and $w(o)$ for each object o of G, a minimum-area tessellation representation Θ for G, such that each tile $\Theta(o)$ has height at least $h(o)$ and width at least $w(o)$ can be constructed in time $O(n)$. In particular, if $h(o) = w(o) = 1$ for each object o of G, then Θ has integer coordinates and area $O(n^2)$.*

4.4   Visibility Representations

Let G be a planar *st*-graph. A *visibility representation* Γ of G draws each vertex v as a horizontal segment, called *vertex-segment* $\Gamma(v)$, and each edge (u, v) as a vertical segment, called *edge-segment* $\Gamma(u, v)$, such that (see Figure 4.10):

- The vertex-segments do not overlap

- The edge-segments do not overlap

- Edge-segment $\Gamma(u, v)$ has its bottom endpoint on $\Gamma(u)$, its top endpoint on $\Gamma(v)$, and does not intersect any other vertex-segment.

A visibility representation of a planar *st*-graph G can easily be constructed from a tessellation representation of G with degenerate vertex-tiles and nondegenerate face-tiles, which can be produced by the algorithm of Theorem 4.2. Indeed, the tessellation representation provides a floorplan for drawing each vertex-segment as the degenerate vertex-tile itself, and each edge-segment as any vertical segment spanning its tile (see Figure 4.10).

Algorithm 4.2 *Visibility* provides a direct construction of a visibility representation for a planar *st*-graph G. For the sake of simplicity, the same notation is used for a vertex-segment of the visibility representation and its corresponding vertex in the graph. The same is done for an edge-segment and its corresponding edge.

An example of the construction obtained by Algorithm 4.2 *Visibility* is shown in Figure 4.11.

Algorithm 4.2 *Visibility*

     Input: planar st-graph G with n vertices

    Output: visibility representation Γ of G with integer

                 coordinates and area $O(n^2)$

1. Construct planar st-graph G^*.

2. Assign unit weights to the edges of G and compute an optimal weighted topological numbering Y of G.

3. Assign unit weights to the edges of G^* and compute an optimal weighted topological numbering X of G^*.

4. For each vertex v, draw the vertex-segment $\Gamma(v)$ at y-coordinate $Y(v)$ and between x-coordinates $X(left(v))$ and $X(right(v)) - 1$. In other words,

    for each vertex v **do**
        draw $\Gamma(v)$ as the horizontal segment with
        $y(\Gamma(v)) = Y(v)$;
        $x_L(\Gamma(v)) = Y(left(v))$;
        $x_R(\Gamma(v)) = Y(right(v)) - 1$;
    endfor

5. For each edge e, draw the edge-segment $\Gamma(e)$ at x-coordinate $X(left(e))$, between y-coordinates $Y(orig(e))$ and $Y(dest(e))$. In other words,

    for each edge e **do**
        draw $\Gamma(e)$ as the vertical segment with
        $x(\Gamma(e)) = X(left(e))$;
        $y_B(\Gamma(e)) = Y(orig(e))$;
        $y_T(\Gamma(e)) = Y(dest(e))$;
    endfor

                                                      $\square$

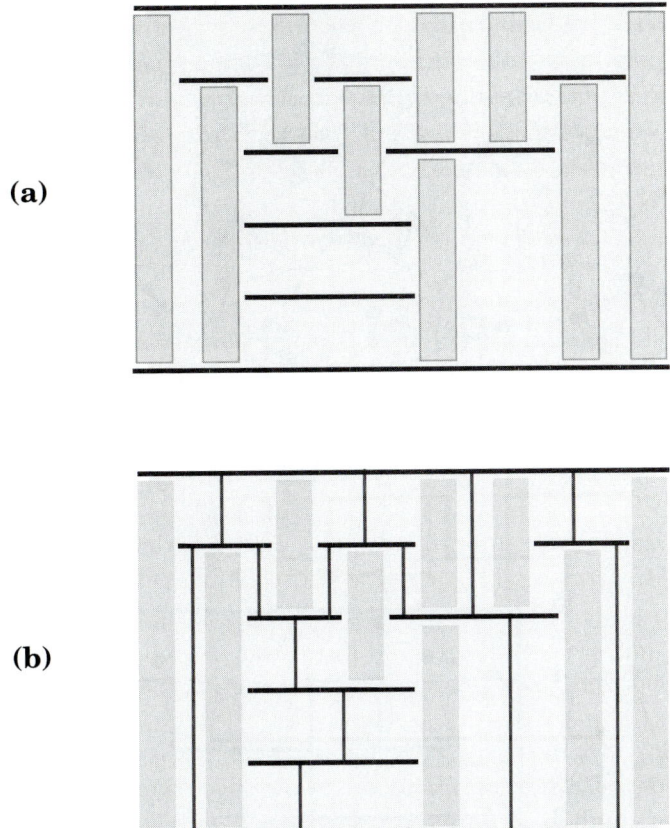

Figure 4.10: Example of construction of a visibility representation from a tessellation representation: (a) tessellation representation of the planar *st*-graph G of Figure 4.3, with degenerate vertex-tiles and nondegenerate face-tiles; (b) visibility representation of G.

The proof of correctness of Algorithm 4.2 *Visibility* is based on the following observations. By Lemma 4.4 and the construction of the algorithm, any two vertex-segments are separated by a horizontal or vertical strip of at least unit width. Also, any two edge-segments on opposite sides of a face are separated by a vertical strip of at least unit width, and no two faces intersect in the representation constructed by the algorithm, except for their common edges. An alternative proof of correctness can be derived by observing that this visibility representation is "drawn inside" a tessellation representation, and can be obtained from it as described at the beginning of this section.

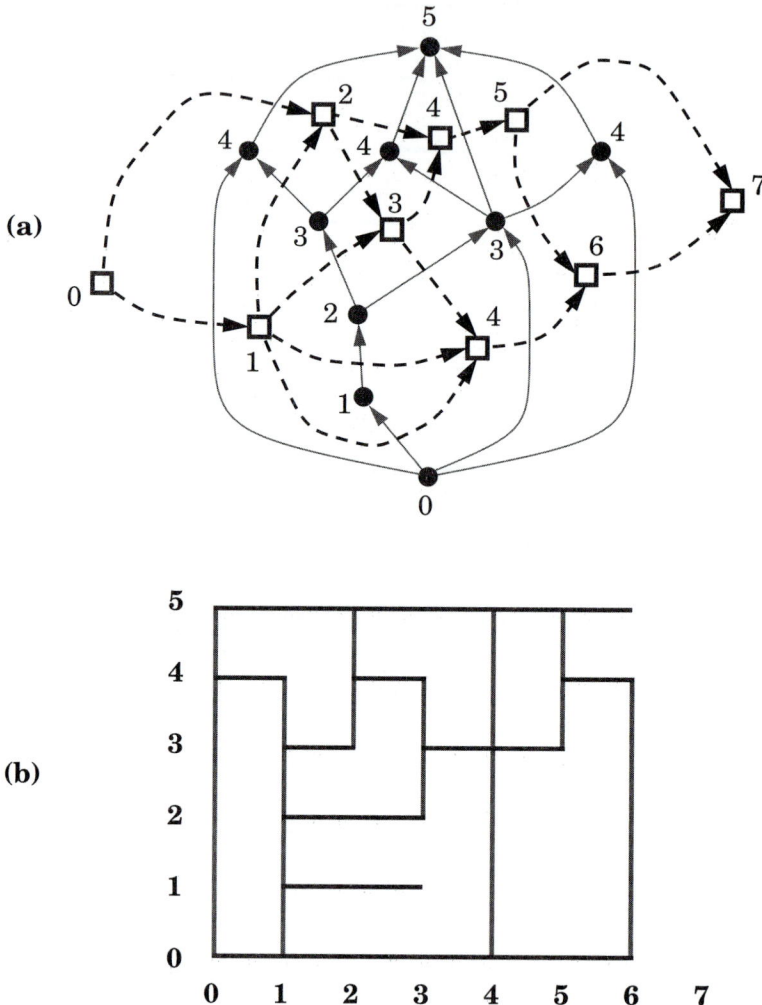

Figure 4.11: Example of a run of Algorithm 4.2 *Visibility*: (a) a planar *st*-graph G, its dual G^*, and the numberings of G and G^*; (b) visibility representation of G constructed by the algorithm.

Clearly, all the steps of Algorithm 4.2 *Visibility* can be executed in $O(n)$ time. Hence, we have:

Theorem 4.3 *Let G be a planar st-graph with n vertices. Algorithm 4.2* Visibility *constructs in $O(n)$ time a visibility representation of G with integer coordinates and $O(n^2)$ area.*

4.5   Constrained Visibility Representations

In this section we present Algorithm 4.3 *Constrained-Visibility*, which constructs a visibility representation of a planar *st*-graph, such that some pre-specified edges are vertically aligned. Such a visibility representation, called *constrained visibility representation*, can be used as a starting point for obtaining orthogonal and polyline drawings with interesting properties, as shown in the rest of this chapter.

Let G be a planar *st*-graph with n vertices. Two paths π_1 and π_2 of G are said to be *nonintersecting* if they are edge disjoint and do not *cross* at common vertices, that is, there is no vertex v of G with edges e_1, e_2, e_3, and e_4 incident in this clockwise order around v, such that e_1 and e_3 are in π_1 and e_2 and e_4 are in π_2. Observe that any two vertex disjoint paths are also nonintersecting.

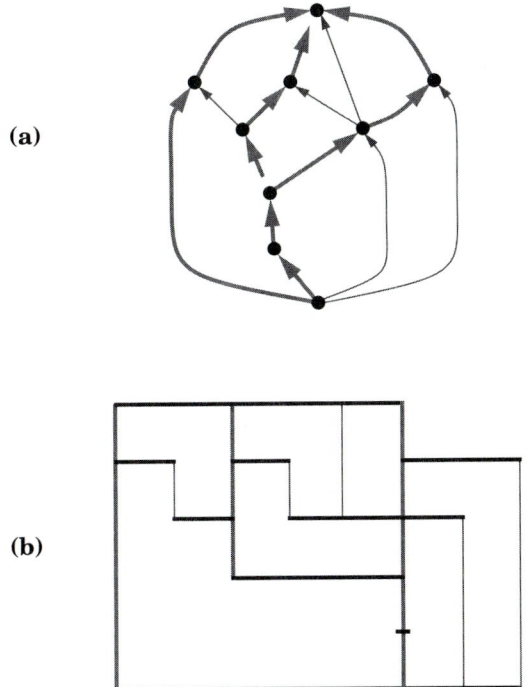

Figure 4.12: Example of a constrained visibility representation: (a) planar *st*-graph G with set Π of paths shown with thick lines; (b) constrained visibility representation of G with respect to Π.

Given a collection Π of pairwise nonintersecting paths of G, we consider the problem of constructing a visibility representation Γ of G, such that, for every path π of Π, the edges of π are vertically aligned. More formally, for any two edges e' and e'' of π, the edge-segments $\Gamma(e')$ and $\Gamma(e'')$ have the same x-coordinate. An example of a constrained visibility representation is given in Figure 4.12.

In order to simplify the description of the algorithm, without loss of generality, we assume that the set Π of nonintersecting paths covers the edges of G. Otherwise, each edge originally not in Π, is inserted in Π as a single-edge path.

We observe that the computations performed by Algorithm 4.3 *Constrained-Visibility* are equivalent to the following construction. First, it modifies G by duplicating each path π in Π, thus forming a new face for each path. Second, it constructs a visibility representation for the modified graph such that the edge-segments of the left side of the boundary of each face are vertically aligned, and two copies of an original vertex are horizontally aligned. Finally, it removes the right copy of every duplicated edge and joins the copies of the duplicated vertices. Figure 4.13 shows an example of a run of Algorithm 4.3 *Constrained-Visibility*.

Notice that every edge e of G has a left and a right face. Also, e belongs to some path in the set Π. Every internal face of G has some path to its left and some path to its right. No path is to the left (resp. right) of s^* (resp. t^*). Hence G_Π contains no directed cycles, has one source s^*, and one sink t^*. Clearly, G_Π is directed and planar. Finally, notice that both s^* and t^* are on the external face of G_Π. Therefore we conclude:

Lemma 4.5 *The digraph G_Π constructed in Step 1 of Algorithm 4.3* Constrained-Visibility *is a planar st-graph.*

From the results described in the previous section, Algorithm 4.3 *Constrained-Visibility* computes a correct visibility representation. Furthermore, each edge e of a path π is assigned the same x-coordinate, $x(\Gamma(e)) = X(\pi)$. The area is clearly $O(n^2)$ and the algorithm takes $O(n)$ time.

Theorem 4.4 *Let G be a planar st-graph with n vertices, and let Π be a set of nonintersecting paths covering the edges of G. Algorithm 4.3* Constrained Visibility *computes in $O(n)$ time a visibility representation of G with integer coordinates and $O(n^2)$ area, such that the edges of every path π in Π are vertically aligned.*

Algorithm 4.3 *Constrained-Visibility*

   Input: planar *st*-graph G with n vertices; set Π of
            nonintersecting paths covering the edges of G

   Output: constrained visibility representation Γ of G
            with integer coordinates and area $O(n^2)$

1. Construct the graph G_Π with vertex set $F \bigcup \Pi$ and edge set $\{(f, \pi)|f = left(e)$ for some edge e of path $\pi\} \bigcup \{(\pi, g)|g = right(e)$ for some edge e of path π $\}$.

   Note that graph G_Π is a planar *st*-graph.

2. Assign unit weights to the the edges of G and compute an optimal weighted topological numbering Y of G, such that $Y(s) = 0$.

3. Assign half-unit weights to the edges of G_Π and compute an optimal weighted topological numbering X of G_Π, such that $X(s^*) = -1/2$.

4. **for each** path π in Π **do**
        for each edge e in π **do**
            draw $\Gamma(e)$ as the vertical segment with
            $x(\Gamma(e)) = X(\pi)$;
            $y_B(\Gamma(e)) = Y(orig(e))$;
            $y_T(\Gamma(e)) = Y(dest(e))$;
        endfor endfor

5. **for each** vertex v **do**
        draw $\Gamma(v)$ as the horizontal segment with
        $y(\Gamma(v)) = Y(v)$;
        $x_L(\Gamma(v)) = \min_{v \in \pi} X(\pi)$;
        $x_R(\Gamma(v)) = \max_{v \in \pi} X(\pi)$;
    endfor

   $\square$

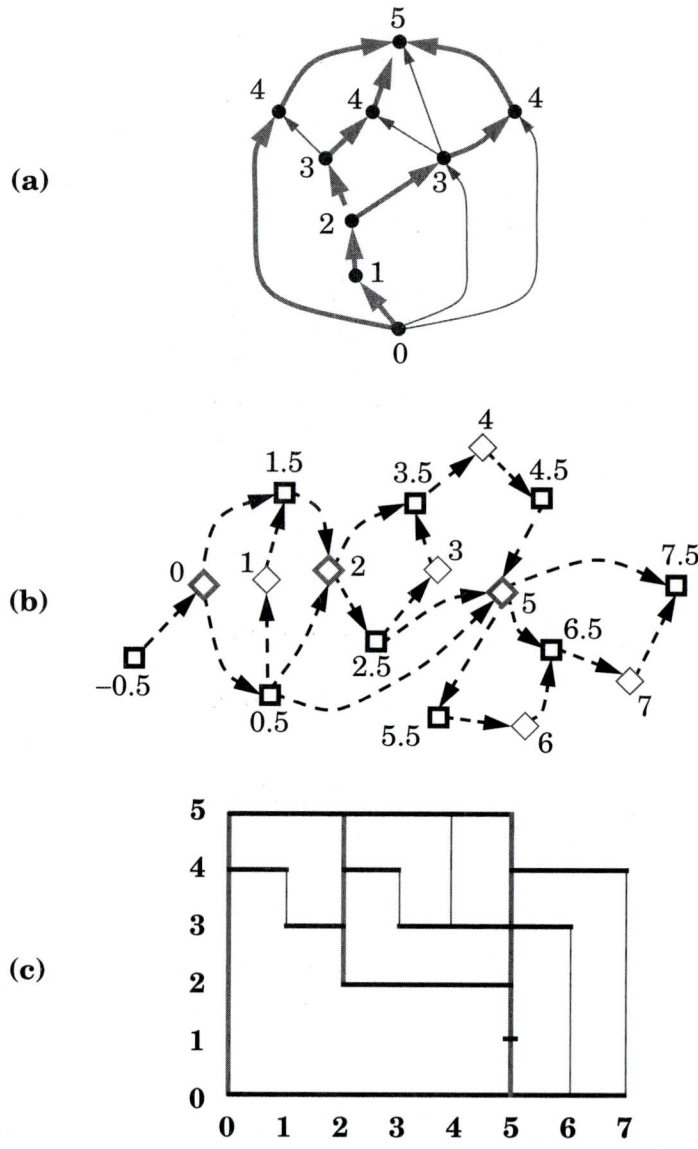

Figure 4.13: Example of constrained visibility representation computed by Algorithm 4.3 *Constrained-Visibility*: (a) planar *st*-graph G, topological numbering of G, and set Π of paths that cover the edges of G, where the paths with at least two edges are drawn with thick lines; (b) digraph G_Π and its topological numbering, where the square vertices represent faces of G and the diamond vertices represent paths of Π; (c) constrained visibility representation of G.

In order to obtain drawings with area $O(n^2)$, we use an optimal weighted topological numbering with unit weights, as shown in Steps 2 and 3 of the algorithm. However, the algorithm works for arbitrary positive edge-weights, and any topological numbering.

4.6 Polyline Drawings

We can construct a planar upward polyline drawing of a planar st-graph G starting from a visibility representation of G as follows. We draw each vertex of G at an arbitrary point of its vertex-segment, and each edge (u, v) of G as a three-segment polygonal chain, whose middle segment is a subset of the edge-segment of (u, v). This construction is formalized in Algorithm 4.4 *Polyline*.

Algorithm 4.4 *Polyline*

    Input: planar st-graph G

    Output: planar upward polyline grid drawing of G

1. Construct a visibility representation Γ of G with integer coordinates.

2. **for each** vertex v **do**

    replace the vertex-segment $\Gamma(v)$ with an arbitrary point

    $P(v) = (x(v), y(v))$ on $\Gamma(v)$

  endfor

3. **for each** edge (u, v) **do**

    if $y(v) - y(u) = 1$ **then** { *short* edge }

      replace the edge-segment $\Gamma(u, v)$ with the segment with

      endpoints $P(u)$ and $P(v)$

    else { *long* edge }

      replace the edge-segment $\Gamma(u, v)$ with the polygonal line

      from $P(u)$ to $P(v)$ through $(x(\Gamma(u, v)), y(u) + 1)$

      and $(x(\Gamma(u, v)), y(v) - 1)$

  endfor

                                                   □

A possible choice for the placement of $P(v)$ is the middle point of vertex-segment $\Gamma(v)$. An example of the polyline drawing obtained with this "median positioning" from the visibility representation of Figure 4.11 is shown in Figure 4.14.a.

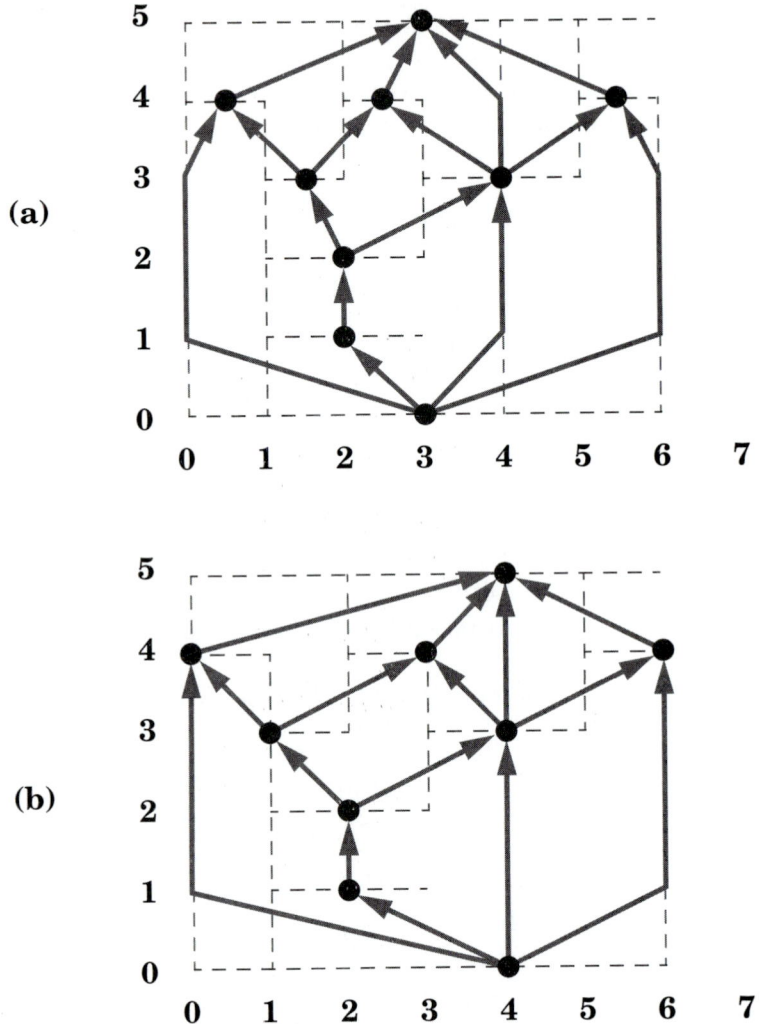

(a)

(b)

Figure 4.14: Polyline drawings constructed by Algorithm 4.4 *Polyline* from the visibility representation of Figure 4.11: (a) median positioning; (b) long-edge positioning with integer coordinates.

Theorem 4.5 *Let G be a planar st-graph with n vertices. Algorithm 4.4* Polyline *constructs in $O(n)$ time a planar upward polyline grid drawing of G with the following properties:*

- *The number of bends is at most $6n - 12$*

- *Every edge has at most two bends.*

Proof: The correctness of the algorithm can be proved with simple geometric considerations. Each edge-segment $\Gamma(u, v)$ is replaced by either a
segment or a polygonal line with at most two bends. Since a planar graph
has at most $3n - 6$ edges, the total number of bends is at most $6n - 12$. □

The above bound on the number of bends can be improved using a
specific visibility representation as input, and a particular choice for the
placement of $P(v)$. Namely, we first construct a visibility representation Γ
of G using Algorithm 4.2 *Visibility*. This guarantees that Γ has at least
$n - 1$ short edges (that is, edges (u, v) with $y(v) - y(u) = 1$). Next, apply
Algorithm 4.4 *Polyline* where, for each vertex v, we place $P(v)$ at the intersection of vertex-segment $\Gamma(v)$ with a long edge incident on v, whenever one
exists. This placement further reduces the number of bends. Additionally,
because of the construction of the visibility representation obtained by Algorithm 4.2 *Visibility*, the height and width of the drawing are bounded by
$O(n)$. Thus we have:

Theorem 4.6 *Let G be a planar st-graph with n vertices. A planar upward
polyline grid drawing of G, with the following properties, can be constructed
in $O(n)$ time:*

- *The drawing has $O(n^2)$ area*

- *The number of bends is at most $(10n - 31)/3$*

- *Every edge has at most two bends.*

An example of polyline drawing, obtained with the "long-edge positioning" of Theorem 4.6 from the visibility representation of Figure 4.11, is
shown in Figure 4.14.b.

The technique above can be extended to constrained visibility representations. Let Γ be a constrained visibility representation for a planar *st*-graph
G and a set of *vertex disjoint* paths Π. Algorithm 4.5 *Constrained-Polyline*
derives a planar upward polyline drawing of G from Γ, such that all the
internal vertices in a path of Π are vertically aligned.

Notice that if there is an edge (u, v) such that $y(v) - y(u) = 2$, then the
two middle points of the polygonal chain associated with (u, v) are coinci-
dent. Figure 4.15 shows the polyline drawing obtained from the constrained
visibility representation shown in Figure 4.13. When a vertex v does not
belong to an aligned path, then any choice of $P(v)$ along $\Gamma(v)$ guarantees

Algorithm 4.5 *Constrained-Polyline*

    Input: planar *st*-graph G; set of vertex disjoint paths
                Π of G

   Output: a planar upward polyline drawing of G, such
                that, for every path π of Π, all the internal
                vertices of π are vertically aligned

1. Construct a constrained visibility representation Γ of G with respect to Π by means of Algorithm 4.3 *Constrained-Visibility*.

2. **for each** vertex v **do**
        replace the vertex-segment $\Gamma(v)$ with a point
        $P(v) = (x(v), y(v))$ on $\Gamma(v)$ as follows:
        if v belongs to a path π of Π **then**
            $x(v) = X(\pi)$;
            $y(v) = Y(v)$;
        else
            choose any point on $\Gamma(v)$
   endfor

3. **for each** edge (u, v) **do**
        if $y(v) - y(u) = 1$ **then** { *short* edge }
            replace the edge-segment $\Gamma(u, v)$ with the segment with
            endpoint $P(u)$ and $P(v)$
        else { *long* edge }
            replace the edge-segment $\Gamma(u, v)$ with the polygonal line
            from $P(u)$ to $P(v)$ through $(x(\Gamma(u, v)), y(u) + 1)$
            and $(x(\Gamma(u, v)), y(v) - 1)$
   endfor

                                                           $\square$

the correctness of the algorithm and a small number of bends (at most two per edge).

Since Algorithm 4.5 *Constrained-Polyline* constructs the output polyline drawing from an intermediate constrained visibility representation, the output drawing has several of the properties of these representations. Recall that a planar *st*-graph with n vertices can have at most $3n - 6$ edges. At least $n - 1$ edges are either short or belong to a path. Hence at most $2n - 5$ edges are drawn with two bends each. Therefore we have:

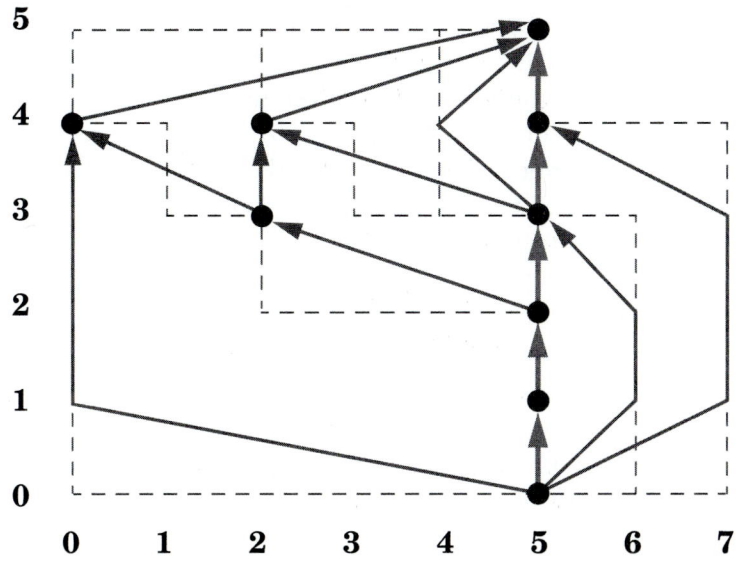

Figure 4.15: Polyline drawing constructed by Algorithm 4.5 *Constrained-Polyline* from the constrained visibility representation of Figure 4.13. Note that we have aligned only one path.

Theorem 4.7 *Let G be a planar st-graph with n vertices, and let Π be a set of vertex disjoint paths of G. Algorithm 4.5* Constrained-Polyline *constructs a planar upward polyline grid drawing Γ for G in O(n) time with the following properties:*

- *For every path π in Π, all the internal vertices of π are vertically aligned*

- *Γ has $O(n^2)$ area*

- *Γ has at most $4n - 10$ bends.*

Algorithm 4.5 *Constrained-Polyline* allows us to effectively visualize specific paths, for example, *critical paths* in PERT diagrams. A PERT *diagram* is a directed acyclic graph whose edges are associated with the tasks of a given project and whose vertices are associated with designated events in the evolution of the project, that is, the start and completion of the various tasks. A PERT diagram has a unique source vertex s, denoting the start of the project, and a unique sink vertex t, denoting the termination of the project. Each edge has a weight which represents the expected duration of the task. The tasks are partially ordered due to technical constraints. Hence, all tasks associated with edges outgoing from a vertex v, can start only if all the tasks associated with the edges incoming in v are completed. The minimum time to complete the entire project is the maximum weight of a path from s to t, and such a path is called a critical path, since delaying any task along that path causes a corresponding delay of the entire project. Therefore, identifying critical paths is very important in planning and monitoring the execution of the project.

Assume that the project starts at time 0. A PERT diagram is usually drawn in such a way that the y direction denotes the flow of time. For example, a vertex v is drawn at a y-coordinate equal to the earliest starting time of the corresponding event, that is, $y(v)$ is the number of edges on a longest path from s to v. Algorithm 4.5 *Constrained-Polyline* allows a PERT diagram to be drawn in such a way that critical paths are effectively displayed along straight lines.

4.7   Dominance Drawings

In this section, we present a drawing algorithm for planar st-graphs with the following features: linear time complexity, small number of bends, small area, detection and display of symmetries, and geometric characterization of the transitive closure by means of the dominance relation between the points associated with the vertices. First, we describe the algorithm for reduced digraphs, and then extend it to the general case.

A *dominance drawing* of a digraph G is a drawing Γ of G, such that, for any two vertices u and v, there is a directed path from u to v in G, if and only if $x(u) \leq x(v)$ and $y(u) \leq y(v)$ in Γ (see Figure 4.16). Notice that these two conditions cannot be simultaneously satisfied with equality since distinct vertices must be placed at distinct points. Dominance drawings have the important feature of characterizing the transitive closure of the digraph by means of the geometric dominance relation among the vertices. A straight-line dominance drawing is upward, but not necessarily strictly upward, because it may have horizontal edges. In this case, a counterclockwise rotation by any angle between $0°$ and $90°$ yields an upward drawing.

4.7.1   Reduced Digraphs

Let G be a reduced planar st-graph with vertex set V and edge set E. Recall that G is embedded in the plane with s and t on the external face. We shall denote with $u \rightarrow v$ a directed path (or the existence of such a path) from

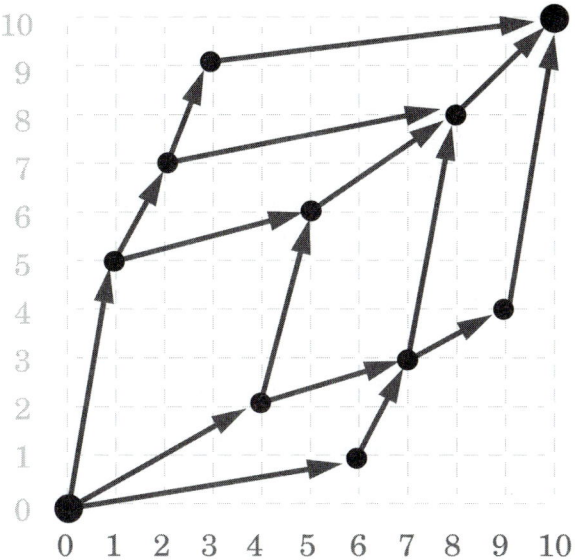

Figure 4.16: An example of a straight-line dominance drawing.

vertex u to vertex v in G. In this subsection, we show how to construct a planar straight-line upward drawing of G.

We will present a lemma that characterizes the relation between dominance drawings and planarity. Some notation is needed. Given a straight-line dominance drawing Γ of a digraph G, consider the point $\Gamma(u) = (x(u), y(u))$ where vertex u is placed. We define the following four regions of the plane (see Figure 4.17)

$$
\begin{aligned}
b(u) &= \{(x, y) : x \leq x(u) \text{ and } y \leq y(u)\} \\
t(u) &= \{(x, y) : x \geq x(u) \text{ and } y \geq y(u)\} \\
l(u) &= \{(x, y) : x < x(u) \text{ and } y > y(u)\} \\
r(u) &= \{(x, y) : x > x(u) \text{ and } y < y(u)\}
\end{aligned}
$$

Lemma 4.6 *Any straight-line dominance drawing Γ of a reduced planar st-graph G is planar.*

Proof: As a contradiction, suppose there is a crossing between edges (u, v) and (w, z) in Γ. Consider edge (u, v). Since G is reduced and Γ is a straight-line dominance drawing, no vertex p is placed in the rectangle defined by

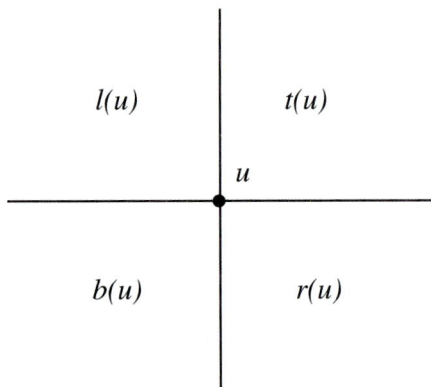

Figure 4.17: Regions $b(u)$, $t(u)$, $l(u)$, and $r(u)$.

points $\Gamma(u)$ and $\Gamma(v)$ (see Figure 4.18).   Otherwise, by the definition of dominance drawing, there would be paths $u \to p$ and $p \to v$, implying that (u, v) is a transitive edge, thus contradicting the fact that G is reduced.

Without loss of generality, assume that $\Gamma(w, z)$ crosses $\Gamma(u, v)$ from left to right.   First, $\Gamma(w)$ cannot be in $b(u)$.   In fact, in this case (w, z) would be transitive with respect to the path consisting of $w \to u$ and $u \to z$. Analogously, z cannot be in $t(v)$.   Hence, the only possible case is that $w \in l(u) - l(v)$ and $z \in r(v) - r(u)$.

Consider paths $s \to u$ and $s \to w$, and let s' be the last (farthest from s) vertex common to both paths. Similarly, let t' be the first (farthest from t) vertex common to paths $v \to t$ and $z \to t$. By the above definitions and the dominance property, G has the following pairwise vertex-disjoint (except in the endpoints) paths (see Figure 4.19)

$$s' \to w, \quad s' \to u, \quad v \to t', \quad z \to t',$$
$$u \to v, \quad w \to z, \quad u \to z, \quad w \to v.$$

Since s and t are on the external face, we can add the edge (s, t) to G, while preserving planarity. It is easy to verify that the paths listed above plus the edge (s, t) form a graph that is homeomorphic to $K_{3,3}$. This fact contradicts the planarity of G.

$\square$

Now we present Algorithm 4.6 *Dominance-Straight-Line*. The algorithm consists of three phases: the first phase, *Preprocessing* sets up a linked data structure; the second phase, *Preliminary Layout*, assigns to each vertex v

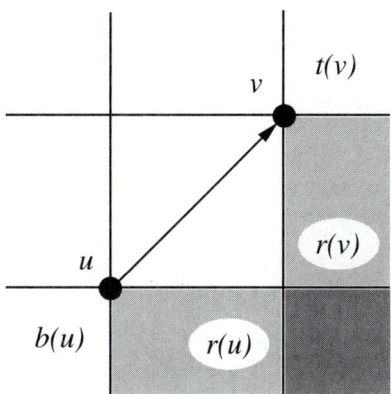

Figure 4.18: Regions around edge (u, v) in the proof of Lemma 4.6.

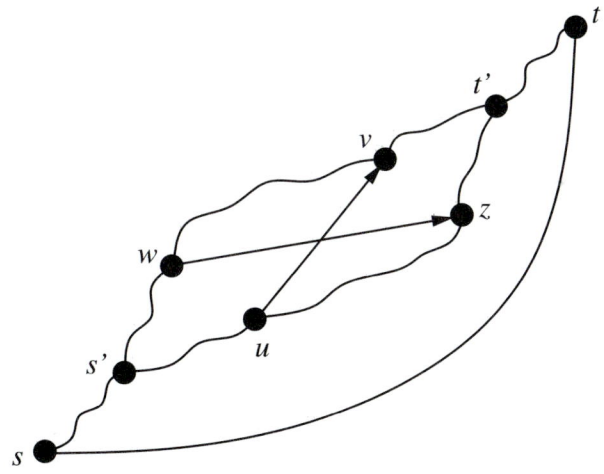

Figure 4.19: A $K_{3,3}$ in the proof of Lemma 4.6.

a distinct X- and Y-coordinate in the range $[0, n - 1]$; the third phase, *Compaction*, adjusts the position of the vertices to reduce the area of the drawing. The Preliminary Layout phase performs essentially two topological sortings of the vertices of G, which scan the successors of each vertex from left to right (e.g., clockwise) and from right to left (e.g., counterclockwise), respectively. The Compaction phase scans the vertices according to the order given by the preliminary X- and Y-coordinates.

Algorithm 4.6 *Dominance-Straight-Line*
    Input: reduced planar *st*-graph G
   Output: straight-line dominance drawing Γ of G

Preprocessing: Set up a linked data structure for G, where each vertex v
points to the list of its outgoing edges sorted according to their clockwise sequence around v. This list is doubly connected by means of
pointers $next(e)$ and $pred(e)$, and is accessed by means of pointers
$firstout(v)$ and $lastout(v)$ to its leftmost and rightmost edge, respectively. Also, v has pointers $firstin(v)$ and $lastin(v)$ to its leftmost and
rightmost incoming edges, respectively. Finally each edge $e = (u, v)$
stores a pointer $head(e)$ to v.

Preliminary Layout: { Assign preliminary coordinates X and Y }

     { Assign preliminary coordinate X }
     Set $count = 0$ and call LabelX(s):
     procedure LabelX($v : vertex$);
     begin
         $X(v) = count$;
         $count = count + 1$;
         if $v \neq t$ **then begin**
            $e = firstout(v)$;
            repeat
               $w = head(e)$;
               if $e = lastin(w)$ **then** LabelX(w);
               $e = next(e)$;
            until $e = nil$
        end
     end;

     { Assign preliminary coordinate Y }
     Set $count = 0$ and call LabelY(s):
     procedure LabelY($v : vertex$);
     begin
         $Y(v) = count$;
         $count = count + 1$;
         if $v \neq t$ **then begin**
            $e = lastout(v)$;
            repeat
               $w = head(e)$;

> **if** $e = firstin(w)$ **then** LabelY(w);
> $e = pred(e)$;
>> **until** $e = nil$
> **end**
end;

Compaction: { Assign final coordinates x and y }

Set up two lists of vertices sorted by increasing X- and Y-coordinate by means of pointers $nextX(v)$ and $nextY(v)$.

{ Assign final coordinate x }
let u be the vertex with $X(u) = 0$;
$x(u) = 0$;
while $nextX(u) \neq nil$ **do begin**
    $v = nextX(u)$;
    if $Y(u) > Y(v)$ **or**
    $(firstout(u) = lastout(u)$ **and** $firstin(v) = lastin(v))$
        then $x(v) = x(u) + 1$
        else $x(v) = x(u)$;
    $u = v$;
end;

{ Assign final coordinate y }
let u be the vertex with $Y(u) = 0$;
$y(u) = 0$;
while $nextY(u) \neq nil$ **do begin**
    $v = nextY(u)$;
    if $X(u) > X(v)$ **or**
    $(firstout(u) = lastout(u)$ **and** $firstin(v) = lastin(v))$
        then $y(v) = y(u) + 1$
        else $y(v) = y(u)$;
    $u = v$;
end;

$\square$

Let u and v be a pair of vertices with consecutive (preliminary) X-coordinates. In general, the (final) x-coordinate is not incremented if (u, v) is an edge, and is incremented otherwise. However, in the special case when (u, v) is the only outgoing edge of u and the only incoming edge of v, the

x-coordinate is incremented. This is done to prevent the possibility that u and v are assigned the same pair of coordinates. Similar considerations can be made for the y-coordinates.

A run of Algorithm *Dominance-Straight-Line* is illustrated in Figure 4.20. The preliminary drawing (X- and Y- coordinates) is shown in Figure 4.20.a. The final drawing (x- and y- coordinates) is shown in Figure 4.20.b. Perhaps the best aesthetic result is obtained by a 45° rotation, as shown in Figure 4.20.c. Given a vertex u of G, we define $B(u)$ (resp. $T(u)$) as the set of vertices distinct from u that can reach (resp. can be reached from) u by a directed path. Also, we define $L(u)$ (resp. $R(u)$) as the sets of vertices that are on the left (resp. right) of every path from s to t through u (see Figure 4.21). Note that $\{u\}$, $B(u)$, $T(u)$, $L(u)$, and $R(u)$ form a partition of the vertices of G.

Lemma 4.7 *The X- and Y-coordinates computed in the Preliminary Layout phase of Algorithm 4.6* Dominance-Straight-Line *have the following properties:*

1. *$X(u) < X(v)$ if and only if $u \in B(v) \cup L(v)$*

2. *$Y(u) < Y(v)$ if and only if $u \in B(v) \cup R(v)$.*

Proof: We give the proof of Property 1. A similar argument holds for Property 2. For the "if" part, observe that the recursive calls of procedure LabelX define a directed spanning tree T of G rooted at s and containing the rightmost incoming edge of each vertex. As a contradiction, suppose that $X(u) > X(v)$. Since vertex u is visited after vertex v by LabelX, vertex u is either on a path from v in T, or it is on a path to the right of the path π from s to v in T. In the first case, we have $v \to u$, which contradicts the hypothesis that $u \in B(v) \cup L(v)$. In the second case, vertex u cannot be in $B(v)$, because no directed path in G can enter vertex v to the right of path π; also, vertex u cannot be in $L(v)$, since it is to the right of the path of G from s to t obtained by extending π with leftmost outgoing edges. The "only-if" part follows from the fact that $u \in B(v) \cup L(v)$ if and only if $v \in T(u) \cup R(u)$. □

From Lemma 4.7 we can deduce that $u \in B(v)$ if and only if both $X(u) \leq X(v)$ and $Y(u) \leq Y(v)$. Thus, we have:

Theorem 4.8 *The drawing of G described by the X- and Y-coordinates computed in the Preliminary Layout phase of Algorithm 4.6* Dominance-Straight-Line *is a straight-line dominance drawing.*

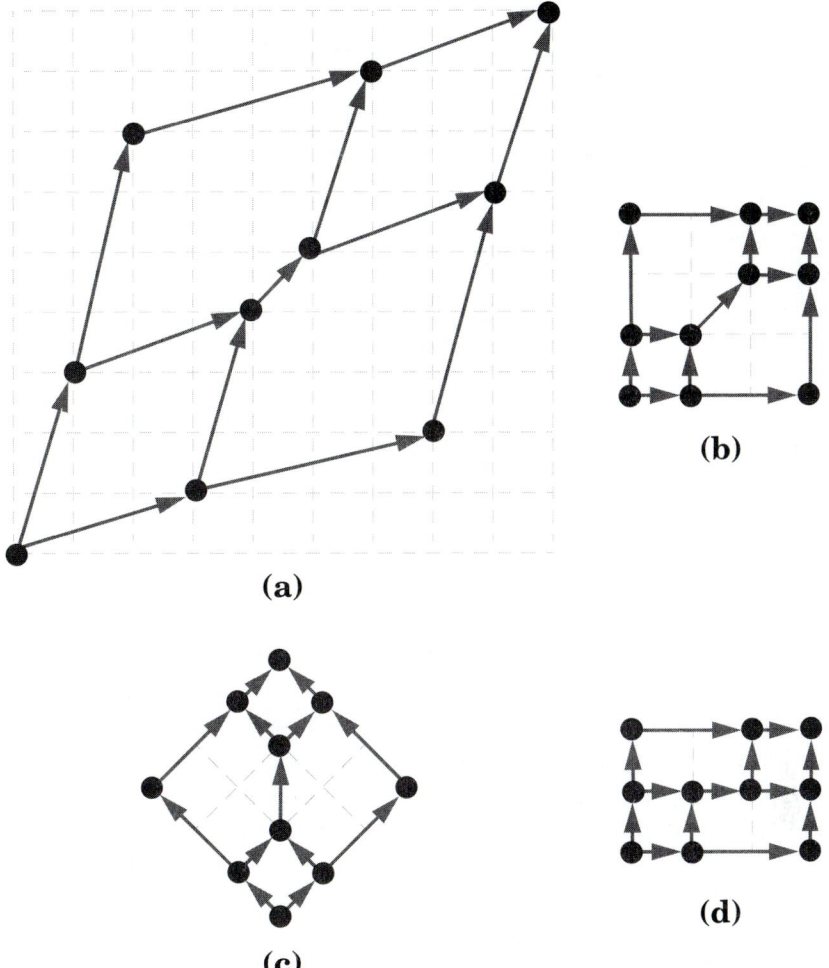

(a)

(b)

(c)

(d)

Figure 4.20: A run of Algorithm 4.6 *Dominance-Straight-Line*: (a) preliminary drawing (X- and Y-coordinates); (b) final drawing (x- and y-coordinates); (c) final drawing rotated by 45°; (d) minimum area drawing.

Lemma 4.8 *Let u and v be a pair of vertices of G such that $X(v) = X(u) + 1$. Then $Y(u) < Y(v)$ if and only if G has an edge from u to v.*

Proof: The "if" part is trivial. For the "only-if" part, suppose that $Y(u) < Y(v)$. Since $X(u) < X(v)$, we have $v \in T(u)$. If (u, v) is not an edge, then the path $(u \to v)$ has a vertex w distinct from u and from v. Hence, $X(u) < X(w) < X(v)$, thus contradicting the hypothesis that $X(v) = X(u) + 1$. $\square$

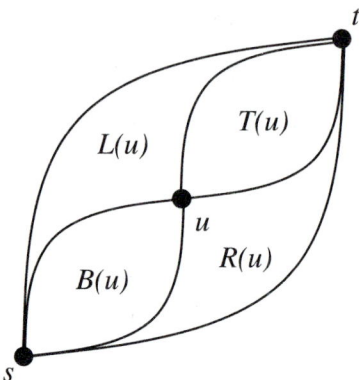

Figure 4.21: Vertex sets $B(u)$, $T(u)$, $L(u)$, and $R(u)$.

Theorem 4.9 *Let G be a reduced planar st-graph with n vertices. Algorithm 4.6* Dominance-Straight-Line *constructs in $O(n)$ time a planar straight-line dominance grid drawing Γ of G with $O(n^2)$ area.*

Proof: By Theorem 4.8, the preliminary drawing given by the X- and Y-coordinates is a straight-line dominance drawing. To also prove that the final drawing Γ given by the x- and y-coordinates is a straight-line dominance drawing, we show that:

1. $u \in B(v) \Rightarrow x(u) \leq x(v)$ **and** $y(u) \leq y(v)$

2. $x(u) < x(v) \Rightarrow u \in B(v) \cup L(v)$

3. $y(u) < y(v) \Rightarrow u \in B(v) \cup R(v)$

4. $x(u) = x(v) \Rightarrow u \in B(v) \cup T(v)$

5. $y(u) = y(v) \Rightarrow u \in B(v) \cup T(v)$

6. No two vertices are drawn at the same point (x, y).

It is immediate to verify that, for any two vertices u and v,

$$X(u) < X(v) \text{ implies that} \leq x(v),$$
$$Y(u) < Y(v) \text{ implies that} y(u) \leq y(v),$$
$$x(u) < x(v) \text{ implies that} X(u) < X(v), \text{ and}$$
$$y(u) < y(v) \text{ implies that} Y(u) < Y(v).$$

Hence, Properties 1–3 follow by Lemma 4.7. Assume that $X(u) < X(v)$ and $x(u) = x(v)$. Let $u = w_1, w_2, \ldots, w_k = v$ be the sequence of vertices with X-coordinate in the range $[X(u), X(v)]$. Since the x-coordinate is not incremented on these vertices, $Y(w_1) < Y(w_2) < \cdots < Y(w_k)$, and hence, $Y(u) < Y(v)$. Since the preliminary drawing is a dominance drawing, we have that $u \in B(v)$. Thus Property 4 is verified, and a similar argument proves Property 5.

Regarding Property 6, assume, as a contradiction, that it does not hold and there are vertices u and v with $x(u) = x(v)$ and $y(u) = y(v)$. By Properties 1–4, we may assume that $X(u) < X(v)$ and $Y(u) < Y(v)$. By Lemma 4.8, all the vertices w, such that $X(u) \leq X(w) \leq X(v)$, form a path from u to v, and all the vertices with Y-coordinate between $Y(u)$ and $Y(v)$ form exactly the same path. Let z be the vertex such that $X(z) = X(v) - 1$ and $Y(z) = Y(v) - 1$. Thus $x(z) = x(v)$ and $y(z) = y(v)$. Since both procedures LabelX and LabelY visit v immediately after z, edge (z, v) must be the only outgoing edge of z and the only incoming edge of v. However, this causes the Compaction phase to increment both x and y at vertex v, contradicting the previous conclusion that $x(z) = x(v)$ and $y(z) = y(v)$.

The area of the drawing Γ is given by $x(t) \cdot y(t)$. Consider the assignment of the x-coordinates. At the end of the Preliminary Layout phase, $X(t) = Y(t) = n - 1$. The compaction step scans the X-list from s to t and, for each pair of consecutive vertices u and v, either $x(v) = x(u)$ or $x(v) = x(u) + 1$. Hence, since $x(s) = 0$, $x(t) \leq n - 1$. Similarly, we have that $y(t) \leq n - 1$.

Concerning the time complexity, procedures LabelX and LabelY traverse each edge twice. At the beginning of the Compaction phase, the two lists can be constructed using a bucket sort. The remaining while-loops take linear time to scan the lists and perform a constant-time test for each vertex. □

4.7.2 Display of Symmetries

Besides producing a dominance drawing, Algorithm *Dominance-Straight-Line* has the important feature of displaying the symmetries and isomorphic parts of the digraph. Before describing these features, we introduce some definitions on symmetries of planar *st*-graphs.

A digraph G is *weakly connected* if its underlying undirected graph is connected. Let G be a planar *st*-graph. An *open component* of G is a maximal weakly-connected subgraph G' of the digraph obtained from G by removing a separation pair $\{p, q\}$, such that G' does not contain s or t. A *closed component* of G is an induced subgraph G' of G, such that (see Figure 4.22):

1. G' is a planar pq-graph

2. G' contains every vertex of G that is on some path from p to q.

3. G' contains every outgoing edge of p, every incoming edge of q, and every incident edge of the remaining vertices of G'.

A *component* of G is either a closed or an open component. Notice that G is a trivial closed component of itself.

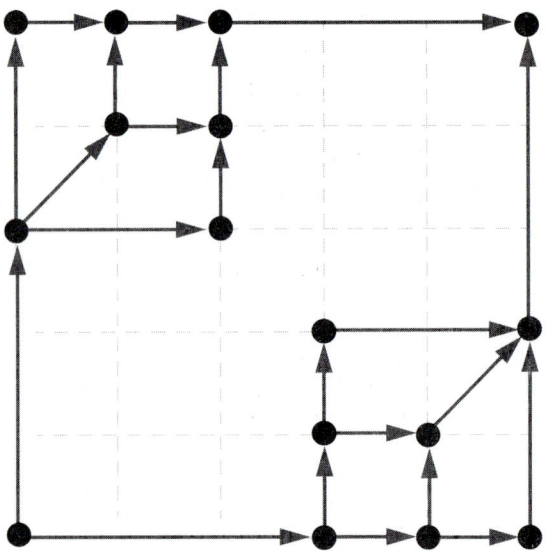

Figure 4.22: Drawing constructed by Algorithm *Dominance-Straight-Line* of a planar st-graph with two rotationally isomorphic components, each of which is axially symmetric.

The digraph obtained from a closed component by removing its source and sink is not necessarily an open component, but, in general, the union of several open components. Also, the digraph obtained from an open component by adding the separation pair is not necessarily a closed component, since Properties 2 and 3 above might not be verified. The concept of open component generalizes the one of subtree of a rooted tree, as follows. Let T be a tree rooted at vertex s. We construct a planar st-graph G_T by connecting all the leaves of T to a new vertex t. It is simple to verify that the subtree of T rooted at a vertex $v \neq s$ is an open component of G_T.

Let C_1 and C_2 be two components of a planar st-graph G that are isomorphic if we ignore the directions of the edges. C_1 and C_2 are said to be *simply isomorphic* if the isomorphism preserves the directions of the edges and the clockwise boundaries of the faces. C_1 and C_2 are said to be *axially isomorphic* if the isomorphism preserves the directions of the edges and inverts the clockwise boundaries of the faces. C_1 and C_2 are said to be *rotationally isomorphic* if the isomorphism inverts the directions of the edges and preserves the clockwise boundaries of the faces. A component is said to be *axially (rotationally) symmetric* if it is axially (rotationally) isomorphic to itself. For example, the digraph of Figure 4.22 has two rotationally isomorphic components, and each such component is axially symmetric.

Let E_L be the set of edges (u, v), such that (u, v) is the rightmost incoming edge of v and the leftmost outgoing edge of u. Let E_R be the set of edges (u, v), such that (u, v) is the leftmost incoming edge of v and the rightmost outgoing edge of u. Also, we define E_H as the set of edges (u, v), such that (u, v) is the only outgoing edge of u and the only incoming edge of v. Observe that $E_H = E_L \cap E_R$. We write $m_L = |E_L|$, $m_R = |E_R|$, and $m_H = |E_H|$. In the example of Figure 4.20, the set E_H contains exactly one edge.

Lemma 4.9 *Let $(u, v) \in E$. Then u and v appear consecutively in the X-list if and only if $(u, v) \in E_L$. Also, u and v appear consecutively in the Y-list if and only if $(u, v) \in E_R$.*

By Lemmas 4.8 and 4.9, the tests for incrementing the x- and y-coordinates in the Compaction step can be rewritten as follows:

$\quad$ **if** $(u, v) \in E_L - E_H$ **then** $x(v) = x(u)$; **else** $x(v) = x(u) + 1$

$\quad$ **if** $(u, v) \in E_R - E_H$ **then** $y(v) = y(u)$; **else** $y(v) = y(u) + 1$.

As shown in the following theorem, Algorithm 4.6 *Dominance-Straight-Line* displays symmetries and isomorphic components.

Theorem 4.10 *Let G be a reduced planar st-graph, and Γ be the corresponding straight-line drawing constructed by Algorithm* Dominance-Straight-Line. *We have:*

1. *Simply isomorphic components of G have drawings in Γ that are congruent up to a translation.*

2. *Axially isomorphic components of G have drawings in Γ that are congruent up to a translation and reflection.*

3. *Rotationally isomorphic components of G have drawings in Γ that are congruent up to a translation and a 180° rotation.*

4. *The drawing of an axially symmetric component of G is symmetric with respect to the straight line that passes through its source and sink.*

5. *The drawing of a rotationally symmetric component of G is symmetric with respect to a 180° rotation around its centroid.*

Proof: In the Preprocessing phase, the vertices of a component are visited consecutively by procedures LabelX and LabelY. Hence, the layout of a component is independent from the rest of the digraph. This proves Property 1. As regards Properties 2 and 4, reversing the orientation of the faces exchanges the set $L(u)$ with $R(u)$, for every vertex u. By Lemma 4.7, this corresponds to exchanging the X-coordinate with the Y-coordinate, and similarly for the final x- and y-coordinates. This yields drawings that are congruent up to a translation and a reflection with respect to a 45°-slope line. Now, we consider Properties 3 and 5. Reversing the direction of the edges exchanges $B(u)$ with $T(u)$ and $L(u)$ with $R(u)$, for every vertex u. Hence, by Lemma 4.7, the X-lists of two rotationally isomorphic components are the reverse of one another, and similarly for the Y-lists. This implies that Properties 3 and 5 hold for the preliminary layout. The sets E_L, E_H, and E_R stay the same after reversing the direction of the edges. Thus the final x- and y-coordinates are incremented for the same pairs of vertices and Properties 3 and 5 hold for the final layout. □

Figure 4.22 shows a drawing produced by Algorithm *Dominance-Straight-Line* that illustrates some of the properties listed in Theorem 4.10.

4.7.3   Minimum Area Dominance Drawings

As shown in Theorem 4.9, Algorithm 4.6 *Dominance-Straight-Line* produces drawings with $O(n^2)$ area. Here we give a tighter upper bound on the area and present a modification of the algorithm that constructs a minimum area drawing among all straight-line dominance drawings of the input planar *st*-graph G.

We recall that the area of the drawing constructed by Algorithm 4.6 *Dominance-Straight-Line* is $x(t) \cdot y(t)$, where t is the sink of G. We can express $x(t)$ and $y(t)$ in terms of n, m_L, m_R, and m_H (see the definitions in the previous section) as follows:

Lemma 4.10 $x(t) = n - 1 - (m_L - m_H)$ *and* $y(t) = n - 1 - (m_R - m_H)$.

Proof: The number of times that the x-coordinate (resp. y-coordinate) is *not* incremented is equal to $m_L - m_H$ (resp. $m_R - m_H$). □

Recall that the area of the drawing constructed by Algorithm 4.6 *Dominance-Straight-Line* is given by $x(t) \cdot y(t)$. Hence, we obtain the following tight bound.

Theorem 4.11 *Algorithm 4.6* Dominance-Straight-Line *produces drawings with area*

$$(n - 1 - (m_L - m_H)) \times (n - 1 - (m_R - m_H)).$$

Suppose that $E_H = \emptyset$. In this case, we can prove that the area of the drawing is optimal. Next, we show how to modify the algorithm to obtain a minimum area drawing in the case when $E_H \neq \emptyset$.

Lemma 4.11 *Given a reduced planar st-graph G such that $E_H = \emptyset$, Algorithm 4.6* Dominance-Straight-Line *produces a minimum area straight-line dominance grid drawing of G.*

Proof: First we observe that any straight-line dominance drawing that preserves the embedding of G must place the vertices of $L(v)$ in $l(v)$ and the vertices of $R(v)$ in $r(v)$. Let v_i be the vertex that is assigned X-coordinate i by the Preliminary Layout phase of Algorithm 4.6 *Dominance-Straight-Line*. By Lemma 4.7, in any drawing of G we have $x(v_i) \leq x(v_{i+1})$. Now consider the $n - m_L$ pairs of vertices $\{v_i, v_{i+1}\}$, such that $Y(v_i) > Y(v_{i+1})$. By Lemma 4.7, $v_{i+1} \in R(v_i)$ and therefore $x(v_{i+1}) > x(v_i)$. We conclude that $x(v_{n-1}) - x(v_0) \geq n - m_L - 1$. A similar argument shows that $y(v_{n-1}) - y(v_0) \geq n - m_R - 1$. Hence, by Theorem 4.11, the drawing constructed by Algorithm 4.6 *Dominance-Straight-Line* has optimal area. □

To take into account the set E_H, we use the following variation of Algorithm 4.6 *Dominance-Straight-Line* (see Figure 4.20.d):

- In the Preprocessing phase we compute m_L and m_R.

- In the Compaction phase we replace the first "if" test with:
  if $(Y(u) > Y(v)$ **or** $(firstout(u) = lastout(u)$ **and**
  $firstin(v) = lastin(v)$ **and** $m_L \leq m_R))$
  and the second "if" test with
  if $(X(u) > X(v)$ **or** $(firstout(u) = lastout(u)$ **and**
  $firstin(v) = lastin(v)$ **and** $m_L > m_R))$.

This variation of the algorithm yields a drawing with area

$$A = (n - 1 - \min(m_L, m_R) + m_H) \times (n - 1 - \max(m_L, m_R)).$$

Clearly for any straight-line dominance drawing of G, we must have an increment of the x- or y-coordinate in correspondence of every edge of E_H. If m_x and m_y are respectively the increments of x and y, with $m_x + m_y = m_H$, the area is at least

$$(n - 1 - m_L + m_x) \times (n - 1 - m_R + m_y).$$

It is easy to see that the minimum of the above quantity is equal to A, and is achieved by setting

$$m_x = \begin{cases} m_H & \text{if } m_L \leq m_R \\ 0 & \text{if } m_L > m_R. \end{cases}$$

This yields the following theorem:

Theorem 4.12 *Let G be a reduced planar st-graph with n vertices. A minimum-area straight-line dominance grid drawing of G can be constructed in $O(n)$ time.*

Note that minimum area drawings may not have the symmetry properties of Theorem 4.10 (see Figure 4.20.d).

4.7.4   General Planar st-Graphs

Algorithm 4.6 *Dominance-Straight-Line* can be extended to general planar *st*-graphs by inserting a dummy vertex on every transitive edge.

The number of bends in the drawing constructed by Algorithm 4.7 *Dominance-Polyline* is equal to the number of transitive edges in the input planar *st*-graph G. In an acyclic digraph with n vertices, at least $n-1$ edges are not transitive. Since G is planar, it has at most $3n - 6$ edges. Hence, G has at most $2n - 5$ transitive edges. Algorithm 4.7 *Dominance-Polyline* has the same symmetry properties of Algorithm 4.6 *Dominance-Straight-Line*. We have:

Theorem 4.13 *Let G be a planar st-graph with n vertices. Algorithm 4.7* Dominance-Polyline *constructs in $O(n)$ time a drawing Γ of G with the following properties:*

Algorithm 4.7 *Dominance-Polyline*
      Input: planar st-graph G
     Output: polyline dominance drawing Γ of G

1. If G is not reduced, replace each transitive edge (u, v) with a chain of two edges, that is, a new vertex x and two new edges (u, x) and (x, v). Let G' be the resulting reduced planar st-graph.

2. Construct a straight-line dominance drawing Γ' of G' using Algorithm *Dominance-Straight-Line*.

3. A polyline dominance drawing Γ of the original digraph G is finally obtained by considering the dummy vertices of Γ' as bends of Γ.   □

1. *Γ is planar, upward, grid, dominance, and polyline*

2. *Γ has $O(n^2)$ area*

3. *Γ has at most $2n - 5$ bends, and every edge has at most one bend;*

4. *Simply isomorphic components of G have drawings in Γ that are congruent up to a translation*

5. *Axially isomorphic components of G have drawings in Γ that are congruent up to a translation and reflection*

6. *Rotationally isomorphic components of G have drawings in Γ that are congruent up to a translation and a 180° rotation*

7. *The drawing of an axially symmetric component of G is symmetric with respect to the straight line that passes through its source and sink*

8. *The drawing of a rotationally symmetric component of G is symmetric with respect to a 180° rotation around its centroid.*

4.8   Drawings of Undirected Planar Graphs

The algorithms of the previous sections for constructing tessellation representations, visibility representations, and upward polyline drawings of planar st-graphs can be extended to draw undirected planar graphs.

Let G be an undirected planar graph. First, we construct a planar embedding of G. This can be done in linear time, using variations of the
known planarity testing algorithms (see Section 3.3). Also, if G is not biconnected, then we augment G to an embedded planar biconnected graph
by adding dummy edges. This also takes linear time (see, e.g., [KB91,
KB92]). Let s and t be two distinct vertices of G on the external face. An
st-numbering for G is a numbering $v_1, v_2, ..., v_n$ of the vertices of G such
that $s = v_1$, $t = v_n$, and every vertex v_j, other than s and t, is adjacent to
at least two vertices v_i and v_k with $i < j < k$. Such a numbering can be
constructed in $O(n)$ time [ET76]. Given an *st-numbering* for G, we orient
every edge of G from the low numbered vertex to the high numbered one
(this orientation is also called a *bipolar orientation*). It is easy to see that
the resulting digraph D is a planar *st-graph* (see Figure 4.23).

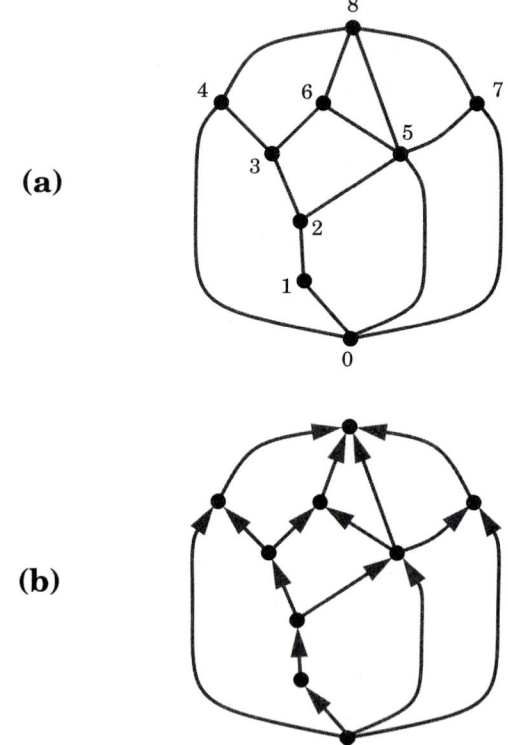

(a)

(b)

Figure 4.23: (a) Biconnected planar graph G and *st-numbering* of G; (b)
bipolar orientation of G induced by the *st-numbering*.

We now apply, to D, one of the algorithms described in the preceding sections for constructing tessellation representations, visibility representations, and upward polyline drawings of planar st-graphs. We derive a corresponding drawing/representation of G by ignoring the directions of the edges and the dummy edges introduced in biconnectivity augmentation.

Theorem 4.14 *Let G be an undirected planar graph with n vertices. The following representations and drawings of G can be constructed in $O(n)$ time:*

- *A tessellation representation with integer coordinates and $O(n^2)$ area.*

- *A visibility representation with integer coordinates and $O(n^2)$ area.*

- *A planar polyline grid drawing with $O(n^2)$ area and at most $(2n - 5)$ bends.*

There are other types of visibility representations of undirected planar graphs that have been studied in the literature. They are mostly of theoretical interest, and are briefly discussed below.

We say that two vertex-segments of a visibility representation are ϵ-*visible* if they can be joined by a vertical strip of nonzero width that does not intersect any other vertex-segment. An ϵ-*visibility representation* for a graph is a visibility representation with the additional property that two vertex-segments are ϵ-visible if and only if the corresponding vertices are adjacent.

We can easily obtain an ϵ-visibility representation for a biconnected planar graph by simply extending the vertex segments of each face f, toward the interior of f, to block the ϵ-visibility between the vertex-segments of $orig(f)$ and $dest(f)$.

If all the cutvertices of a connected planar graph can be placed on the boundary of the external face, then the ϵ-visibility representations for each biconnected component can be placed so that they will not create extraneous visibilities. Conversely, if a planar graph admits an ϵ-visibility representation, then there exists an embedding of the graph such that all the cutvertices appear on the boundary of the external face. In fact, since any face of a planar graph can be made external, we have the following theorem [TT86, Wis85]:

Theorem 4.15 *A planar graph G admits an ϵ-visibility representation if and only if there exists a planar embedding of G, such that all cutvertices of G appear on the boundary of the same face.*

In other words, if we augment G by adding a new vertex and connecting it to every cutvertex, then G admits an ϵ-visibility representation if and only if the new graph is planar. This alternative characterization can be used in order to test, in linear time, whether G admits an ϵ-visibility representation [TT86].

A *strong-visibility representation* for a graph G is a visibility representation for G with the additional property that two vertex-segments are visible if and only if the corresponding vertices of G are adjacent. Clearly, any visibility representation of a maximal planar graph is also a strong-visibility representation. However, the problem of determining whether a given planar graph G admits a strong-visibility representation is NP-complete, even if G is triconnected [And92]. If G is four-connected however, then G admits a a strong-visibility representation which can be computed in linear time [TT86].

4.9   Planar Orthogonal Drawings

In this section, we present Algorithm 4.8 *Orthogonal-from-Visibility* for constructing planar orthogonal drawings. This algorithm uses visibility representations as an intermediate construction. Because of the nature of orthogonal drawings, we consider only graphs with vertices of degree less than or equal to four.

An example of a run of Algorithm 4.8 *Orthogonal-from-Visibility* is given in Figure 4.25.

In the orthogonal drawing constructed by Algorithm 4.8 *Orthogonal-from-Visibility*, there are at most two bends per vertex distinct from s and t, and at most four bends for s and t (see Figure 4.24). Hence, the total number of bends is at most $2n + 4$. Clearly, the area of the drawing is about the same as the area of the constrained visibility representation, that is $O(n^2)$. All the steps of the algorithm take $O(n)$ time. Therefore, we have:

Theorem 4.16 *Let G be a biconnected planar graph with n vertices of degree at most four. Algorithm 4.8* Orthogonal-from-Visibility *constructs in $O(n)$ time a planar orthogonal grid drawing of G with $O(n^2)$ area and at most $2n + 4$ bends. Also, each edge has at most two bends, except for two edges that have each at most four bends.*

Algorithm 4.8 *Orthogonal-from-Visibility* can be extended to general planar graphs, as shown in [TT87, TT89a], where techniques for reducing the

---

Algorithm 4.8 *Orthogonal-from-Visibility*

    Input: biconnected planar graph G with n vertices of
                degree at most four
  Output: planar orthogonal grid drawing of G

1. Construct a planar embedding of G and orient its edges such that the resulting digraph D is a planar st-graph.

2. Create a set of $n - 2$ directed paths of D associated with the vertices of D distinct from s and t, as follows: The path π_v associated with vertex v consists of two edges e' and e'' where: if v has two incoming edges, then e' is the leftmost incoming edge of v and e'' is the rightmost outgoing edge of v; while if v has either one or three incoming edges, e' is the median incoming edge of v and e'' is the median outgoing edge of v. Unify paths sharing edges, which yield a set Π of nonintersecting paths.

3. Using Algorithm 4.3 *Constrained-Visibility*, construct a constrained visibility representation Γ of D, with respect to the set Π of paths, such that Γ has integer coordinates.

4. Construct a planar orthogonal grid drawing of G as follows:

   - For each vertex v distinct from s and t, draw v at the intersection $P(v)$ of vertex segment $\Gamma(v)$, with the edge segments of path π_v (see Figure 4.24.a).

   - Draw vertex s (resp. t) at the intersection of its vertex segment with the edge segment of its median outgoing (resp. incoming) edge (see Figure 4.24.b).

   - For each edge $e = (u, v)$, such that u and v are distinct from s and t, draw e as an orthogonal chain through the following points: $P(u)$, the intersection of $\Gamma(u)$ and $\Gamma(e)$, the intersection of $\Gamma(e)$ and $\Gamma(v)$, and $P(v)$. The chain consists of three segments, where the first and last segment may be empty.

   - Edges incident to s or t are drawn as shown in Figure 4.24.b.
   $\square$

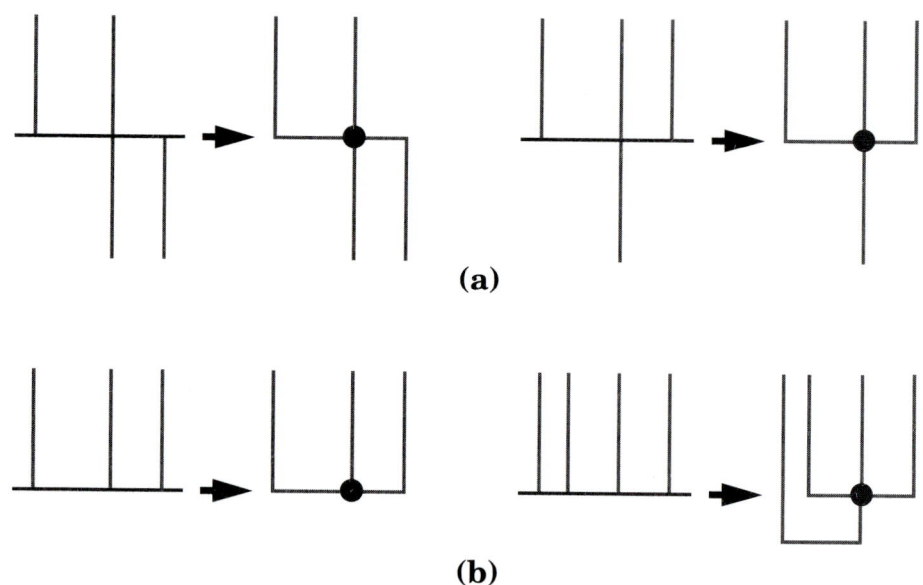

(a)

(b)

Figure 4.24: Drawing vertices and edges in Step 4 of Algorithm 4.8 *Orthogonal-from-Visibility*: (a) drawing of a vertex distinct from s and t; (b) drawing of s and t.

number of bends in an orthogonal drawing are also presented (see Section 5.7).

4.10　Planar Straight-Line Drawings

One of the classic mathematical problems of graph drawing is to construct a straight-line planar drawing of a planar graph. A classic result independently established in [Far48, Ste51, Wag36], shows that every planar graph admits a planar straight-line drawing. (The proof of Lemma 6.4 uses the technique of [Far48].) This result also follows from Steinitz's theorem on convex polytopes in three dimensions [SR34].

The problem of constructing planar straight-line drawings of planar graphs has also been solved, for example, by the barycenter algorithm of Tutte described in Section 10.2. However, these researchers were more concerned with proving the existence of straight-line drawings than with designing algorithms to create them. In particular, all the algorithms prior to 1988 have poor resolution. Namely, the output drawings contain ver-

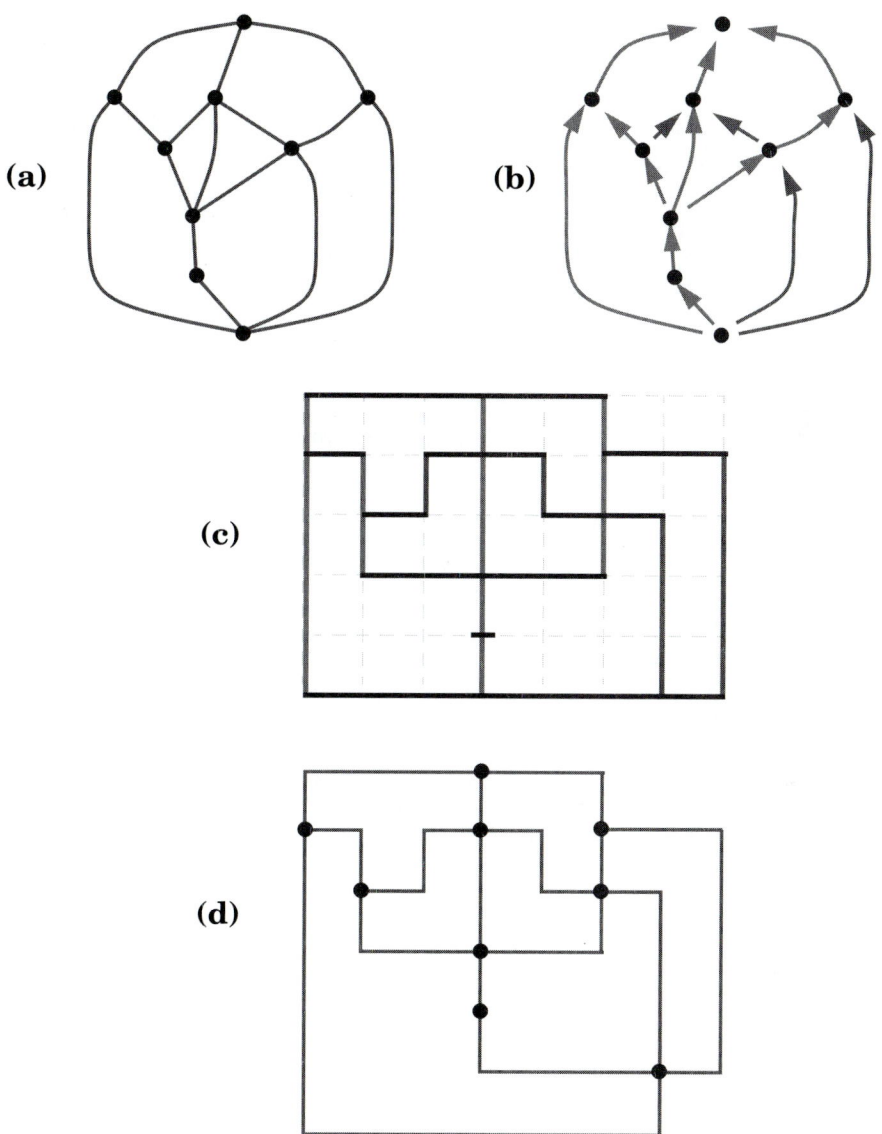

Figure 4.25: An example of a run of Algorithm 4.8 *Orthogonal-from-Visibility*: (a) planar graph G; (b) orientation D of G and set Π of nonintersecting paths; (c) constrained visibility representation Γ of D; (d) orthogonal drawing of G.

tices which are exponentially close together, which implies that they have exponential area if a minimum unit distance between vertices is specified. This resolution problem limits the applications of these classic techniques for visualization purposes.

de Fraysseix, Pach and Pollack [dFPP90] and Schnyder [Sch90] independently show the following fundamental result.

Theorem 4.17 *Every n-vertex planar graph has a planar straight-line grid drawing with $O(n^2)$ area.*

The proof of this theorem by [dFPP90] uses an orientation technique. The graph is first oriented and then the drawing is created, one vertex at a time, in the order specified by the orientation. The proof by [Sch90] exploits the properties of a partial order defined over the vertices, edges, and faces of a maximal planar graph.

An example of a planar straight-line drawing constructed by the algorithm of [dFPP90] is show in Figure 4.26.

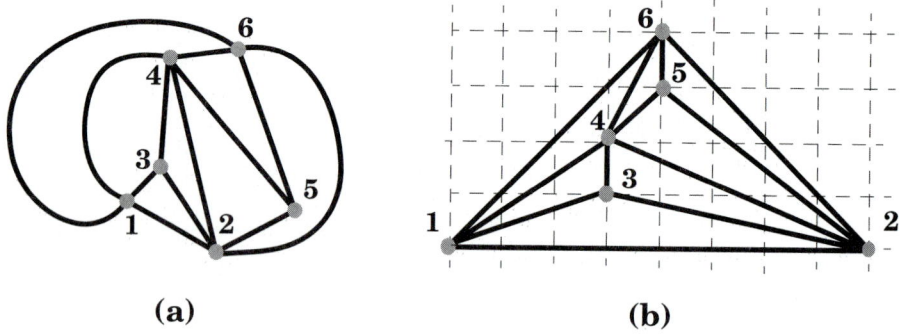

(a)   **(b)**

Figure 4.26: Example of a planar straight-line grid drawing with quadratic area.

4.11   Exercises

1. Prove that the following statements are equivalent for a digraph G:

   - G is acyclic
   - G admits a topological numbering
   - G admits a topological sorting.

2. Show that a topological sorting is unique if and only if the digraph has a directed path that visits every vertex.

3. Prove that the digraph G^* defined in Section 4.2 is a planar st-graph.

4. Prove Lemma 4.4.

5. Construct a tessellation representation of the planar st-graph of Figure 4.22 using Algorithm 4.1 *Tessellation*.

6. Construct a minimum-area tessellation representation of the planar st-graph of Figure 4.3, such that $h(o) \geq 1$ and $w(o) \geq 3$, for every object o (vertex, edge, or face), using the algorithm of Theorem 4.2.

7. Give complete proofs of Theorems 4.1 and 4.2.

8. Give a complete proof of the bound on the number of bends given in Theorem 4.6.

9. Give a proof of Property 2 of Lemma 4.7.

10. Construct a visibility representation of the planar st-graph of Figure 4.22 using Algorithm 4.2 *Visibility*.

11. Choose a set of nonintersecting paths covering the planar st-graph G of Figure 4.22, and construct a constrained visibility representation G using Algorithm 4.3 *Constrained-Visibility*.

12. Construct a planar upward polyline grid drawing of the planar st-graph of Figure 4.22 using Algorithm 4.4 *Polyline* and the long-edge positioning for the vertices.

13. Choose a path π from the source to the sink of the planar st-graph G of Figure 4.22, and construct a planar upward polyline grid drawing of G, such that the internal vertices of π are vertically aligned, using Algorithm 4.5 *Constrained-Polyline*.

14. Let G be a planar st-graph. Construct two subgraphs T_L and T_R of G as follows:

   - T_L is obtained by selecting for each vertex $v \neq s$ of G, the rightmost incoming edge of v.
   - T_R is obtained by selecting for each vertex $v \neq s$ of G, the leftmost incoming edge of v.

(a) Show that T_L and T_R are trees rooted at vertex s.

(b) Show that the X- and Y-coordinates of a vertex v, computed in the Preliminary Layout phase of Algorithm 4.6 *Dominance-Straight-Line*, are equal to the ranks of vertex v in a preorder traversal of T_L and T_R, respectively, where we assume that the children of a node are visited from left to right, and that the ranks start at 0.

15. Implement Algorithm *Dominance-Polyline*.

16. Construct a polyline dominance drawing of the planar st-graph of Figure 4.3 using Algorithm *Dominance-Polyline*.

17. Construct a planar polyline grid drawing of the planar graph G of Figure 4.23.a, by orienting it into a planar st-graph, using an st-numbering that is different from the one shown in Figure 4.23.a.

18. Give a complete proof of Theorem 4.16.

Chapter 5

Flow and Orthogonal Drawings

Network flow techniques can be used to solve a variety of planar graph drawing problems. In a planar polyline drawing, the angles formed by the edges at the vertices and at the bends satisfy geometric properties that can be naturally expressed with a flow model. Namely, we can view angles as a "commodity" that is produced by the vertices and consumed by the faces.

An important aesthetic for planar orthogonal drawings is the minimization of the number of bends (see Section 2.1 and Figure 5.1). In this chapter, we present a graph drawing method based on network flow techniques, which constructs a planar orthogonal drawing of an embedded planar graph with minimum number of bends. We show that minimizing bends in planar orthogonal drawings can be modeled as a minimum cost flow problem on a flow network derived from the graph and its embedding. In this flow network, each unit of flow corresponds to a $\pi/2$ angle, the vertices are producers of four units of flow, the faces consume an amount of flow proportional to the number of angles in their interior, and each bend transfers a unit of flow across its incident faces. By giving unit cost to the flow associated with bends, a drawing with the minimum number of bends corresponds to a flow of minimum cost. This yields a quadratic-time algorithm for bend minimization. This technique was first presented in [Tam87], with variations, refinements, and extensions given in [FK96, Tam85, TDB88, TTV91a]. Linear-time algorithms for constructing planar orthogonal drawings with $O(1)$ bends per edge, but that do not guarantee the minimum number of bends, are given in Chapter 4. Note that it is NP-hard to minimize bends over all possible embeddings of a planar graph [GT95] (see

Appendix A). Polynomial-time algorithms exist only for special classes of planar graphs [DLV93] (see Appendix A). Linear-time algorithms for constructing orthogonal drawings of general (nonplanar) graphs are given in Chapter 8. The techniques presented in this chapter can also be used for drawing general nonplanar graphs by means of a preliminary planarization step (see Section 7.1).

Recall that only graphs whose vertices have degree at most four admit a planar orthogonal drawing. Hence, throughout this chapter, unless otherwise specified, we consider only graphs with vertices of degree at most four.

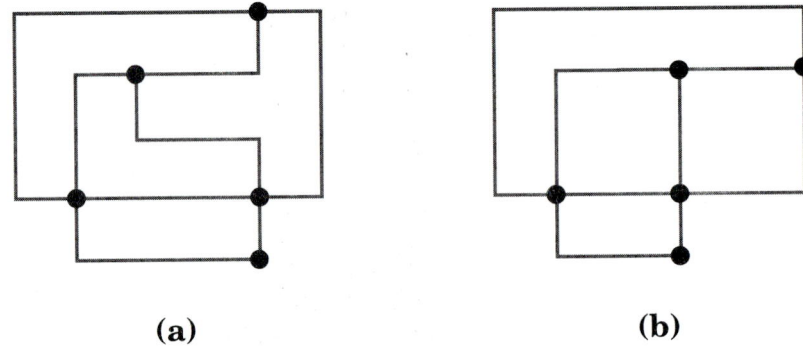

(a)   **(b)**

Figure 5.1: Two planar orthogonal drawings of the same embedded planar graph: (a) drawing with 9 bends; (b) drawing with 6 bends. The drawing in part (b) has the minimum number of bends.

This chapter is organized as follows. In Section 5.1, we give preliminary definitions on angles in orthogonal drawings. In Section 5.2, we introduce the concept of orthogonal representation, which defines the "shape" of an orthogonal drawing in terms of angles, without considering the actual lengths of the edges. A network flow model for the problem of constructing planar orthogonal drawings of embedded planar graphs is defined in Section 5.3. The problem of constructing an orthogonal drawing with a given orthogonal representation is studied in Section 5.4. In Section 5.5, we give the algorithm for minimizing the number of bends in a planar orthogonal drawing. The algorithm is able to support a variety of constraints, as shown in Section 5.6. Additional applications of the flow model are given in Section 5.7. Finally, in Section 5.8, we show how to apply the techniques to produce drawings of planar graphs with degree greater than four, using a drawing convention similar to the orthogonal grid convention.

Three drawings constructed with the techniques presented in this chapter are shown in Figures 5.2–5.4.

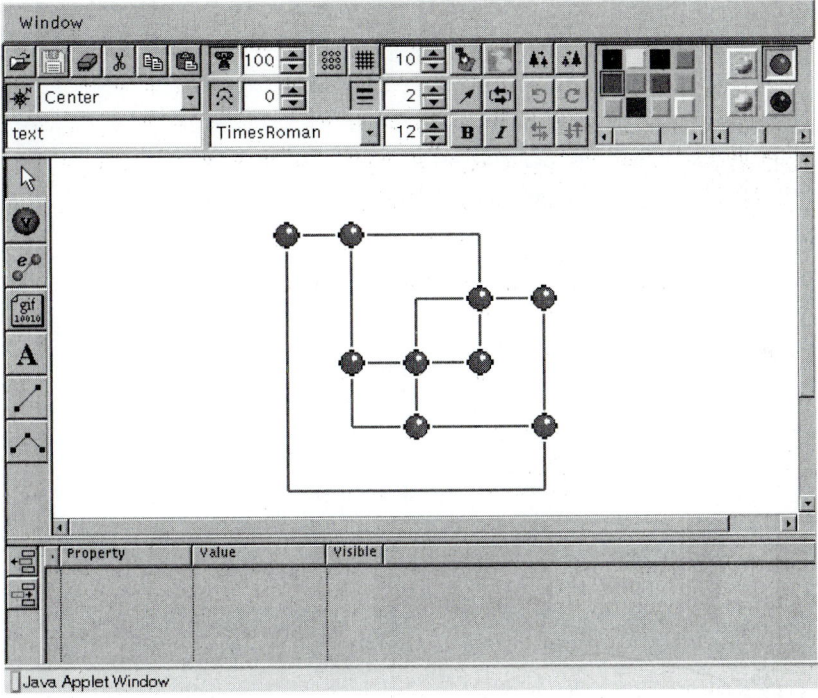

Figure 5.2: An orthogonal drawing constructed by the `Graph Drawing Server`. (Courtesy of S. Bridgeman.)

5.1 Angles in Orthogonal Drawings

Let Γ be a planar orthogonal drawing of an embedded planar graph G. There are two types of angles in Γ:

- Angles formed by two edges incident on a common vertex, called *vertex-angles*

- Angles formed by bends (that is, angles formed by consecutive edge segments of the same edge), called *bend-angles*.

The following properties are immediate (see Figures 5.5 and 5.6):

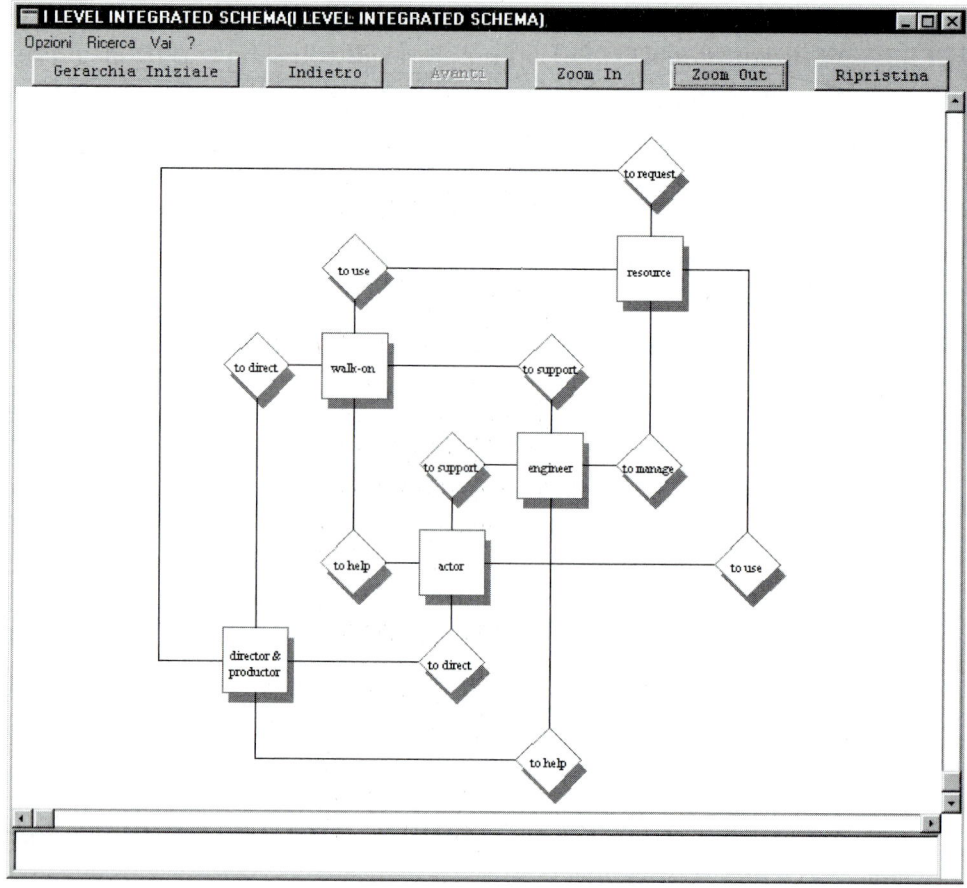

Figure 5.3: An orthogonal drawing of an entity-relationship diagram created by the JBG software. It contains one crossing that has been introduced by a planarization algorithm. (Courtesy of M. Simoncelli.)

Lemma 5.1 *In a planar orthogonal drawing, the sum of the measures of the vertex-angles around a vertex is equal to* 2π.

Lemma 5.2 *Let f be an internal face of a planar orthogonal drawing. The sum of the measures of the vertex-angles and bend-angles inside face f is equal to* $\pi(p-2)$, *where p is the total number of such angles. If f is the external face, then the above sum is equal to* $\pi(p+2)$.

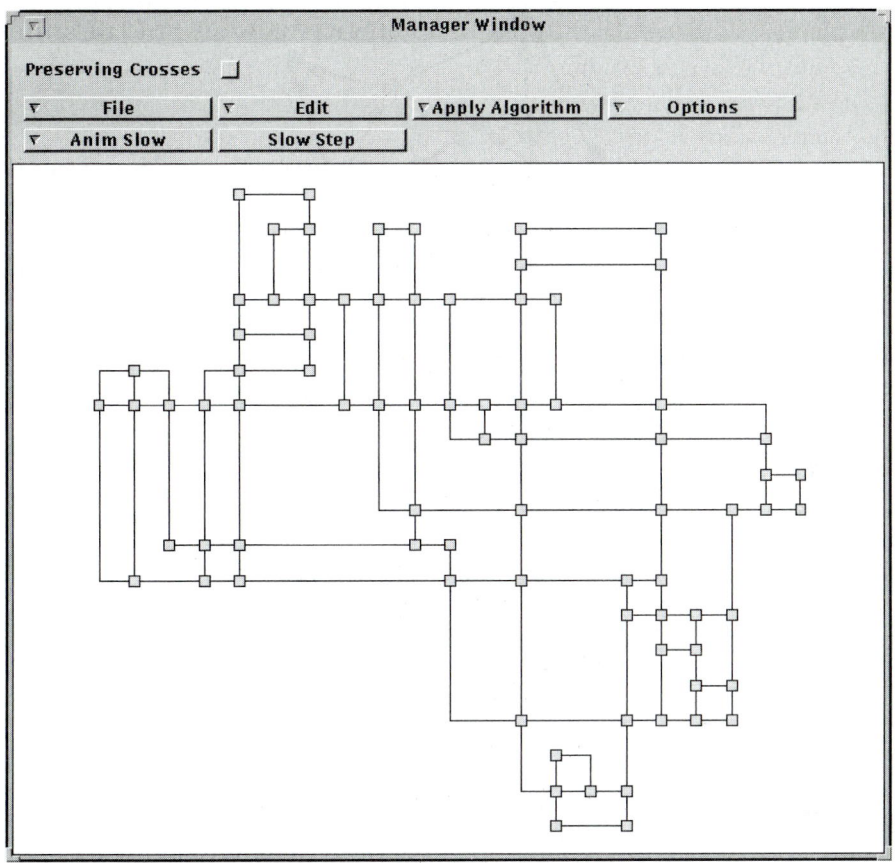

Figure 5.4: An orthogonal drawing of a graph with 80 vertices created by the `GDToolkit` software. (Courtesy of W. Didimo, A. Leonforte, and M. Patrignani.)

5.2 Orthogonal Representations

In this section, we introduce the concept of orthogonal representation, which captures the notion of "orthogonal shape" of a planar orthogonal drawing, by taking into account angles but disregarding edge lengths.

Let G be an embedded planar graph with vertices of degree at most four. We denote with $a(f)$ the total number of vertex-angles inside face f of G. If G is biconnected, then $a(f)$ is equal to the number of vertices (edges) of f. For each (undirected) edge e of G with endpoints u and v, the two possible orientations (u, v) and (v, u) of edge e are called *darts*. A dart is

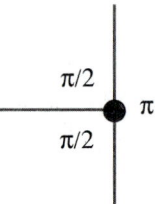

Figure 5.5: Angles around a vertex (vertex-angles) in a planar orthogonal drawing.

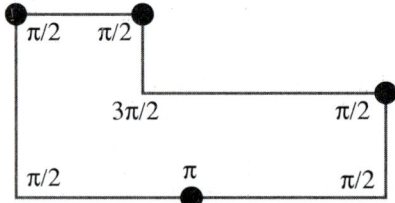

Figure 5.6: Angles inside a face (face-angles) in a planar orthogonal drawing.

said to be *counterclockwise* with respect to face f if f is on the left hand side when traversing the dart in the direction of its orientation. We denote with $D(v)$ the set of darts that begin at vertex v, and with $D(f)$ the set of counterclockwise darts on face f.

Given a planar orthogonal drawing Γ of G, we define values α and β associated with the darts of G as follows (see Figure 5.7.a):

- $\alpha(u,v) \cdot \pi/2$ is the angle at vertex u formed by the first segments of dart (u,v) and the next dart counterclockwise around u

- $\beta(u,v)$ is the number of bends along dart (u,v) with the $\pi/2$ angle on the left hand side.

An orthogonal representation of G describes an equivalence class of planar orthogonal drawings of G with "similar shape," that is, with the same α and β values associated with the darts of G. More formally, we say that an *orthogonal representation* of G is an assignment of integer values $\alpha(u,v)$ and $\beta(u,v)$, to each dart (u,v) of G, that satisfy the following properties (see Lemmas 5.1 and 5.2):

- $1 \leq \alpha(u, v) \leq 4$

- $\beta(u, v) \geq 0$

- For each vertex u, the sum of $\alpha(u, v)$ over all the darts oriented away from u is equal to four, that is,

$$\sum_{(u,v)\in D(u)} \alpha(u, v) = 4$$

- For each internal face f, the sum of $\alpha(u, v) + \beta(v, u) - \beta(u, v)$ over all the counterclockwise darts (u, v) on face f is equal to $2a(f) - 4$, that is,

$$\sum_{(u,v)\in D(f)} \alpha(u, v) + \beta(v, u) - \beta(u, v) = 2a(f) - 4$$

- For the external face h, the above sum is equal to $2a(h) + 4$, that is,

$$\sum_{(u,v)\in D(h)} \alpha(u, v) + \beta(v, u) - \beta(u, v) = 2a(h) + 4.$$

In Figure 5.7, we show three planar orthogonal drawings of a graph with the same orthogonal representation. Note that the orthogonal representation describes the "shape" of an orthogonal drawing, up to permuting the order of the bends along each edge. In particular, two orthogonal drawings with the same orthogonal representation have the same number of bends (equal to the sum of the β values over all the darts). Conversely, in Section 5.4, we show that given an orthogonal representation H, there exists a planar orthogonal drawing with orthogonal representation H that can be constructed in linear time.

5.3 The Network Flow Model

In this section, we present a network flow model for the problem of constructing planar orthogonal drawings of embedded planar graphs. This model views angles as a "commodity" that is "produced" by the vertices, "transported" between faces by the edges through their bends, and eventually "consumed" by the faces. Hence, the nodes of the network are the vertices and faces of the graph. Since all angles we deal with have measure $k\pi/2$, with $1 \leq k \leq 4$, we establish the convention that a unit of flow represents a $\pi/2$ angle. We shall see that the formulas of Lemmas 5.1 and 5.2 express the "conservation" of flow at vertices and faces, respectively.

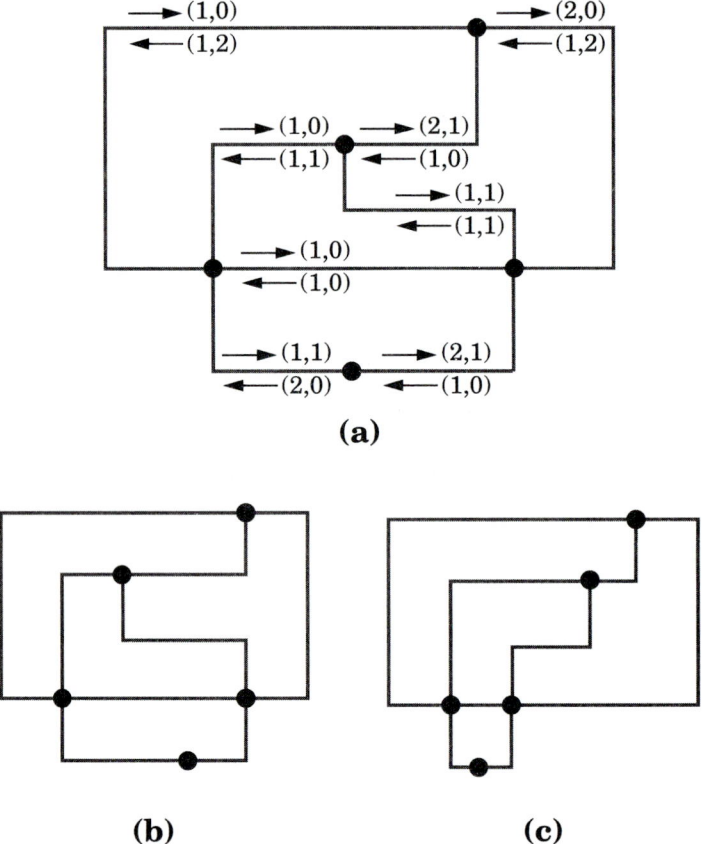

Figure 5.7: Three planar orthogonal drawings with the same orthogonal representation. Each dart (u, v) of the drawing in part (a) is labeled with the pair $(\alpha(u, v), \beta(u, v))$.

We need to introduce some terminology to discuss networks and flow. A *network* $\mathcal{N}$ is a digraph whose vertices are called *nodes* and whose edges are called *arcs*, such that:

- Each source (resp. sink) v has a production (resp. consumption) denoted $\sigma(v)$. The total amount of production of the sources is equal to the total consumption of the sinks.

- Each arc (u, v) is labeled with:

    - a *lower bound* $\lambda(u, v)$

> – a *capacity* $\mu(u, v)$
>
> – a *cost* $\chi(u, v)$.

A *flow* ϕ in $\mathcal{N}$ associates a nonnegative integer $\phi(u, v)$, with each arc (u, v). Flow $\phi(u, v)$ cannot exceed the capacity of (u, v) and cannot be less than the lower bound of (u, v). Also, for each node of $\mathcal{N}$ that is not a source or a sink, the sum of the flows of the incoming arcs is equal to the sum of the flows of the outgoing arcs.

The *cost of the flow* ϕ in $\mathcal{N}$ is the sum of $\chi(u, v)\phi(u, v)$ over all the arcs of $\mathcal{N}$. The *value of the flow* in $\mathcal{N}$ is the sum of the flows reaching the sinks. The *minimum cost flow problem* is stated as follows. Given a network $\mathcal{N}$, find a flow ϕ in $\mathcal{N}$, such that the cost of ϕ is minimum.

We associate a flow network $\mathcal{N}$, whose nodes have supplies and demands, and whose arcs each have a lower bound λ, a capacity μ, and a cost χ, with an embedded planar graph G as follows (see Figure 5.8):

- The nodes of $\mathcal{N}$ are the vertices and faces of G

- A vertex-node v of $\mathcal{N}$ produces flow $\sigma(v) = 4$

- A face-node of $\mathcal{N}$ consumes flow $\sigma(f) = 2a(f) - 4$ if f is an internal face, and flow $\sigma(h) = 2a(h) + 4$ if h is the external face

- For each dart (u, v) of G, with faces f and g on its left and right, respectively, $\mathcal{N}$ has two arcs (u, f) and (f, g), where:

    - arc (u, f) has lower bound $\lambda(u, f) = 1$, capacity $\mu(u, f) = 4$, and cost $\chi(u, f) = 0$ (see Figure 5.8.a)

    - arc (f, g) has lower bound $\lambda(f, g) = 0$, capacity $\mu(f, g) = +\infty$, and cost $\chi(f, g) = 1$ (see Figure 5.8.b).

The thought behind the definition of flow network $\mathcal{N}$ is as follows (see Figure 5.9):

- The flow in arc (u, f) associated with dart (u, v) represents the quantity $\alpha(u, v)$, that is, the measure of an angle formed at vertex u inside face f; the lower bound and capacity indicate that such an angle must be at least $\pi/2$ and at most 2π; the cost is zero since such an angle is at a vertex and not at a bend

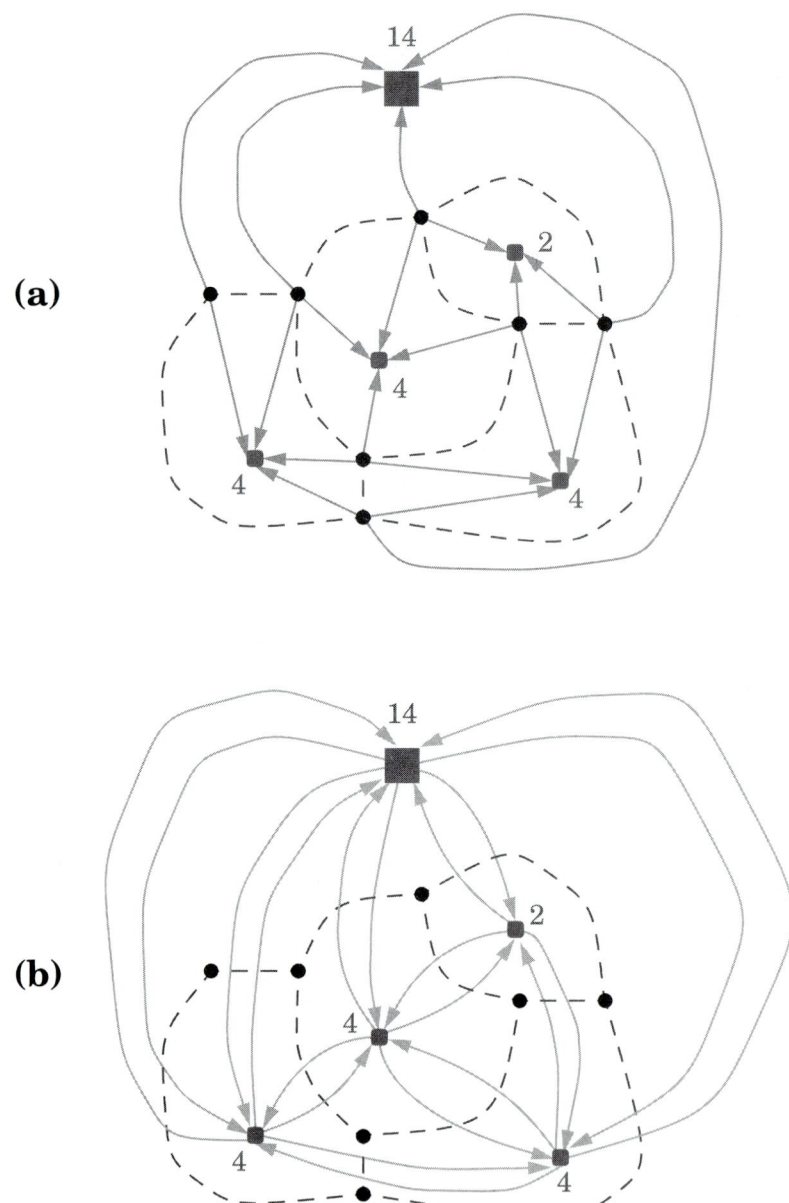

Figure 5.8: Network $\mathcal{N}$ associated with an embedded planar graph G (shown with dashed lines). Each face-node f of $\mathcal{N}$ is labeled with the amount of flow $\sigma(f)$ consumed: (a) arcs of $\mathcal{N}$ from vertex-nodes to face-nodes; (b) arcs of $\mathcal{N}$ between face-nodes.

- The flow in arc (f, g) associated with dart (u, v) represents the quantity $\beta(u, v)$, that is, the number of bends with the $\pi/2$ angle in face f along an edge between faces f and g; the lower bound and capacity indicate that such a number must be nonnegative and can be unbounded; the cost is one since each unit of flow in such an arc corresponds to a bend

- The conservation of flow at a vertex-node represents the property expressed in Lemma 5.1

- The conservation of flow at a face-node represents the property expressed in Lemma 5.2.

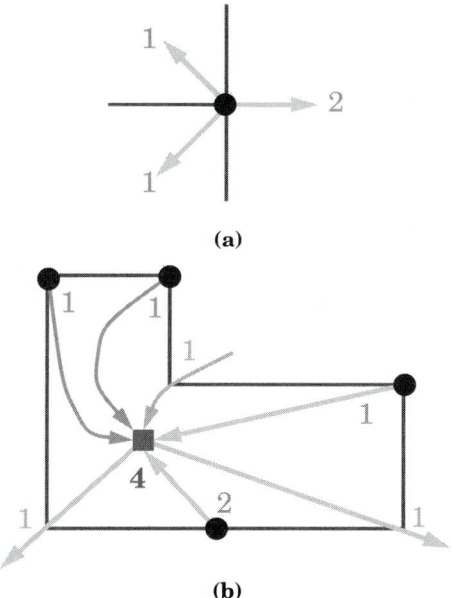

Figure 5.9: Correspondence between flow in network $\mathcal{N}$ and orthogonal representation of G: (a) vertex-node; (b) face-node.

The total amount of flow supplied by the vertex-nodes is equal to the total amount of flow consumed by the face-nodes. Indeed, let n, m, and r be the number of vertices, edges, and faces of G, respectively. By Euler's formula [BM76], we have $n - m + r - 2 = 0$. Therefore

$$\sum_v \sigma(v) - \sum_f \sigma(f) \;=\; \sum_v 4 - \sum_f (2a(f) - 4) - 8$$

$$
\begin{aligned}
&= \quad 4n - 4m + 4r - 8 \\
&= \quad 4(n - m + r - 2) \\
&= \quad 0.
\end{aligned}
$$

The number of nodes of $\mathcal{N}$ is $n + r \leq m + 2 \leq 2n + 2$, and the number of arcs of $\mathcal{N}$ is twice the number of darts of G, that is, $4m \leq 8n$. Note that $\mathcal{N}$ is planar but has bidirectional arcs between pairs of face-nodes. It is straightforward to compute $\mathcal{N}$ from G. Thus, we have:

Lemma 5.3 *Let G be an embedded planar graph with n vertices. The flow network $\mathcal{N}$ associated with G has $O(n)$ nodes and arcs, and can be constructed from G in $O(n)$ time.*

The correspondence between orthogonal representations and flows is formalized in the following theorem.

Theorem 5.1 *Let G be an embedded planar graph, and $\mathcal{N}$ be the flow network associated with G. For a dart (u, v) of G, let (u, f) and (f, g) be the associated arcs of $\mathcal{N}$. The following relations uniquely associate an orthogonal representation of G (given by values α and β) with a flow ϕ in network $\mathcal{N}$:*

- $\phi(u, f) = \alpha(u, v)$

- $\phi(f, g) = \beta(u, v).$

Also, the cost of flow ϕ is equal to the number of bends of the associated orthogonal representation of G.

In the example of Figure 5.10, we show the flow associated with a given orthogonal representation.

Algorithm 5.1 *Orthogonalize* computes an orthogonal representation with the minimum number of bends for an embedded planar graph G. It is based on Lemma 5.3 and Theorem 5.1.

Theorem 5.2 *Let G be an embedded planar graph with n vertices. Algorithm 5.1* Orthogonalize *computes an orthogonal representation of G, with the minimum number of bends, in time $O(T(n))$, where $T(n)$ is the time for computing a minimum cost flow in the flow network $\mathcal{N}$ associated with G.*

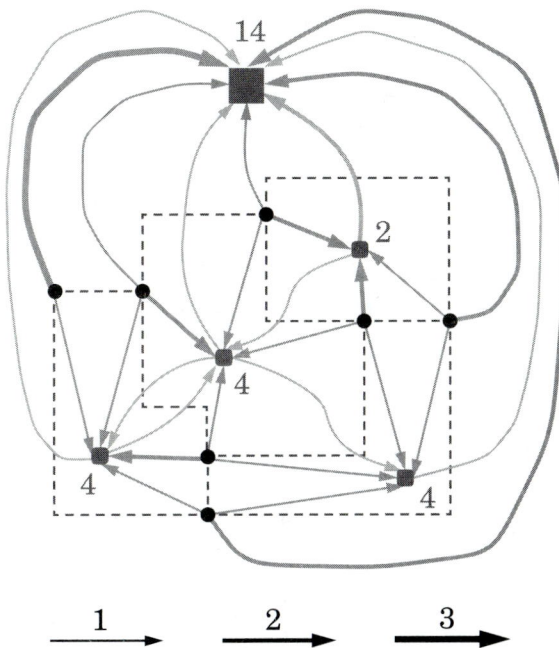

Figure 5.10: Example of flow ϕ associated with a planar orthogonal representation (drawn with dashed lines). Only the arcs with nonzero flow are shown. The thickness of the arc is proportional to the amount of flow. Each face-node f is labeled with the amount of flow $\sigma(f)$ consumed.

Algorithm 5.1 *Orthogonalize*

　　Input: 　embedded planar graph G with n vertices of maximum degree four

　Output: 　orthogonal representation of G with the minimum number of bends

1. Construct the flow network $\mathcal{N}$ associated with G (Lemma 5.3).

2. Compute a flow ϕ of minimum cost for network $\mathcal{N}$.

3. Compute the orthogonal representation of G associated with ϕ (Theorem 5.1).

$\square$

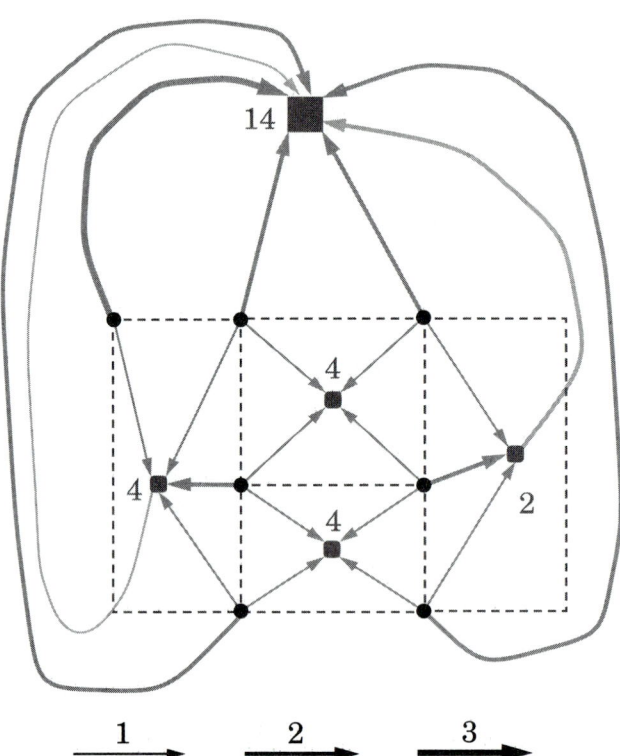

Figure 5.11: Example of a planar orthogonal representation with the minimum number of bends (drawn with dashed lines) associated with a flow ϕ of minimum cost. Only the arcs with nonzero flow are shown. The thickness of the arc is proportional to the amount of flow. Each face-node f is labeled with the amount of flow $\sigma(f)$ consumed.

In Figure 5.11, we show the orthogonal representation, with the minimum number of bends, associated with a flow of minimum cost.

A simple algorithm for computing a minimum cost flow in network $\mathcal{N}$ is based on the standard technique of augmenting the flow along minimum cost paths [AMO93]. It runs in time $T(n) = O(n^2 \log n)$ using $O(n)$ space. A more complex algorithm, which exploits the sparsity of network $\mathcal{N}$, runs in time $T(n) = O(n^{7/4} \log n)$ using $O(n)$ space [GT97b].

5.4 Compaction of Orthogonal Representations

In this section, we consider the problem of *compacting* an orthogonal representation, that is, of constructing an orthogonal grid drawing with a given orthogonal representation, such as the one produced by Algorithm 5.1 *Orthogonalize*. We want to assign lengths to the segments of the edges of the orthogonal representation, such that there are no crossings or overlaps among the vertices and edges. We aim at keeping the area small, while using only integer values for the segment lengths, hence the name "compaction." We will show that a drawing with area $O((n + b)^2)$ can be constructed in $O(n + b)$ time, where n and b denote the number of vertices and bends in the orthogonal representation, respectively.

The algorithm for the compaction problem deals separately with horizontal and vertical segments. We begin by describing the algorithm for the special case where each face in the orthogonal representation has the shape of a rectangle, and then consider the general case.

5.4.1 Orthogonal Representations with Rectangular Faces

Let G be an embedded planar graph with n vertices, and H be an orthogonal representation of G, such that each face of H has the shape of a rectangle (see Figure 5.12). We have that H has at most four bends, which can only be placed at the four "corners" of the external face. Any other bend would be incompatible with the requirement that all faces have a rectangular shape. Hence, the segments of H correspond to the edges of G, except possibly for at most eight segments incident on the bends of the external face.

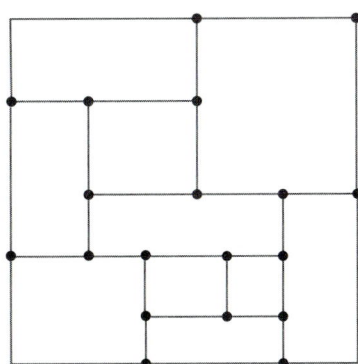

Figure 5.12: Example of orthogonal representation with rectangular faces.

We can formally express the fact that an internal face f has rectangular shape with the conditions $\alpha(u,v) \leq 2$ and $\beta(v,u) = 0$ for each dart $(u,v) \in D(f)$. Conversely, the external face h has rectangular shape if $\alpha(u,v) \geq 2$ and $\beta(u,v) = 0$ for each dart $(u,v) \in D(h)$.

Algorithm 5.2 *Tidy-Rectangle-Compact* uses a flow model of the compaction problem. Namely, it constructs two flow networks, one for the horizontal segments, and the other for the vertical segments. We shall describe the network N_{hor} for the horizontal segments (see Figure 5.13). The other network N_{ver} is analogous (see Figure 5.14).

Algorithm 5.2 *Tidy-Rectangle-Compact*

    Input: embedded planar graph G with n vertices of maximum degree four; orthogonal representation H of G, such that all the faces have rectangular shape

   Output: planar orthogonal grid drawing Γ of G with orthogonal representation H and minimum height, width, area, and total edge length

1. Construct flow networks N_{hor} and N_{ver} associated with H.

2. Compute minimum cost flows for N_{hor} and N_{ver}.

3. Set the length of each segment of H equal to the flow in the corresponding arc of N_{hor} or N_{ver}.

                                                                       □

Network N_{hor} has a node associated with each internal face plus two special nodes, denoted s and t, representing the "lower" and "upper" region of the external face, respectively. Also, N_{hor} has an arc (f,g) for every pair of faces f and g that share a horizontal segment e, with f below g. The flow in arc (f,g) represents the length of segment e. Hence, arc (f,g) has lower bound $\lambda(f,g) = 1$, capacity $\mu(f,g) = +\infty$, and cost $\chi(f,g) = 1$. Figures 5.13 and 5.14 show a flow of minimum cost for N_{hor} and N_{ver}, respectively.

The following properties of network N_{hor} are immediate. N_{hor} is planar and acyclic, with a unique source and a unique sink, both on the external face. This implies that N_{hor} is a planar st-graph (see Section 4.2). Also, N_{hor} has $O(n)$ nodes and arcs.

Clearly, given an orthogonal drawing of G with orthogonal representation

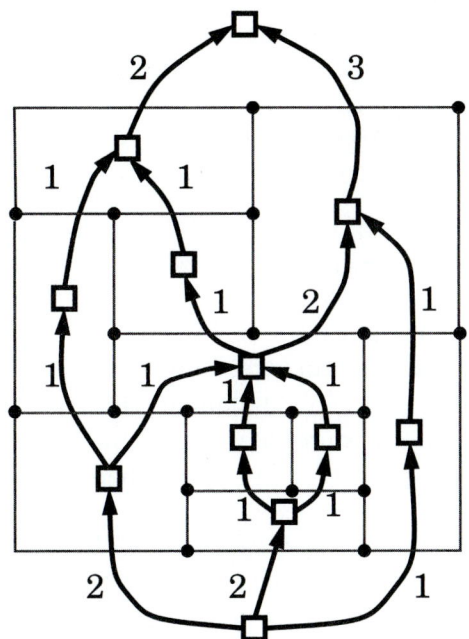

Figure 5.13: Network N_{hor} for the orthogonal representation of Figure 5.12, and a minimum cost flow for N_{hor}.

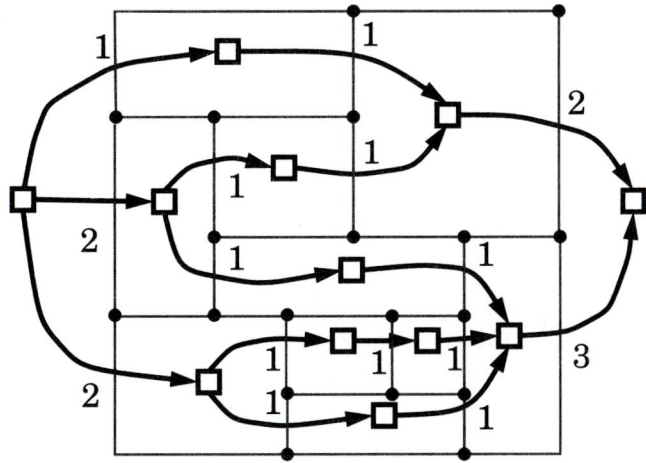

Figure 5.14: Network N_{ver} for the orthogonal representation of Figure 5.12, and a minimum cost flow for N_{ver}.

H and integer segment lengths, we can immediately compute a flow for N_{hor} (and N_{ver}) by setting the flow in each arc equal to the length of its associated segment. Note that:

- The flow value for N_{hor} (N_{ver}) is equal to the width (height) of the drawing

- The sum of the costs of the flows in N_{hor} and N_{ver} is equal to the total edge length of the drawing.

For example, the flows of Figures 5.13 and 5.14 can be obtained from the drawing of Figure 5.16.a. The converse is also true. Indeed, the conservation of flow at each node of N_{hor} (N_{ver}) signifies that the top and bottom (left and right) side of each rectangle have the same length. This implies the assigned lengths give a consistent drawing. Therefore, we have:

Lemma 5.4 *Given flows for networks N_{hor} and N_{ver}, setting the length of each segment of H equal to the flow of the corresponding arc in N_{hor} or N_{ver} yields a planar orthogonal drawing Γ of G with orthogonal representation H. Also, the width (height) of Γ is equal to the value of the flow in N_{hor} (N_{ver}), and the total edge length of Γ is equal to the sum of the costs of the flows in N_{hor} and N_{ver}.*

By Lemma 5.4, the compaction problem for an orthogonal representation with rectangular faces can be reduced to a minimum-cost flow computation. This compaction method is summarized in Algorithm 5.2 *Tidy-Rectangle-Compact* that computes minimum cost flows for networks N_{hor} and N_{ver} (see Figures 5.13 and 5.14) to construct a drawing with minimum height, width, area, and total edge length (see Figure 5.16.a).

The correctness of Algorithm 5.2 *Tidy-Rectangle-Compact* follows from Lemma 5.4. The time complexity of Steps 1 and 3 is $O(n)$ time; Step 2 takes $O(n^{7/4} \log n)$ [GT97b] time (see the discussion after Theorem 5.2).

Now we present a different compaction algorithm that runs in linear time and minimizes the height, width, and area of the drawing, but does not guarantee the minimum total edge length.

Let N_{hor}^* be the digraph obtained from G and H by (see Figure 5.15):

- Replacing (at most four) bends with fictitious vertices

- Orienting the horizontal edges from left to right

- Contracting maximal paths of vertical edges to a vertex.

Digraph N_{hor}^* is a planar st-graph (see Section 4.2). We call the vertices of N_{hor}^* *vertical bars*. Note that N_{hor}^* is the "dual planar st-graph" of N_{hor} (see Section 4.2). We perform an analogous construction to obtain planar st-graph N_{ver}^*, whose vertices are associated with maximal paths of horizontal edges, called *horizontal bars*. Digraphs N_{hor}^* and N_{ver}^* each have $O(n)$ vertices and edges, where n is the number of vertices of G.

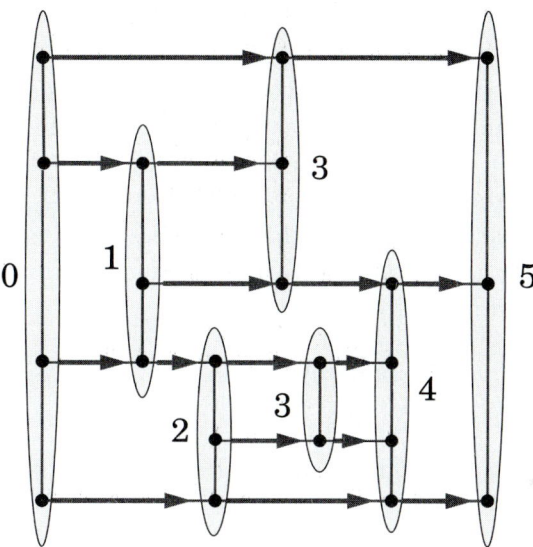

Figure 5.15: Digraph N_{hor}^* for the orthogonal representation of Figure 5.12. Each vertex of N_{hor}^* is shown as a shaded oval. The vertex labels show an optimal weighted topological numbering with respect to unit edge weights.

We can use topological numberings (see Section 4.1) of planar st-graphs N_{hor}^* and N_{ver}^* to compute flows in N_{hor} and N_{ver}.

Lemma 5.5 *Given an integer topological numbering X (Y) of N_{hor}^* (N_{ver}^*), a flow ϕ for N_{hor} (N_{ver}) can be constructed by setting $\phi(f,g) = X(b'') - X(b')$ $(\phi(f,g) = Y(b'') - Y(b'))$, where b' and b'' are the vertical (horizontal) bars containing the left (bottom) and right (top) endpoint of the horizontal (vertical) segment associated with arc (v,f), respectively. Also, the value of flow ϕ is equal to the difference between the maximum and minimum X (Y) value.*

By Lemma 5.5, a flow in N_{hor} (N_{ver}) of minimum value can be constructed from an optimal weighted topological numbering of N_{hor}^* (N_{ver}^*)

with respect to unit edge weights (see Section 4.1). Hence, by Lemma 5.4, we obtain a planar orthogonal grid drawing of G with minimum width, height, and area. This compaction method is summarized in Algorithm 5.3 *Fast-Rectangle-Compact*. An example of a run of Algorithm 5.3 *Fast-Rectangle-Compact* is shown in Figure 5.16.b.

Algorithm 5.3 *Fast-Rectangle-Compact*

   Input: embedded planar graph G with n vertices of maximum degree four; orthogonal representation H of G, such that all the faces have rectangular shape

   Output: planar orthogonal grid drawing Γ of G with orthogonal representation H and minimum height, width, and area

1. Construct planar st-graphs N^*_{hor} and N^*_{ver} and assign unit weights to their edges.

2. Compute optimal weighted topological numberings X and Y of N^*_{hor} and N^*_{ver}, respectively.

3. Set the length of each horizontal segment e of H equal to $X(b'') - X(b')$, where b' and b'' are the vertical bars of N^*_{hor} containing the left and right endpoint of segment e, respectively.

4. Set the length of each vertical segment e of H equal to $Y(b'') - Y(b')$, where b' and b'' are the horizontal bars of N^*_{ver} containing the bottom and top endpoint of segment e, respectively.

$\square$

We summarize with the following theorem:

Theorem 5.3 *Given an embedded planar graph G with n vertices of degree at most 4, and an orthogonal representation H of G, such that all the faces have rectangular shape, Algorithm 5.3 Fast-Orthogonal-Compact constructs a planar orthogonal grid drawing of G, with minimum height, width, and area, in $O(n)$ time.*

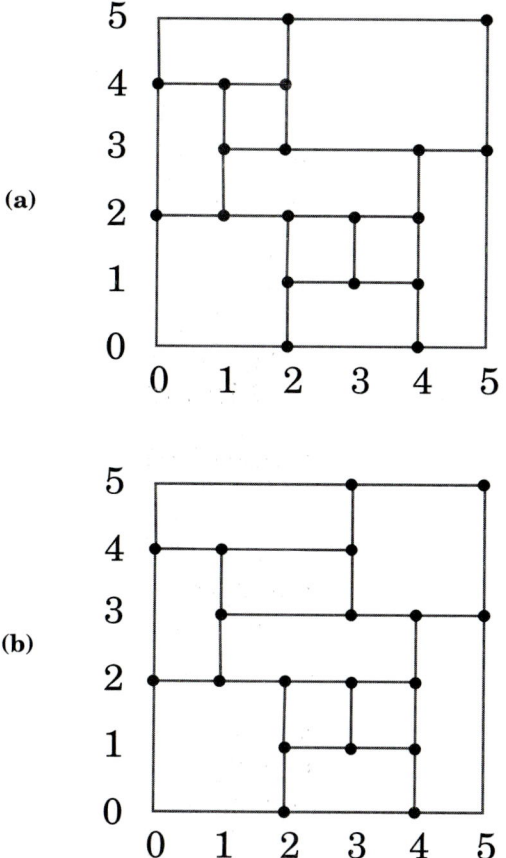

Figure 5.16: Examples of compaction of the orthogonal representation of Figure 5.12: (a) drawing produced by Algorithm 5.2 *Tidy-Rectangle-Compact* using the flows shown in Figures 5.13 and 5.14; (b) drawing produced by Algorithm 5.3 *Fast-Rectangle-Compact* using the topological numbering shown in Figure 5.15.

5.4.2   General Orthogonal Representations

In this section, we show how to compact general orthogonal representations, where the regions do not necessarily have a rectangular shape. We "refine" the orthogonal representation into one whose regions have a rectangular shape by introducing "invisible" dummy edges, and then apply one of the compaction algorithms of the previous section.

Let G be an embedded planar graph with n vertices, and H be an orthogonal representation of G. A *rectangular refinement* of H is an orthogonal representation H' of a graph G', such that (see Figure 5.17):

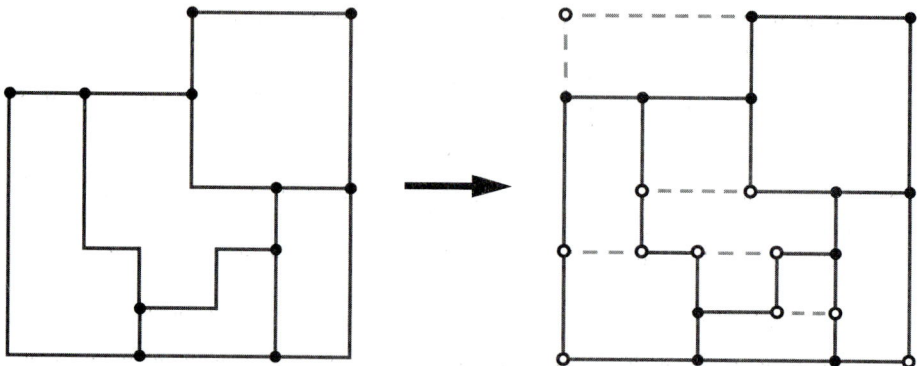

Figure 5.17: Example of rectangular refinement.

- G' is obtained from G by a sequence of the following operations:

    - add an isolated vertex
    - insert a vertex along an edge
    - add an edge.

- The "subrepresentation" of H' associated with G is the same as H.

- The regions of H' have rectangular shape.

Clearly, a drawing of G' with orthogonal representation H' contains a drawing of G with orthogonal representation H. In this section, we show that a rectangular refinement H' of H always exists and can be efficiently computed.

The construction of H' starts by inserting a vertex at each bend of H. Next, we consider each face in turn. Let f be an internal face. If f has rectangular shape, nothing has to be done. Otherwise, we proceed as follows (see Figure 5.18):

1. For each edge e of f, let $next(e)$ be the edge following e when traversing the boundary of f counterclockwise, and let $corner(e)$ be the common vertex of e and $next(e)$.

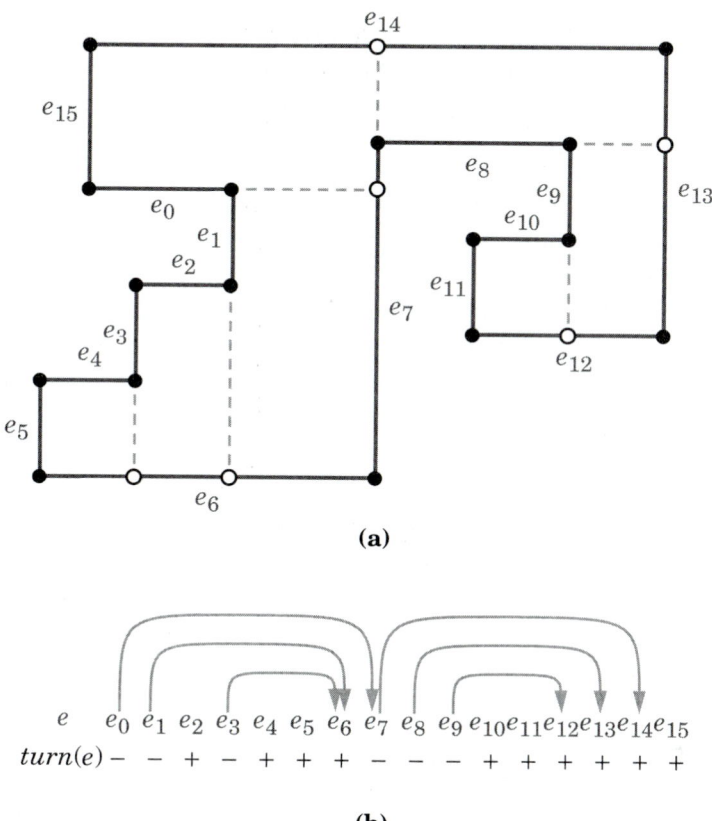

(a)

(b)

Figure 5.18: Example of "refinement" of an internal face into rectangles. Edges $extend(e)$ are dashed in part (a). Edges $front(e)$, for each e with $turn(e) = -1$, are indicated by arrows in part (b).

2. For each edge e of f, we set $turn(e) = +1$ if e and $next(e)$ form a left turn, $turn(e) = 0$ if e and $next(e)$ are aligned, and $turn(e) = -1$ if e and $next(e)$ form a right turn.

3. For each edge e, find the first edge e' following e counterclockwise, such that the sum of the *turn* values for all the edges between e (included) and e' (excluded) is equal to 1, and set $front(e) = e'$.

4. For each edge e, such that $turn(e) = -1$ (i.e., e and $next(e)$ form a right turn), insert a vertex $project(e)$ along edge $front(e)$, and add edge $extend(e) = (corner(e), project(e))$. Update H' by establishing that

$extend(e)$ has no bends, and e and $extend(e)$ are aligned. If $front(e') =$ $front(e'') = e''$, for distinct edges e' and e'', then we establish that $project(e')$ follows $project(e'')$ counterclockwise, if and only if e', e'', and $front(e')$ form a counterclockwise sequence.

The above algorithm "refines" internal face f into a collection of rectangular faces. Its correctness can be proved as follows. First, $front(e)$ is defined for every edge e, since by Lemma 5.2, $\sum_e turn(e) = 4$.   Assume, as a contradiction, that two newly inserted edges $extend(e')$ and $extend(e'')$ "cross", that is, going counterclockwise we encounter in order e', e'', $front(e')$, and $front(e'')$ (see Figure 5.19). This contradicts the definition of $front$ (see Figure 5.18).

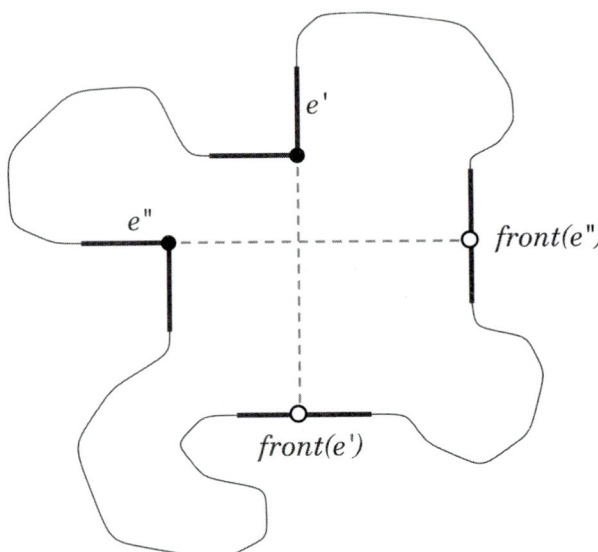

Figure 5.19: Showing by contradiction that $extend(e')$ and $extend(e'')$ cannot cross.

The refinement of the external face can be done with a variation of the above algorithm. Now, we have that $\sum_e turn(e) = -4$, so that $front(e)$ may not be defined for every edge e. To handle the edges with $front$ undefined, we add a "rectangle" around the external face, and we "extend" such edges by "projecting" them onto the sides of the rectangle (see Figure 5.20).

It is easy to see that the refined orthogonal representation H' has $O(n+b)$ vertices, where b is the number of bends of H. Also, the refinement algorithm can be implemented in linear time by keeping the vertices encountered in

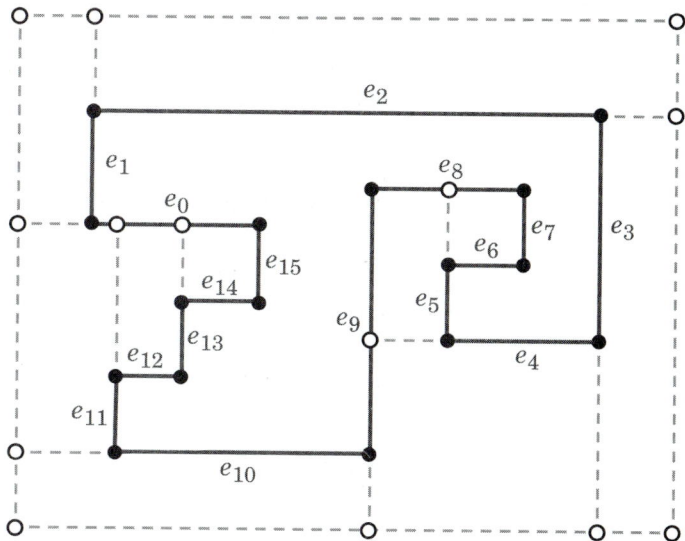

Figure 5.20: Example of "refinement" of the external face into rectangles.

the traversal of each face in a stack. Therefore, by combining Algorithm 5.3 *Fast-Orthogonal-Compact* with the refinement strategy above, we obtain:

Theorem 5.4 *Given an embedded planar graph G with n vertices of degree at most 4, and an orthogonal representation H of G with b bends, a planar orthogonal drawing of G with integer coordinates and area $O((n + b)^2)$ can be constructed in $O(n + b)$ time.*

If we use Algorithm 5.2 *Tidy-Rectangle-Compact* instead of Algorithm 5.3 *Fast-Orthogonal-Compact*, then the total edge length of the drawing would probably be smaller, but the time complexity would increase to $O(n^{7/4} \log n)$.

5.5 An Orthogonal Drawing Algorithm that Minimizes the Number of Bends

Using the building blocks provided by Sections 5.3 and 5.4, we can construct Algorithm 5.4 *Optimal-Orthogonal*, the complete algorithm for creating a planar orthogonal drawing, with a minimum number of bends.

Recall that it may be possible to obtain a drawing with smaller total edge length by using Algorithm 5.2 *Tidy-Orthogonal-Compact* instead of Algorithm 5.3 *Fast-Orthogonal-Compact*.

Algorithm 5.4 *Optimal-Orthogonal*

    Input: embedded planar graph G with n vertices of
                degree at most four

  Output: planar orthogonal grid drawing Γ of G with
                area $O(n^2)$ and the minimum number of bends

1. Construct an orthogonal representation H of G with the minimum number of bends by means of Algorithm 5.1 *Orthogonalize*.

2. Refine H into an orthogonal representation H' with rectangular faces.

3. Construct a planar orthogonal grid drawing Γ' of H' by means of Algorithm 5.3 *Fast-Orthogonal-Compact*.

4. Obtain from Γ' a planar orthogonal grid drawing Γ of G by ignoring the fictitious edges and vertices introduced in the refinement step.   □

Since the minimum number of bends in a planar orthogonal drawing is $O(n)$ (see Table A.7), the compaction can be carried out in $O(n)$ time. Thus the time complexity of Algorithm 5.4 *Optimal-Orthogonal* is dominated by the minimum cost flow computation. We summarize the main result of this section in the following theorem:

Theorem 5.5 *Given an embedded planar graph G with n vertices of degree at most four, Algorithm 5.4* Optimal-Orthogonal *constructs a planar orthogonal grid drawing of G with area $O(n^2)$ and the minimum number of bends, in $O(T(n))$ time,, where $T(n)$ is the time for computing a minimum cost flow in the flow network $\mathcal{N}$ associated with G.*

We recall that $T(n) = O(n^{7/4} \log n)$ [GT97b] and that $T(n) = O(n^2 \log n)$ can be achieved with a simple algorithm (see the discussion after Theorem 5.2).

Algorithm 5.4 *Optimal-Orthogonal* can be used in the orthogonalization step of the topology-shape-metrics approach for constructing orthogonal drawings of general (nonplanar) graphs outlined in Section 2.3.

5.6 Constraints

Algorithm 5.4 *Optimal-Orthogonal* can be easily modified to support user-defined constraints of the following types on the drawing:

- *Vertex-angle Constraints*: Upper and lower bounds on a vertex-angle, that is, on $\alpha(u, v)$, for a dart (u, v)

- *Bend Constraints*: Upper and lower bounds on the bends of an edge e, that is, upper and lower bounds on $\beta(u, v)$ and $\beta(v, u)$ for the darts (u, v) and (v, u) of edge e.

These constraints can be imposed by modifying the capacities and lower bounds of the arcs of $\mathcal{N}$ associated with appropriate darts. For example, to prescribe at most two bends on an edge e with darts (u, v) and (v, u), we set the capacity of the arcs (f, g) and (g, f) of $\mathcal{N}$, associated with the faces f and g on the left of (u, v) and (v, u), equal to two respectively, that is, $\mu(f, g) = \mu(g, f) = 2$. Note that a set of vertex-angle and bend constraints allows us to prescribe the orthogonal representation of a subgraph. The time complexity of Algorithm 5.4 *Optimal-Orthogonal* is not affected by the use of the constraint satisfaction mechanism.

In Fig. 5.21, we show a drawing with the minimum number of bends subject to bend constraints requiring two given edges to have zero bends.

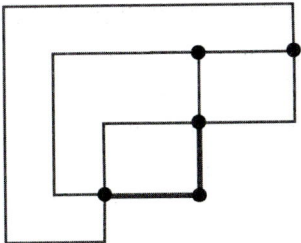

Figure 5.21: Planar orthogonal drawing of the embedded planar graph of Figure 5.1. The drawing has the minimum number of bends subject to bend constraints requiring that the two edges drawn with thick lines have zero bends. Imposing this constraint causes the minimum number of bends to increase from 6 to 8.

5.7   Bend Minimal Drawings

In this section, we present additional applications of the flow model introduced in Section 5.3. We provide a characterization of planar orthogonal drawings with the minimum number of bends (Theorem 5.6). This characterization opens a different avenue for bend minimization. Suppose that we have an orthogonal representation with a nonminimum number of bends, for example, from Algorithm 4.8 *Orthogonal-from-Visibility* (see Theorem 4.16). We can apply the characterization to give *bend-stretching* transformations that reduce the number of bends.

Let Γ be a planar orthogonal drawing. A vertex- or face-angle of Γ measuring $\pi/2$, π, or $3\pi/2$ is called *inflex*, *flat*, or *reflex*, respectively. An oriented closed simple curve C, drawn onto Γ, defines an *elementary transformation* of Γ if it intersects vertices only by entering from flat or reflex angles. The elementary transformation is obtained by "transporting" a $\pi/2$ angle across each vertex and edge intersected by C (see Figure 5.22). For each vertex v traversed by C, the transformation subtracts $\pi/2$ from the angle where C enters, and it adds $\pi/2$ to the angle where C exits. Also, for each intersection of C with an edge e, if C traverses e at a bend entering from the reflex angle, then the transformation removes that bend. Otherwise (C traverses e entering from an inflex or a flat angle), it adds to e a bend with the reflex angle on the side where C exits.

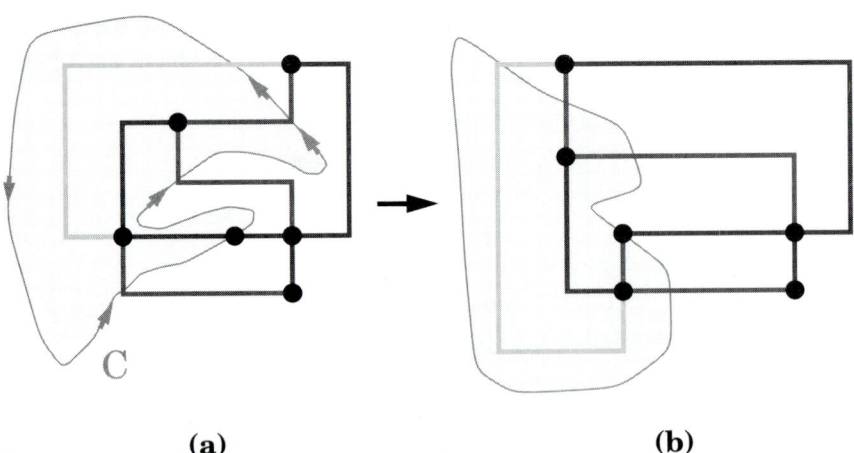

(a)   **(b)**

Figure 5.22: Example of an elementary transformation: (a) initial drawing and closed curve C with $reflex(C) = 3$, $flat(C) = 1$, $inflex(C) = 0$, and $\Delta(C) = -2$; (b) final drawing with two fewer bends.

Let $reflex(C)$, $flat(C)$, and $inflex(C)$ be the number of edges that are traversed by C entering from a reflex, flat, and inflex angle, respectively. Note that we do not take into account traversals of vertices. The variation in the number of bends caused by the elementary transformation defined by C is given by (see Figure 5.22)

$$\Delta(C) = flat(C) + inflex(C) - reflex(C).$$

Curve C is said to be *trivial* if it intersects only one edge (going back and forth between two faces) and $\Delta = 0$ (see Figure 5.23). The elementary transformation defined by a trivial curve does not change the drawing.

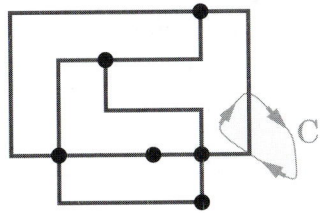

Figure 5.23: Example of a trivial curve with $\Delta = 0$.

In the correspondence between orthogonal representations of G and flows in network $\mathcal{N}$ established by Theorem 5.1, a curve C, defining an elementary transformation, corresponds to an augmenting cycle (see [AMO93]) in $\mathcal{N}$ with cost Δ. Since a minimum cost flow has no negative-cost augmenting cycles, Γ has the minimum number of bends if and only if $\Delta \geq 0$ for every curve. Also, a minimum cost flow is unique if and only if it has no zero-cost augmenting cycles (see [AMO93]). Hence, we conclude that the orthogonal representation of Γ is the unique orthogonal representation of G with the minimum number of bends if and only if, for every curve C, $\Delta > 0$.

Theorem 5.6 *A planar orthogonal drawing Γ of an embedded planar graph G of maximum degree at most 4 has the minimum number of bends if and only if, for every curve C defining an elementary transformation, we have $\Delta(C) \geq 0$. Also, the orthogonal representation of Γ is the unique orthogonal representation of G with the minimum number of bends if and only if, for every nontrivial curve C defining an elementary transformation, $\Delta(C) > 0$.*

Theorem 5.6 suggests an alternative algorithm for computing an orthogonal drawing, with the minimum number of bends, for an embedded planar

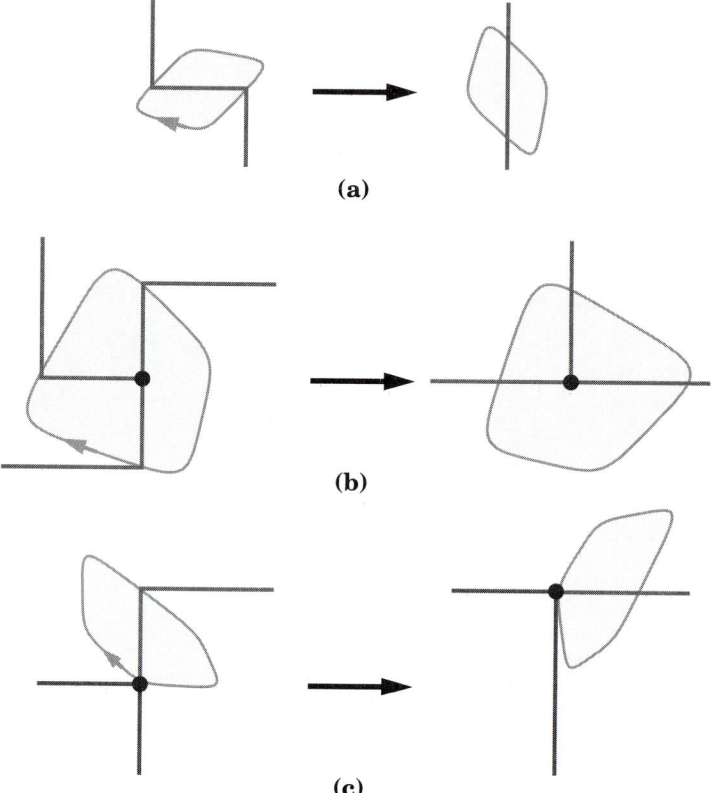

(a)

(b)

(c)

Figure 5.24: Bend-stretching transformations.

graph G with n vertices. Start with an $O(n)$-bend drawing Γ, for example, the one constructed by Algorithm 4.8 *Orthogonal-from-Visibility* (see Theorem 4.16), and then remove bends by means of $O(n)$ elementary transformations with $\Delta < 0$. This algorithm is inefficient, since testing whether Γ admits such an elementary transformation is equivalent to finding a negative-cost augmenting cycle in the flow network $\mathcal{N}$ associated with the orthogonal representations of G, which takes $O(n^2)$ time (see [AMO93]).

There are however, special cases of elementary transformations with $\Delta < 0$ that can be efficiently detected in linear time by a simple visit of the orthogonal representation. In Figure 5.24, we show three such elementary transformations, called *bend-stretching transformations*, which were introduced in [TT89a]. In Figure5.25, we show an example of the improvement obtained by performing bend-stretching transformations.

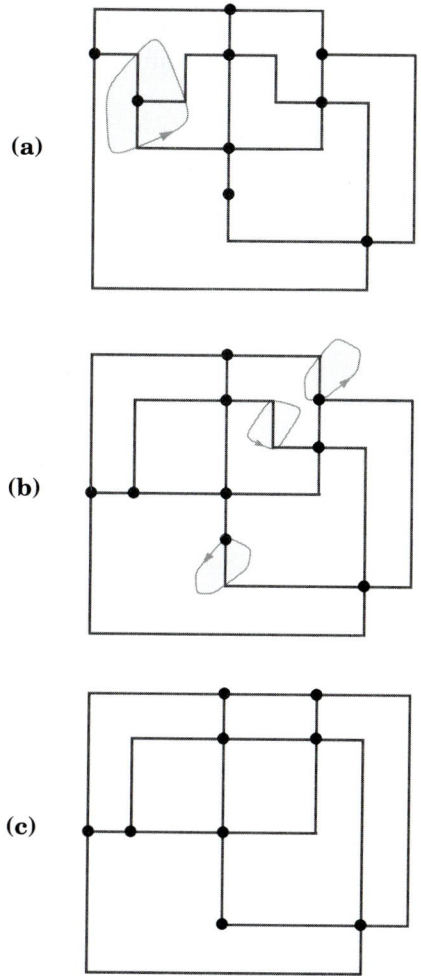

Figure 5.25: Example of the improvement obtained by performing a sequence of four bend-stretching transformations on a planar orthogonal drawing: (a) initial drawing (same as part (d) of Figure 4.25); (b) intermediate drawing after one transformation; (c) final drawing after three transformations.

Two drawings constructed with the techniques presented in this chapter are shown in Figure 5.26. The same graph is drawn with two different algorithms. The drawing on the left has been constructed by first applying a variation of Algorithm 4.8 *Orthogonal-from-Visibility* and then perform-

ing bend stretching transformations. The drawing on the right has been
constructed with a variation of Algorithm 5.4 *Optimal-Orthogonal*. The
technique used for the first drawing is faster than the technique used for the
second drawing. However, the second drawing is more readable.

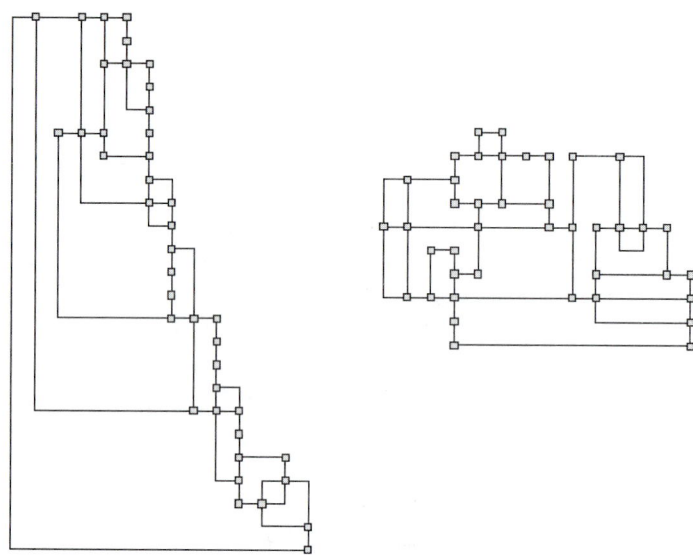

Figure 5.26: Two orthogonal drawings of the same graph created by the
`GDToolkit` software. (Courtesy of W. Didimo, A. Leonforte, and M. Patrignani.)

5.8   Extension to General Planar Graphs

Algorithm 5.4 *Optimal-Orthogonal* is applicable only to planar graphs with
vertices of degree at most four. In this section, we show how to extend
the algorithm to general planar graphs. For this purpose, we extend the
definition of orthogonal drawing to general graphs, by allowing vertices of
degree greater than four to be represented by rectangles with horizontal and
vertical sides. Related work appears in [FK96].

Let G be an embedded planar graph. For each vertex v of degree $d > 4$,
we expand G into a cycle $C(v)$ of d vertices $v_1, v_2, \ldots, v_d$, where each vertex
v_i becomes incident to one of the edges formerly incident on v. Cycle $C(v)$ is
called the *expansion cycle* of vertex v. Let G' be the graph obtained from G

by the above expansion procedure. Graph G' is an embedded planar graph with vertices of degree at most four. In particular, a vertex of an expansion cycle has degree three.

We construct a planar orthogonal drawing Γ' of graph G', subject to the constraint that each edge of an expansion cycle has zero bends, using the constrained variation of Algorithm 5.4 *Optimal-Orthogonal* described in Section 5.6.

Lemma 5.6 *In drawing Γ', each expansion cycle $C(v)$ is drawn as a rectangle with horizontal and vertical sides.*

Proof: Let f be the face of G' bounded by $C(v)$, and let u be a vertex of $C(v)$. Since u has degree three, each angle incident of u measures at most π. Also, the bend constraints cause every edge of $C(v)$ to be drawn as a horizontal or vertical straight-line segment. Thus the drawing of cycle $C(v)$ in Γ' is a polygon with horizontal and vertical sides that has internal angles measuring either $\pi/2$ or π. We conclude that $C(v)$ is drawn as a rectangle. □

We can view Γ' as a planar orthogonal drawing of graph G, such that the representation of every vertex v is a rectangle with horizontal and vertical sides. Note that such a drawing of G is not guaranteed to have the minimum number of bends.

5.9 Exercises

1. Prove Lemma 5.2.

2. Show that in a planar orthogonal drawing with the minimum number of bends, no edge has two bends with a $\pi/2$ angle on opposite sides.

3. Show that the graph of Figure 5.11 has more than one planar orthogonal representation with the minimum number of bends.

4. Prove that networks N_{hor} and N_{ver} are planar st-graphs.

5. Give a complete proof of Theorem 5.4.

6. Apply Algorithm 5.4 *Optimal-Orthogonal*, showing all steps, to:

   (a) The graph of Figure 5.1.a

   (b) The graph of Figure 5.17

(c) The graph of Figure 5.24.

7. Show how to modify Algorithm 5.4 *Optimal-Orthogonal* to give two new algorithms:

   (a) An algorithm which constructs a drawing with the minimum number of bends subject to a prescribed orthogonal representation for a subgraph.

   (b) An algorithm which constructs a drawing, such that a given edge has a prescribed shape, specified by the sequence of left and right turns of its bends.

8. Show that the planar orthogonal drawing of Figure 5.24 does not have the minimum number of bends using an elementary transformation.

Chapter 6

Flow and Upward Planarity

When considering acyclic digraphs, the notion of planarity needs to be refined to take into account the fact that such digraphs are usually drawn *upward*, that is, with the edges monotonically increasing in the vertical direction. Namely, we recall that a digraph is *upward planar* if it admits a drawing that is at the same time planar and upward (see Section 2.1). Planarity and acyclicity are necessary but not sufficient conditions for upward planarity (see Figure 6.1).

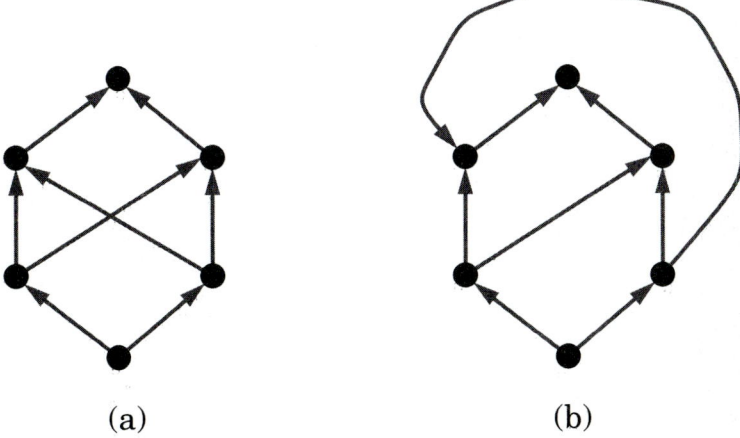

(a)   (b)

Figure 6.1: Two drawings of a planar acyclic digraph that is not upward planar: (a) an upward drawing which is not planar; (b) a planar drawing which is not upward.

This chapter addresses the upward planarity problem for digraphs. The study of upward planarity has fascinating connections with fundamental graph-theoretic and order-theoretic properties such as connectivity and dimension (see, e.g., [Riv93]).

In Section 6.1, we describe a characterization that relates upward planarity with planar *st*-graphs. In upward planarity, angles play a role similar to their role in orthogonal drawings; this is the subject of Section 6.2. The concepts presented in Section 6.2 find application in Section 6.3, where we present a polynomial time algorithm to test upward planarity of embedded acyclic digraphs [BDLM94]. The test consists of determining the existence of a planar upward drawing with the given embedding. This is modeled by a flow problem, where the sources and sinks of the digraph produce "large" angles that are consumed by the faces.

In Sections 6.4 and 6.5, we present a polynomial time algorithm to test upward planarity of single source acyclic digraphs [BDMT98, HL96]. In Section 6.6, we show that, while testing whether a digraph admits a planar drawing or an upward drawing can be done in linear time, combining the two properties makes the problem NP-complete [GT95]. The NP-completeness proof is based on a flow model. In Section 6.7, we complete the chapter by addressing several other aspects of upward planarity.

Algorithms for constructing drawings of general (nonplanar) acyclic digraphs are presented in Chapter 9.

6.1   Inclusion in a Planar *st*-Graph

The following theorem gives a simple characterization of upward planarity [DT88, Kel87].

Theorem 6.1 *Let G be a digraph. The following statements are equivalent:*

1. *G is upward planar.*

2. *G admits an upward planar straight-line drawing.*

3. *G is the spanning subgraph of a planar st-graph.*

For example, the digraph of Figure 6.2.a is upward planar because adding to it some edges yields the planar *st*-graph shown in Figure 6.2.b.

The remainder of this section consists of a proof of Theorem 6.1. First, we show that Statement 1 implies Statement 3. Next, we show that Statement 3 implies Statement 2. Obviously, Statement 2 implies Statement 1, which completes the proof.

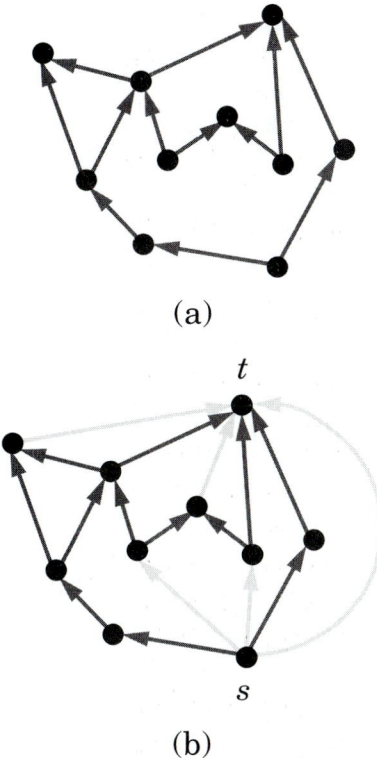

(a)

(b)

Figure 6.2: (a) An upward planar digraph G. (b) Planar st-graph obtained from G by adding the light edges.

We illustrate the proof that Statement 1 implies Statement 3 in Figure 6.3. Consider an upward planar straight-line drawing of G, and call s a source of G with lowest y-coordinate, and t a sink of G with highest y-coordinate. At a sink $v \neq t$, we start drawing a new edge upward. If we encounter an existing edge e, then we follow its route closely, to avoid other edges, until we reach $w = dest(e)$. This adds a new edge (v, w) that preserves planarity and acyclicity and "cancels" former sink v. This procedure needs a minor modification if a vertical ray emanating upward from v does not intersect any edge. By repeating this step, we are able to cancel all the sinks, except t. A similar procedure allows us to cancel all the sources, except s. Finally, we add the edge (s, t).

The proof that Statement 3 implies Statement 2 is as follows. Given a planar st-graph G' including G, we construct a planar upward straight-line

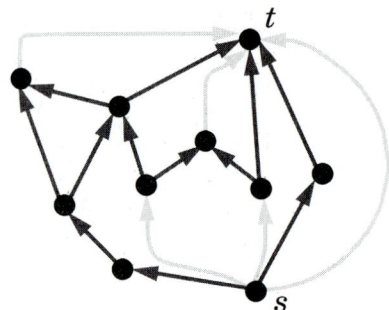

Figure 6.3: Construction showing that Statement 2 implies Statement 3 in Theorem 6.1.

drawing of G in three steps:

1. We add edges to G', such that the resulting digraph G'' is a planar st-graph with all faces consisting of three edges.

2. We construct an upward planar straight-line drawing of G''.

3. We remove the edges that do not belong to G from the drawing of G''.

Let f be a face of a planar st-graph G'. We recall that by Lemma 4.1, f consists of two directed paths P_l and P_r from $orig(f)$ to $dest(f)$. The construction of Step 1 is based on the following lemmas.

Lemma 6.1 *Let P be either P_l or P_r, $P = (v_1, \ldots, v_k)$, where $v_1 = orig(f)$ and $v_k = dest(f)$, and assume that $k \geq 4$. Then either edge (v_1, v_{k-1}) or edge (v_2, v_k) can be added to G' within face f, such that the resulting embedded digraph is a planar st-graph.*

Lemma 6.2 *If f is an internal face and both P_l and P_r have at least three vertices, then the embedded digraph, obtained by adding edge (v_l, v_r) to G' within face f, where v_l (v_r) is a vertex of P_l (P_r) distinct from $orig(f)$ and $dest(f)$, is a planar st-graph.*

If G' does not have the edge (s, t), then we add it. If (s, t) is not on the external face, then we change the embedding of G', such that (s, t) is on the external face. If G' has a face f with more than three edges, then either Lemma 6.1 or Lemma 6.2 applies. Hence, we can add an edge to G' within face f. We repeat this edge-addition process until all the faces have three edges.

The construction for Step 2 is given in Lemma 6.4. Some geometric definitions are needed. Let $X = (v_0, \ldots, v_k)$ be a simple polygon, where the sequence of vertices is counterclockwise, and p a point inside X. A vertex v_i of X is said to be *visible* from p, if the segment pv_i lies entirely inside X. A vertex v_i is said to be *properly visible* from p if it is visible from p and the interior of the segment pv_i does not intersect X. The *kernel* of X is the set of points p from which all vertices of X are visible. Notice that the concept of visibility used here (visibility in any direction), is different from the one of the definition of visibility representation (visibility in the vertical direction) given in Chapter 4. The *left half-plane* of an edge (v_i, v_{i+1}) of X is defined as the half plane on the left of the straight line through (v_i, v_{i+1}), oriented from v_i to v_{i+1}. The *wedge* of a vertex v_i of X is defined as the intersection of the left half-planes of the edges incident upon v_i (see Figure 6.4.a). The kernel of X is equal to the intersection of the left half-planes of its edges, or, equivalently, to the intersection of the wedges of its vertices [YB61]. Using this characterization of the kernel and continuity arguments, we can prove the following lemma (see Figure 6.4.b).

Lemma 6.3 *Let v_i be a vertex of a simple polygon X, such that:*

- *v_i belongs to the kernel of X*

- *The remaining vertices of X, except v_{i-1} and v_{i+1}, are properly visible from v_i.*

Then there exists a disk D centered at v_i such that the intersection of D and the wedge of v_i is contained in the kernel of X.

Lemma 6.4 *Let G be a planar st-graph with all faces consisting of three edges. Given any upward planar straight-line drawing Δ for the external face of G, there exists an upward planar straight-line drawing of G with the external face drawn as Δ.*

Proof: The proof is by induction on the number n of vertices of G. The basis of the induction, $n = 3$, is immediate, since Δ is a drawing of G. Now we assume that the theorem holds for graphs with fewer than n vertices. Let v be a vertex of G that is not on the external face, and let χ be the undirected cycle of the neighbors of v. We distinguish two cases.

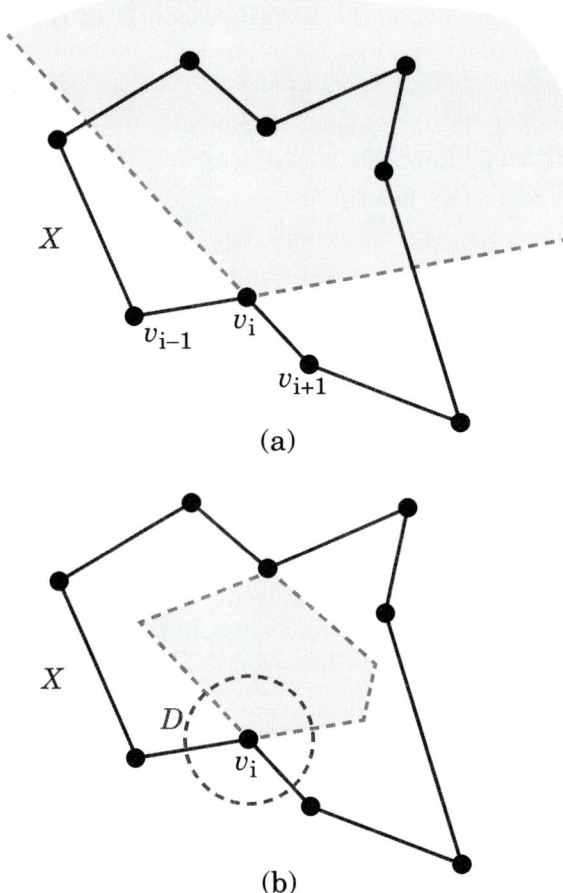

Figure 6.4: (a) Wedge of vertex v_i in polygon X. (b) Illustration of Lemma 6.3.

Case 1. If χ has a chord, that is, an edge (u, w) joining two vertices non-consecutive in χ, then the undirected cycle $\lambda = (u, v, w)$ partitions G into subgraphs sharing cycle λ, where we denote the external subgraph with G_1 and the internal subgraph with G_2. We have that G_1 and G_2 are planar st-graphs with fewer than n vertices and with all faces consisting of three edges (see Figure 6.5). By the inductive hypothesis, we can construct an upward planar straight-line drawing Γ_1 of G_1, with the external face drawn as Δ. Let Λ be the subdrawing of cycle λ in Γ_1. We again use the inductive hypothesis to construct an upward planar straight-line drawing Γ_2 of G_2, with the external face drawn as

Λ. The union of Γ_1 and Γ_2 is an upward planar straight-line drawing of G, with the external face drawn as Δ.

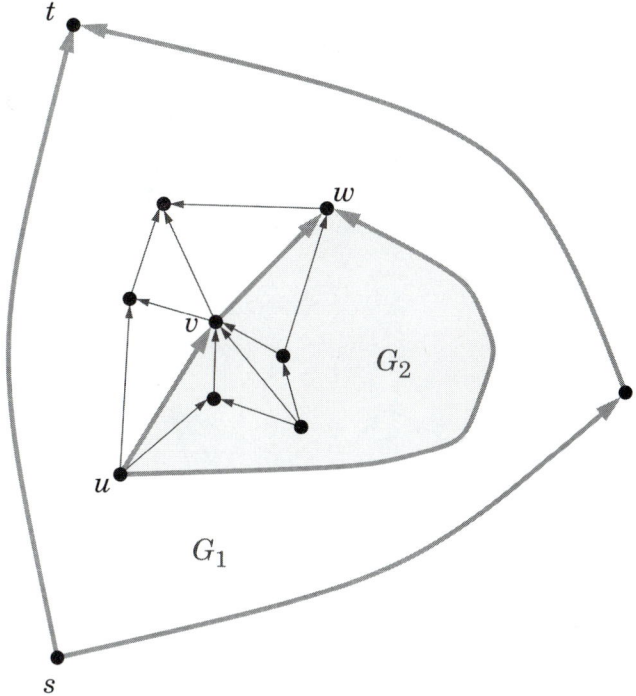

Figure 6.5: Subgraphs G_1 and G_2 in Case 1 of the proof of Lemma 6.4.

Case 2. Otherwise (χ has no chords). Let u be a predecessor of v, such that there is no directed path from u to any other predecessor of v. Note that, given a topological numbering of G (see Section 4.1), u can be chosen as the predecessor of v with the highest number. We contract edge (u, v) into vertex u (see Figure 6.6). Namely, we remove vertex v together with its incident edges, and add new edges between u and each vertex w of χ nonadjacent to u, where we add the edge (u, w) if w was a successor of v, and add edge (w, u) if w was a predecessor of v.

The above choice of u and Lemma 4.2 ensure that the resulting graph G' is a planar st-graph with $n - 1$ vertices and all faces consisting of three edges. We apply the inductive hypothesis to construct an upward planar straight-line drawing Γ' of G', with the external face drawn as Δ. To complete the construction, we have to remove the new

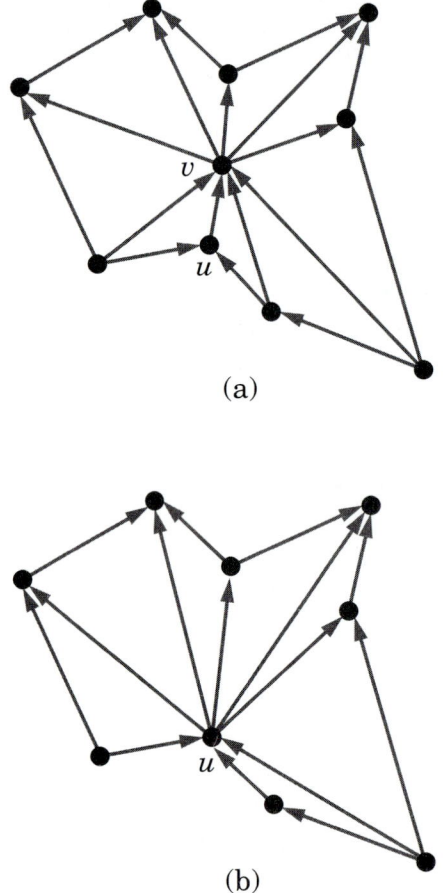

(a)

(b)

Figure 6.6: Contraction of vertex v into vertex u in Case 2 of the proof of Lemma 6.4: (a) before the contraction; (b) after the contraction.

edges and reinsert vertex v inside the polygon X of Γ' corresponding to cycle χ. A legal placement for vertex v must satisfy the following requirements:

1. Every vertex of X must be properly visible from v.

2. Vertex v is below its successors and above its predecessors.

Because of our construction, polygon X and vertex v satisfy the hypotheses of Lemma 6.3. Therefore, there exists a disk D centered at v, such that the intersection S of D and the wedge of v is contained in the kernel of X. Clearly, placing v in the interior of S satisfies requirement 1. It remains to show that v can be placed inside S so that requirement 2 is also satisfied. Let y' be the minimum y-coordinate of a successor of v in Γ'. Requirement 2 is satisfied by placing v at any interior point of S with y-coordinate less than y'.

$\square$

Lemma 6.4 immediately implies that Statement 2 of Theorem 6.1 implies Statement 3. We have completed the proof of Theorem 6.1.

Note that it is easy to prove directly that Statement 3 of Theorem 6.1 implies Statement 1. Namely, given a planar st-graph G' including G as a spanning subgraph, we construct a planar upward polyline drawing of G', using one of the algorithms for drawing planar st-graphs presented in Chapter 4 (see, e.g., Theorem 4.5) and then remove the edges that do not belong to G from the drawing of G'.

As shown in [GT93], a variation of the strategy given in the proof of Lemma 6.4 yields an $O(n)$-time algorithm for constructing an upward planar straight-line drawing of an n-vertex planar st-graph. However, while such drawings are desirable for their simplicity, their area requirement may be prohibitive for visualization applications. In fact, in Section 11.1, it is shown that there exists a family G_n of upward planar digraphs, such that G_n has $2n + 2$ vertices, and any planar straight-line upward drawing of G_n has area $\Omega(2^n)$. This result holds under any resolution rule that prevents drawings from being arbitrarily scaled down (e.g., integer vertex coordinates).

Testing whether an n-vertex digraph G is a planar st-graph can be easily done in $O(n)$ time by separately testing that:

- G has a single source s and a single sink t

- G plus the edge (s, t) is planar (as an undirected graph)

- G is acyclic.

Acyclicity can be tested in $O(n)$ time by means of an elementary depth-first-search method (see, e.g., [CLR90]). Planarity can also be tested in $O(n)$ time (see Section 3.3 and [HT74]). Hence, Theorem 6.1 yields an exponential-time (albeit linear-space) upward planarity testing algorithm, which consists of adding all the possible subsets of edges, and testing whether each of the resulting digraphs is a planar st-graph.

Theorem 6.2 *Upward planarity testing is in NP.*

See [Riv93] for an alternative proof of Theorem 6.2.

6.2   Angles in Upward Drawings

This section presents a characterization of upward planarity for embedded digraphs [BD91, BDLM94]. This characterization yields a polynomial time upward planarity testing algorithm for embedded digraphs presented in Section 6.3.

Let G be an embedded digraph. A vertex of G is *bimodal* if the cyclic sequence of its incident edges can be partitioned into two (possibly empty) linear sequences, one consisting of incoming edges and the other consisting of outgoing edges. If all its vertices are bimodal, then G is *bimodal*. The following lemma can be easily proved by elementary geometry.

Lemma 6.5 *An embedded digraph is upward planar only if it is bimodal.*

Note that a planar st-graph is bimodal. This immediately follows either from Lemma 4.2, or from Lemma 6.5, and the fact that a planar st-graph is upward planar.

We recall some terminology. We say that an embedded planar digraph is upward planar if it admits an upward planar drawing with the given embedding. The *angles* of an embedded planar digraph are the pairs of consecutive edges incident on the same vertex. Such angles are mapped to geometric angles in a straight-line drawing of the digraph. We slightly enlarge this definition as follows. If a vertex has exactly one incident edge e, we call the pair e, e an angle. This corresponds to an angle of 2π in a drawing. An *internal vertex* of a digraph is a vertex that is not a source or a sink.

Consider an assignment of labels from the set {*small, large*} to the angles formed by pairs of incoming or outgoing edges of G. The intuitive meaning of the labels is to indicate whether the angle is smaller or larger than π in an upward planar straight-line drawing of G. Let p be either a vertex or a face of G. We denote the number of angles of p with label *large* and *small* with $L(p)$ and $S(p)$, respectively. The following lemma is simple to prove.

Lemma 6.6 *The following two consistency properties hold for any upward planar straight-line drawing of a digraph G:*

$$
L(v) = \begin{cases} 0 & \text{if } v \text{ is an internal vertex,} \\ 1 & \text{if } v \text{ is a source or a sink.} \end{cases}
$$

$$
L(f) - S(f) = \begin{cases} -2 & \text{if } f \text{ is an internal face,} \\ +2 & \text{if } f \text{ is the external face.} \end{cases}
$$

A labeling that respects the consistency properties of Lemma 6.6 is illustrated in Figure 6.7.

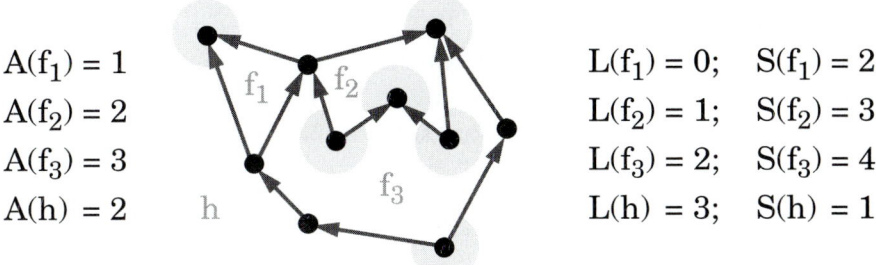

$A(f_1) = 1$ $L(f_1) = 0$; $S(f_1) = 2$

$A(f_2) = 2$ $L(f_2) = 1$; $S(f_2) = 3$

$A(f_3) = 3$ $L(f_3) = 2$; $S(f_3) = 4$

$A(h) = 2$ $L(h) = 3$; $S(h) = 1$

Figure 6.7: Large and small angles in an upward planar straight-line drawing. The large angles are indicated. Note that the consistency properties of Lemma 6.6 are verified by the labeling.

Let $A(f)$ be the number of angles in face f formed by pairs of incoming edges ($A(f)$ is also equal to the number of angles in face f formed by pairs of outgoing edges). The values $A(f)$ are determined by the embedding and are independent from the drawing (see Figure 6.7). Clearly, for any labeling, we have

$$L(f) + S(f) = 2A(f)$$

for every face f.

Thus the consistency properties of Lemma 6.6 can be rewritten in the following format, where only large angles are taken into account.

Lemma 6.7 *The following two consistency properties hold for any upward planar straight-line drawing of a digraph G:*

$$L(v) \;\; = \;\; \begin{cases} 0 & \textit{if } v \textit{ is an internal vertex,} \\ 1 & \textit{if } v \textit{ is a source or a sink.} \end{cases}$$

$$L(f) \;\; = \;\; \begin{cases} A(f) - 1 & \textit{if } f \textit{ is an internal face,} \\ A(f) + 1 & \textit{if } f \textit{ is the external face.} \end{cases}$$

Motivated by the above formulation, we now consider an assignment Φ that maps each vertex v, which is a source or a sink, to a face $\Phi(v)$ incident on v, and we denote with $\Phi^{-1}(f)$ the set of vertices assigned to face f. We say that assignment Φ is *consistent* if there exists a face h, such that

$$|\Phi^{-1}(f)| \;=\; \begin{cases} A(f) - 1 & \text{if } f \neq h, \\ A(f) + 1 & \text{if } f = h. \end{cases}$$

Assigning vertex v to face $f = \Phi(v)$ corresponds to giving label *large* to the angle formed by v in f, and a consistent assignment corresponds to a labeling with external face h that respects the consistency properties of Lemma 6.7. In Figure 6.8, we show the consistent assignment associated with the labeling of Figure 6.7.

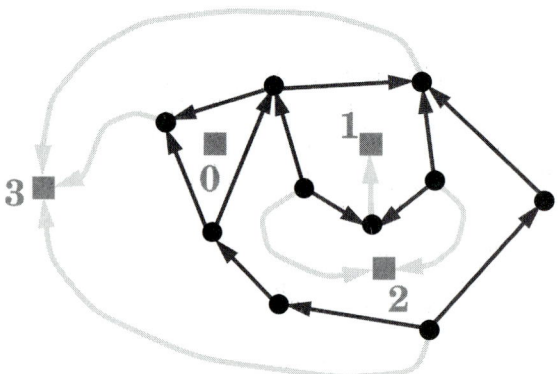

Figure 6.8: The consistent assignment associated with the labeling of Figure 6.7. Small squares represent the faces. The quantity $A(f) - 1$ is shown next to each internal face f. The quantity $A(h) + 1$ is shown next to the external face h.

The following lemma can be deduced from Lemma 6.7.

Lemma 6.8 *An embedded bimodal digraph is upward planar only if it admits a consistent assignment of sources and sinks to faces.*

The necessary conditions given in Lemmas 6.5–6.8 are also sufficient. Namely, given an embedded bimodal digraph G and a consistent assignment Φ of sources and sinks to faces of G, Algorithm 6.1 *Assign-Upward* constructs a planar st-graph that includes G as a spanning subgraph.

In order to describe Algorithm 6.2 *Saturate-Face*, we need to introduce some definitions. A *source-switch* (*sink-switch*) of a face f is a source (sink) of f. A *switch* of f is either a source-switch or a sink-switch of f. Observe that a source (sink) is a source-switch (sink-switch) in all its incident faces; an internal vertex is a switch in all its incident faces but two.

Algorithm 6.1 *Assign-Upward*

    Input: embedded bimodal digraph G with n vertices; consistent assignment Φ of sources and sinks to faces of G

   Output: planar st-graph G' that includes G as a spanning subgraph

1. For each face f of G, execute Algorithm 6.2 *Saturate-Face* on (f). This algorithm inserts new edges that "cancel" some sources and sinks of G.

2. Let s be a source, and t be a sink assigned to the external face h. Connect, with new edges, to s all the sources not canceled in the previous step, and to t all the sinks not canceled in the previous step.

                 □

We associate, to each face f of G, a circular sequence σ_f of symbols obtained by traversing f clockwise and assigning s_L and t_L (*L*-symbols) to source-switches and sink-switches labeled L (large) in f, and s_S and t_S (*S*-symbols) to source-switches and sinks-switches labeled S (small) in f. If f is an internal face, by Lemma 6.7, σ_f contains $A(f) - 1$ *L*-symbols and $A(f) + 1$ *S*-symbols.

Algorithm 6.2 *Saturate-Face* works as follows. It looks in σ_f for *canonical* subsequences. A canonical subsequence has one *L*-symbol followed by two *S*-symbols. When one of such canonical subsequences is found, then one edge is added to G in f; f is split into two new faces f' and f'', and σ_f is split into two new sequences $\sigma_{f'}$ and $\sigma_{f''}$. Figure 6.9 gives an example of the behavior of Algorithm 6.2 *Saturate-Face*. Observe that this technique is structurally similar to the refinement of an orthogonal representation into one whose regions have a rectangular shape, as given in Section 5.4.

Lemma 6.9 *Given an embedded bimodal planar digraph G, with n vertices and a consistent assignment Φ of sources and sinks to faces of G, Algorithm 6.1* Assign-Upward *constructs a planar st-graph that includes G as a spanning subgraph in $O(n)$ time.*

Proof: Algorithm 6.2 *Saturate-Face* applied to face f inserts edges between pairs of vertices of f. We show that each edge insertion preserves planarity, acyclicity, and bimodality. Furthermore, we show that after all edge insertions have been performed, the resulting embedded digraph G' has exactly

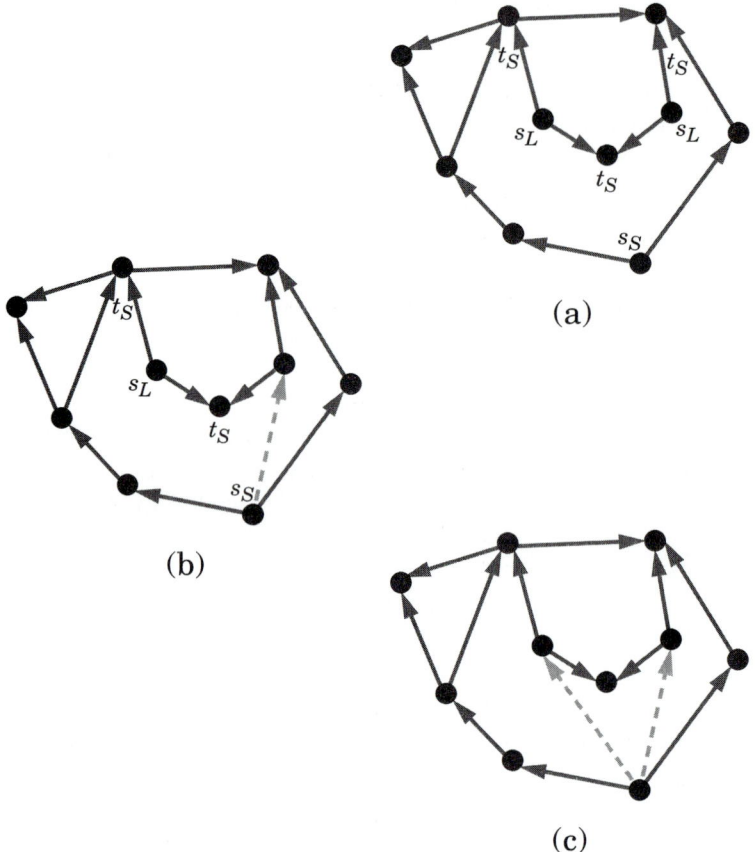

Figure 6.9: An example of execution of Algorithm 6.2 *Saturate-Face*: (a) initial configuration; (b) after the first edge insertion; (c) final configuration after the second edge insertion.

one source s and one sink t on the same face. Hence, G' is a planar st-graph that includes G.

Planarity and Acyclicity: As far as planarity is concerned, each edge is inserted inside a face. Hence, it does not cause crossings.

Now we prove that each edge insertion preserves the acyclicity of the digraph. The proof is by contradiction. Suppose that a simple directed cycle C is obtained after the insertion of edge (z, x) (see Figure 6.10) in the bimodal digraph G', derived from G after a number of sources and sinks have been eliminated. Suppose that both x and z are source-

Algorithm 6.2 *Saturate-Face*

>   *Input:*   embedded bimodal digraph G; face f of G
>   equipped with a circular sequence σ_f of sym-
>   bols
>   *Output:* embedded bimodal digraph G where some
>   faces have been split

1. If f has exactly one source-switch and one sink-switch (i.e., $|\sigma_f| = 2$) then return

2. Find a canonical subsequence (x, y, z) in σ_f composed by one L-symbol followed by two consecutive S-symbols; let v_x, v_y, and v_z be the vertices associated with symbols x, y, and z, respectively

3. Split f into two faces f' and f'' by inserting one edge; f'' consists of the part of f containing v_x, v_y and v_z plus the new edge; f'' has only one source and only one sink; two cases are possible depending on (x, y, z):

   - $(x, y, z) = (s_L, t_S, s_S)$: Add edge (v_z, v_x); f' consists of the part of f that does not contain v_y plus the new edge (v_z, v_x); observe that v_x is not a source of the new digraph and $\sigma_{f'}$ is obtained from σ_f by replacing the subsequence s_L, t_S, s_S with s_S.

   - $(x, y, z) = (t_L, s_S, t_S)$: Add edge (v_x, v_z); f' consists of the part of f that does not contain v_y plus the new edge (v_x, v_z); observe that v_x is not a sink of the new digraph and $\sigma_{f'}$ is obtained from σ_f by replacing the subsequence t_L, s_S, t_S with t_S.

4. Apply *Saturate-Face* to face f'.

$\square$

---

switches of f (the case where x and z are sink switches is analogous). Let Φ' be the consistent assignment for G', where z is not assigned to f while x is assigned to f. Denote by p_0 the path of G' from x to z, such that C is the union of path p_0 and edge (z, x). In order to have a cycle through x and z, z cannot be a source in G'.

Now consider the path p_1 of f from x to z containing sink-switch y. Two cases are possible.

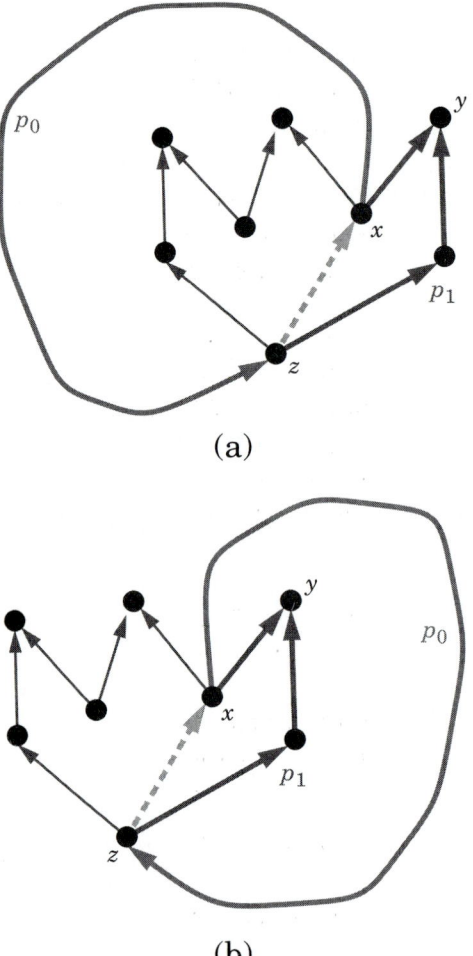

Figure 6.10: Cycles in the proof of Lemma 6.9.

Case 1. Paths p_0 and p_1 are vertex disjoint (but for the endvertices x and z). The concatenation of p_0 and p_1 is a circuit γ with $A(\gamma) = 1$, since it contains only the switches x and y. If γ is external to f, then Φ' assigns γ to x (see Figure 6.10.a), a contradiction. Otherwise, Φ' assigns γ to y (see Figure 6.10.b), again a contradiction.

Case 2. Paths p_0 and p_1 share one or more vertices distinct from x and z. Observe that the common vertices all lie on the directed path from x to y, otherwise C would not be simple. Let w be the last common vertex on the directed path from x to y; w and y are distinct vertices, otherwise a cycle was already present before the insertion of the edge (z, x). Let p'_0 be the path from w to z on the cycle and let p'_1 be the path from w to z on the face f, containing y. The concatenation γ of p'_0 and p'_1 is a circuit with $A(\gamma) = 1$, since it contains only the switches w and y. If γ is internal to f, then y is assigned to γ in Φ', a contradiction. Otherwise, w is a source in the embedded graph G' and has to be assigned to γ in Φ', yielding again a contradiction.

Bimodality: After the insertion of edge (z, x), the resulting embedding is still bimodal. Suppose that vertices z and x are both source-switches (the other case is analogous). Edge (z, x) is the only incoming edge of x. Thus all the outgoing edges of x appear consecutively in the embedding. Now consider vertex z. Edge (z, x) is inserted between two consecutive outgoing edges of z, which preserves the bimodality of the embedding.

The Consistent Assignment Invariant: After the insertion of edge (z, x), the assignment is modified as follows:

- All the sources and the sinks that are assigned to f by Φ and are still sources and sinks after the addition of (z, x) are assigned by Φ' to f'.

- All the remaining sources and sinks are assigned by Φ' as by Φ.

Hence, it is immediate to verify that assignment Φ' is consistent.

Single Source and Sink: We have to show that, after all edge insertions have been performed, the resulting digraph has exactly one source and one sink, both on the external face.

First, we prove that after Algorithm 6.2 *Saturate-Face* is performed on one internal face, all the faces that are obtained from that face contain exactly one source-switch and one sink-switch, both labeled S. We show that if an internal face f has more than one source-switch and sink-switch, then it is always possible to find one of the two canonical subsequences of Algorithm 6.2 *Saturate-Face* in σ_f. Because of the presence of $A(f) + 1$ S-symbols over the $2A(f)$ symbols of σ_f, it is always possible to find a subsequence of one L-symbol followed by two S-symbols. Observe that the canonical subsequences are exactly the subsequences consisting of one L-symbol followed by two consecutive

S-symbols. Hence, only a vertex on the external face can be a source or a sink after the process has been performed on all the internal faces.

When Algorithm 6.2 *Saturate-Face* is applied to the external face h, since the number of assigned sources and sinks is now $A(h) + 1$, the procedure stops when the final circular sequence σ_h is composed by $k \geq 0$ S-symbols and $k+2$ L-symbols. Since no two S-symbols appear consecutively in the sequence, the final sequence has the following structure in terms of S- and L-symbols: $\sigma_h \equiv L_1, \sigma_1, L_2, \sigma_2$, where σ_1 and σ_2 are two alternating sequences of S- and L-symbols. Each of σ_1 and σ_2 starts with an S-symbol and ends with an L-symbol. Observe that the L-symbols of one of the two alternating subsequences refer to sources while the L-symbols of the other subsequence refer to sinks.

The time complexity of Algorithm 6.2 *Saturate-Face*(f) is linear in the number of vertices of f. A simple implementation consists of pushing the L-symbols onto a stack while traversing σ_f. Hence, Algorithm 6.1 *Assign-Upward* takes $O(n)$ time.   □

Theorem 6.3 *An embedded digraph G with external face h is upward planar if and only if it is acyclic, bimodal, and admits a consistent assignment Φ of sources and sinks to faces. Also, given Φ, a planar st-graph that includes G as a spanning subgraph can be constructed in $O(n)$ time.*

Proof: The "only if" part follows immediately from Lemmas 6.5–6.8. The "if" part and the computational result are a consequence of Lemma 6.9 and Theorem 6.1.   □

As an example, Theorem 6.3 can be used to prove that the digraph of Figure 6.1 is not upward planar, as illustrated in Figure 6.11.

6.3 Upward Planarity Testing of Embedded Digraphs

Now we present an algorithm for testing whether an embedded digraph is upward planar. The algorithm is based on the characterization of Theorem 6.3.

To test whether an embedded digraph G admits a consistent assignment of sources and sinks to faces for a given choice of external face h, we construct a bipartite flow network $\mathcal{B}_h$ as follows (see Figure 6.12):

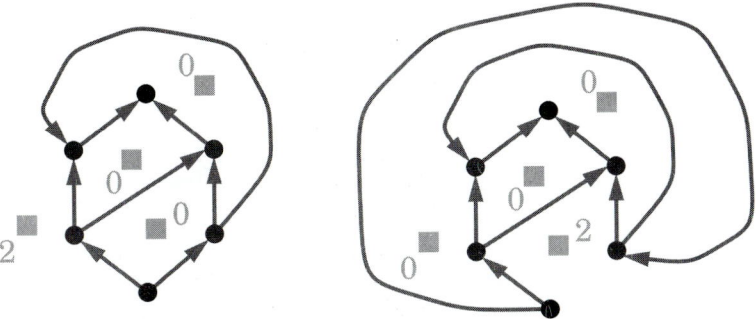

Figure 6.11: An embedded digraph that is bimodal but does not admit a consistent assignment of sources and sinks to faces, for any choice of the external face.

- The nodes of network $\mathcal{B}_h$ are the sources, sinks, and faces of G. The sources and sinks of G are the sources of network $\mathcal{B}_h$, and each supplies a unit of flow. Each face f of G is a sink of network $\mathcal{B}_h$, with demand equal to $A(f) - 1$ units of flow if $f \neq h$, and equal to $A(f) + 1$ units of flow if $f = h$.

- Network $\mathcal{B}_h$ has an arc (v, f) if v is a source or sink of G on face f.

A *flow* in network $\mathcal{B}_h$ is an assignment of values 0 or 1 to the arcs of $\mathcal{B}_h$, such that, for each source v of $\mathcal{B}_h$, the sum of the values assigned to the outgoing arcs of v is less than or equal to the supply of v, and for each sink f of $\mathcal{B}_h$, the sum of the values assigned to the incoming arcs of f is less than or equal to the demand of f. The value of a flow in $\mathcal{B}_h$ is the sum of the values assigned to its arcs.

We summarize the properties of $\mathcal{B}_h$ in the following lemma.

Lemma 6.10 *The bipartite flow network $\mathcal{B}_h$, associated with an embedded n-vertex digraph G and a face h of G, has $O(n)$ vertices. Also, G admits a consistent assignment of sources and sinks to faces, subject to h being the external face, if and only if $\mathcal{B}_h$ admits a flow of value r, where r is the number of sources and sinks of G.*

Constructing network $\mathcal{B}_h$ takes $O(n)$ time, where n is the number of vertices of G. The existence of a flow for $\mathcal{B}_h$ can be tested in $O(rn)$ time by means of r flow augmentations (for the standard augmenting path method to solve network flow problems, see, e.g., [CLR90]). Hence, we can test the

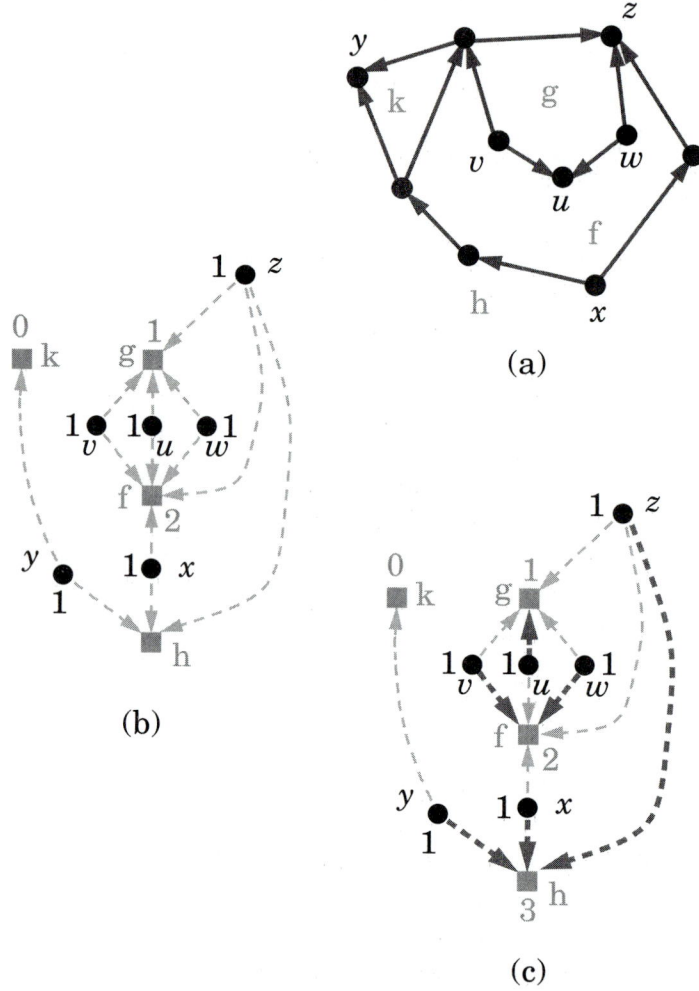

Figure 6.12: (a) The embedded digraph G of Figure 6.2. (b) The network $\mathcal{B}_h$ associated with G and external face h. The nodes of $\mathcal{B}_h$ are labeled with their supplies or demands. (c) Example of flow in network $\mathcal{B}_h$. The thick arcs have unit flow and give a consistent assignment of sources and sinks to faces in G.

upward planarity of G in $O(n^2 r)$ time by repeating the above procedure for all the $O(n)$ possible choices of the external face h.

Now we show that the time complexity can be reduced to $O(nr)$ using Algorithm 6.3 *Embedded-Upward-Planar-Test*.

Algorithm 6.3 *Embedded-Upward-Planar-Test*

  Input: embedded planar bimodal digraph G with n
         vertices

  Output: set of admissible external faces in a planar up-
         ward drawing of G

1. Construct flow network $\mathcal{B}$, which is the same as $\mathcal{B}_h$, except that each face f has demand $A(f) - 1$. Note that flow network $\mathcal{B}$ is independent from the choice of external face.

2. Test whether $\mathcal{B}$ admits a flow of value $r - 2$. If not, then return the empty set (G is not upward planar, for any choice of the external face).

3. For each face f, which is a sink of $\mathcal{B}$, increase its demand by two units, and test whether the flow of value $r - 2$ in $\mathcal{B}$ can be augmented by two units.

4. Return the set of all the faces of G for which the augmentation test of Step 3 is successful.

$\square$

Let n be the number of vertices of G, and let r be the number of its sources and sinks. Step 1 takes $O(n)$ time. Step 2 can be performed with $r - 2$ flow augmentations, each taking $O(n)$ time, and hence, runs in $O(nr)$ time. In Step 3, at most two augmentations are performed for each face. Hence, Step 3 takes $O(nr)$ time. Finally, Step 4 takes $O(n)$ time. We conclude that Algorithm 6.3 *Embedded-Upward-Planar-Test* runs in $O(nr)$ time.

By Theorem 6.3, the complete upward planarity test algorithm for an embedded digraph G consists of first testing whether G is acyclic and bimodal, which takes $O(n)$ time, and then using Algorithm 6.3 *Embedded-Upward-Planar-Test* to test whether G admits a consistent assignment of sources and sinks to its faces. This takes $O(nr)$ time.

Theorem 6.4 *Let G be an embedded digraph with n vertices and r sources and sinks. We can test whether G is upward planar in $O(nr) = O(n^2)$ time.*

Since a triconnected planar digraph has a unique embedding (see Chapter 1), we can exploit the above algorithm to test its upward planarity.

However, an improvement on the time performance can be obtained using the following lemma.

Lemma 6.11 *Let G be a planar embedded acyclic triconnected digraph. Let r be the number of sources and sinks of G. The number of faces of G that have at least one source and one sink is $O(r)$.*

Proof: Let G' be the digraph defined as follows. The vertices of G' are the sources and sinks of G. For each face f of G, that contains at least one source and one sink, one of the sources and one of the sinks of f are arbitrarily selected and an edge between them is inserted in the edge set of G'.

The number of faces of G that have at least one source and one sink is equal to the number of edges of G'.

Since G is triconnected, an edge between two vertices x and y of G' can be inserted at most twice, otherwise x and y would result in a separating pair of G. Hence, G' is a graph with multiple edges with at most two edges for each pair of vertices and without self-loops.

Furthermore, by construction, G' is planar, hence, it has at most $6r - 12$ edges.   □

Observing that the only meaningful external faces are those that have at least one source and one sink, we can conclude that the number of external faces that have to be taken into account by our algorithm is $O(r)$. We have:

Theorem 6.5 *Let G be a triconnected planar digraph with n vertices and r sources and sinks. We can test whether G is upward planar in $O(n + r^2) = O(n^2)$ time.*

6.4 Optimal Upward Planarity Testing of Single-Source Embedded Digraphs

In this section, we describe a characterization of upward-planarity and a related optimal upward-planarity testing algorithm for single-source embedded digraphs [BDMT98].

Given an embedded digraph G, with a single source s, we define the undirected *face-sink graph* $\mathcal{F}$ of G as follows:

- The vertices of $\mathcal{F}$ are: (1) the faces of G and (2) the vertices of G that are sink-switches for at least one face of G.

- Graph $\mathcal{F}$ has an edge (f, v) if and only if the vertex v is a sink-switch of face f.

The edges of graph $\mathcal{F}$ incident on a vertex v, which is a sink of G, represent the possible assignments of v to the faces of G (see Section 6.2). In Figure 6.13.b, we show the face-sink graph $\mathcal{F}$ of the embedded single-source digraph G of Figure 6.13.a. Note that, in this example, where G is upward planar, $\mathcal{F}$ is a *forest*, that is, a collection of trees.

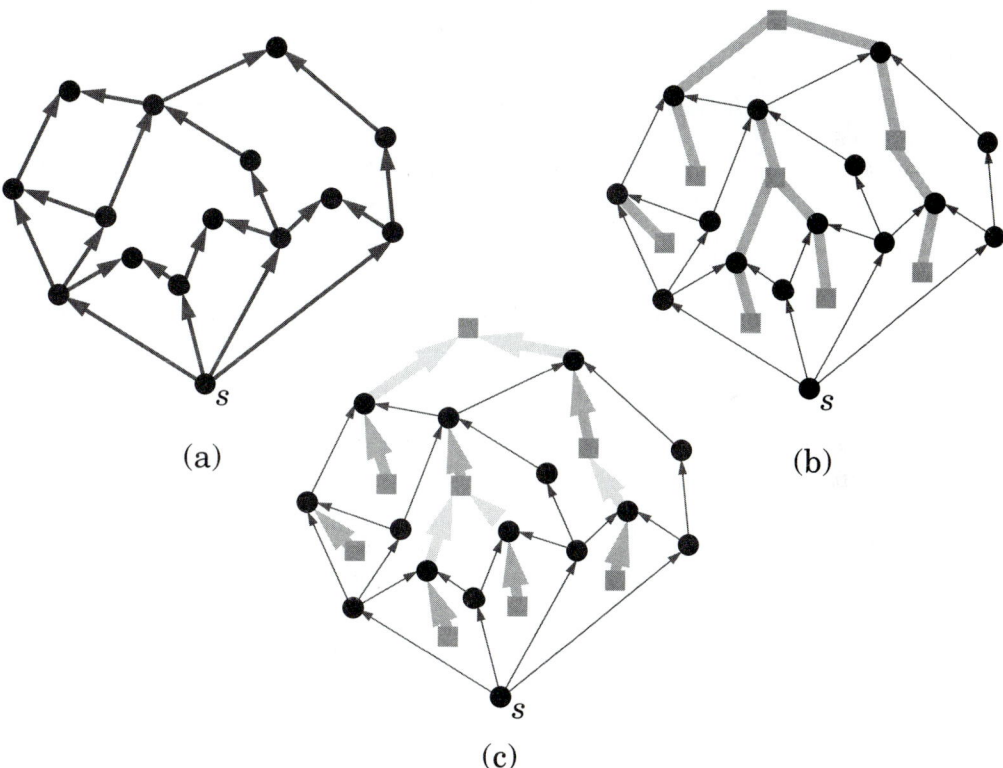

Figure 6.13: (a) An embedded single-source digraph G. (b) The face-sink graph $\mathcal{F}$ of G, shown with light-blue edges. (c) A consistent assignment of the source and sinks of G to its faces (shown with yellow edges), and the corresponding rooting of the trees of $\mathcal{F}$.

Figure 6.13.c shows a consistent assignment of the source and sinks of G to the faces. This assignment corresponds to rooting each tree of $\mathcal{F}$ and orienting its edges from child to parent. Namely, a sink v is assigned to a face f if and only if v is a child of f in the rooted tree containing v and f. We also notice that the roots of all but one tree (denoted with $\mathcal{T}$) are internal vertices of G. Tree $\mathcal{T}$ does not contain any internal vertex of G and is rooted at the external face h.

Figure 6.13 illustrates of the following theorem. A proof can be found ins [BDMT98].

Theorem 6.6 *Let G be an embedded single-source digraph, and h a face of G. Digraph G is upward planar, subject to h being the external face, if and only if all the following conditions are satisfied:*

1. *The source of G is on the boundary of face h.*

2. *The face-sink graph $\mathcal{F}$ of G is a forest.*

3. *One tree $\mathcal{T}$ of $\mathcal{F}$ has no internal vertices of G, while the remaining trees have exactly one internal vertex.*

4. *Face h is a vertex of tree $\mathcal{T}$.*

An additional example for Theorem 6.6 is given in Figure 6.14. While Conditions 1–3 of Theorem 6.6 are satisfied, Condition 4 is not satisfied because face h is in a tree of $\mathcal{F}$ that contains an internal vertex.

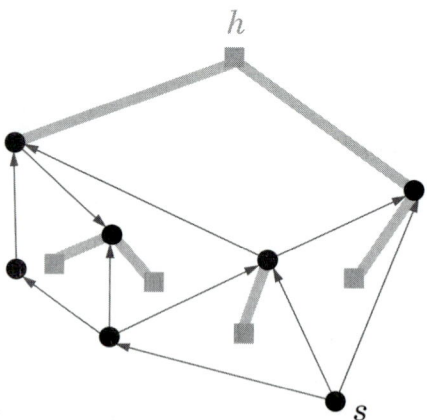

Figure 6.14: An embedded single-source digraph that is not upward planar and its face-sink graph.

Theorem 6.6 yields Algorithm 6.4 *Embedded-Single-Source-Upward-Planar-Test* for testing the upward planarity of an embedded single-source digraph G [BDMT98].

Algorithm 6.4 *Embedded-Single-Source-Upward-Planar-Test*
   Input: embedded planar bimodal digraph G with n
              vertices
   Output: set of admissible external faces in a planar up-
              ward drawing of G

1. Test whether G is acyclic and bimodal. If either of these properties is not verified, then return "not upward planar."

2. Construct the face-sink graph $\mathcal{F}$ of G.

3. Check Conditions 2 and 3 of Theorem 6.6. If these conditions are not verified, then return "not upward planar," else let $\mathcal{T}$ be the tree of Condition 3.

4. Report the set of faces of G that contain the source s of G (Condition 1) and are vertices of tree $\mathcal{T}$ (Condition 4). If this set is empty, then return "not upward planar;" else return "upward planar."

   □

Algorithm 6.4 *Embedded-Single-Source-Upward-Planar-Test* can be easily implemented in $O(n)$ time.

Theorem 6.7 *Let G be an embedded single-source digraph with n vertices. We can test whether G is upward planar in $O(n)$ time.*

By applying Theorem 6.7 to the embedded digraph G of Figure 6.14, we conclude that G is not upward planar (for any choice of the external face).

6.5   Optimal Upward Planarity Testing of Single-Source Digraphs

In this section, we present a decomposition strategy for testing the upward planarity of single-source digraphs, which was originally proposed in [HL96], and later improved in [BDMT98].

To start with, it is easy to prove that the blocks of a single-source digraph can be separately tested.

Lemma 6.12 *A connected single-source digraph G is upward planar if and only if all the blocks of G are upward planar.*

By Lemma 6.12, we restrict our attention to a biconnected single-source digraph G. The basic idea is to decompose G into its triconnected components [HT73] and test each of them separately for upward planarity, with certain constraints imposed on them to ensure that merging the triconnected components back together preserves upward planarity. Recall that the upward planarity of a triconnected digraph can be efficiently tested (Theorem 6.5 and Theorem 6.7).

Let G be a biconnected digraph. A *split pair* of G is either a separation pair or a pair of adjacent vertices. A *split component* of a split pair $\{u, v\}$ is either an edge (u, v) or a maximal subgraph C of G, such that $\{u, v\}$ is not a split pair of C. The decomposition is performed by splitting the digraph G into split components with respect to a separation pair, and recursively decomposing each split component. Each split component is constrained by attaching to it a certain digraph, called a *marker*, which represents the rest of the digraph. There are four type of markers, as shown in Figure 6.15.

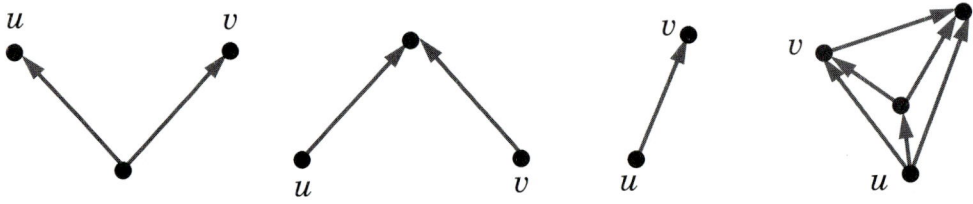

Figure 6.15: Markers.

Suppose that G has two split components, $\vec{H}$ and $\vec{K}$, with respect to a separation pair $\{u, v\}$. We augment each of $\vec{H}$ and $\vec{K}$ with an appropriate marker that represents the other split component, and recursively test each of them for upward planarity. The markers have a twofold purpose:

- When testing a split component for upward planarity, they take into account the "shape" of the other split component

- They ensure that each digraph in the decomposition process is biconnected and has a single source.

For example, consider the biconnected single-source digraph G shown in Figure 6.16.a, which is not upward planar. The split components of G with respect to $\{u, v\}$, shown in Figure 6.16.b and Figure 6.16.c, are each upward planar. By adding the appropriate markers, we obtain the augmented split components shown in Figure 6.16.d and Figure 6.16.e. Note that the augmented split component of Figure 6.16.e is not upward planar, as can be shown by applying Theorem 6.7. This indicates that G is not upward planar.

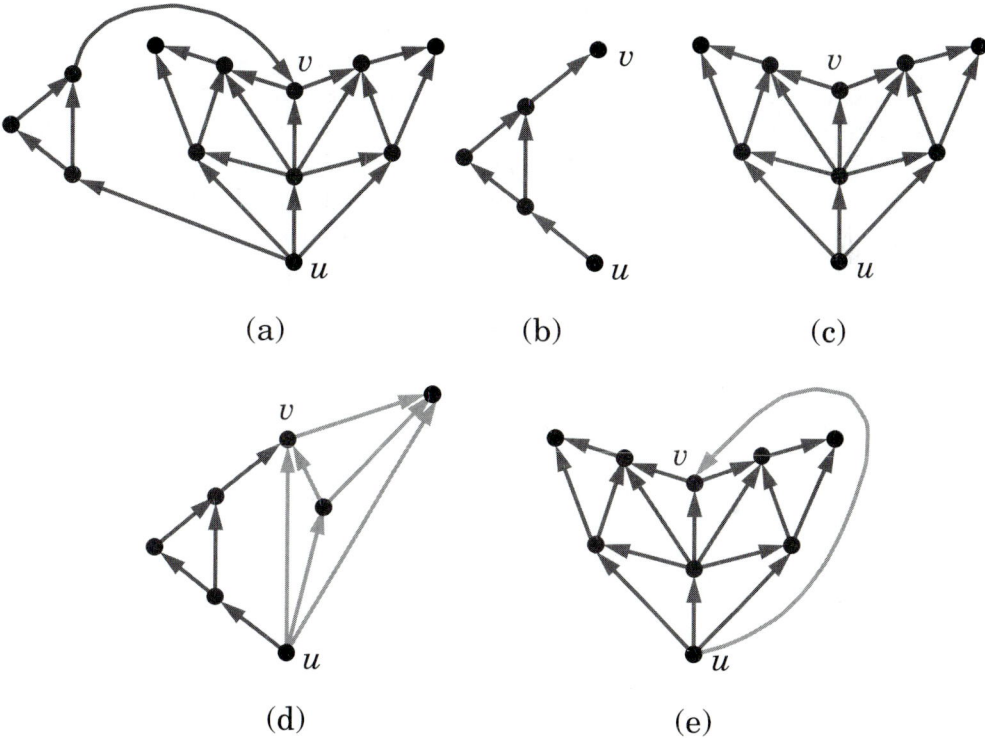

Figure 6.16: (a) A biconnected single-source digraph G with a separation pair u, v. (b) Split-component $\vec{H}$ of G with respect to u, v. (c) Split-component $\vec{K}$ of G with respect to u, v. (d) Split-component $\vec{H}$ augmented with the appropriate marker (shaded). (e) Split-component $\vec{K}$ augmented with the appropriate marker (shaded).

In addition to the markers, we must take into account the inside-outside relationship of the split components with respect to the external face. For example, if we determine that in any upward planar drawing of a split component the separation pair does not appear on the external face, then we must test the other split component for upward planarity, subject to the separation-pair appearing on the external face. Hence, in the decomposition process we should keep track of vertices that are constrained to appear on the external face.

In [HL96], an $O(n^2)$ time upward planarity testing algorithm for single-source digraphs is presented. It is based on the above decomposition strategy. In [BDMT98], the time complexity is reduced to $O(n)$ by combining a linear-time algorithm for triconnected single source-digraphs (Theorem 6.7) with an improved decomposition strategy, which is outlined below.

The *SPQR-tree* ([DT90]) $T(G)$ of a biconnected graph (or digraph) G, describes the arrangement of its triconnected components (see Figure 6.17). The decomposition tree $T(G)$ is an unrooted tree whose nodes are of four types: S, P, Q, and R. Each edge of $T(G)$ is associated with an edge or separation pair of G, and each node μ of $T(G)$ is associated with a multigraph, called the *skeleton* of μ. A P-node corresponds to a parallel composition of split components with respect to a separation pair (see Figure 6.18.a), and its skeleton is a bundle of parallel edges. An S-node corresponds to a cyclic arrangement of split components and separation pairs (see Figure 6.18.b), and its skeleton is a cycle. An R-node corresponds to a maximal triconnected homeomorphic subgraph of G, which is its skeleton (see Figure 6.17.c). A Q-node corresponds to an edge of G, and its skeleton consists of two parallel edges. Note that the edge directions are ignored in the definition of SPQR-tree.

The upward planarity testing algorithm of [BDMT98] first replaces each edge of the skeletons by a *gadget* (playing the same role as the marker of [HL96]), which is either a directed edge or a *peak* (see Figure 6.19), and tests each augmented skeleton for upward planarity, marking those gadgets that can appear on the external face in a planar upward drawing.

The existence of a compatible inside-outside relationship between skeletons is then tested using the SPQR-tree. Namely, the nesting of the skeletons is represented by a rooting of the SPQR-tree $T(G)$. If node ν is the parent of node μ, then the skeleton of ν is "outer" and the skeleton of μ "inner" in the embedding of G. Of course, this can be done only if the gadget of the skeleton of μ representing the split component of the skeleton of ν is marked. Also, the source s of G must appear in the outermost skeleton (i.e., at the root of $T(G)$).

In the example of Fig 6.17, only the skeleton of node μ_3 contains the source s. Hence, $T(G)$ must be rooted at μ_3. However, this implies that the gadget e of the skeleton of node μ_2, associated with the split component of the skeleton of μ_3, must appear on the external face in an upward planar drawing. This is impossible, as can be shown by applying Theorem 6.7. Thus, the single-source digraph of Fig 6.17.a is not upward planar.

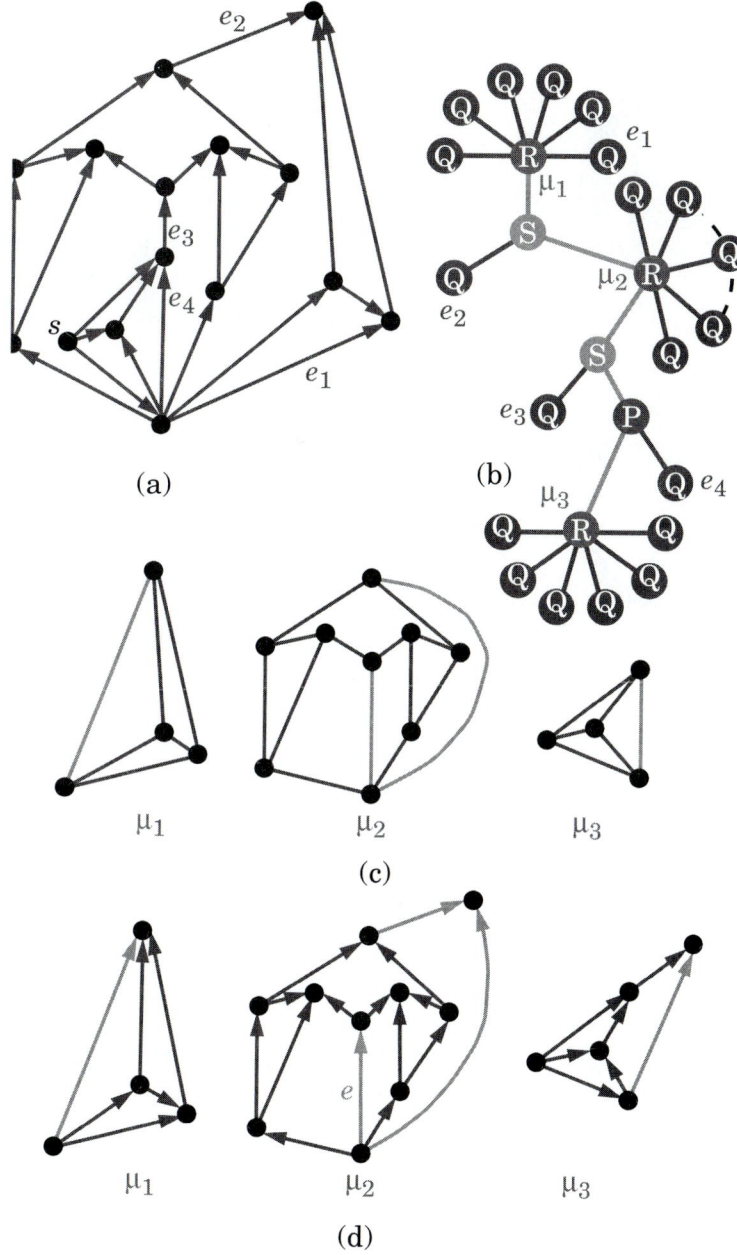

Figure 6.17: (a) A biconnected single-source digraph G. (b) The SPQR-tree $T(G)$ of G. The edges of $T(G)$ that correspond to the edges and separation pairs of G are shown as red and light blue lines respectively. (c) Skeletons of the R-nodes of $T(G)$. The light blue edges correspond to split components. (d) Augmented skeletons of the R-nodes of $T(G)$. The gadgets representing split components are shown by light blue lines.

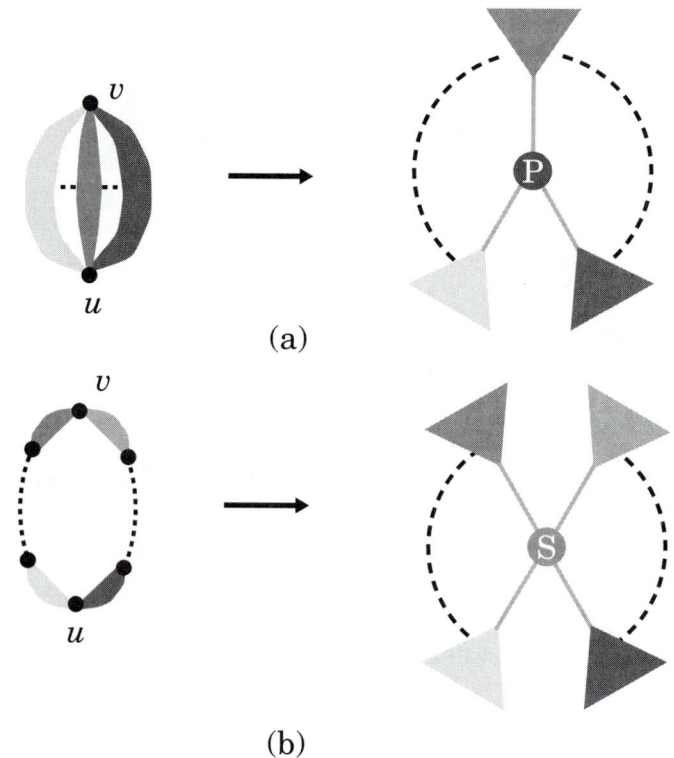

Figure 6.18: (a) Schematic illustration of a P-node. (b) Schematic illustration of an S-node.

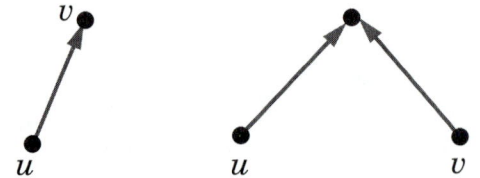

Figure 6.19: The edge and peak gadgets.

Theorem 6.8 *Let G be a single-source digraph with n vertices. We can test whether G is upward planar in $O(n)$ time.*

6.6 Upward Planarity Testing is NP-complete

In this section, we overview the proof in [GT95] that upward planarity testing is NP-complete. The proof is a reduction from the following well-known NP-complete problem [GJ79]:

NOT-ALL-EQUAL-3-SAT: Given a set of clauses with three literals each, is there a truth assignment, such that each clause has at least one true literal and one false literal?

Section 6.6.1 describes some special graphs called *tendrils* and *wiggles* that are used in the reduction. A reduction from NOT-ALL-EQUAL-3-SAT to an auxiliary flow problem is given in Section 6.6.2. Section 6.6.3 describes the reduction from the auxiliary flow problem to the upward planarity testing problem.

6.6.1 Tendrils and Wiggles

In this section, we define several digraphs that will be used as gadgets in our reductions.

In Figure 6.20.a, we show *tendril T_k ($k \geq 1$)*, which is an acyclic digraph with $k + 1$ sources and $k + 1$ sinks. We also define tendril T_0 as a a digraph consisting of a single edge. Tendril T_k ($k \geq 0$) has a designated source and a designated sink, called the *poles* of T_k. We consider transformations where a directed edge (u, v) of a digraph is replaced with a tendril T_k, in which the source is identified with u and the sink with v.

Lemma 6.13 *Tendril T_k is upward planar.*

In any upward planar drawing of T_k, the external face consists of two paths between s and t. One such path, called *outer path*, has $2k$ large angles and no small angles, and the other path, called *inner path*, has $2k$ small angles and no large angles. When a tendril replaces an edge of an embedded planar digraph, the outer path becomes a subpath of a face, and we say that the *contribution* of the outer path to the face is $+2k$. Similarly, we say that the contribution of the inner path to its face is $-2k$.

Figure 6.20.b shows a *wiggle W_k*, which is an acyclic digraph consisting of a chain of $2k + 1$ edges whose orientation alternates along the chain. The extreme vertices of W_k, a source and a sink, are called the *poles* of W_k. We consider transformations where a directed edge (u, v) of an embedded digraph is replaced with wiggle W_k, where s is identified with u and t with

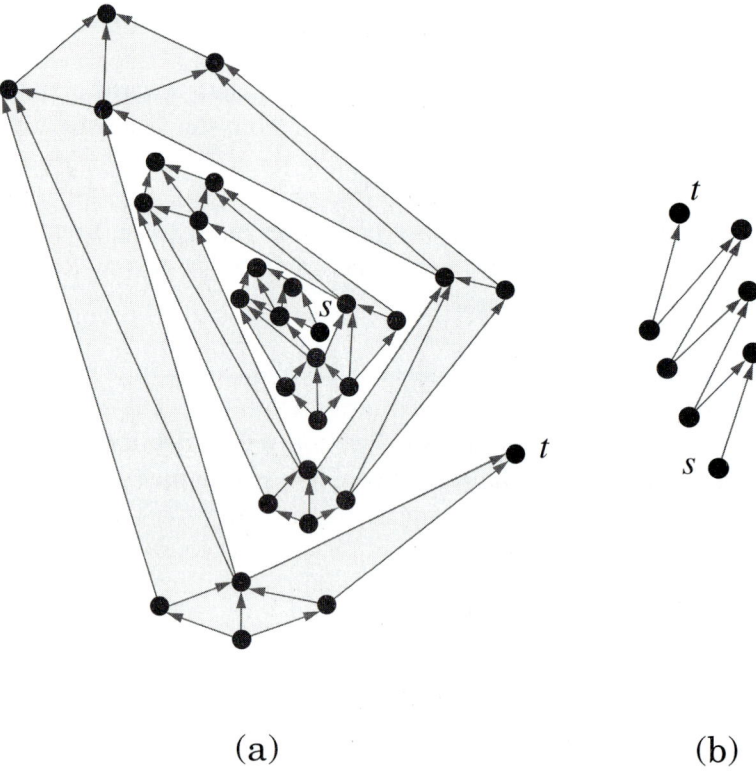

(a)   (b)

Figure 6.20: (a) Tendril T_3. (b) Wiggle W_3.

v. Given an upward drawing of W_k, we say that the *contribution* of W_k to a face f containing W_k, is the number of large angles minus the number of small angles of W_k in f. Clearly, W_k can be upward embedded to give to f any contribution $2i$ with $0 \leq i \leq k$. Note that if W_k gives contribution c to a face, it gives contribution $-c$ to the other face it belongs to.

6.6.2   An Auxiliary Undirected Flow Problem

In this section, we define two auxiliary flow problems and show that they are equivalent to NOT-ALL-EQUAL-3-SAT under polynomial-time reductions.

A *switch-flow network* is an undirected flow network $\mathcal{N}$, where each edge is labeled with a range $[c' \cdots c'']$ of nonnegative integer values, called the *capacity range* of the edge. For simplicity, we denote the capacity range $[c \cdots c]$ with $[c]$. A *flow* for a switch-flow network is an orientation and an assignment of integer "flow" values to the edges of the network. A *feasible flow* is a flow that satisfies the following two properties:

Range Property: The flow assigned to an edge is an integer within the capacity range of the edge.

Conservation Property: The total flow entering a vertex from the incoming edges is equal to the total flow exiting the vertex from the outgoing edges.

Starting from an instance S of NOT-ALL-EQUAL-3-SAT, we construct a switch-flow network $\mathcal{N}$ as follows (see Figure 6.21). Let the literals of S be denoted with $x_1, y_1, \ldots, x_n, y_n$, where $y_i = \overline{x_i}$, and the clauses of S be denoted with $c_1, \ldots, c_m$. Let θ be a positive integer parameter. We denote the number of occurrences of literals x_i and y_i in the clauses of S with α_i and β_i $(i = 1, \ldots, n)$, respectively. Note that $\sum_{i=1}^{n}(\alpha_i + \beta_i) = 3m$. Also, we define $\gamma_i = (2i - 1)\theta$ and $\delta_i = 2i\theta$ $(i = 1, \ldots, n)$. Network $\mathcal{N}$ has a *literal vertex* for each literal of S and a *clause vertex* for each clause of S, plus a special dummy vertex z. There are three types of edges in $\mathcal{N}$:

Literal Edges: Joining pairs of literals associated with the same boolean variable. The capacity range of literal edge (x_i, y_i) is $[\alpha_i \gamma_i + \beta_i \delta_i]$.

Clause Edges: Joining each literal to each clause. The capacity range of clause edge (x_i, c_j) is $[\gamma_i]$ if $x_i \in c_j$, and $[0]$ otherwise. The capacity range of clause edge (y_i, c_j) is $[\delta_i]$ if $y_i \in c_j$, and $[0]$ otherwise.

Dummy Edges: Joining each literal and each clause to the dummy vertex. The capacity ranges of dummy edges (z, x_i) and (z, y_i) are $[\beta_i \delta_i]$ and $[\alpha_i \gamma_i]$, respectively. The capacity range of dummy edge (z, c_j) is $[0 \cdots \eta_j - 2\theta]$, where η_j is the sum of the capacities of the clause edges incident on c_j.

The construction of network $\mathcal{N}$ from S is straightforward and can be carried out in $O(nm)$ time.

A feasible flow in network $\mathcal{N}$ corresponds to a satisfying truth assignment for S. Namely, a literal is true whenever its incident literal edge is incoming in the feasible flow (see Figure 6.21.b) and its incident clause edges, with nonzero capacity range, are outgoing. Also, the three clause edges with nonzero capacity range incident on a clause vertex c_j cannot be all incoming or all outgoing, because of the conservation property at vertex c_j and the choice of capacity range for the dummy edge incident on c_j. We obtain:

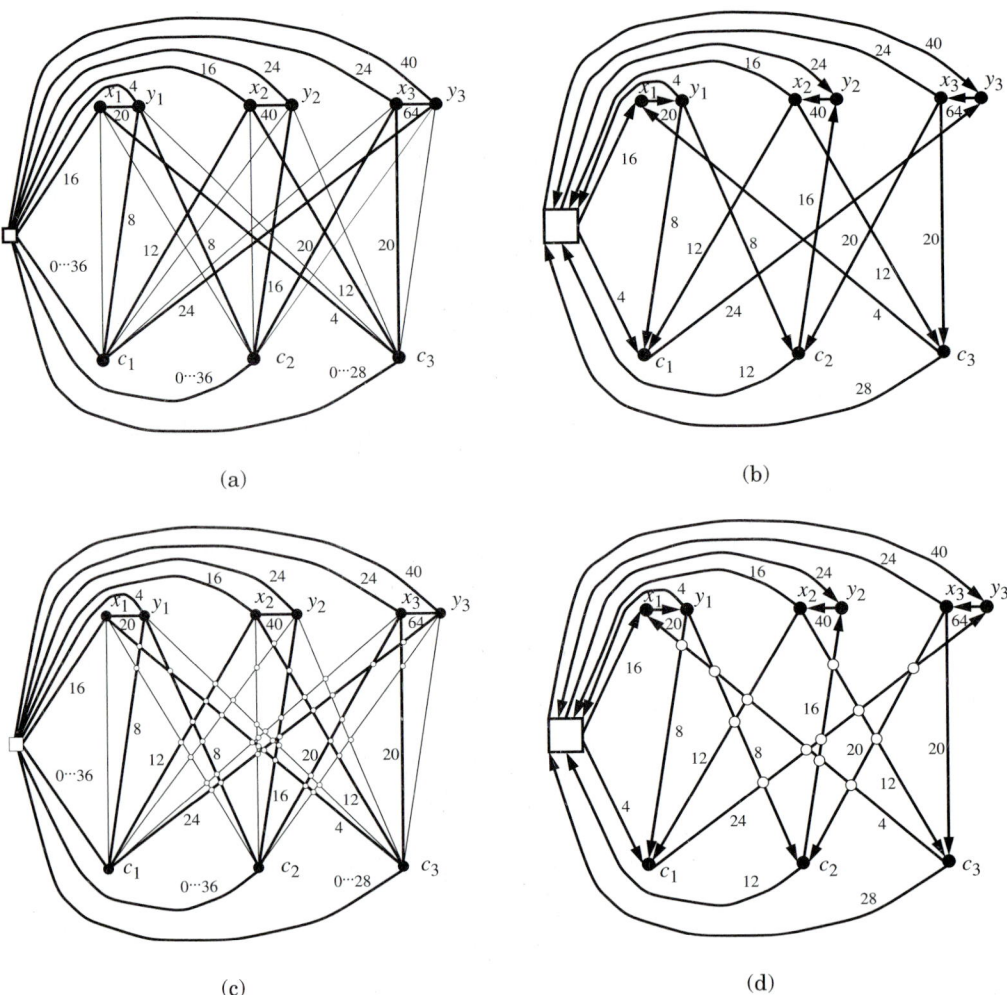

Figure 6.21: (a) Switch-flow network $\mathcal{N}$ with parameter $\theta = 4$, associated with the the NOT-ALL-EQUAL-3-SAT instance $\mathcal{S}$, with clauses $c_1 = y_1 x_2 y_3$, $c_2 = y_1 y_2 x_3$, and $c_3 = x_1 x_2 x_3$. The clause edges with zero capacity range are shown with thin lines. (b) Feasible flow for $\mathcal{N}$ corresponding to the satisfying truth assignment (y_1, x_2, x_3) for $\mathcal{S}$. Only the edges with nonzero flow are shown. (c) Planar switch-flow network $\mathcal{P}$ associated with $\mathcal{S}$. The edges with zero capacity range are shown with thin lines. (d) Feasible flow for $\mathcal{P}$ corresponding to the satisfying truth assignment (y_1, x_2, x_3) for $\mathcal{S}$. Only the edges with nonzero flow are shown.

Lemma 6.14 *An instance $\mathcal{S}$ of* NOT-ALL-EQUAL-3-SAT *is satisfiable if and only if the associated switch-flow network $\mathcal{N}$ admits a feasible flow. Also, given a feasible flow for $\mathcal{N}$, a satisfying truth assignment for $\mathcal{S}$ can be computed in $O(nm)$ time, where n and m are the number of variables and clauses of $\mathcal{S}$, respectively.*

Now, starting from $\mathcal{N}$, we construct a planar switch-flow network $\mathcal{P}$ consisting of $O(n^2m^2)$ vertices in $O(n^2m^2)$ time. Network $\mathcal{P}$ has the property that network $\mathcal{N}$ admits a feasible flow if and only if network $\mathcal{P}$ admits a feasible flow, and a feasible flow for $\mathcal{N}$ can be computed from a feasible flow for $\mathcal{P}$ in $O(n^2m^2)$ time.

$\mathcal{P}$ is constructed as follows (see Figure 6.21). First, we construct a drawing of $\mathcal{N}$, such that the literal vertices and the clause vertices are arranged on two parallel lines, and crossings occur only between clause edges. Next, we replace the crossings formed by the clause edges with new vertices, called *crossing* vertices. We call *fragment edges* the edges introduced by the splitting of the clause edges. Each fragment edge inherits the capacity range of the originating clause edge.

Using Lemma 6.14, we obtain the main result of this section.

Theorem 6.9 *Given an instance $\mathcal{S}$ of* NOT-ALL-EQUAL-3-SAT *with n variables and m clauses, the associated planar switch-flow network $\mathcal{P}$ has $O(n^2m^2)$ vertices and edges, and can be constructed in $O(n^2m^2)$ time. Instance $\mathcal{S}$ is satisfiable if and only if network $\mathcal{P}$ admits a feasible flow. Also, given a feasible flow for $\mathcal{P}$, a satisfying truth assignment for $\mathcal{S}$ can be computed in $O(n^2m^2)$ time. Moreover, if $n \geq 3$ and $m \geq 3$, then $\mathcal{P}$ is triconnected.*

6.6.3 Upward Planarity Testing

In this section, we show how to reduce the problem of computing a feasible flow in the planar switch-flow network $\mathcal{P}$, associated with a NOT-ALL-EQUAL-3-SAT instance $\mathcal{S}$, to the problem of testing the upward planarity of a suitable digraph. We set parameter θ equal to 4.

Now, we construct an orientation $\vec{\mathcal{P}}$ of $\mathcal{P}$ as follows (see Figure 6.22):

- Every literal edge (x_i, y_i) is oriented from x_i to y_i.

- Every fragment edge is oriented away from the clause vertex and towards the literal vertex.

- Every dummy edge incident on a literal vertex is oriented towards the dummy vertex, and every dummy edge incident on a clause vertex is oriented towards the clause vertex.

By Theorem 6.9, S has at least three clauses and variables each. We construct the dual digraph $\vec{\mathcal{D}}$ of $\vec{\mathcal{P}}$ by orienting every dual edge of $\mathcal{D}$ from the face on the left to the face on the right of the primal edge (see Figure 6.22).

Lemma 6.15 *The dual digraph $\vec{\mathcal{D}}$ of $\vec{\mathcal{P}}$ is upward planar, triconnected, acyclic, and has exactly one source and one sink, denoted with s and t.*

Starting from digraph $\vec{\mathcal{D}}$, we construct a new digraph $\vec{\mathcal{G}}$ by replacing the edges of $\vec{\mathcal{D}}$ with subgraphs (tendrils or wiggles), as follows (see Figure 6.23):

- Every edge of $\vec{\mathcal{D}}$ that is the dual of a literal edge, fragment edge, or dummy edge incident on a literal vertex, is replaced with tendril T_c, where $[c]$ is the capacity range of the dual edge. Note that c is a multiple of parameter θ.

- Every edge of $\vec{\mathcal{D}}$ that is the dual of a dummy edge incident on a clause vertex is replaced with wiggle W_c, where $[0 \cdots c]$ is the capacity range of the dual edge.

The vertices of $\vec{\mathcal{G}}$ that are also in $\vec{\mathcal{D}}$ are called *primary vertices*. The remaining vertices of $\vec{\mathcal{G}}$ are called *secondary vertices*. By Lemma 6.15 and the construction of digraph $\vec{\mathcal{G}}$, all the drawings of $\vec{\mathcal{G}}$ are obtained by choosing one of the two possible flips for each tendril.

Lemma 6.16 *Digraph $\vec{\mathcal{G}}$ is upward planar if and only if the tendrils can be flipped and the wiggles can be arranged such that for every face the total contribution of the tendrils and wiggles is zero.*

The proof of Lemma 6.16 uses the result of Theorem 6.3.

We establish the following correspondence between digraph $\vec{\mathcal{G}}$ and network $\mathcal{P}$ (see Figure 6.23): the faces of $\vec{\mathcal{G}}$ correspond to the vertices of $\mathcal{P}$; the tendrils and wiggles of $\vec{\mathcal{G}}$ correspond to the the edges of $\mathcal{P}$; flipping a tendril of $\vec{\mathcal{G}}$ corresponds to orienting an edge of $\mathcal{P}$; the contribution of a tendril or wiggle of $\vec{\mathcal{G}}$ corresponds to the flow in an edge of $\mathcal{P}$; the balance of the contributions of the tendrils and wiggles in the faces of $\vec{\mathcal{G}}$ corresponds to the conservation of flow at the vertices of $\mathcal{P}$.

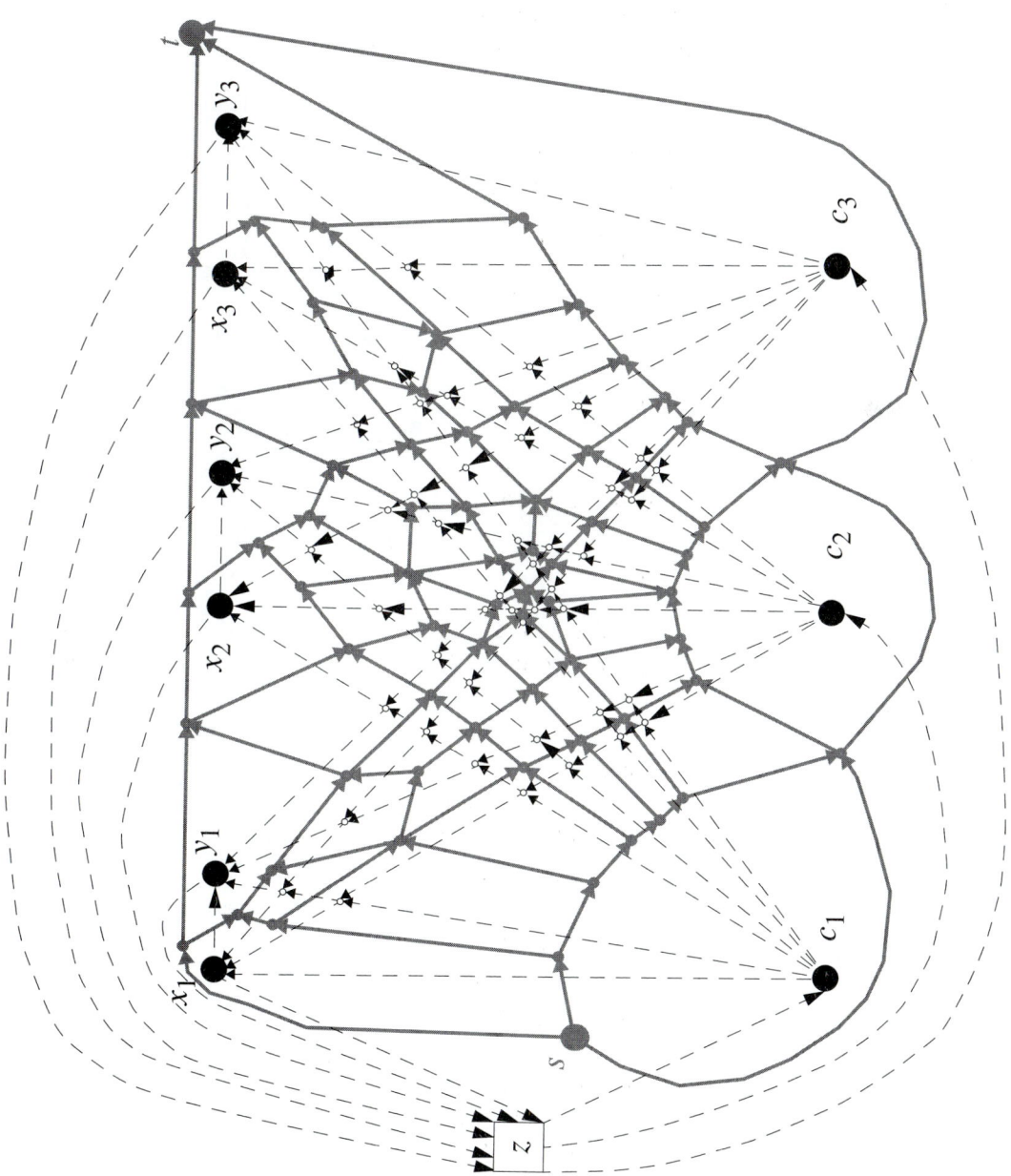

Figure 6.22: Orientation $\vec{\mathcal{P}}$ (drawn with dashed lines) of the network $\mathcal{P}$ shown in Figure 6.21.c and dual digraph $\vec{\mathcal{D}}$ (drawn with solid lines) of $\vec{\mathcal{P}}$.

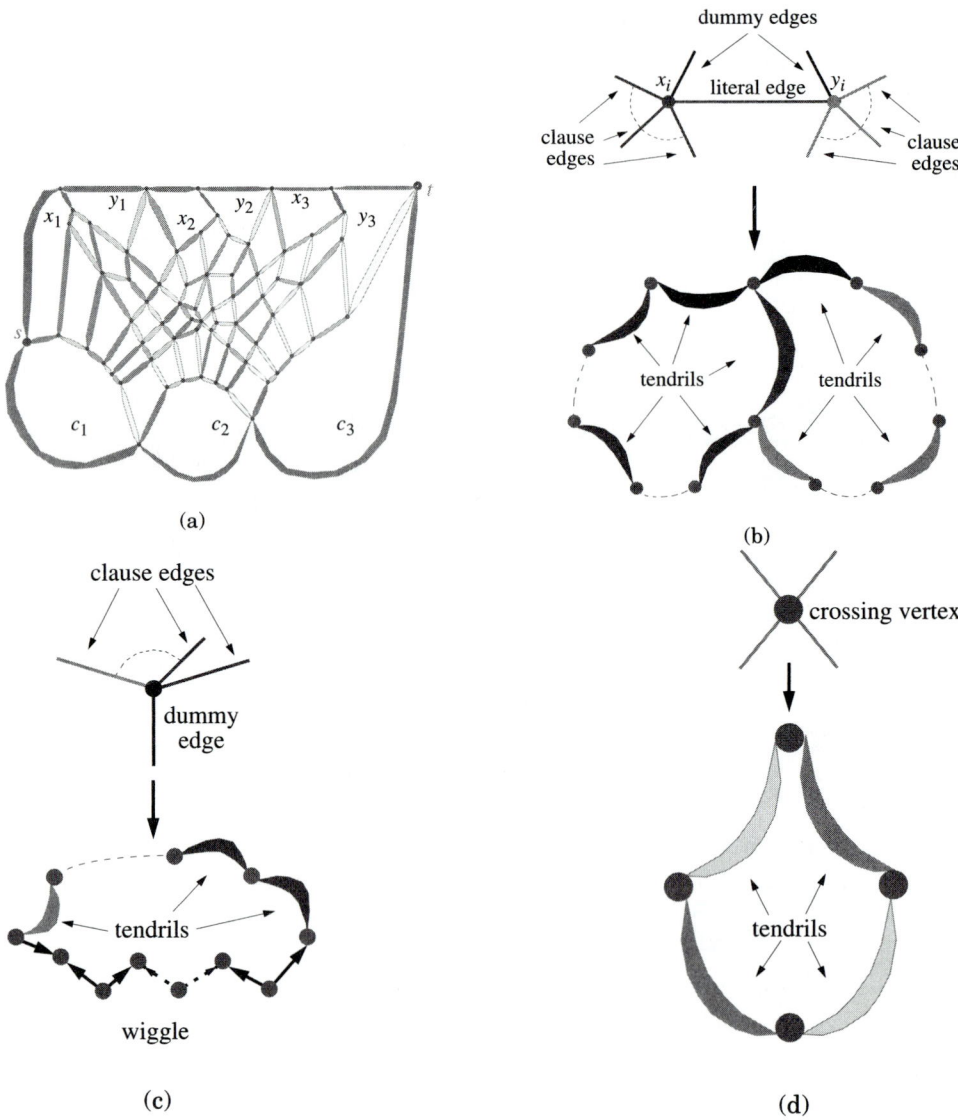

Figure 6.23: Schematic illustration of: (a) digraph $\vec{\mathcal{G}}$ obtained from $\vec{\mathcal{D}}$ by replacing edges with tendrils and wiggles; (b) the two faces of $\vec{\mathcal{G}}$ associated with literal vertices x_i and y_i of $\mathcal{P}$; (c) the face of $\vec{\mathcal{G}}$ associated with a clause vertex of $\mathcal{P}$; (d) the face of $\vec{\mathcal{G}}$ associated with a crossing vertex of $\mathcal{P}$.

Theorem 6.10 *Given an instance S of* NOT-ALL-EQUAL-3-SAT *with n variables and m clauses and the associated planar switch-flow network $\mathcal{P}$, digraph $\vec{G}$, associated with S and $\mathcal{P}$, has $O(n^3 m^2)$ vertices and edges, and can be constructed in $O(n^3 m^2)$ time. Instance S is satisfiable and network $\mathcal{P}$ admits a feasible flow if and only if digraph $\vec{G}$ is upward planar. Also, given an upward planar drawing for $\vec{G}$, a feasible flow for $\mathcal{P}$ and a satisfying truth assignment for S can be computed in $O(n^3 m^2)$ time.*

From Theorems 6.2, 6.9, and 6.10 we conclude:

Corollary 6.1 *Upward planarity testing is NP-complete.*

6.7 Further Issues in Upward Planarity

We complete the chapter by addressing several other aspects of upward planarity.

6.7.1 Outerplanar Digraphs

A graph is said to be *outerplanar* if it is planar and it admits an embedding, such that all the vertices are on the same face. In [Pap95], it is shown that upward planarity testing can be efficiently performed for outerplanar digraphs. The algorithm exploits the fact that the dual of an embedded outerplanar graph is a tree.

Theorem 6.11 *Let G be an embedded outerplanar digraph with n vertices. We can test whether G is upward planar in $O(n)$ time.*

Theorem 6.12 *Let G be an outerplanar digraph with n vertices. We can test whether G is upward planar in $O(n^2)$ time.*

6.7.2 Forbidden Cycles for Single-Source Digraphs

Thomassen [Tho89] characterizes the upward planarity of embedded digraphs with a single source in terms of certain forbidden (undirected) cycles. This characterization is used in the algorithm in [HL96].

Theorem 6.13 *An embedded digraph G is upward planar if and only if it is acyclic and there is a choice of external face, such that:*

- *The source of G is on the external face*

- *Every undirected cycle C of G has a vertex which becomes a sink after removing all the edges outside C.*

Note that the choice of external face determines what is inside and outside a cycle. The necessity of the condition is easy to verify by considering the vertex of C with highest y-coordinate, in an upward planar drawing of G (see, e.g., Figure 6.7).

Theorem 6.13 provides an alternative proof of the fact that the digraph of Figure 6.1, which has a unique embedding, is not upward planar, as shown in Figure 6.24.

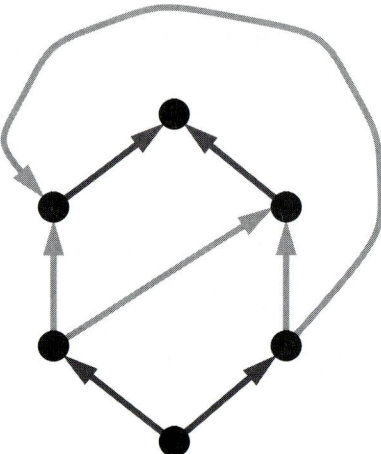

Figure 6.24: Example of forbidden cycle (shown with shaded lines) in the embedded digraph of Figure 6.1.b.

How to apply Theorem 6.13 to test the upward planarity of an embedded single-source digraph is shown in [HL96].

6.7.3   Forbidden Structures for Lattices

We say that an ordered set is planar if its covering digraph (*Hasse diagram*) is upward planar (refer to [Bir67] for standard terminology on ordered sets). Testing upward planarity of digraphs and planarity of ordered sets are equivalent problems. Namely, it is easy to see that a digraph G is upward planar if and only if the ordered set with *covering digraph* obtained from G by inserting a vertex along every transitive edge is planar.

An important consequence of the fact that the digraph G of Figure 6.1 is not upward planar is that an upward planar digraph cannot contain a subgraph homeomorphic to G. This observation implies the following result [Bir67, p. 32, Ex. 7(a)].

Theorem 6.14 *The ordered set induced by an upward planar digraph with one source and one sink is a lattice, that is, a bounded planar ordered set is a lattice.*

A Kuratowski-type characterization of planar lattices in terms of forbidden sublattices is given in [KR75]. Namely, they define a family $\mathcal{L}$ of nonplanar lattices (see Figure 6.25) and show that $\mathcal{L}$ is the minimal obstruction set, under sublattice containment, for upward planarity.

Theorem 6.15 *A lattice is planar if and only if it contains no (order) sublattice isomorphic to a lattice from the family $\mathcal{L}$. Moreover, $\mathcal{L}$ is the minimum such family.*

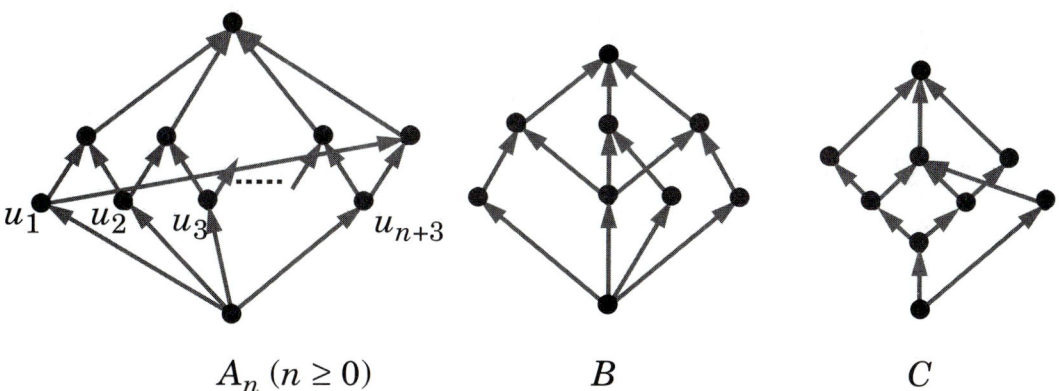

$$A_n \ (n \geq 0) \qquad\qquad B \qquad\qquad C$$

Figure 6.25: Some of the nonplanar lattices in the set $\mathcal{L}$ of Theorem 6.15.

Platt [Pla76] characterizes the planarity of a lattice in terms of the planarity of an undirected graph related to its covering digraph.

Theorem 6.16 *A lattice is planar if and only if the undirected graph obtained from its covering digraph, by ignoring the orientation of the edges and adding an edge between the source and sink, is planar.*

Lempel, Even, and Cederbaum [LEC67] relate the planarity of biconnected undirected graphs to the upward planarity of acyclic digraphs with one source and one sink. Recall from Section 4.8 that a *bipolar orientation* of an undirected graph G is an acyclic digraph with exactly one source and one sink, which is obtained from G, by orienting its edges. A biconnected graph admits a bipolar orientation with adjacent source and sink.

Theorem 6.17 *Let G be a biconnected graph, and G' be a bipolar orientation of G with adjacent source and sink. Thus G is planar if and only if G' is upward planar.*

The planarity of lattices is also characterized by the (order) dimension [BFR71].

Theorem 6.18 *A lattice is planar if and only if it has dimension at most two.*

6.7.4   Some Classes of Upward Planar Digraphs

Several classes of planar digraphs whose members are always upward planar have been identified.

Theorem 6.19 *All the digraphs in the following classes are upward planar:*

- *Digraphs whose underlying undirected graph is a forest*

- *Planar st-graphs*

- *Series-parallel digraphs*

- *Planar bipartite digraphs [DLR90].*

6.8   Exercises

1. Give examples of planar acyclic digraphs with one source and one sink that are not upward planar.

2. Give an example of a planar acyclic digraph that is not upward planar and whose blocks are upward planar.

3. Prove Lemma 6.12.

4. Prove that digraphs whose underlying undirected graphs are a forest are upward planar.

5. Prove that acyclic digraphs whose underlying undirected graphs are a simple cycle are upward planar.

6. Let P be a simple polygon without horizontal sides. A *peak* is a vertex v of P, such that its incident sides are both above or both below the horizontal line through v. Prove that the number of peaks that have a convex angle inside P is equal to the number of peaks that have a concave angle inside P plus 2.

7. Give a linear time algorithm to test whether a planar acyclic digraph has a bimodal planar embedding.

8. Apply Algorithm 6.3 *Embedded-Upward-Planar-Test* to test the upward planarity of the embedded digraph of Figure 6.13.a.

9. Let G be a digraph, such that a reorientation of its edges results in a series-parallel digraph. Prove or disprove: G (with the original orientation of its edges) is upward planar.

10. Give a "reasonable" definition of the equivalence classes of upward planar drawings.

Chapter 7

Incremental Construction

Several methods used in graph drawing rely on an incremental construction strategy, where a drawing or an intermediate representation (e.g., planar embedding) is constructed by adding vertices and edges one at a time, possibly applying some greedy optimization at each step. Incremental construction strategies are motivated, not only by algorithmic choices, but also by the need to support the interactive updates performed by the user.

This chapter gives incremental techniques for two graph drawing problems. In Section 7.1, we outline a simple incremental planarization technique. In Section 7.2, we present an interactive orthogonal drawing method.

7.1 Planarization

Planarization techniques are motivated by the availability of many efficient and well-analyzed drawing algorithms for planar graphs (see, e.g., Chapter 2). If the graph is nonplanar, it is transformed into a planar graph by means of a preliminary planarization step that replaces each crossing with a fictitious vertex, and then a drawing method for planar graphs is applied.

Finding the minimum number of crossings and finding a maximum planar subgraph are both NP-hard problems (see Section A.6). Hence, existing planarization algorithms use heuristics. Work on planarization and related techniques includes [CHT93, CNS79, Dji95, DT96, EFG82, JLM97, JTS86, JTS89, Kan92b, La 94, MS78, Men92, NT84, OT81].

7.1.1   Incremental Planarization

A *planarization operation* for a graph consists of adding a new vertex x and replacing a pair (a, b), (c, d) of nonadjacent edges with the four edges (a, x), (b, x), (c, x) and (d, x). The operation is illustrated in Figure 7.1. Intuitively, a planarization operation adds a fictitious vertex x, at which the edges (a, b) and (c, d) cross. A *planarization* G' of a graph G is a planar graph obtained from G by a sequence of planarization operations. It is easy to show that every graph has a planarization.

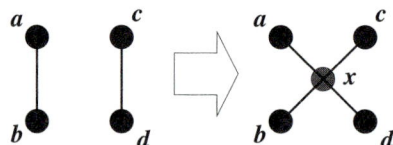

Figure 7.1: Planarization operation.

Algorithm 7.1 *Planarize* is a simple algorithm for finding a planarization of a graph. It uses an algorithm for finding a planar subgraph as a subroutine (see Figure 7.2).

Step 1 of Algorithm 7.1 *Planarize* computes a *maximal* planar subgraph of the input graph. The best available algorithm for the *maximum* planar subgraph problem is described in [JM96]. This method has a solid theoretical foundation in polyhedral combinatorics, and achieves good results in practice, despite its worst-case exponential running time.

Step 2 can be performed in $O(n)$ time with a variation of a planarity testing algorithm (see Section 3.3). Step 3 computes a shortest path algorithm in a planar graph. This step can be implemented in $O(n')$ time, where n' is the current number of vertices of G' [KRRS94]. Note that n' may be $\Omega(n^4)$. However, in many applications, graphs are sparse and "almost planar," and n' is much smaller.

7.1.2   Constraints in Incremental Planarization

Several constraints of topological nature can be supported within the Algorithm 7.1 *Planarize*, including:

- Preventing crossings on edges

- Placing vertices on the external boundary.

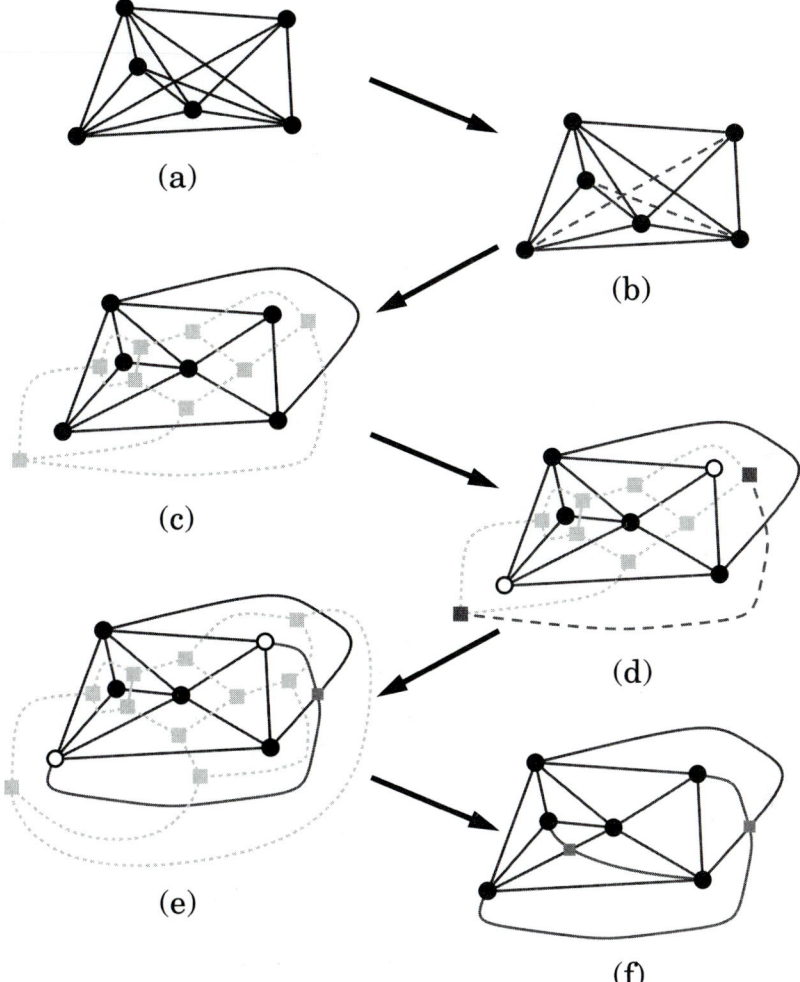

Figure 7.2: Simple planarization method: (a) initial graph; (b) partition of the edges into planar (solid) and nonplanar (dashed); (c) dual graph (dotted) used to route the nonplanar edges; (d) shortest path in the dual graph for a nonplanar edge; (e) embedding and dual graph after the insertion of a nonplanar edge; (e) final planarized graph.

In order to prevent the edges of a given subset E^* from having crossings, we modify Steps 1 and 3 of Algorithm 7.1 *Planarize* as follows:

- In Step 1, we try adding the edges of E^* first, so that a maximal subset of them will be in the planar subgraph computed by this step.

Algorithm 7.1 *Planarize*
     Input: graph G
    Output: planarization G' of G

1. Compute a maximal planar subgraph S of the input graph G, and partition the edges into "planar" and "nonplanar" accordingly (see Figure 7.2.b), as follows:

   - Start with subgraph G' consisting only of the vertices of G, but no edges

   - For each edge e of G, if the graph obtained by adding e to G' is planar, then add e to G' and classify e as "planar," else reject e and classify it as "nonplanar."

2. Construct a planar embedding of the planar subgraph G', and the dual graph of S (see Figure 7.2.c).

3. Add to G' the nonplanar edges, one at at time, each time minimizing the number of crossings. This is done as follows for a nonplanar edge (u, v):

   - Find a shortest (least number of edges) path in the dual graph of the current embedding G' from the faces incident to u to the faces incident to v (see Figure 7.2.d).

   - Add the nonplanar edge and update G' and its dual (see Figure 7.2.e).

                                                         □

- In Step 3, we place a large "crossing cost" on the edges of E^*.

In order to constrain a given subset of vertices V^* to be on the external boundary, we can add a fictitious vertex v^* to the graph and fictitious edges connecting v^* to all the vertices in V^*. We then impose the aforementioned constraint of preventing crossings on the edges incident on v^* (see Figure 7.3).

7.2   Interactive Orthogonal Drawing

Many applications require human interaction during the design process, where the user is given the ability to alter the graph as the design pro-

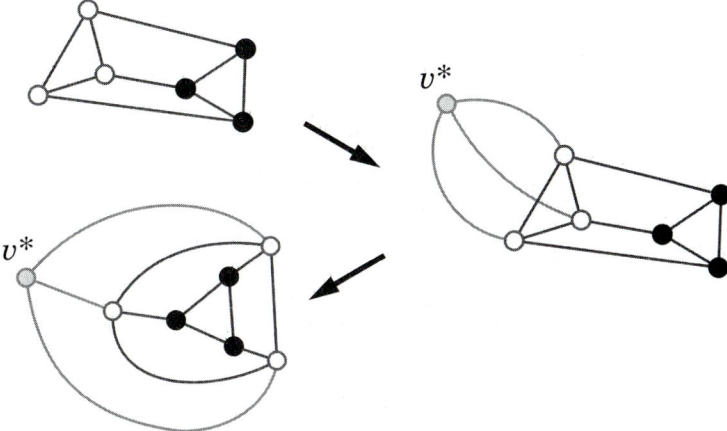

Figure 7.3: Constraining vertices to be on the external face.

gresses. *Interactive*, or *dynamic*, graph drawing addresses the problem of maintaining a drawing of a graph while the user is interactively modifying the graph. If an insertion, deletion, or move operation is performed on the graph, then the new graph should be redrawn. Running any drawing algorithm on the new graph will result in a new drawing, which may be vastly different from the previous one. This is an inefficient use of time and resources from two points of view:

(a) The machine must spend considerable computational resources to run the algorithm on the new graph.

(b) The user may need to spend considerable cognitive effort in trying to relate the new drawing to the previous one.

A systematic approach to dynamic graph drawing, especially as it relates to problem (a), appears in [CDTT95]. The focus of the approach is to perform queries and updates on an implicit representation of the drawing. Algorithms are presented for maintaining drawings of trees, series-parallel digraphs, and planar *st*-graphs. Most updates of the data structures require logarithmic time.

Problem (b) is equally important. Consider Figure 7.4. Suppose that the user has the graph in Figure 7.4.a on the screen, and the user adds the edge (b, c). If a planarity-based algorithm is used to recompute the drawing, then the shape of the drawing will change dramatically to avoid the edge crossing, as in Figure 7.4.b. This dramatic change destroys the user's "mental map," that is, the mental image of the drawing. From the user's point of view, it would be better to simply accept the edge crossing for the sake of preserving the mental map, as in the drawing of Figure 7.4.c. Models for the mental map, as well as some layout adjustment methods which preserve the mental map, were introduced in [MELS95].

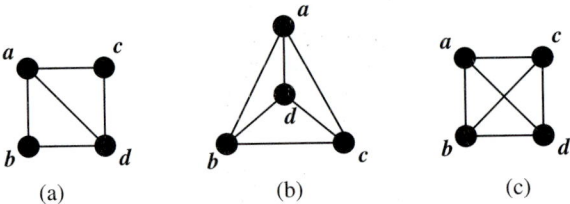

(a)   (b)   (c)

Figure 7.4: The transition from (a) to (b) destroys the user's mental map; the transition from (a) to (c) does not.

This section describes interactive techniques from [PT, PT96, PST97] for orthogonal graph drawing. The techniques address both problem (a) and problem (b), that is, they are efficient, and they preserve the user's mental map. Furthermore, the drawings have good aesthetic qualities: the number of bends and the area are both bounded. Section 7.2.1 introduces the scenaria: the allowable interactive operations and models for the user's "mental map." The following two sections present two incremental drawing methods based on these scenaria. Section 7.2.1 compares the methods.

There are several other studies of incremental graph drawing methods. A technique for restructuring a layered drawing of a tree (see Section 3.1.2) in time proportional to its height is presented in [Moe90]. An interactive drawing system for layered drawings is presented in [Nor96]. Interactive graph drawing methods based on force-directed methods and constraint resolution are presented in [RMS97, ECH97]. Further interactive orthogonal drawing techniques are presented in [BK97, Föß97, MHT93, PT, PT96, PST97].

7.2.1   Interactive Drawing Scenaria

Software which supports interactive graph drawing features should be able to: (a) create a drawing of a given graph under some layout standard (e.g., orthogonal, straight line, etc.), and (b) give the user the ability to interact with the drawing in the following ways:

- Insert an edge between two specified vertices

- Insert a vertex along with its incident edges

- Delete edges, vertices or sets of vertices, or edges

- Move a vertex

- Move a set of vertices and edges.

There are various factors which affect the decisions that an interactive drawing system takes at each moment a user request is posted and before the next drawing is displayed. Some of these factors are the following:

- The amount of control the user has upon the position of a newly inserted vertex.

- The amount of control the user has on how a new edge will be routed in the current drawing connecting two vertices of the current graph.

- How different the new drawing will be, with respect to the current drawing.

Based on these factors, we propose the following scenaria for interactive graph drawing:

1. The *full-control scenario*. The user has full control over the position of a new vertex in the current drawing. The control can range from specifying lower and upper bounds on the x- and y-coordinates that the new vertex will have, to providing the exact desired coordinates to the system. The edges can be routed by the user or by the system.

2. The *draw-from-scratch scenario*. Here, every time a user request is posted, the new graph is drawn using one of the popular drawing techniques. Apart from the fact that this scenario gives rather slow interactive drawing systems, the new drawing may be completely different form the current drawing, that is, the user's mental map may be destroyed.

3. The *relative-coordinates scenario*. The general shape of the current drawing remains the same. The coordinates of some vertices and edges may change by a small constant, because of the insertion of a new vertex and its incident edges (somewhere in the middle of the current drawing), and the insertion of a constant number of rows and columns. The relative ordering of vertices in the x and y directions does not change, and, to some extent, the user's mental map is preserved.

4. The *no-change scenario*. In this approach, the coordinates of the already placed vertices, bends, and edges *do not change at all*. In order to achieve such a property, specific invariants need to be maintained after each insertion. In this scenario, the user's mental map is strongly preserved.

A practical technique for the incremental restructuring of an orthogonal drawing, after an edge insertion under the relative-coordinates scenario, is presented in [MHT93]. In the following, we present two methods that incrementally construct an orthogonal drawing under the relative-coordinates and no-change scenaria, respectively [PT, PT96, PST97]. Related methods are presented in [BK97, Föß97].

The Relative-Coordinates Scenario

In this scenario, every time a new vertex is about to be inserted into the current drawing, the system makes a decision about the coordinates of the vertex and the routing of its incident edges. New rows and columns may be inserted anywhere in the current drawing in order for this routing to be feasible. The coordinates of the new vertex (say v), as well as the locations of the new rows and/or columns, will depend on the following:

- The degree of v (at the time of insertion).

- For each vertex u that is adjacent to v, which directions (i.e., up, down, right, or left) around vertex u can be used by the new edges.

- Whether or not the required routing of edges can be done utilizing segments of existing rows or columns that are free (not covered by an edge).

- Our optimization criteria.

Deletions of vertices and edges can be done trivially by simply removing them from the drawing. After several deletions, a compaction step (see Section 5.4) may be necessary in order to reduce the area occupied by the drawing. A move can be implemented via a deletion followed by a subsequent insertion.

When we use the relative-coordinates scenario in an interactive system, we can start from an existing drawing of a graph, or we can start from scratch, that is from an empty graph. In either case, we assume that the insertion of any vertex/edge under this scenario will not increase the number of connected components of the current graph. The only exception to this is when a single vertex is inserted into an empty graph. Any other vertex inserted during an update operation will be connected to at least one vertex of the current drawing.

Let us assume that v is the next vertex to be inserted in the current graph during an update operation. The number of vertices in the current graph connected to v is called the *local degree* of v. From the discussion above, it follows that we only consider the case where an inserted vertex has local degree one, two, three, or four, except for the first vertex inserted in an empty graph. If the user wishes to insert a new vertex that has local degree zero, then this vertex is placed in a temporary location and it will be inserted automatically in the future, when some new insertions of vertices increase its (local) degree.

Assume that vertex v is about to be inserted in the current graph. For each one of the vertices of the current drawing that is adjacent to v, the system checks the possible directions around these vertices that new edges may be inserted or routed. The target is to minimize the number of new rows or columns that have to open up in the current drawing, as well as the number of bends that appear along the routed edges.

There are many different cases because there are many possible combinations. First, we will give examples of some of the best and worst cases one might encounter, and then, we will see in more detail how v is inserted when its local degree is one, two, three, or four. In the example shown in Figure 7.5.a, vertices u_1 and u_2 have a *free edge* (i.e., grid edge not covered by a graph edge) up and to the right respectively. In this case, no new rows/columns are needed for the insertion of vertex v and no new bends are introduced.

On the other hand however, in the example shown in Figure 7.5.b, all four vertices u_1, u_2, u_3, and u_4 have pairwise opposite direction free edges. The insertion of new vertex v requires the insertion of three new rows and three new columns in the current drawing. Additionally, eight bends are introduced. Vertices u_1, u_2, u_3, and u_4 have general positions in Figure 7.5.b, and we can see that edge (v, u_4) has four bends. We can avoid the four-bend edge, if we insert vertex v as shown in Figure 7.5.c. The total number of new rows, columns and bends is still the same, but the maximum number of bends per edge is now three. For a more even distribution of the bends of the edges adjacent to vertex v, we may choose to insert vertex v as shown in Figure 7.5.d, where every edge has exactly two bends (three new rows and three new columns are still required). Notice, though, that the approach described in Figure 7.5.d for inserting vertex v, is not always possible (e.g., we cannot have this kind of insertion if vertices u_1, u_2, u_3, and u_4 are in the same row or column).

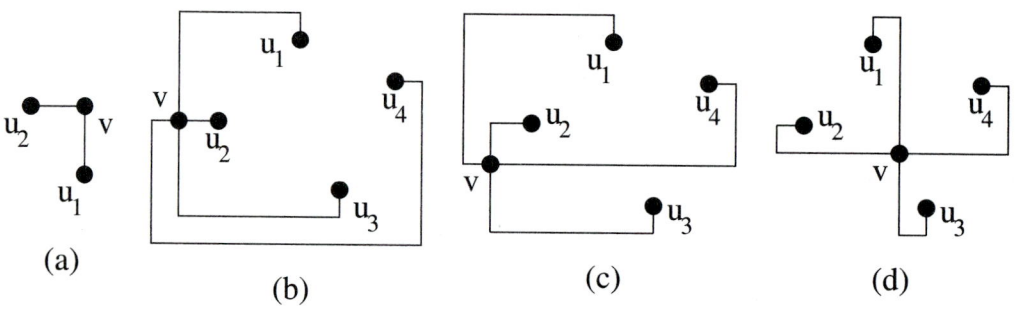

Figure 7.5: Insertion of v: (a) no new row or column is required; (b)–(d) three new rows and three new columns are required, with a maximum of four bends per edge in (b), three bends per edge in (c), and two bends per edge in (d).

Let v be the next vertex to be inserted. There are many cases, if we are interested in an exhaustive analysis, and it is relatively easy to enumerate all of them for each insertion. We distinguish the following main cases for vertex v:

1. v has local degree one. If u is the vertex of the current drawing that is adjacent to v, we draw an edge between u and v. Edge (u, v) uses a direction (up, right, bottom, or left) that is not taken by some other edge incident to u. This is depicted in Figure 7.6.a, and this insertion requires at most either a new row or a new column. No new bend is inserted.

2. v has local degree two. In the best case, the insertion requires no new rows, columns or bends as shown in Figure 7.5.a. In the worst case, though, two new rows and one new column, or one new row and two new columns, and three new bends might be required (see Figure 7.6.b).

3. v has local degree three. In the worst case, the insertion requires a total of four new rows and columns, and five new bends. In Figure 7.6.c, we show an example of such an insertion that requires one new row, three new columns and five new bends.

4. v has local degree four. The worst case requires a total of six new rows and columns, however, at most four of them can be either rows or columns. Also, eight new bends may be introduced, in the worst case. We have already discussed an example, which is depicted in Figure 7.5.c. In Figure 7.6.d, we show another case, where two new rows, four new columns and eight new bends are introduced.

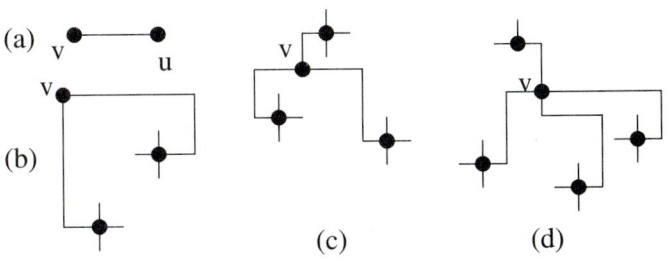

Figure 7.6: Inserting v when its local degree is (a) one, (b) two, (c) three, and (d) four.

In Figure 7.7, we show an orthogonal drawing of a graph drawn under the relative-coordinates scenario we just described.

Lemma 7.1 *Assume that n vertices are inserted into an orthogonal drawing of a graph with height h and width w, using the interactive graph drawing scheme under the relative-coordinates scenario. These insertions add up to $8n$ new bends and result in a new drawing with area at most*

$$\left(\frac{h+w}{2} + 3n\right)^2.$$

Proof: Assume that all n inserted vertices have local degree four, and each one of them falls into one of the worst cases described above, in terms of rows, columns, and bends introduced. This means that each insertion introduces eight new bends and a total of six new rows and columns. Let h' and w' be the height and the width, respectively, of the graph after the n vertex insertions are completed. Therefore, $h' + w' = h + w + 6n$. The area of the final drawing $h' \times w'$ is maximized when

$$h' = w' = \frac{h'+w'}{2} = \frac{h+w}{2} + 3n.$$

Hence, the result follows. $\qquad\square$

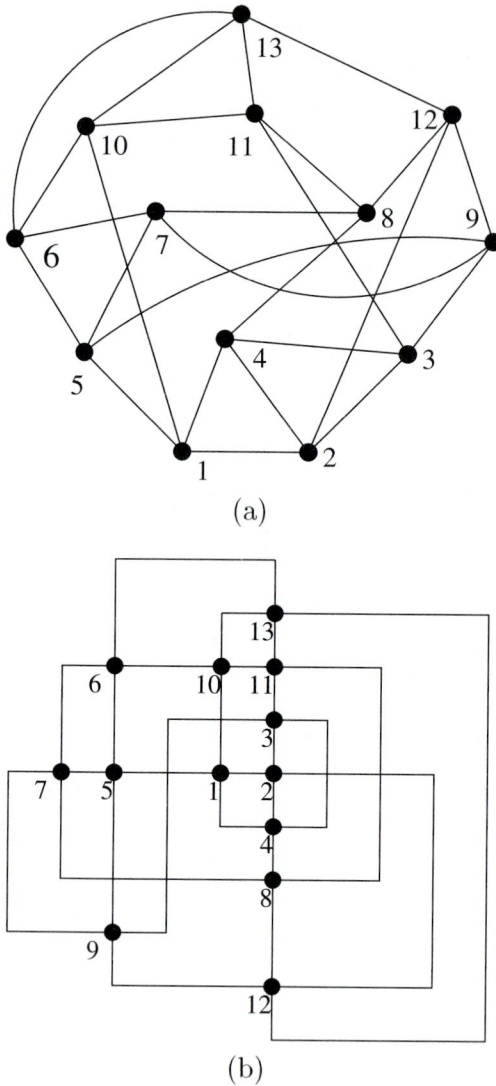

Figure 7.7: (a) A graph G of maximum degree four that is interactively constructed by adding vertices $1, 2, \ldots, 13$. (b) Orthogonal grid drawing of G constructed by the interactive graph drawing scheme under the relative-coordinates scenario. Notice that no edge has more than three bends. In fact, there is only one edge with three bends (i.e., edge $(12, 13)$), whereas all the other edges have two bends or less.

In the rest of this section, we assume that, when we use the interactive graph drawing scheme under the relative-coordinates scenario, we start from scratch, that is the given graph is empty. According to the discussion in the beginning of this section, the relative-coordinates scenario guarantees that the graph that is being built is always connected after any vertex insertion. Let $n_1(t)$, $n_2(t)$, $n_3(t)$, and $n_4(t)$ denote the number of vertices of local degree one, two, three, and four, respectively, that have been inserted up to time t. Also, let $n(t)$ be the total number of vertices that have been inserted up to time t. Clearly, we have

$$n_1(t) + n_2(t) + n_3(t) + n_4(t) = n(t) - 1. \tag{7.1}$$

We now analyze the number of bends. From the description of the interactive graph drawing scheme under the relative-coordinates scenario, at most six new rows and columns are opened as a result of a vertex insertion (see Figures 7.5.b–d and 7.6.d). Figures 7.5 and 7.6 cover the worst cases in terms of rows, columns, and bends required for a single vertex insertion, and for all possible local degrees of the inserted vertex. From these figures, we also observe the following:

- There can be at most three bends along any edge of the drawing (see Figure 7.5.c)

- The bends along an edge are introduced at the time of insertion of the vertex that is incident to that edge.

From Figures 7.5 and 7.6 and from the discussion above, it follows that at most three new bends are introduced when a vertex of local degree two is inserted, at most five new bends when a vertex of local degree three is inserted, and at most eight new bends when a vertex of local degree four is inserted. No new bend is introduced when a vertex of local degree one is inserted. In other words, if $B(t)$ is the total number of bends at time t, it holds that

$$B(t) \leq 3n_2(t) + 5n_3(t) + 8n_4(t). \tag{7.2}$$

Furthermore, the total number of edges at time t is

$$n_1(t) + 2n_2(t) + 3n_3(t) + 4n_4(t) \leq 2n(t). \tag{7.3}$$

Subtracting (7.1) from (7.3), and multiplying by 3, we obtain

$$3n_2(t) + 6n_3(t) + 9n_4(t) \leq 3n(t) + 3. \tag{7.4}$$

From (7.2) and (7.4), we obtain the following upper bound on $B(t)$

$$B(t) \leq 3n(t) + 3. \tag{7.5}$$

With a more complex analysis (see Exercise 2), one can prove that $B(t) \leq 3n(t) - 1$.

Regarding the area of the drawing at time t, we can infer the following facts from Figures 7.5 and 7.6:

- When a vertex with local degree one is inserted, either a new row or a new column is required.

- When a vertex with local degree two is inserted, either two new rows and one new column are required, or one new row and two new columns are required.

- When a vertex with local degree three is inserted, a total of at most four new rows and columns are required.

- When a vertex with local degree four is inserted, a total of at most six new rows and columns are required.

Let $h(t)$ and $w(t)$ denote the height and the width, respectively, of the drawing at time t. Then, it holds that

$$h(t) + w(t) \leq n_1(t) + 3n_2(t) + 4n_3(t) + 6n_4(t) \tag{7.6}$$

If we multiply both sides of (7.3) by $\frac{3}{2}$, we have

$$\frac{3}{2}n_1(t) + 3n_2(t) + \frac{9}{2}n_3(t) + 6n_4(t) \leq 3n(t). \tag{7.7}$$

Hence, by (7.6) and (7.7), we obtain

$$h(t) + w(t) \leq 3n(t). \tag{7.8}$$

This implies that the area $A(t)$ at time t is at most

$$A(t) \leq \frac{9}{4}n(t)^2 = 2.25n(t)^2.$$

We summarize the above analysis in the following theorem.

Theorem 7.1 *Consider a graph G of maximum degree four that is constructed, starting from an isolated vertex, by means of a sequence of operations that add to G a vertex and one or more edges incident on it. Let $n(t)$ be the number of vertices of G at time t. The interactive graph drawing scheme under the relative-coordinates scenario maintains, at any time t, an orthogonal grid drawing of G with the following properties:*

- *Each edge has at most three bends*

- *The total number of bends is at most $3n(t) - 1$*

- *The area is at most $2.25n(t)^2$.*

Also, after each operation, the coordinates of any vertex or bend are shifted by a total amount of at most six units along the x and y axes.

The scenario described in this section maintains the general shape of the current drawing after an update takes place. The coordinates of vertices and bends of the current drawing may shift by a total amount of at most six units along the x and y axes, as a result of an update operation. This change does not affect the number of bends of the current drawing. This scenario works well when we build a graph from scratch (incremental setting), or we are presented with a drawing (which was produced by any algorithm) and we want our interactive system to update it.

The No-Change Scenario

In the no-change scenario, the drawing system *never* changes the positions of vertices and bends of the current drawing; it just increments the drawing by adding the new elements. As in the previous scenario, our scheme produces an orthogonal drawing under the assumption that the maximum degree of any vertex at any time is less than or equal to four. We assume that we build a graph from scratch in such a way that the graph is always connected.

Let u be a vertex of the current drawing, and let v be the next vertex to be inserted. In our scheme, there are four possible ways to draw the edge connecting u to v, which are schematically illustrated in Figure 7.8.a. Each one is called a *route* of vertex u. Vertex u has up to two routes *to the right*, through edges e_1 and e_2, and up to two routes *to the bottom*, through edges e_3 and e_4. Namely, vertex u has a route to the right if and only if there is no edge of the current graph using the portion of the row of u to the right of u (edge e_2) or the portion of the column of u above u (edge e_1). Similarly, u has a route to the bottom if and only if there is no edge of the current graph using the portion of the column of u below u (edge e_3) or the portion of the row of u to the left of u (edge e_4). The routes of vertex u through edges e_2 and e_3 are said to be *direct*.

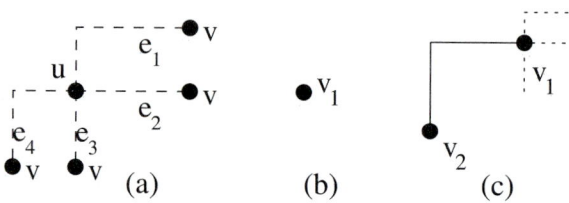

Figure 7.8: (a) Possible routes of a vertex u of the current drawing. (b)–(c) Inserting the first two vertices in an empty graph.

When a vertex is inserted, it is connected to some vertices that have already been placed. The local degree of a vertex that is about to be inserted into the current drawing is defined in the same way as in the relative-coordinates scenario presented in the previous section. Since the graph is always connected, we only consider the case where an inserted vertex has local degree one, two, three, or four. Let us assume that v_i is the next vertex to be inserted in the current drawing. Let r_i be the number of edges incident on v_i that are drawn along nondirect routes. We distinguish the following cases:

1. v_i has local degree one (see Figure 7.9). Let e be the edge incident on v_i. We introduce at most r_i bends and $r_i + 1$ rows and/or columns. In Figure 7.9.a, vertex v_i has one direct route to the bottom and two routes to the right. In Figure 7.9.b, vertex v_i has one direct route to the right and two routes to the bottom.

2. v_i has local degree two (see Figure 7.10). There are four cases. We show two cases in Figure 7.10. The other two cases are symmetric and are treated in a similar fashion. We introduce at most $r_i + 2$ bends and at most $r_i + 2$ rows and/or columns. Vertex v_i has one direct route to the right and one direct route to the bottom.

3. v_i has local degree three (see Figure 7.11). There are eight cases. All cases, however, can be treated by considering just two cases, as shown in Figure 7.11. The remaining cases are symmetric and are treated in a similar fashion. We introduce at most $r_i + 3$ bends and at most

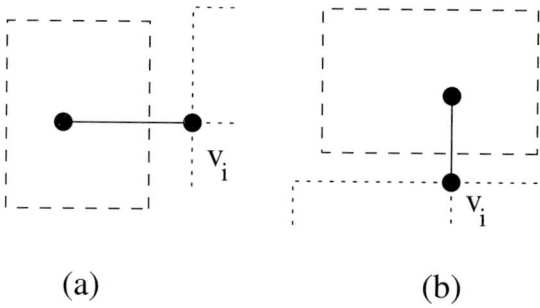

(a)   (b)

Figure 7.9: Insertion of vertex v_i with local degree one.

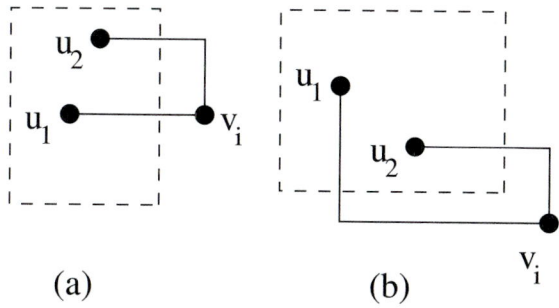

(a)   (b)

Figure 7.10: Insertion of vertex v_i with local degree two: (a) both neighbors of v_i have a route to the right (bottom); (b) one neighbor has a route to the right and the other neighbor has a route to the bottom.

$r_i + 2$ rows and/or columns. Vertex v_i has one direct route either to the right or to the bottom.

4. v_i has local degree four (see Figure 7.12). There are sixteen cases. All cases, however, can be treated by considering just three cases, as shown in Figure 7.12. The symmetric cases are treated in a similar fashion. We introduce at most $r_i + 6$ bends and at most $r_i + 4$ rows and/or columns.

In Figure 7.13, we show an example of a drawing constructed by the interactive graph drawing scheme under the no-change scenario.

Theorem 7.2 *Consider a graph G of maximum degree four that is constructed, starting from an isolated vertex, by means of a sequence of operations that add to G a vertex and one or more edges incident on it. Let $n(t)$ be*

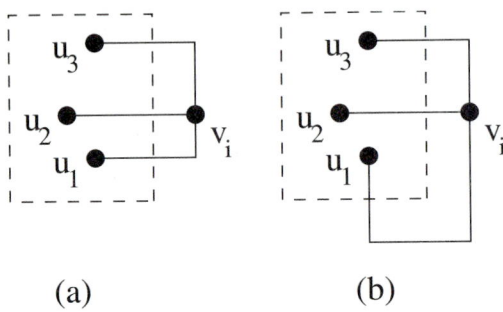

(a)   (b)

Figure 7.11: Insertion of vertex v_i with local degree three: (a) all the neighbors of v_i have a route to the right (bottom); (b) two neighbors have a route to the right (bottom) and the other neighbor has a route to the bottom (right).

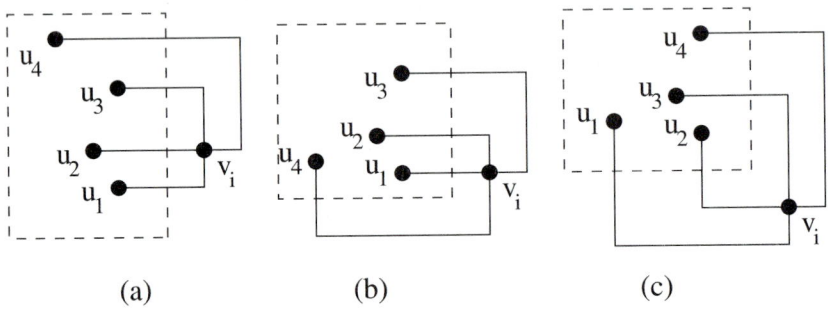

(a)   (b)   (c)

Figure 7.12: Insertion of vertex v_i with local degree four: (a) all the neighbors of v_i have a route to the right (bottom); (b) three neighbors have a route to the right (bottom) and one neighbor has a route to the bottom (right); (c) two neighbors have a route to the right (bottom) and the other two neighbors have a route to the bottom (right).

the number of vertices of G at time t. The interactive graph drawing scheme, under the no-change scenario, maintains, at any time t, an orthogonal grid drawing of G with the following properties:

- *Every edge has at most three bends*

- *The total number of bends at time t is at most $\frac{8}{3}n(t) + 2$;*

- *The area at time t is at most $(\frac{4}{3}n(t))^2$.*

Also, every insertion operation takes constant time.

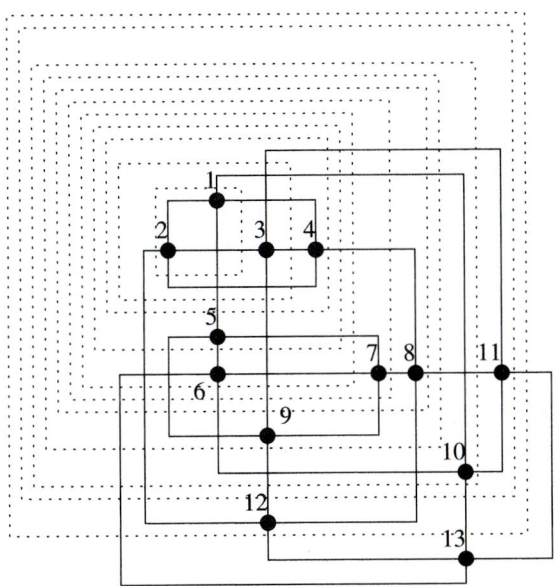

Figure 7.13: Drawing of the graph of Figure 7.7.a constructed by the interactive graph drawing scheme under the no-change scenario. The final drawing has width 10, height 11, and 24 bends. The dotted boxes delimit the drawing at each intermediate step.

Proof: By the description of the scenario, each edge is drawn with at most three bends. Let $n_1(t)$, $n_2(t)$, $n_3(t)$, and $n_4(t)$ denote the number of vertices of local degree one, two, three, and four, respectively, that have been inserted up to time t. Let $B(t)$ be the number of bends at time t, we have

$$B(t) \leq 2n_2(t) + 3n_3(t) + 6n_4(t) + \sum_{i=2}^{n(t)} r_i. \qquad (7.9)$$

When inserting vertex v_i, an edge (u, v_i) incident on v_i can be drawn along a nondirect route only if $u = v_1$ or u has local degree one. At most two edges incident on v_1 are drawn along a nondirect route. Also, each vertex of local degree one will contribute at most one nondirect route. Thus, we have

$$\sum_{i=2}^{n(t)} r_i \leq n_1(t) + 2. \qquad (7.10)$$

By (7.9)–(7.10), we obtain

$$B(t) \leq n_1(t) + 2n_2(t) + 3n_3(t) + 6n_4(t) + 2 \leq 2n(t) + 2n_4(t) + 2. \qquad (7.11)$$

In order to establish an upper bound for $B(t)$, we compute the maximum number of vertices of local degree four that can be inserted up to time t under any insertion sequence. The number of edges incident on the vertices of local degree four up to time t is $4n_4(t)$. Let $m'(t)$ be the number of the remaining edges at time t. It holds that $m'(t) + 4n_4(t) \leq 2n(t)$. Notice that $n_4(t)$ is maximized when $m'(t)$ is minimized. Since the graph has to be connected at time t, it holds that $m' \geq n(t) - n_4(t)$. Hence, we obtain

$$n_4(t) \leq \frac{n(t)}{3}. \tag{7.12}$$

Thus, by (7.11), we obtain

$$B(n) \leq \frac{8}{3}n(t) + 2.$$

We now discuss the area of the drawing. Let $P(t)$ be the half perimeter (width plus height) of the drawing at time t. By the description of the scenario, we have

$$P(t) \leq n_1(t) + 2n_2(t) + 2n_3(t) + 4n_4(t) + \sum_{i=2}^{n(t)} r_i. \tag{7.13}$$

By (7.10), we obtain

$$P(t) \leq 2n_1(t) + 2n_2(t) + 2n_3(t) + 4n_4(t) + 2 = 2n_4(t) + 2n(t). \tag{7.14}$$

By (7.12) and (7.14), we conclude that

$$P(t) \leq \frac{8}{3}n(t).$$

The area at time t is at most $\left(\frac{P(t)}{2}\right)^2$, that is, at most $(\frac{4}{3}n(t))^2$. $\square$

An implementation of the interactive drawing scheme should try to do the following whenever possible:

- Reuse rows and columns on which other vertices have been previously placed.

- Use all direct routes first before using nondirect routes.

For example, when vertex 9 was inserted in the drawing of Figure 7.13, the column of vertex 2 was reused. Hence, in practice, the area and number of bends are typically smaller than the theoretical bounds given in Theorem 7.2.

Comparison

The analyses of the relative-coordinates and no-change scenaria, presented in the previous sections, suggests that the performance of the no-change scenario is better than that of the relative-coordinates scenario, in terms of area and number of bends. This is true only in the worst-case.

The no-change scenario guarantees that the current drawing is never altered, since any vertex insertion and edge routing takes place around it. Another advantage of the no-change scenario is that each update operation takes constant time.

In the relative-coordinates scenario, the general shape of the drawing is maintained after each update operation. Redrawing the whole graph after an update operation requires linear time, since the coordinates of many vertices and bends of the current graph may be shifted (by a total amount of at most six units along the two axes). However, the relative-coordinates scenario has one important feature: it gives the user the ability to insert a vertex into any existing orthogonal drawing. This is due to the fact that no invariants are maintained by this scenario.

Both the relative-coordinates and the no-change scenaria can be extended to the case where the current graph is allowed to become disconnected during the interactive drawing process. For more details see [PT96, PST97].

An experimental study, comparing the performance of the two scenaria on a data set containing over 8000 graphs of maximum degree four, revealed the following:

- The relative-coordinates scenario always exhibited better performance than no-change in terms of both area and number of bends.

- The practical behavior of the two scenaria was much better than their established theoretical worst-case bounds, in most cases. In other words, the worst case did not happen very frequently.

An extensive description of the experimental results, along with heuristics on the placement of vertices, appears in [PST97].

Figure 7.14 shows two drawings constructed by an interactive graph drawing system under the relative-coordinates scenario. Figure 7.15 shows two drawings constructed by an interactive graph drawing system under the no-change scenario.

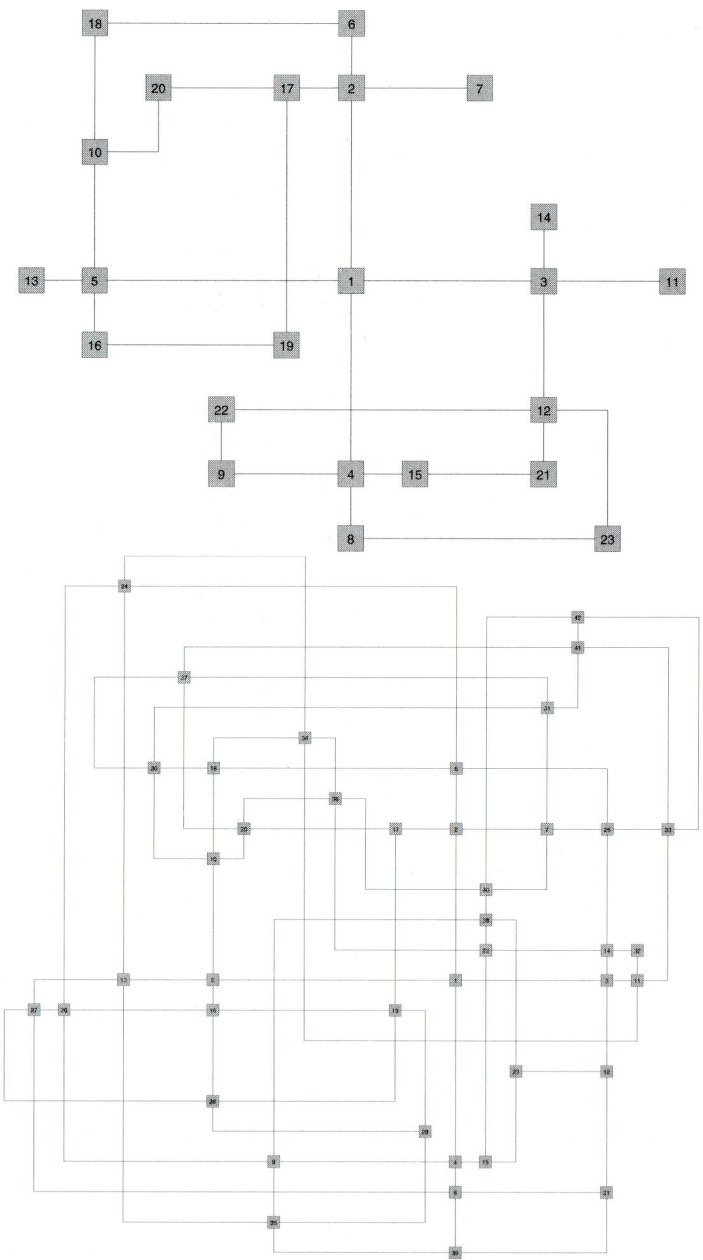

Figure 7.14: Two orthogonal drawings constructed by an interactive graph drawing system under the relative-coordinates scenario. The vertex numbers indicate the order of insertion. (Courtesy of J. Six.)

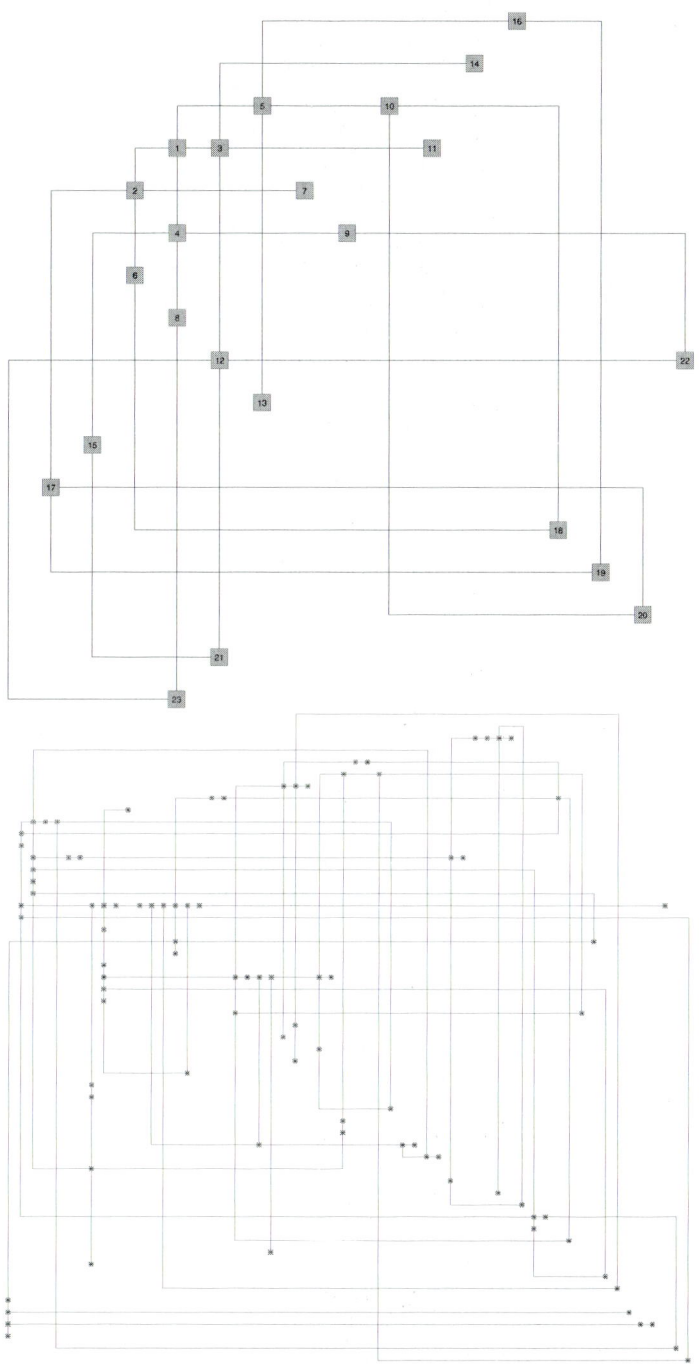

Figure 7.15: Two orthogonal drawings constructed by an interactive graph drawing system under the no-change scenario. The vertex numbers indicate the order of insertion. (Courtesy of J. Six.)

7.3   Exercises

1. Algorithm 7.1 *Planarize* is a simple algorithm for finding a planarization of a graph. The quality of the resulting planarization depends on several factors. Describe them and give best and worst case examples.

2. Prove the bound $B(t) \leq 3n(t) - 1$ on the number of bends of the drawing produced by the interactive graph drawing scheme under the relative-coordinates scenario given in Theorem 7.1. A possible approach consists of solving a linear program over variables n_1, n_2, n_3, and n_4, where the function to maximize is $3n_2 + 5n_3 + 8n_4$.

3. Show that the expression $n_1(t) + 3n_2(t) + 4n_3(t) + 6n_4(t)$ appearing in (7.6) is maximized for $n_1(t) = n_3(t) = 0$, $n_2(t) = n(t) - 2$, and $n_4(t) = 1$.

4. Show that the upper bounds on the number of bends and on the area given in Theorem 7.2 are tight.

5. The following (noninteractive) algorithm constructs an orthogonal drawing of a given graph G with n vertices:

   (a) Compute a numbering $v_1, \ldots, v_n$ of the vertices of G, such that the subgraph induced by $v_1, \ldots, v_i$ is connected for each $i = 1, \ldots, n$

   (b) Incrementally draw G by inserting $v_1, \ldots, v_n$, using the interactive graph drawing scheme under the relative-coordinates scenario.

   Develop a suitable numbering scheme for (5a) that yields better bounds than those given in Theorem 7.1.

6. Repeat Exercise 5 using the no-change scenario instead of the relative-coordinates scenario in (5b). Develop a suitable numbering scheme for (5a) that yields better bounds than those given in Theorem 7.2.

7. Extend the interactive graph drawing scheme under the relative-coordinates scenario so that it works for graphs with degree higher than four. Make reasonable assumptions. Discuss the trade-offs.

8. Is it possible to extend the interactive graph drawing scheme under the no-change scenario so that it works for graphs with degree higher than four? What assumptions are needed? Discuss the trade-offs.

Chapter 8

Nonplanar Orientations

The techniques presented in Chapters 4 and 5 rely heavily on the topology of planar graphs. If a graph is not planar, then these techniques require a planarization step (see Section 7.1). This introduces a potentially large number (up to $O(n^4)$) of fictitious vertices. Their number influences the complexity of the drawing algorithm, and their placement influences the quality of the final drawing.

The techniques in this chapter construct orthogonal grid drawings of nonplanar graphs without a planarization step. They first orient a given graph, then draw it, one vertex at a time, following the order of the orientation. This approach has been followed in several algorithms that achieve good bounds in terms of both the number of bends and the required area.

In Section 8.1, we describe an algorithm that produces an orthogonal grid drawing of an n-vertex biconnected graph of maximum degree four that needs at most $0.77n^2$ area and at most $2n + 4$ bends. Each edge has at most two bends. The algorithm uses a "pairing" technique: vertices are paired in order to use the same row or column.

This algorithm is extended to the case of simply connected (i.e., not necessarily biconnected) graphs of maximum degree four in Section 8.2. The bounds for area and bends are the same as for biconnected graphs. This work appeared in [PT95, PT97c, PT98]. Similar techniques have been presented in [BK94].

An algorithm that constructs drawings of graphs whose vertices have degree greater than four is described in Section 8.3. Given a graph with m edges, this algorithm constructs drawings with width at most $m-1$, height at most $\frac{m}{2} + 2$, and at most one bend per edge. This work appeared in [Pap96, PT97b]. Related work can be found in [Bie97].

8.1   Biconnected Graphs

In this section, we present an algorithm for obtaining orthogonal grid drawings of general (nonplanar) biconnected graphs of maximum degree four. A simple general method for producing such drawings is as follows:

- The graph is first *st*-ordered.

- The first vertex is placed and columns are allocated for each of its incident edges.

- Next, the vertices are placed on the grid consecutively, according to their order in the *st*-ordering.

- At each step, a vertex v is placed on a new row.

- When vertex v is drawn, we also draw all its incoming edges using the already allocated columns.

- The outgoing edges of v are drawn by allocating a new column for each outgoing edge. These columns will be used later.

As we will discuss later, this method can be implemented to run in linear time. The drawings produced require area at most $n \times n$ and at most $2n + 4$ bends, with at most two bends per edge.

Next we present an algorithm that follows the above method and achieves the same bound for the number of bends as the one described above. However, due to a clever vertex placement, it achieves better bounds in terms of area. The goal of the algorithm is to *reuse* as many rows and columns as possible by carefully placing vertices. This is done by finding pairs of vertices that can share a row or column in the final drawing.

We distinguish between two different kinds of pairs:

- *Row Pairs:*

    - both vertices of such a pair share the same row in the final drawing of G, or

    - the vertices of such a pair are placed in two different rows but their placement results in reusing one row (e.g., one of them shares the same row with one or more other vertices, which either belong to another pair or do not belong to any pair at all).

In either case, we reuse a row.

- *Column Pairs:* The two vertices of such a pair are placed in such a way that a column is reused in the final drawing of G. A column is reused when at least two different edges (incident to the vertices) use it. Thus we reuse a column.

Let G be a (perhaps nonplanar) biconnected graph of maximum degree four. First we compute an st-numbering for G, with a vertex s as the source and a vertex t as the sink, and use the numbering to orient the graph. A vertex with a incoming and b outgoing edges is called an a-b vertex ($1 \leq a, b \leq 4$). For example, a vertex with one incoming and two outgoing edges, is a 1-2 vertex. The goal of the algorithm is to create pairs of vertices of G, so that every 1-2, 1-3, and 2-2 vertex is a member of exactly one such pair.

In order to simplify our presentation, we *condense* G as follows. After the st-numbering is complete, we scan the graph G looking for 1-1 vertices whose outgoing edge enters a 1-2 or a 1-3 vertex. We *absorb* these vertices into a single edge until no 1-2 or 1-3 vertex has a 1-1 vertex as its (unique) immediate predecessor. No double edges are introduced when these 1-1 vertices are (temporarily) removed from G. Notice that this step does not alter the number of incoming and outgoing edges for each vertex that has not been absorbed. Let us use the notation G' for the condensed graph, and n' for its number of vertices. We then modify the st-numbering of G', such that there are no gaps in the st-number sequence assigned to the vertices of G' as a result of the removal of these vertices from G.

The row and column pairs described above can be formed in various ways. Next we present Algorithm 8.1 *Form-Pairs* that aims to create as many pairs as possible. A *regular graph* of degree four is a graph such that all the vertices have degree four. We will show that this algorithm works well since it creates at least $\lceil \frac{n-2}{4} \rceil$ pairs for any regular graph of degree four. It considers the vertices of G' in reverse order of the st-numbering and produces pairs starting with the vertex immediately before the sink t. If a vertex already belongs to a pair, the vertex is *assigned*, otherwise it is *unassigned*. The next unassigned vertex to be considered is always a 1-2, 1-3, or 2-2 vertex and it is paired with some other lower numbered vertex in G'. The assignment of the 1-2, 1-3, and 2-2 vertices of G' to pairs is called *pairing* of G'. The vertex of a pair with the lowest st-number of the two is called the *first* vertex of the pair, and the other is called the *second* vertex.

In the rest of this chapter, when we talk about a *predecessor* of a vertex in G or G' with respect to the st-numbering, we mean the immediate predecessor of this vertex.

Algorithm 8.1 *Form-Pairs*

  Input: graph G of maximum degree four
  Output: pairing of the vertices of the condensed
         graph G'

1. Compute an *st*-numbering of G.

2. Condense G by absorbing degree two vertices, as described above.

3. $i = n' - 1$.

4. **while** $i > 2$ **do**

    (a) Consider vertex v_i according to a decreasing order of the *st*-numbering

    (b) **if** v_i is a 1-1, 2-1, or 3-1 vertex **then**
        - $i = i - 1$

    (c) **else if** v_i is a 1-2 or 1-3 vertex **then**
        - form a pair containing vertices v_{i-1} and v_i
        - $i = i - 2$

    (d) **else if** v_i is a 2-2 vertex **then**

        i. Find the smallest j such that either
            A. v_{i-j} is not a 1-1, 2-1, or 3-1 vertex, or
            B. v_{i-j} is a predecessor of v_i
        ii. form a pair containing vertices v_{i-j} and v_i
        iii. $i = i - j - 1$

    end while

    □

Algorithm 8.1 *Form-Pairs* assigns every 2-2, 1-2, and 1-3 vertex v_i to one pair, where $3 \leq i \leq n'-1$. Vertex v_2 (which is a 1-1 or 1-2 or 1-3 vertex) may or may not be paired with another vertex; this depends on both the graph and the *st*-numbering. In Step 4(c), every 1-2 or 1-3 vertex v_i is always paired with vertex v_{i-1}. If vertex v_i is a 2-2 vertex, then Algorithm 8.1 *Form-Pairs* pairs v_i with some vertex v_j, where j is the highest number less than i so that v_j is one of the following types:

- 1-1 vertex which is also a predecessor of v_i

- 2-1 vertex which is also a predecessor of v_i

- 3-1 vertex which is also a predecessor of v_i

- 2-2 vertex

- vertex

- vertex.

The algorithm pairs all 2-2, 1-2, and 1-3 vertices, except possibly for v_2, since v_2 and v_3 cannot be 3-1 vertices. Now we discuss how to place the pairs on the grid. Let $\langle v_i, v_j \rangle$ be a pair $(j < i)$ formed by Algorithm 8.1 *Form-Pairs*. Vertex v_j might be a predecessor of v_i, or the two vertices might not have a predecessor-successor relationship. If the latter is the case, they are called *independent*. Various types of pairs are drawn in a different fashion as follows:

1. If v_i is a **2-2 vertex**, then we distinguish three cases for v_j:

   (a) v_j is a **2-2 vertex**. Here we have a column pair.

      - If v_j is a predecessor of v_i, then there is a column that is closed by placing v_j (i.e., an edge incident to v_j is completed and the rest of the column originally allocated to this edge is now free). Hence, the column can be reused, as shown in Figure 8.1.a.
      - If v_i and v_j are independent, then we can always reuse one column regardless of the arrangement of the columns of the incoming edges of v_i and v_j (see Figures 8.1.b and 8.1.c for two examples). Notice that in this case, in order to reuse a column, we sometimes have to place v_i in a row below v_j. This placement is possible since v_i and v_j are independent. One can visualize this case by exchanging the labels of v_i and v_j in Figure 8.1.b.

   (b) v_j is a **1-1, 2-1, or 3-1 vertex** and a predecessor of v_i.

      - If v_j is a 2-1 or 3-1 vertex, a column can be reused (i.e., we have a column pair), as shown in Figure 8.1.d.
      - Otherwise, if v_j is a 1-1 vertex, then the two vertices can share the same row (i.e., we have a row pair) as shown in Figure 8.1.e.

(c) v_j is a **1-2 or 1-3 vertex**. Here there are two subcases:

- If v_j is a predecessor of v_i, then v_i can be placed in the same row as v_j, that is, we have a row pair. In fact, it can be placed at the intersection point of the row of v_j and the edge coming from the other predecessor of v_i, as shown in Figure 8.2.a. Notice that because of the pairing algorithm, the other predecessor of v_i, say v_k, is such that $k < j$.

- If v_i and v_j are independent, then we have a column pair. In fact, vertex v_j can be placed in the row immediately above the row of v_i, thus reusing the column of the edge terminating at v_i, as shown in Figure 8.2.b.

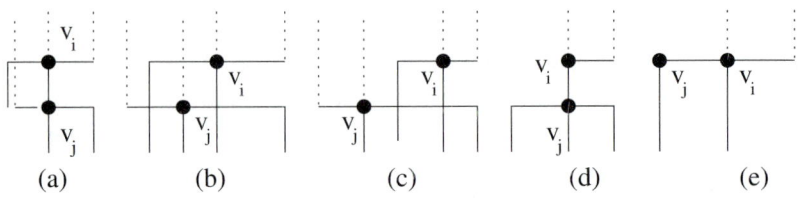

(a)   (b)   (c)   (d)   (e)

Figure 8.1: Vertex v_i is of type 2-2 and a column is reused when: (a) v_j is a 2-2 vertex and v_i's predecessor; (b),(c) v_j is independent of v_i; (d) v_j is 2-1 or 3-1 and v_i's predecessor; (e) a row is shared when v_j is 1-1.

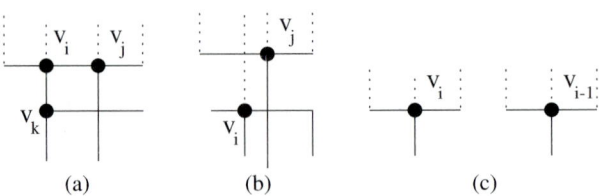

(a)   (b)   (c)

Figure 8.2: (a) Vertices v_i and v_j share the same row. (b) Vertex v_j is placed in a row above v_i and a column is reused. (c) Vertices v_i and v_{i-1} are independent and share the same row.

2. If v_i is a **1-2 or 1-3 vertex**, then it is always paired with vertex v_{i-1}. We distinguish four cases for v_{i-1}:

(a) If v_{i-1} is a **2-2, 2-1, or 3-1 vertex** then we have a column pair. Vertex v_i is placed in a row above the row of v_{i-1} and a column is reused as described in Cases 1(a) and 1(b) above.

(b) If v_{i-1} is a **1-2 or 1-3 vertex** and vertices v_i and v_{i-1} are independent, then we have a row pair. In this case, vertices v_i and v_{i-1} are placed in the same row, as shown in Figure 8.2.c.

(c) If v_{i-1} is a **1-2 or 1-3 vertex**, v_{i-1} is v_i's predecessor, and both of the following conditions hold, then we have a row pair.

- Either v_i is connected later to another vertex, say v_j, which is 1-1, 1-2, or 1-3; or v_i is connected later to a 2-2 vertex v_j, which is either the second vertex of a pair of type 1(c) shown in Figure 8.2.a, or the second vertex of a pair of type 1(b) shown in Figure 8.1.e.

- The edge (v_{i-1}, v_i) has not absorbed any 1-1 vertices from the original graph G.

In this case, v_i and v_{i-1} are placed in the same row, as shown in Figure 8.3. We only have to ensure that edge e will connect to v_j in the future, as shown in Figure 8.3. Every edge is bent at most twice. Also notice that the total number of bends for both v_i and v_{i-1} is the same as if these two vertices were placed in two different rows.

(d) The final case is when v_{i-1} is a **1-2 or 1-3 vertex**, v_{i-1} is a predecessor of v_i and at least one of the two conditions described in the previous case does not hold. As can be seen by Figures 8.4.a and b, although v_i and v_{i-1} are placed in two different rows, a row is still reused. So v_{i-1} and v_i form a row pair.

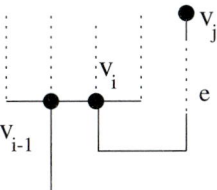

Figure 8.3: Vertices v_i and v_{i-1} share the same row and edge e will connect to an appropriate future vertex, as described in pair type 2(c).

Recall that in order to simplify our description, we absorbed some degree two vertices. After the drawing of G' is complete, we need to restore those vertices. They can usually be placed on bends or on grid points (i.e., points

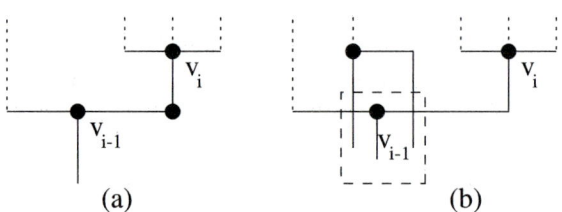

Figure 8.4: (a) Vertex v_{i-1} shares the same row with a 1-1 vertex which is placed on the bend of edge (v_{i-1}, v_i). (b) Vertex v_i shares the same row with the vertex which will be placed next in the drawing.

of integer coordinates that do not have a crossing). In the extreme case where this is not possible, new rows are introduced as needed. Notice that the pairing of the vertices of G' "transfers" to G. All the other vertices of the drawing maintain their positions, that is the rows and columns in which they are placed.

Algorithm 8.2 *Four-Orthogonal* presents a formal description of the technique.

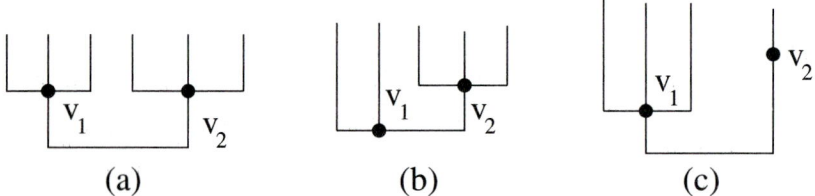

Figure 8.5: v_1 and v_2 placed by Algorithm 8.2 *Four-Orthogonal*: (a) v_1 and v_2 can be placed in the same row; (b) the placement of v_1 and v_2 when v_1 has degree three; (c) the placement of v_1 when v_2 is assigned to a pair.

Figure 8.6.a shows a regular degree four graph with 13 vertices and Figure 8.6.b shows the orthogonal grid drawing that the algorithm produces for it. Notice that vertices 1 and 2, 3 and 4, and 6 and 7 are placed in the same row. Also, the pairs $\langle 10, 8 \rangle$, $\langle 5, 4 \rangle$, and $\langle 3, 2 \rangle$ reuse one column each. A total of four bends are saved in the rows where vertices 3 and 4, and 6 and 7 are placed. The drawing has height 11 and width 10.

Next we prove two intermediate results about the number of columns and rows of the drawings produced by Algorithm 8.2 *Four-Orthogonal*.

Algorithm 8.2 *Four-Orthogonal*

> *Input:*
>   biconnected graph G of maximum degree four
> *Output:* orthogonal grid drawing of G

1. Compute an *st*-numbering of G.

2. Run Algorithm 8.1 *Form-Pairs* and let G' be the resulting condensed graph.

3. (a) **if** v_2 does not belong to a pair in which it shares a row with another vertex, **then** place vertices v_1 and v_2 in the same row (see Figure 8.5.a).

   (b) **if** v_1 and/or v_2 have degree less than four, **then** the placement of v_1 and v_2 might require one or two rows. Figure 8.5.b shows the case where v_1 had degree three and v_2 has degree four. Notice that in this case, there is only one bend along edge (v_1, v_2).

   (c) **if** v_2 is assigned to a pair, **then** we place v_1 as shown in Figure 8.5.c (if v_1 has degree four). Vertex v_2 will be placed when its pair is considered.

4. **repeat**

   (a) Consider the next vertex v_i according to the *st*-numbering of G'.

   (b) **if** v_i has not already been placed, **then**:

      i. **if** vertex v_i is unassigned, **then** place v_i in a new row. Connect v_i with each vertex v_j ($j < i$), such that (v_j, v_i) is a directed edge of G'. Allocate as many columns as needed, depending on v_i's outdegree.

      ii. **if** vertex v_i is assigned to a pair, **then** place v_i along with the other vertex in the pair, following the placement rules described above for the specific type of pair.

   until the only remaining vertex is $v_{n'}$.

5. Insert $v_{n'}$ in a new row. **if** $v_{n'}$ is of degree four, **then** there is an incoming edge that enters $v_{n'}$ from the top and bends twice. This edge is chosen to be the one that connects to $v_{n'-1}$.

6. Restore the degree two vertices of G that were absorbed in Algorithm 8.1 *Form-Pairs*, as described above.

□

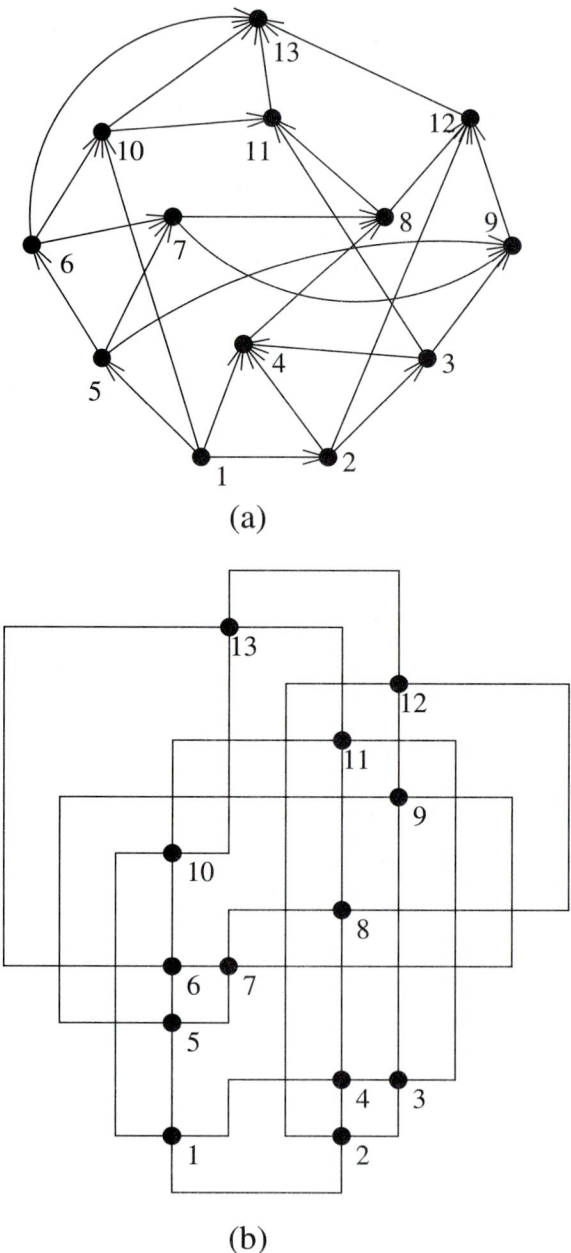

Figure 8.6: (a) *st*-numbering of an example graph. (b) Orthogonal grid drawing of the graph shown in part (a) produced by Algorithm 8.2 *Four-Orthogonal*.

Lemma 8.1 *Suppose that there is a total of p_1 column pairs, p_2 unassigned degree two vertices, p_3 unassigned degree three vertices in G, and that $k_1 = p_1 + p_2 + \frac{p_3}{2}$. Then the width of the drawing of G output by Algorithm 8.2 Four-Orthogonal is at most $n + 1 - k_1$.*

Proof: When we place a vertex v of $G = (V, E)$ with $outdeg(v)$ outgoing edges, we increase the width of the current drawing by $outdeg(v) - 1$. Since all vertices of G other than v_n have at least one outgoing edge, the width of the drawing can be at most

$$\sum_{v \in V - \{v_n\}} (outdeg(v) - 1) \le m - n + 1.$$

For each one of the p_1 column pairs of G, there is exactly one vertex of the pair which reuses some column for one of its outgoing edges. This means that the width of the drawing is at most $m - n + 1 - p_1$. Let us assume that there is a total of p_3 unassigned degree three vertices of G (these are 2-1 vertices), and a total of p_2 unassigned degree two vertices of G (this includes the vertices that were temporarily removed from G). It follows that the total number of edges of G can be at most

$$m \le 2n - p_2 - \frac{p_3}{2}.$$

If we use this bound for the edges of G in the above expression for the width of the drawing of G, it follows that the width is at most

$$2n - n + 1 - (p_1 + p_2 + \frac{p_3}{2}),$$

or $n + 1 - k_1$, where $k_1 = p_1 + p_2 + \frac{p_3}{2}$.   □

Lemma 8.2 *Suppose that there are k_2 row pairs of vertices in G. Then the height of the drawing of G output by Algorithm 8.2 Four-Orthogonal is at most $n + 1 - k_2$, when $k_2 \ge 1$, or n when $k_2 = 0$.*

Proof: Suppose that we have a total of k_2 row pairs in G. Vertex v_n requires one extra row if it is of degree four. Vertex v_1 also requires an extra row if it is of degree four and is not able to share the same row with v_2. All the other vertices of G are placed in separate rows. Hence, the height of the final embedding of G is at most $n + 1 - k_2$.

If there are no row pairs in the graph (i.e., $k_2 = 0$), then the placement of vertices v_1 and v_2 requires at most two rows (see Figures 8.5.a and b), according to Step 3 of Algorithm 8.2 *Four-Orthogonal*. Since vertex v_1 does not require any extra row, it follows that the height G is n when $k_2 = 0$. $\square$

Next we refine our analysis of the area requirement of Algorithm 8.2 *Four-Orthogonal*. In order to obtain worst case bounds, we consider graphs that contain the maximum number of edges, namely regular graphs of degree four.

The graph may have at most one 4-0 vertex and at most one 0-4 vertex. Let us assume that the graph has one 4-0 vertex, one 0-4 vertex, and x_{3-1} 3-1 vertices. Intuitively, in order to maximize the number of 3-1 vertices the following has to occur: (a) the number of the remaining types of vertices (other than 3-1) is minimized, and (b) the remaining vertices have as many outgoing edges as possible. This implies that the remaining vertices must be of type 1-3 only. Let x_{1-3} be their number. Since the number of outgoing edges is equal to the number of incoming edges, we have

$$4 + 3x_{1-3} + x_{3-1} = x_{1-3} + 3x_{3-1} + 4.$$

It also holds that

$$x_{3-1} + x_{1-3} + 2 = n.$$

Solving this system of equations we obtain that the number of vertices of type 4-0, 0-4, and 3-1 is at most $\lfloor \frac{n+2}{2} \rfloor$. This implies the following lemma:

Lemma 8.3 *Consider a biconnected graph of maximum degree four along with an st-numbering. Then the number of vertices of type 4-0, 0-4, and 3-1 is at most $\lfloor \frac{n+2}{2} \rfloor$.*

We are ready now to discuss the properties of the drawings produced by Algorithm 8.2 *Four-Orthogonal*.

Theorem 8.1 *Let G be an n-vertex biconnected graph with maximum degree four. Algorithm 8.2 Four-Orthogonal constructs an orthogonal grid drawing Γ of G in $O(n)$ time with the following properties:*

- *The area of Γ is at most $0.77n^2 + O(n)$*

- *The total number of bends in Γ is at most $2n + 4$*

- *No edge has more than two bends.*

Proof: From Lemmas 8.1 and 8.2, the area of the drawing of $G = (V, E)$ output by Algorithm 8.2 *Four-Orthogonal* is at most: $(n+1-k_1) \times (n+1-k_2)$. Also, the total number of vertices in G of degree two, three, and those with degree four that are of type either 1-3 or 2-2, is at least $\lceil \frac{n-2}{2} \rceil$ (see Lemma 8.3). Since all vertices of this type are either paired (see Algorithm 8.1 *Form-Pairs*) or contribute to the reduction of the number of columns (see proof of Lemma 8.1), it holds that $k_1 + k_2 \geq \lceil \frac{n-2}{4} \rceil$. The area is maximized when $k_1 = k_2 = \frac{n-2}{8}$. Thus the area is at most

$$\left(\frac{7n}{8} + \frac{5}{4}\right) \times \left(\frac{7n}{8} + \frac{5}{4}\right) = 0.77n^2 + 2.18n + 1.56 \approx 0.77n^2.$$

Each vertex v inserted in the drawing introduces $deg(v) - 2$ bends, with the exception of vertices v_1, v_2, v_n, and the vertices which form a pair of the type shown in Figure 8.3. In that figure, we can see that one of the two 1-3 vertices (v_{i-1}) introduces one bend, and the other one (v_i) introduces three bends. When we have pairs like this, we may assume, for the sake of the analysis, that each one of the two 1-3 vertices introduces two bends, since the combined total is still four bends. Vertices v_1 and v_2 introduce $deg(v_1) + deg(v_2) - 2$ bends and v_n introduces at most four bends. Hence, the total number of bends is at most

$$\sum_{v \in V} (deg(v) - 2) + 4 = 2m - 2n + 4.$$

Since the number of edges can be at most $2n$ (if our graph is regular of degree four), it follows that the total number of bends introduced by Algorithm 8.2 *Four-Orthogonal* is at most $2n + 4$.

Finally, notice that because of the construction of the drawing, no edge bends more than twice.

Now we discuss the time complexity of Algorithm 8.2 *Four-Orthogonal*. Since new rows and columns are continually inserted in the drawing, it is important to be able to maintain and update the data structures efficiently. The insertion of new rows poses no problems, since they are always inserted on top of the existing current drawing. New columns however are arbitrarily inserted anywhere in the current drawing. For this reason, we need to be able to keep track of the relative order among all the columns. We use the data structure and algorithms for the order maintenance problem proposed by Dietz and Sleator [DS87], that support the following operations in $O(1)$ time:

- *Insert(x,y):* Insert item y after item x. Item y must not be in the list already.

- *Delete(x):* Delete item x from the list.

- *Order(x,y):* Return true if item x is before item y in the list, otherwise return false.

This implies that the total running time of Algorithm 8.2 *Four-Orthogonal* is linear.   □

In the next section, we will discuss how to extend the results of this section to simply connected graphs. In order to accomplish this, we need to reduce the bound on the total number of bends to $2n + 2$ with a minor adjustment of the drawing. In the rest of this section, we discuss practical issues such as using a simpler data structure, the expected number of bends/area, and the effects of *st*-numberings on the resulting drawings.

As we discussed in the proof of the above theorem, the time complexity assumes the use of the Dietz and Sleator data structure, which is complicated. Alternatively, the use of a simple balanced binary search tree data structure will suffice for updates and column order queries. However, the time complexity of the algorithm will increase to $O(n \log n)$, since each such operation will require $O(\log n)$ time.

In practice, the number of bends in drawings produced by Algorithm 8.2 *Four-Orthogonal* is expected to be less than $2n + 4$:

- When a 2-2 vertex is placed in the same row as its 1-2 or 1-3 predecessor, then two bends and one column are saved. We call these *good* row pairs.

- Two bends and one column are saved in the case where we have a pair of two 1-3 vertices, say v_i and v_j, and v_j is placed in a row above v_i. Thus, if the vertex which is placed in the row of v_j is a 2-2, 2-1, or 3-1 type and has v_j as its predecessor, two extra bends are saved. We also call these good row pairs. We will use the existence of at least one good row pair in the next section in order to improve the obtained bounds.

- If we have a pair of type 2(c) in which the second vertex is 1-2, then the placement of this pair, as described in Figure 8.3, will save one bend.

This means that we expect the total number of bends to be less than the upper bound of Theorem 8.1. Also, note that the area required by the drawings produced by Algorithm 8.2 *Four-Orthogonal*, is typically better than what Theorem 8.1 claims for two reasons:

- The total number of 1-1, 1-2, 1-3, 2-2, and 2-1 type vertices is often larger than $\frac{n}{2}$.

- In the proof of Theorem 8.1, we only considered vertices of type 1-1, 1-2, 1-3, 2-2, and 2-1 to determine the total area. When pairs are formed, we typically expect some vertices of type 3-1 to participate as the first vertex in some column pairs of type 1(b) or 2(a). If this is the case, then the total number of pairs is further increased.

In fact, experimentation on the performance of Algorithm 8.2 *Four-Orthogonal* revealed that the area and shape of the produced drawings depends heavily on the specific *st*-numbering that is employed [PT95].

- One *st*-numbering algorithm (resembling Depth First Search) produced drawings in which the height was larger than the width, but the area was no more than $0.65n^2$.

- A second *st*-numbering algorithm (resembling Breadth First Search) produced more squarish drawings, with shorter edges, but the column reuse was not as good as in the case of the first type. As a result, the area was larger, but never more than $0.72n^2$.

Finally, in all these experiments the number of bends was at most $2n$, and for large graphs it was significantly lower than $2n$. Figures 8.7 and 8.8 show two drawings constructed by an implementation of Algorithm 8.2 *Four-Orthogonal*.

If the given graph has maximum degree three, then one can obtain better bounds for the area and bends of the drawings. Namely, there is a linear-time algorithm that produces drawings with at most $\lfloor \frac{n}{2} \rfloor + 3$ bends, and at most $\frac{1}{4}n^2$ area. Moreover, there is at most one edge that bends twice [PT95, PT97c, PT98].

8.2 Extension to Connected Graphs

In this section, we show how to extend the above approach to all connected graphs. The technique is based on breaking the graph into its blocks, which has been successfully employed by various authors (see e.g., [BK94, PT95, TT89b]). The *block cutvertex tree* of graph G has a B-node for each block of G, and a C-node for each cutvertex of G. Edges in the block cutvertex tree connect each B-node μ to the C-nodes associated with the cutvertices in the block of μ.

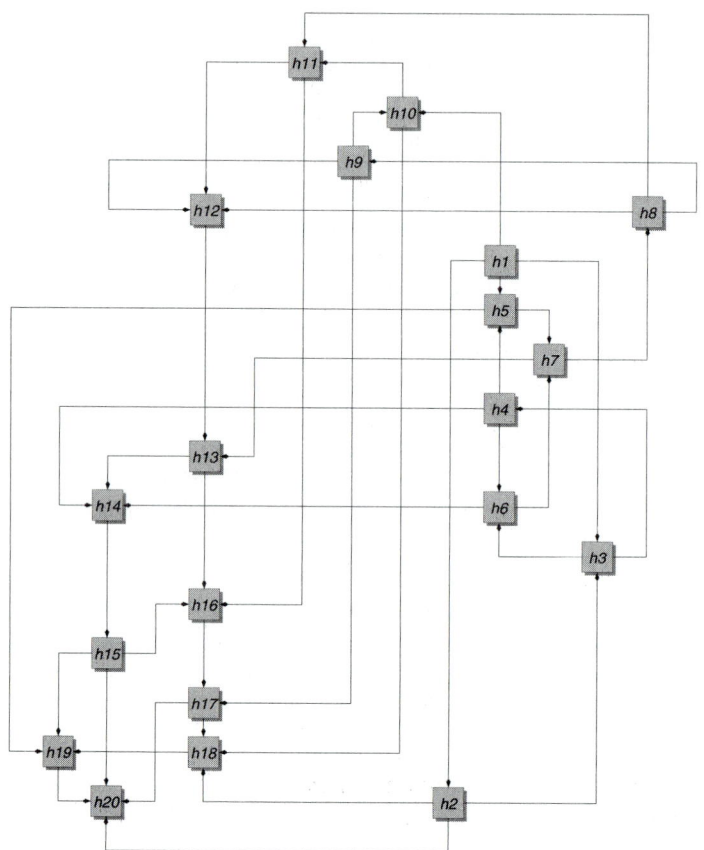

Figure 8.7: Orthogonal drawing constructed by an implementation of Algorithm 8.2 *Four-Orthogonal.* (Courtesy of A. Papakostas.)

In order to extend the bounds obtained in the previous section to one-connected graphs, we have to guarantee that when Algorithm 8.2 *Four-Orthogonal* draws any block the height and width of the drawing is at most n and the number of bends is at most $2n + 2$.

Notice that in the worst case it is possible for Algorithm 8.2 *Four-Orthogonal* to produce a drawing with $2n + 4$ bends and/or width $n + 1$. This can happen only if the following hold:

- The graph is regular of degree four

- There is no good row pair in the graph. Recall that good row pairs save one column and two bends, as described in the paragraph following the proof of Theorem 8.1.

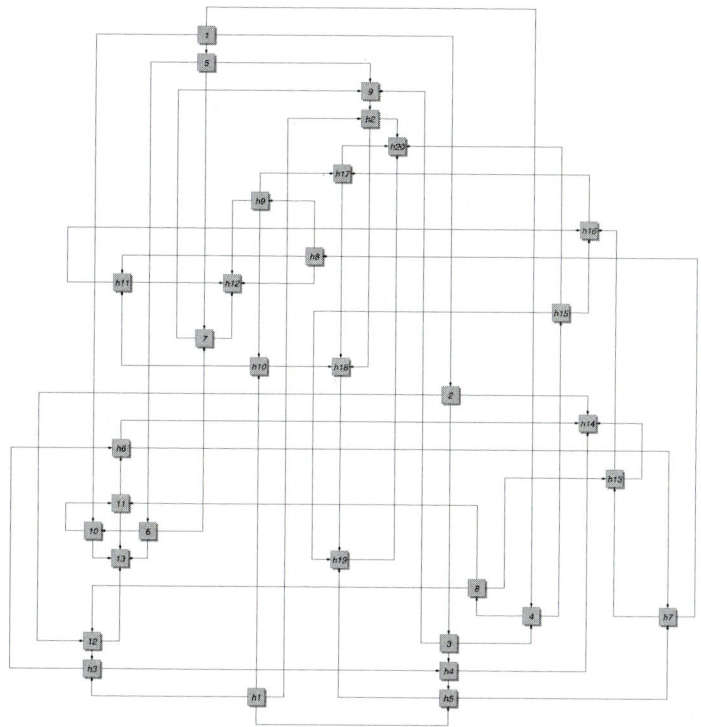

Figure 8.8: Orthogonal drawing constructed by an implementation of Algorithm 8.2 *Four-Orthogonal*. (Courtesy of A. Papakostas.)

We now show that it is possible to avoid these two cases. Consider a regular biconnected graph G with degree four. Let us assume that after running Algorithm 8.1 *Form-Pairs* on G, there are no good row pairs. In this case, the drawing of G, produced by Algorithm 8.2 *Four-Orthogonal*, may have $2n + 4$ bends and $n + 1$ width (this is especially true if there are column pairs). Here we describe a technique which forces a good row pair in the pairing of the vertices of G. The target is to generate at least one good row pair even at the price of breaking other pairs.

Suppose there is no good row pair. We scan the vertices of G following the st-numbering, until we find the first vertex v that is not a 1-3 vertex. We distinguish two cases for v:

1. Vertex v is a **2-2 vertex**. Let u be the highest numbered predecessor of v. Vertices v and u do not belong to the same pair, since in that case, we would have a good row pair. We break the pair that v is in,

and pair v with u. This new pair is of type 1(c) (the case shown in Figure 8.2.a). Notice that in order to form the new pair, we have to break the pair that u was previously assigned to. However, doing so will not increase the width or the total number of bends.

2. Vertex v is a **3-1 vertex**. We break any pair that v might have been assigned to with another higher numbered vertex. We check the highest numbered 1-3 predecessor of v, say u (notice that, since v has three incoming edges, u cannot be vertex v_2). Vertex u has been paired with another 1-3 vertex, and u is the second vertex in that pair, as a result of the running of Algorithm 8.1 *Form-Pairs*. This pair is now treated as a pair of type 2(d), and v will be placed in the same row as u.

From the above, it follows that, if we have a regular degree four biconnected graph G, then we can place one 2-2 or 3-1 vertex in the same row as its highest numbered predecessor (vertex u in the above description). We accomplish this by forming a new row pair of type either 1(c) (u is the first vertex and v is the second vertex of the pair), or 2(d) (u is the second vertex of the pair, v becomes an unassigned vertex and is placed in u's row). In either case, the row pair is a good row pair and the resulting drawing has at most $2n + 2$ bends. Also, the width of the drawing is at most n. Notice that although we might have to break two existing pairs, the new good row pair that we form saves one row, one column, and two bends. Therefore we have:

Theorem 8.2 *Let G be an n-vertex biconnected graph with maximum degree four. The above variation of Algorithm 8.2 Four-Orthogonal constructs an orthogonal grid drawing Γ of G in $O(n)$ time with the following properties:*

- *The area of Γ is at most $0.77n^2 + O(n)$*

- *The total number of bends in Γ is at most $2n + 2$*

- *No edge has more than two bends.*

Algorithm 8.2 *Four-Orthogonal* can be extended to connected graphs of maximum degree four. Suppose that we have such a graph G. We split G into its blocks and produce the block cutvertex tree of G. Next, we apply the variation of Algorithm 8.2 *Four-Orthogonal* as described in Theorem 8.2 on each block separately. Then we put the blocks together to form the final drawing. We use an inductive approach for constructing the drawing of G.

In the base case, we apply Algorithm 8.2 *Four-Orthogonal* on a biconnected graph. In the induction step we consider a subtree of the block cutvertex tree of G and we split the subtree into a block G_0 (i.e., the root of the subtree) and the connected (but not necessarily biconnected) subgraphs $G_1, G_2, \ldots G_q$. According to the induction hypothesis, each G_i is already drawn. Hence, the process of drawing G reduces to drawing G_0 and merging each G_i at the appropriate places.

Figure 8.9 shows how the blocks are placed together. The proof of correctness of this technique is rather long and is based on maintaining some invariants during the drawing process. A detailed description of the technique and its proof can be found in [PT97c, PT98].

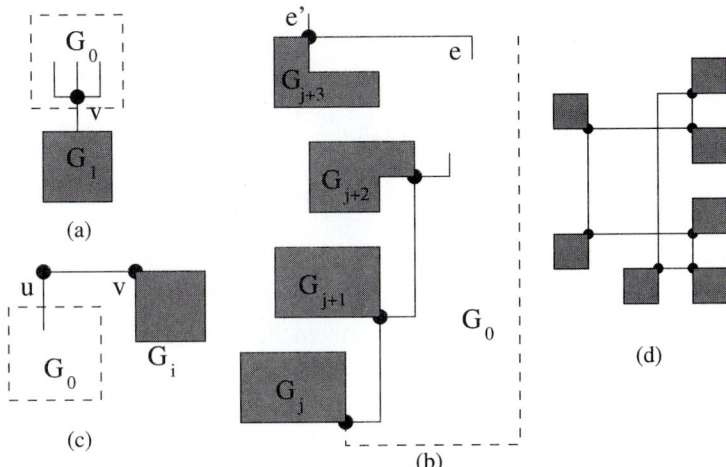

Figure 8.9: (a) G_0 continues the drawing of G_1. (b) Examples of subgraph rotation, placement and column reuse. (c) Reusing row(s) when G_i is connected to G_0 through a bridge. (d) Drawing of a graph whose G_i's are small size graphs (each G_i here is a triangle).

Theorem 8.3 *Let G be an n-vertex connected graph with maximum degree four. We can construct an orthogonal grid drawing Γ of G in $O(n)$ time with the following properties:*

- *The area of Γ is at most $0.77n^2 + O(n)$*

- *The total number of bends in Γ is at most $2n + 2$*

- *No edge has more than two bends.*

The technique of splitting a connected graph G into its blocks has been used in several algorithms in order to prove upper bounds [BK94, PT95, PT97c, PT98, TT89b]. Due to the nature of Algorithm 8.2 *Four-Orthogonal,* we can apply a simpler strategy in order to obtain orthogonal grid drawings of connected graphs using an *augmentation technique:*

1. Insert a new (fictitious) vertex t_S into graph G and connect it with all leaf blocks of the block cutvertex tree of G. Connect t_S to vertices, preferably of degree less than four, of each leaf block. The augmented graph G' is biconnected.

2. Compute an st-numbering of G' choosing as the source a vertex, preferably of degree less than four, and sink t_S.

3. Next remove t_S. Notice that the vertices of G are numbered so that there is one source and many sinks (equal to the number of leaf blocks in the block cutvertex tree of G).

4. Finally run Algorithm 8.2 *Four-Orthogonal* on G.

The above algorithm produces drawings whose height, width, and number of bends increase proportionally to the number of sinks, in the worst case. Hence, the upper bounds of Theorem 8.3 do not hold. However, it is much easier to implement.

8.3   Drawing Graphs of Degree Higher than Four

The above techniques can be extended to draw graphs of degree higher than four, by expanding each vertex of high degree into a chain of vertices of degree four, as discussed in [BK94]. Special care is needed to number such vertices consecutively and not to pair them during the pairing step of Algorithm 8.2 *Four-Orthogonal.* Unfortunately, the resulting drawings tend to be unnecessarily tall.

To overcome this problem, we present a technique that is specifically designed for drawing graphs of degree higher than four. Each vertex is drawn as a *rectangular box.* We call the boundary edges of a box *sides.* Figure 8.10.a shows a box with its four sides, *top, left, bottom,* and *right.* Each side has a number of *connectors* where all the edges of the graph incident to the vertex are attached. Each connector point can be incident to only one edge (except for the four corner connectors, which can be incident to two edges).

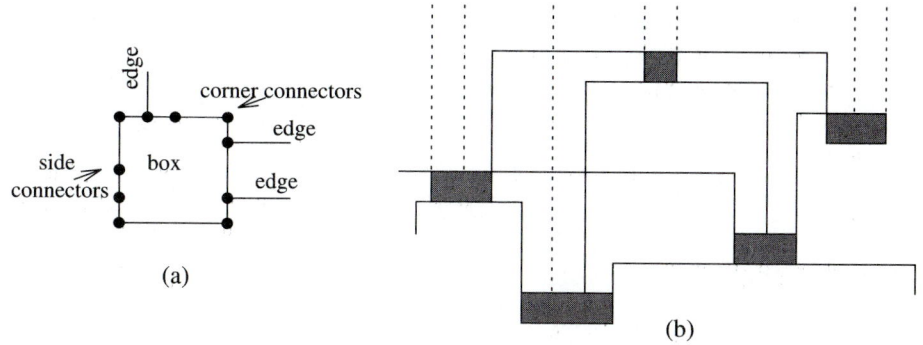

Figure 8.10: (a) A box with its sides and connectors. (b) Part of an orthogonal drawing produced by the simple algorithm described in this section.

When a box is used to represent a vertex in an orthogonal grid drawing, its sides lie on grid lines and its connectors have integer coordinates. Also, the perimeter of the box is sufficiently large, so that all the incident edges can be attached to different connectors of the box boundary. We present a simple algorithm for producing orthogonal grid drawings. The algorithm inserts the vertices in the drawing, one vertex at a time. For simplicity, we assume that the given graph is biconnected, and that an st-numbering has been computed on the graph. As before, the edges of the graph are directed from lower to higher numbered vertices. The size of each vertex v is decided when v is the next vertex to be inserted in the drawing. The box size depends on the number of incoming and outgoing edges of v.

All outgoing edges of vertex v are attached to the top side connectors (see Figure 8.11.a). This implies that the width of the box is at least equal to the number of outgoing edges of the vertex. If the box has only one

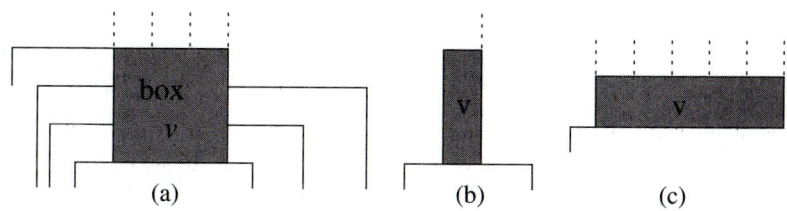

Figure 8.11: Various types of box v: (a) Seven incoming and four outgoing edges; (b) only one outgoing edge; (c) only one incoming edge.

outgoing edge, we still use two columns for the box (i.e., a box with width one, see Figure 8.11.b). We also use a box of width one for the sink.

The incoming edges of v are split between the right and left side connectors. More specifically, if v has $indeg(v)$ incoming edges, then $\lfloor \frac{indeg(v)}{2} \rfloor$ incoming edges are attached to the right side and the remaining $\lceil \frac{indeg(v)}{2} \rceil$ incoming edges are attached to the left side connectors of box v (see Figure 8.11.a). If v has only one incoming edge, we still use two rows for the box (i.e., a box with height one, see Figure 8.11.c). We also use a box of height one for the source. Each incoming edge of v originally has vertical direction, since it is an outgoing edge of some other box which has already been placed. Then it bends only once, and finally assumes horizontal direction before it is attached to the appropriate side connector of box v.

At most $\lceil \frac{indeg(v)}{2} \rceil$ new rows and $outdeg(v)$ (i.e., number of outgoing edges of v) new columns need to be opened up when the algorithm inserts the next vertex v. Vertices with only one outgoing (incoming) edge are the exception, since two new columns (rows) need to open up for their boxes.

Before we describe how the boxes are placed, we give some definitions. If v is the next vertex to be inserted, we locate the incoming edges of v and the columns to which they are assigned. The vertices of the drawing where v's incoming edges come from, are v's *predecessors*. Let us first assume that $indeg(v)$ is even. Since all the columns of the current drawing are always ordered from left to right, there are two columns c_1 and c_2 holding the incoming edges e_1 and e_2, respectively, of v with the following properties:

- c_1 is to the left of c_2.

- There are $\frac{indeg(v)}{2} - 1$ columns holding incoming edges of v to the left of c_1.

- There are $\frac{indeg(v)}{2} - 1$ columns holding incoming edges of v to the right of c_2.

Edges e_1 and e_2 are called *median incoming edges* of vertex v; more specifically, e_1 is the *left median incoming edge* and e_2 is the *right median incoming edge* of v.

If $indeg(v)$ is odd, there is only one median incoming edge e. In this case, if c is the column holding e, then there are $\lfloor \frac{indeg(v)}{2} \rfloor$ columns holding incoming edges of v to the left and right of c. The function of the median incoming edge(s) is to establish where to split the incoming edges between the left and right side of v.

When the algorithm places vertex v, it first creates the box of v, and then it opens up the appropriate number of new columns between the median incoming edges of v. Next it opens up new rows above the current drawing, and places box v there. If v has only one median incoming edge, then the box of v is placed to the right of this edge. Figure 8.11.b shows some vertices placed by the above algorithm, as part of a larger drawing. If we are given an n-vertex m-edge biconnected graph, then the following theorem holds for the above algorithm:

Theorem 8.4 *Given a biconnected graph G with m edges, and an st-numbering, the above algorithm produces an orthogonal grid drawing Γ of G in $O(m)$ time with the following properties:*

- *The perimeter of each vertex is proportional to the degree of the vertex.*

- *The width of Γ is at most $m+n_{out1}$, and the height is at most $\frac{m}{2}+\frac{n_{odd}}{2}+n_{in1}+n_{in2}$, where n_{out1} is the number of vertices with one outgoing edge, n_{odd} is the number of vertices with an odd number of incoming edges, n_{in1} is the number of vertices with one incoming edge, and n_{in2} is the number of vertices with two incoming edges.*

- *Each edge has at most one bend.*

Proof: Similar to the proof of Theorem 8.1, we use the data structure and algorithms for the order maintenance problem proposed by Dietz and Sleator [DS87], that support the operations in $O(1)$ time. This means that the median incoming edge(s) can be computed in $O(indeg(v))$ time, using a linear-time median finding algorithm (see, e.g. [CLR90]), where v is the vertex that is being inserted. Hence, the total running time of the algorithm is $O(m)$.

The bounds on the area and the number of bends of the drawing follow from the above discussion. More specifically, the width is obtained by the total number of outgoing edges, which is m, and the fact that vertices with one outgoing edge require two columns. The height is obtained by observing that the number of rows is equal to half the total number of incoming edges, which is $\frac{m}{2}$, plus extra rows based on the following two facts: vertices with one or two incoming edges require two rows; a vertex v with an odd number of incoming edges requires $\frac{indeg(v)}{2}+\frac{1}{2}$ rows. $\square$

The reason that we do not attach any incoming edges to the bottom side of the vertex (except the corner connectors) is twofold. The incoming edges of a vertex are not necessarily on contiguous grid columns, and if some incoming edge were using the bottom side of v, then we would have to horizontally stretch the box which this edge was coming from (say u) to create space for the rest of the outgoing edges of u. This would create vertices whose perimeter might not be proportional to the degree of each vertex.

The above algorithm can be improved by allowing vertices to share (or reuse) rows and columns, in a fashion similar to the pairing technique described in Section 8.1. Also, vertices of degree one, two, and some vertices of degree three and four, are represented by points. The results of these improvements are summarized in the following theorem:

Theorem 8.5 *Let G be a graph with m edges, and an st-numbering, There exists an algorithm that produces an orthogonal grid drawing of G, by representing the high degree vertices as boxes. The running time of the algorithm is $O(m)$. The produced orthogonal drawing has the following properties:*

- *The perimeter of each vertex is proportional to the degree of the vertex.*

- *The width is at most $m - 1$.*

- *The height is at most $\frac{m}{2} + 2$.*

- *Each edge has at most one bend.*

- *The total number of bends is at most $m - n_{b-1}$, where n_{b-1} is the number of vertices with one outgoing edge.*

In Figure 8.12, we show an example of a 12-vertex and 31-edge nonplanar graph G, drawn by an algorithm with the properties described in Theorem 8.5. For more details on this approach and the proof of Theorem 8.5, see [PT97b].

8.4   Exercises

1. Draw the graph of Figure 8.6, using Algorithm 8.2 *Four-Orthogonal*, without doing the pairing step. Compare the area and the number of bends between the two drawings.

2. Use three different *st*-numberings for the vertices of the graph of Figure 8.6 and draw it using Algorithm 8.2 *Four-Orthogonal*. Observe the different properties of the drawings.

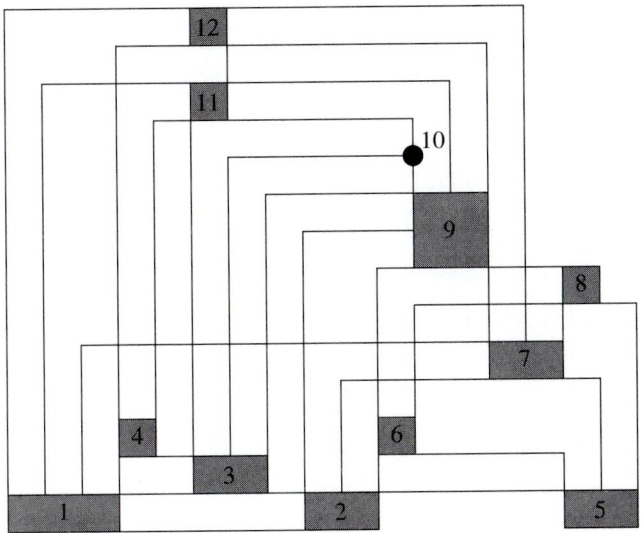

Figure 8.12: An orthogonal drawing of a graph of high degree.

3. Let G be a graph with an even number n of vertices. Suppose that G has $n/2$ vertices of degree three and $n/2$ vertices of degree four. Customize Algorithm 8.2 *Four-Orthogonal* so that it produces the best possible drawing (in terms of area and number of bends) for G. What are the bounds? Prove your answer.

4. Let G be an n-vertex planar graph with a given embedding. Modify Algorithm 8.2 *Four-Orthogonal* so that the produced drawing respects the given embedding. Prove bounds on the area and number of bends of the drawing.

5. Consider the algorithm described at the end of Section 8.2. Show that, choosing the lowest degree vertex from each leaf block to connect to the fictitious sink t_S, results in drawings with low area and few bends. In fact, assume that each leaf block has exactly one vertex of degree two. Prove bounds on the area and number of bends of the resulting drawing.

Chapter 9

Layered Drawings of Digraphs

This chapter presents the hierarchical approach for creating polyline drawings of digraphs with vertices arranged in horizontal layers, as outlined in Section 2.4. The method was presented in 1981 by Sugiyama, Tagawa and Toda [STT81], and several subsequent methods [GKNV93, Car80, ES91, GNV88, GM89, Mes88, MRH91, PT90] are closely related. These methods are highly intuitive and can be applied to any digraph, regardless of its graph-theoretic properties. Thus they are attractive in practice, and variations of them may be found in several existing systems. Examples are given in Figures 9.1–9.4.

The hierarchical approach consists of three steps:

- *Layer Assignment*: (described in Section 9.1) Assigns vertices to horizontal layers, and thus determines their y-coordinate.

- *Crossing Reduction*: (described in Section 9.2) Orders the vertices within each layer to reduce the number of edge crossings.

- *Horizontal Coordinate Assignment*: (described in Section 9.3) Determines an x-coordinate for each vertex.

If the input digraph contains directed cycles, then a preprocessing step is needed:

- *Cycle Removal*: (described in Section 9.4) Temporarily reverses the direction of a subset of the edges to make the digraph acyclic.

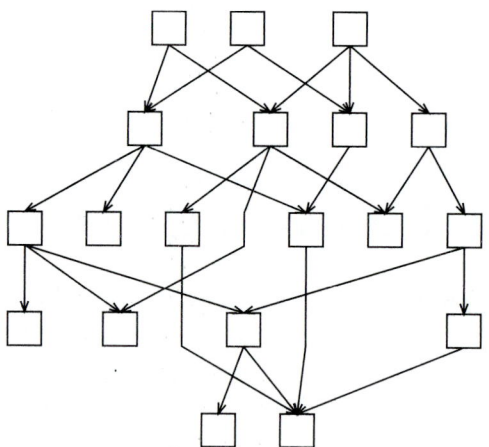

Figure 9.1: A layered drawing constructed by `D-Abductor`. (Courtesy of K. Misue.)

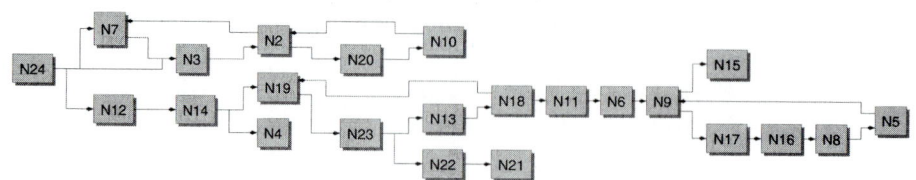

Figure 9.2: A layered drawing created by the `Tom Sawyer Toolkit`. (Courtesy of Tom Sawyer Software.)

267

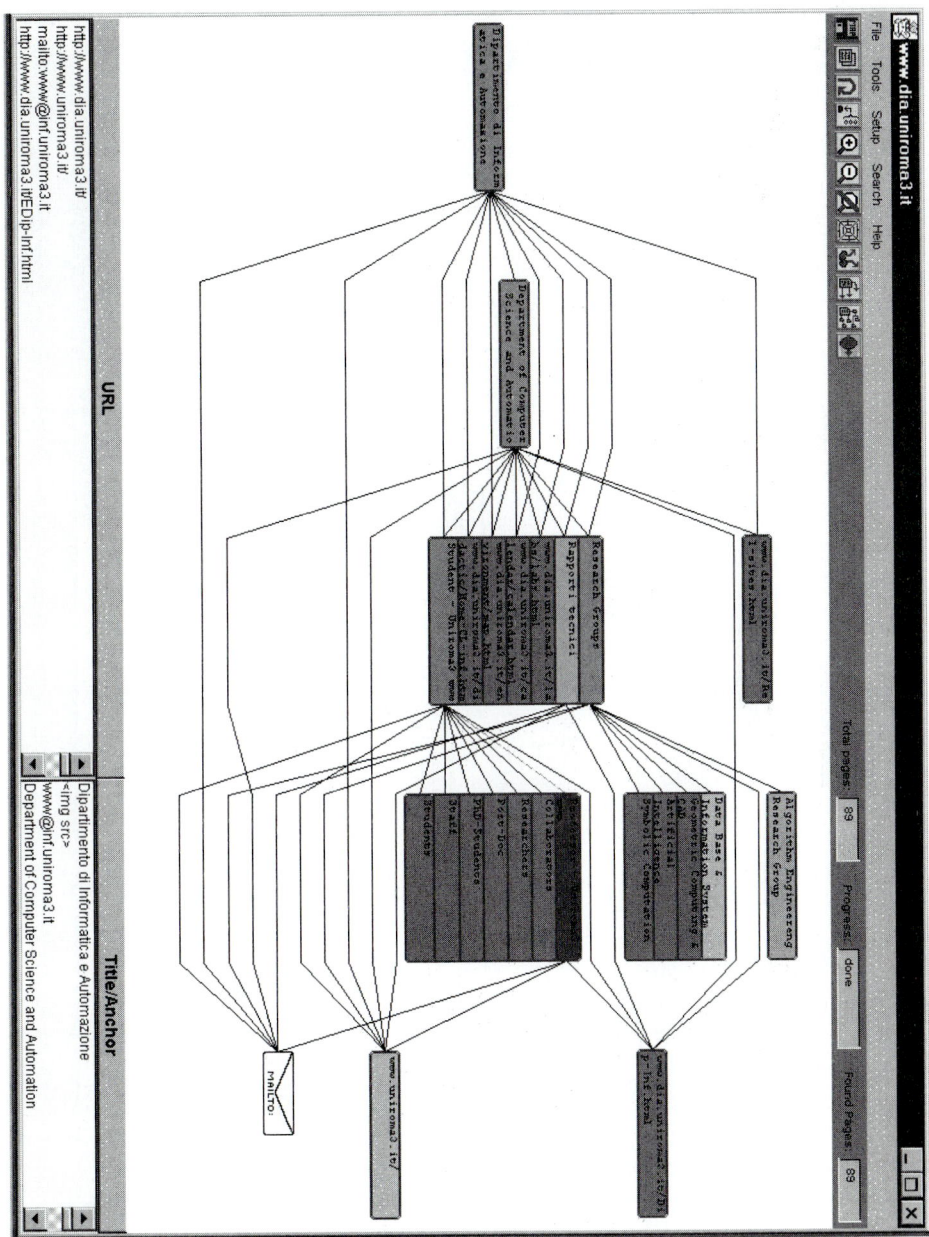

Figure 9.3: A layered drawing created by `Ptolomaeus` software. This represents the structure of a web site. (Courtesy of R. Lillo and F. Vernacotola.)

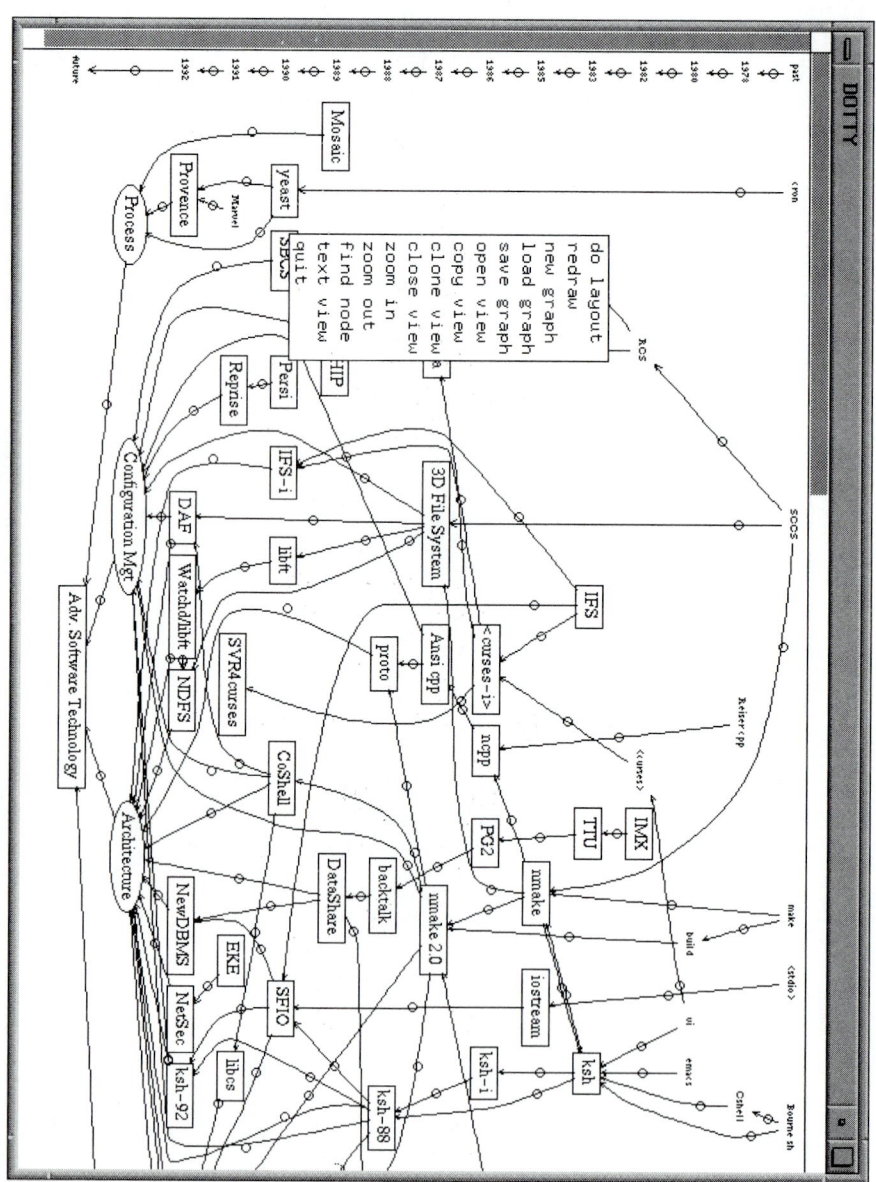

Figure 9.4: A layered drawing constructed by dotty. (Courtesy of S. North.) Observe that polyline edges are converted to splines.

9.1 Layer Assignment

The target of this step is to assign a y-coordinate to each vertex.

To discuss the issues involved in layer assignment, some terminology is required. Suppose that $G = (V, E)$ is an acyclic digraph. A *layering* of G is a partition of V into subsets L_1, L_2, ..., L_h, such that if $(u, v) \in E$, where $u \in L_i$ and $v \in L_j$, then $i > j$. An acyclic digraph with a layering is a *layered digraph*. The *height* of a layered digraph is the number h of layers. We also say that the digraph is an *h-layered digraph*. The *width* of the digraph is the number of vertices in the largest layer, that is, $\max_{1 \leq i \leq h} |L_i|$. The *span* of an edge (u, v) with $u \in L_i$ and $v \in L_j$ is $i - j$. The digraph is *proper* if no edge has a span greater than one.

Note that the concept of layering of an acylic digraph is related to topological numbering and sorting (see Section 4.1).

Layered digraphs normally adopt the *layered drawing* convention. More specifically, we draw vertices in layer L_i on the horizontal line $y = i$, as shown in Figure 9.5.

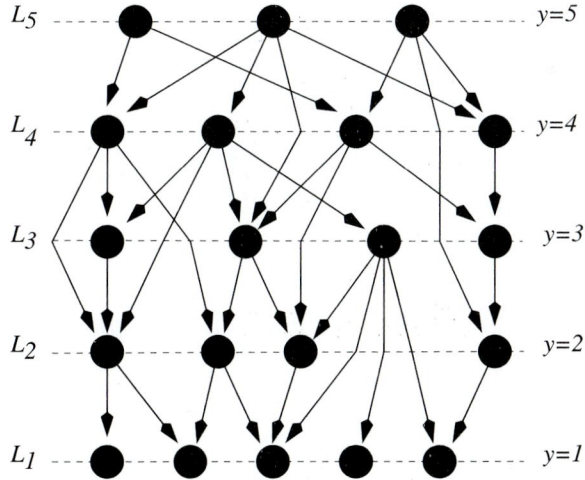

Figure 9.5: Example of a layered drawing of a digraph.

In some applications, the vertices are preassigned to layers. For example, the diagram in Figure 9.6 shows the prerequisite structure of a Computer Science degree. In this case, a student's progress is measured by the y-coordinates of the nodes.

However, in many applications the vertices have not been preassigned to layers. The aim of the layer assignment step is to transform an acyclic

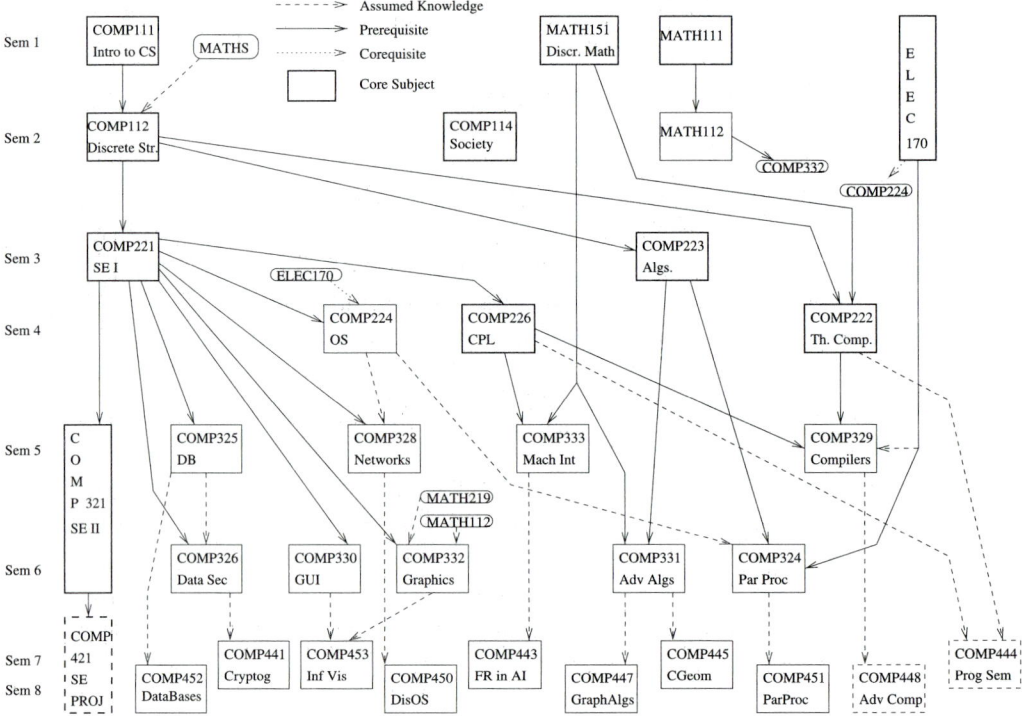

Figure 9.6: Layered drawing of a digraph showing prerequisites between courses. (courtesy of B. Beresford-Smith).

digraph into a layered digraph. There are three important requirements of the layering:

1. The layered digraph should be compact. This means that its width and height should be small. The distance between layers is a constant. Thus a lower bound on the height is the maximum number of edges in a path from a source (vertex of indegree zero) to a sink (vertex of outdegree zero). Section 9.1.1 describes a simple method which meets this lower bound on height, but ignores width. Section 9.1.2 describes a method which takes both height and width into account.

2. The layering should be proper. This is easily achieved by inserting "dummy vertices" along the long edges, as follows. We replace each edge (u, v) of span $k > 1$ with a path $(u = v_1, v_2, \dots, v_k = v)$, adding

the *dummy vertices* $v_2, v_3, \ldots, v_{k-1}$ (see Figure 9.7). The dummy vertices are needed because the crossing reduction step in Section 9.2 assumes that the digraph is proper (it is difficult to handle crossings involving edges of span greater than one).

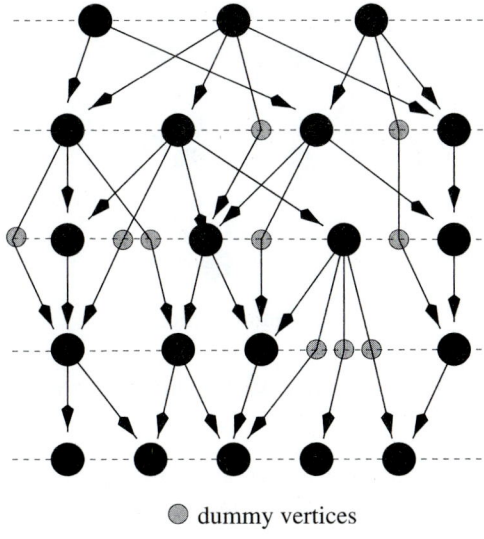

dummy vertices

Figure 9.7: Adding dummy vertices (drawn as small circles) to break up long edges in the layered digraph of Figure 9.5.

3. The number of dummy vertices should be small. If there are $O(n)$ edges, each with span $O(n)$, then the number of dummy vertices is quadratic (see Figure 9.8). There are several reasons to avoid a layering with a large number of dummy vertices:

- The time used by subsequent steps of the layering approach depends on the total number of vertices, dummy plus real.

- Bends in the edges in the final drawing occur only at dummy vertices. Readability increases when the number of bends decreases. Although some straightening can be achieved at the horizontal coordinate assignment step, it is desirable to alleviate the problem by reducing the number of dummy vertices.

- The number of dummy vertices on an edge measures the y extent of the edge. It is easier for the eye to follow short edges than long edges.

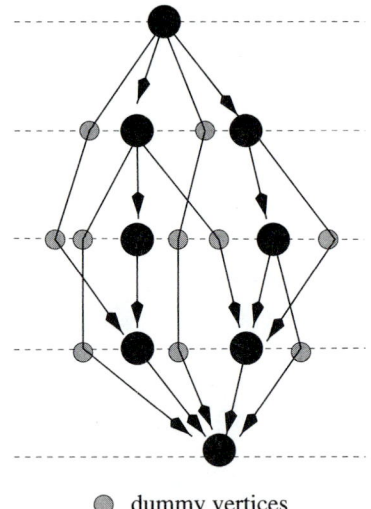

◯ dummy vertices

Figure 9.8: A layering with many dummy vertices.

A technique that computes a layering to minimize the number of dummy vertices is described in Section 9.1.3.

9.1.1   The Longest Path Layering

The longest path layering first places all sinks in layer L_1, then each remaining vertex v is placed in layer L_{p+1}, where the longest (maximum number of edges) path from v to a sink has length p. An example of a drawing using a longest path layering is shown in Figure 9.9.

This layering has two attractive properties.

- It can be computed in linear time because the digraph is acyclic.

- It uses a minimum number of layers, that is, the height of the layering is minimal.

The main drawback of the longest path layering is that it may give drawings that are too wide. For example, the lower layers in Figure 9.9 are relatively wide. Section 9.1.2 considers this problem.

9.1.2   Layering to Minimize Width

The longest path layering minimizes height. However, compactness of the final drawing depends on both width and height.

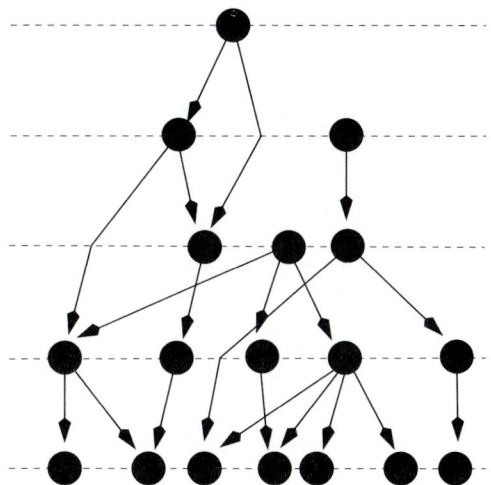

Figure 9.9: A longest path layering.

Unfortunately, the problem of finding a layering with minimum width, subject to having minimum height, is NP-complete for the following reason. Suppose that each vertex of an acyclic digraph G represents a unit-time task to be performed on one of the processors of a multiprocessor. An edge (u, v) in G represents a precedence constraint that u must precede v. This is illustrated in Figure 9.10.

The *precedence-constrained multiprocessor scheduling problem* is to assign each task to one of W processors, so that all tasks are completed in time H. This can be done if and only if G has a layering of width W and height H. The NP-completeness of the layer assignment problem can be thus derived from the NP-completeness of the multiprocessor scheduling problem [GJ79].

The connection with multiprocessor scheduling suggests heuristics for layering. In particular, we now describe Algorithm 9.1 *Coffman-Graham-Layering* [CG72], from the theory of multiprocessor scheduling. This algorithm takes a reduced digraph G (see section 4.7.1) and a positive integer W as input. It returns a layering of G with width at most W. The aim of the algorithm is to ensure that the height of the layering is kept small, and some performance guarantees for the height have been proven [LS77]. Note that the restriction of the input to reduced digraphs is not significant, since transitive edges do not affect the width of a layering.

At this stage, it is approriate to comment that the width of a layering, as defined above, does not take the width of dummy vertices into account.

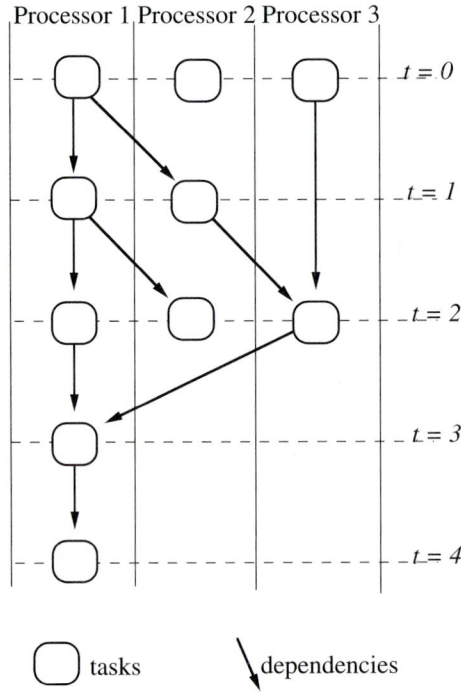

Figure 9.10: Layering and scheduling.

This is a convenient assumption that is accurate only when the size of the real vertices is considerably larger than the space occupied by the dummy vertices. In most applications, the assumption is justified because the real vertices are rectangles with a reasonable amount of text. See, for example, Figure 9.11. In the case when the real vertices are small, we must adjust the Coffman-Graham algorithm to take this into account.

Algorithm 9.1 *Coffman-Graham-Layering* has two phases; the first orders the vertices, and the second assigns vertices to layers. The algorithm uses an order defined on finite sets of positive integers as follows. If S is a finite set of positive integers, then let $\max(S)$ denote the largest element of S. Then $S < T$ if either:

- $S = \emptyset$ and $T \neq \emptyset$, or

- $S \neq \emptyset$, $T \neq \emptyset$, and $\max(S) < \max(T)$, or

- $S \neq \emptyset$, $T \neq \emptyset$, $\max(S) = \max(T)$, and $S - \{\max(S)\} < T - \{\max(T)\}$.

Algorithm 9.1 *Coffman-Graham-Layering*

    Input: reduced digraph $G = (V, E)$, and a positive
                  integer W

    Output: layering of G of width at most W

1. Initially, all vertices are unlabeled.

2. **for** $i = 1$ **to** $|V|$ **do**

    (a) Choose an unlabeled vertex v, such that $\{\pi(v) : (u, v) \in E\}$ is minimized

    (b) $\pi(v) = i$.

3. $k = 1$; $L_1 = \emptyset$; $U = \emptyset$.

4. **while** $U \neq V$ **do**

    (a) Choose $u \in V - U$, such that every vertex in $\{v : (u, v) \in E\}$ is in U, and $\pi(u)$ is maximized

    (b) **if** $|L_k| < W$ **and** for every edge (u, w), $w \in L_1 \cup L_2 \cup \ldots L_{k-1}$ **then** add u to L_k
        else $k = k + 1$, $L_k = \{u\}$

    (c) Add u to U.

                                                  □

In fact, this is simply a lexicographic order, where the largest item of the set is the most significant, for example, $\{1, 4, 7\} < \{3, 8\}$, and $\{3, 4, 9\} < \{1, 5, 9\}$.

The first phase of the algorithm orders the vertices by assigning a positive integer label $\pi(u)$ to each vertex. First label 1 is assigned to a source u, so that $\pi(u) = 1$. After labels $1, 2, \ldots, k - 1$ have been assigned to vertices, label k is assigned to a vertex v, such that:

(1) No label has been assigned to v yet

(2) Labels have been assigned to all vertices u for which $(u, v) \in E$

(3) Among vertices satisfying (1) and (2) above, the set of labels of immediate predecessors of v (that is, $\{\pi(u) : (u, v) \in E\}$) is minimized in the lexicographic ordering "$<$" defined above.

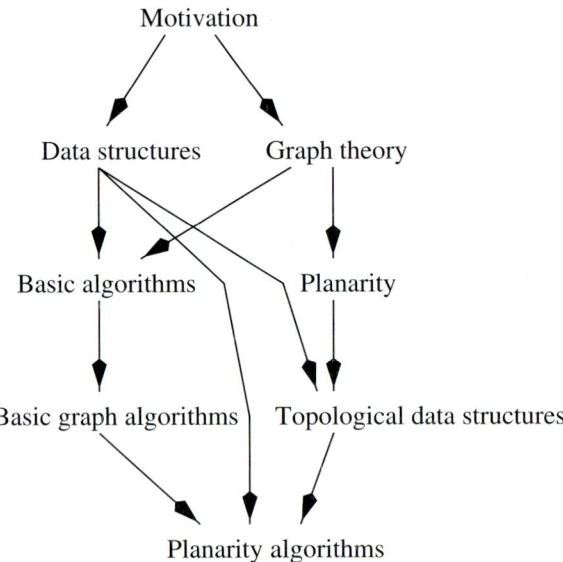

Figure 9.11: A layering in which real vertices are large in comparison to dummy vertices.

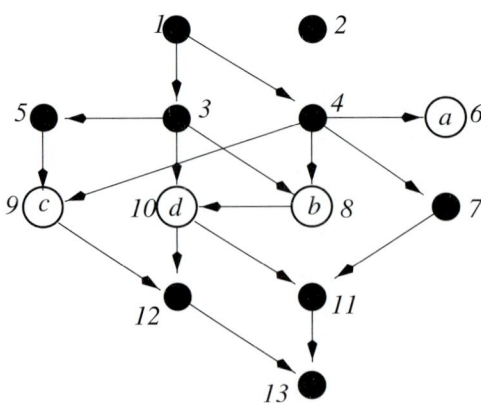

Figure 9.12:   Labels computed by Algorithm 9.1 *Coffman-Graham-Layering*. Note that vertex a is labeled before vertex b because $\{4\} < \{3, 4\}$, and vertex c is labeled before vertex d because $\{4, 5\} < \{3, 7\}$.

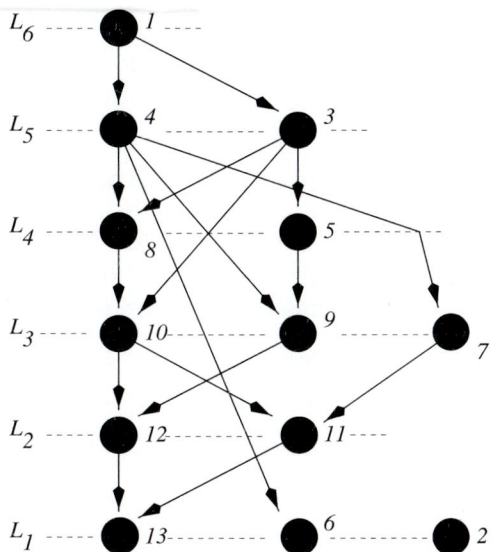

Figure 9.13: Layers computed by Algorithm 9.1 *Coffman-Graham-Layering*.

A digraph labeled by this procedure is illustrated in Figure 9.12.

The second phase of Algorithm 9.1 *Coffman-Graham-Layering* fills the layers with vertices, ensuring that no layer receives more than W vertices. We start with the bottom layer L_1 and proceed to the top layer L_h. To fill L_k, we choose a vertex v which has not been placed in a layer yet, and for which all vertices u with $(v, u) \in E$ have been placed in one of the layers $L_1, L_2, \ldots L_{k-1}$. If there is more than one such vertex, then we choose the one with the largest label. If there are no such vertices or layer L_k becomes full (that is, $|L_k| = W$), then we proceed to the next layer L_{k+1}. The layering with $W = 3$, produced for the digraph in Figure 9.12, is illustrated in Figure 9.13.

It can be shown [LS77] that the height of the layering output by Algorithm 9.1 *Coffman-Graham-Layering* is not too large, in the following sense. Let h_{min} be the minimum height of a layering of width W. Then the height h of the layering satisfies

$$h \leq (2 - \frac{2}{W})h_{min}.$$

Recall that the notion of *width* used here does not take dummy vertices into account, because dummy vertices have very small width in comparison to real vertices (which may contain significantly long text strings). Nevertheless, as mentioned above, dummy vertices do incur some cost. The next section shows how to minimize the number of dummy vertices.

9.1.3   Minimizing the Number of Dummy Vertices

Surprisingly, we can compute a layering in polynomial time that minimizes the number of dummy vertices [GKNV93]. Suppose that each vertex u of an acyclic digraph $G = (V, E)$ has a y-coordinate $y(u)$, which satisfies the following properties:

1. $y(u)$ is an integer for each vertex u.

2. $y(u) \geq 1$ for each vertex u.

3. $y(u) - y(v) \geq 1$ for each $(u, v) \in E$.

Such a function y defines a layering with $L_m = \{u \in V : y(u) = m\}$. Denote by f the sum of the vertical spans of the edges in this layering minus the number of edges, that is

$$f = \sum_{(u,v) \in V} (y(u) - y(v) - 1).$$

Note that f measures the total vertical extent of all the edges. Further, f is the number of dummy vertices in a layering defined by y.

The layer assignment problem is reduced to choosing y-coordinates to minimize f, subject to the conditions (1), (2), and (3). This is an integer linear programming problem. It is shown in [GKNV93] that the corresponding relaxed linear programming problem has an integer solution.

In fact, we can intuitively see why there is an integer solution, as follows. Suppose that for some vertex u, the value $y(u)$ of an optimal solution of the corresponding linear program is not an integer. Geometrically, this means that u is positioned strictly between the line $y = \lfloor y(u) \rfloor$ and the line $y = \lceil y(u) \rceil$. Denote $\lfloor y(u) \rfloor$ by y_u. Inequality (3) above ensures that no neighbor of u lies between the lines $y = y_u$ and $y = y_u + 1$.

If $outdeg(u) > indeg(u)$, then the value of f gets no larger if we move u down a little. As long as there are no edges (u, v) with $y(v) > y_u - 1$, we can move u all the way down to the line $y = y_u$, without violating the constraints (2) and (3) (see Figure 9.14).   In other words, f does not increase if the noninteger $y(u)$ is rounded down. If we are careful about the order in which the vertices are moved, then we can move all vertices with $outdeg(u) >$

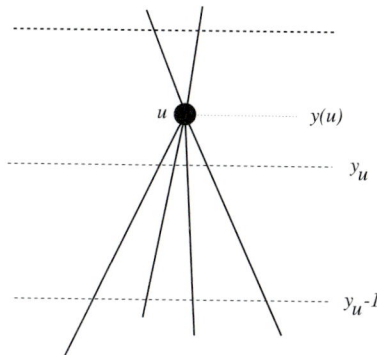

Figure 9.14: Moving a vertex downward.

$indeg(u)$ downward to an integral y-coordinate. A symmetric argument can be used for the case $outdeg(u) < indeg(u)$ and, if $outdeg(u) = indeg(u)$, then we can move u either way. Hence, we can change each noninteger y to an integer, without violating the constraints or increasing f.

Further, this linear programming problem can be solved efficiently in several ways (see [GKNV93]).

9.1.4 Remarks on the Layer Assignment Problem

To achieve compactness, the multiprocessor scheduling methods are quite effective for the following reason. In most drawings, vertices are not simple points, but are rectangles with horizontal text labels. Thus the inter-vertex spacing in the horizontal direction is usually larger than in the vertical direction. This makes the demand on width more important than the demand on height, and multiprocessor scheduling methods are effective for drawings where the preferred direction is top to bottom. However, for drawings where the preferred direction is left to right, the longest path layering may be competitive.

In practice, the dummy vertex minimization methods not only give shorter edge lengths and fewer dummy vertices, but also tend to give relatively compact layerings.

Unfortunately, combining the goals of minimizing the height of a drawing and minimizing the number of dummy vertices leads quickly to NP-completeness [Lin92].

9.2   Crossing Reduction

In this section, we consider the problem of drawing a layered digraph with a small number of crossings. We assume that the layering step has been executed, and so the input to the crossing reduction step is a proper layered digraph.

The number of edge crossings in a drawing of a layered digraph does not depend on the precise position of the vertices, but only on the ordering of the vertices within each layer. Thus the problem of reducing edge crossings is the combinatorial one of choosing an appropriate vertex ordering for each layer, not the geometric one of choosing an x-coordinate for each vertex. Although this combinatorialization conceptually simplifies the problem, it remains difficult. In fact, the problem of minimizing edge crossings in a layered digraph is NP-complete, even if there are only two layers [GJ83]. Also, it is NP-complete even if there is only one nondummy vertex in each layer [MNKF90].

A variety of heuristics have been used to reduce crossings. This section discusses several such heuristics. First, we outline the *layer-by-layer sweep*, which is the general format of most techniques. The most critical part of the layer-by-layer sweep is an algorithm for the two-layer crossing problem, that is, a technique for reducing crossings between two layers. We examine some techniques for solving this problem in detail.

9.2.1   The Layer-by-Layer Sweep

The layer-by-layer sweep method can be described as follows. First, a vertex ordering of layer L_1 is chosen. Then, for $i = 2, 3, \ldots, h$, the vertex ordering of layer L_{i-1} is held fixed while reordering the vertices in layer L_i, to reduce crossings between edges whose endpoints are in layer L_{i-1} and layer L_i.

Note that this method presupposes a solution to a problem of the following form. Given a fixed vertex ordering of layer L_{i-1}, choose a vertex ordering of layer L_i to minimize the number of edge crossings. This problem is called the *two-layer crossing problem*. The analysis of the two-layer crossing problem is the subject of much of the remainder of this section.

There are several variations of the basic layer-by-layer sweep. For instance, we can hold the vertex orderings of both L_{i-1} and L_{i+1} fixed, while reordering the vertices of layer L_i to reduce crossings between layers L_{i-1}, L_i and L_{i+1}. Other variations include ways of sweeping. We can sweep top to bottom, bottom to top, and continue to do several sweeps, until the number of crossings does not decrease. However, for each of these variations, the two-layer crossing problem is fundamental and has received a great deal of attention in the literature [Cat88, EK86, EW94, JM97, Mak88a, Mak88b, War77b].

A two-layered digraph is a bipartite digraph $G = (L_1, L_2, E)$, which consists of disjoint sets L_1 and L_2 of vertices and a set $E \subseteq L_1 \times L_2$ of edges.

Although the aim of this step is to *order* each layer, it is convenient to specify vertex orderings for L_1 and L_2, by giving a unique x-coordinate $x_i(u)$ for each vertex $u \in L_i$, $i = 1, 2$. The number of crossings in a drawing of G specified by x_1 and x_2 is denoted by $cross(G, x_1, x_2)$, and the minimum number of crossings subject to the vertices of L_1 being ordered by x_1 is denoted by $opt(G, x_1)$. Note that

$$opt(G, x_1) = \min_{x_2} cross(G, x_1, x_2).$$

Using this terminology, the *two-layer crossing problem* may be stated as follows.

> Given a two-layered digraph $G = (L_1, L_2, E)$ and an ordering x_1 of L_1, find an ordering x_2 of L_2, such that $cross(G, x_1, x_2) = opt(G, x_1)$.

Unfortunately the two-layer crossing problem is NP-complete [EW94]. The remainder of this subsection discusses three basic heuristic methods for the two-layer crossing problem.

A simple observation is important for all three of these methods: if u and v are vertices in L_2, then the number of crossings between edges incident with u and edges incident with v depends only on the relative positions of u and v and not on the other vertices. This observation motivates the notion of crossing number defined below [EK86, War77b]. Suppose that u and v are vertices in L_2. The *crossing number* c_{uv} is the number of crossings that edges incident with u make with edges incident with v, when $x_2(u) < x_2(v)$. More formally, for $u \neq v \in L_2$, c_{uv} is the number of pairs $(u, w), (v, z)$ of edges with $x_1(z) < x_1(w)$. For convenience, we also define $c_{uu} = 0$ for all $u \in L_2$. For example, Figure 9.15 shows a drawing of a two-layered digraph and the crossing numbers for each pair of vertices in the top layer.

Note that the crossing numbers can be used to compute $cross(G, x_1, x_2)$, and to give a lower bound for $opt(G, x_1)$, as in the following simple lemma.

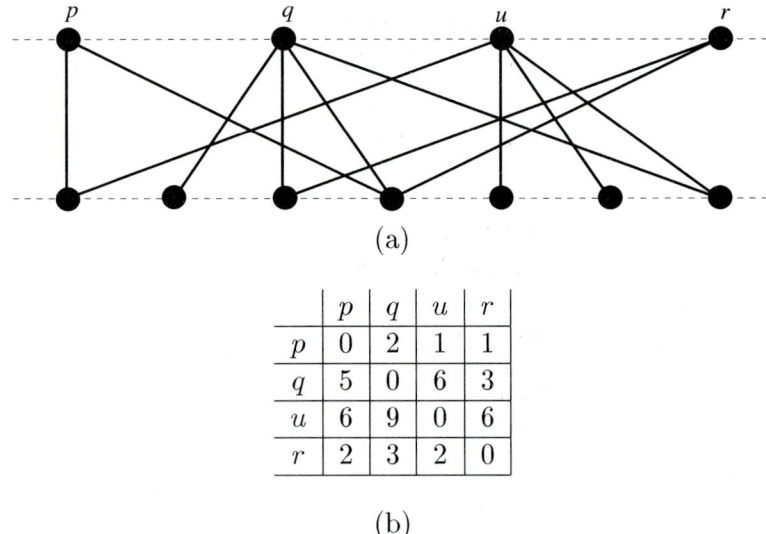

(a)

	p	q	u	r
p	0	2	1	1
q	5	0	6	3
u	6	9	0	6
r	2	3	2	0

(b)

Figure 9.15: (a)Drawing of a two layer digraph. (b) Crossing numbers for each pair of vertices in the top layer.

Lemma 9.1 *If $G = (L_1, L_2, E)$ is a two layer digraph and x_1 and x_2 are orderings of L_1 and L_2 respectively, then*

$$cross(G, x_1, x_2) = \sum_{x_2(u) < x_2(v)} c_{uv}. \tag{9.1}$$

Further

$$opt(G, x_1) \geq \sum_{u,v} \min(c_{uv}, c_{vu}), \tag{9.2}$$

where the sum is over all unordered pairs $\{u, v\}$ of vertices of the top layer.

Proof: The identity (9.1) is immediate. For inequality (9.2), note that every ordering of L_2 (including an optimal ordering) has either $x_2(u) < x_2(v)$ or $x_2(v) < x_2(u)$. □

9.2.2   Sorting Methods

The aim of an algorithm for the two-layer crossing problem is to sort the vertices in L_2 into an order that minimizes the number of crossings. This can be exploited to give a few simple methods. Each requires computation of the crossing numbers. This can be done by a naive algorithm in $O(|E|^2)$ time, and be reduced to $O\left(\sum_{u,v} c_{uv}\right)$, with a little effort (see Exercises).

The first, called Algorithm 9.2 *Adjacent-Exchange*, exchanges adjacent pairs of vertices, using the crossing numbers, in a way similar to bubble-sort.

Algorithm 9.2 *Adjacent-Exchange*

    Input: two-layered digraph $G = (L_1, L_2, E)$ and a vertex order x_1 for L_1

   Output: vertex order x_2 for L_2

1. Choose an initial order for L_2.

2. **repeat**

         Scan the vertices of L_2 from left to right, exchanging an adjacent pair u, v of vertices, whenever $c_{uv} > c_{vu}$

     until the number of crossings does not reduce.

                                                               □

Since c_{uv} depends only on the relative positions of u and v, there is no need to change the values of the crossing numbers. Thus we can implement each scan of the vertices at Step 2 of Algorithm 9.2 *Adjacent-Exchange*, in $O(|L_2|)$ time, and there are $O(|L_2|)$ scans; the time complexity of Algorithm 9.2 *Adjacent-Exchange* is $O(|L_2|^2)$.

For some pathological inputs, Algorithm 9.2 *Adjacent-Exchange* can give poor results (see Figure 9.16).

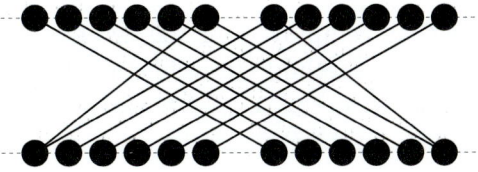

Figure 9.16: Worst case for the adjacent-exchange method.

We can also use a method reminiscent of quick-sort, called *Split*. We choose a *pivot vertex* $p \in L_2$, and place each vertex $u \neq p \in L_2$ to the left of p if $c_{up} < c_{pu}$, and to the right of p otherwise. The algorithm is then applied recursively to the sets of vertices to the left and right of p. Algorithm 9.3 *Split* has worst case time complexity $O(|L_2|^2)$ but, (like quick-sort) in practice, it runs in $O(|L_2| \log |L_2|)$ time.

Algorithm 9.3 *Split*

      Input: two-layered digraph $G = (L_1, L_2, E)$, an order
                     x_1 for L_1
    Output: vertex order x_2 for L_2

    if L_2 is not empty **then**

      (a) Choose a pivot vertex $p \in L_2$.

      (b) $V_{left} = \emptyset$; $V_{right} = \emptyset$

      (c) **foreach** vertex $u \in L_2$ such that $u \neq p$ **do**

              if $c_{up} \leq c_{pu}$
              then place u in V_{left}
              else place u in V_{right}

      (d) Recursively apply the algorithm to the digraphs induced by V_{left} and V_{right}, and output the concatenation of the outputs of these two applications.

                                                           $\square$

Several methods similar to Algorithms 9.2 *Adjacent-Exchange* and 9.3 *Split* are described in [EK86]. All require precomputation of the crossing array and thus have nonlinear time complexity. In the next section, we present two methods that run in linear time.

9.2.3   The Barycenter and Median Methods

The most common methods employed for the two-layer crossing problem are variations of the *barycenter* method. Roughly speaking, the x-coordinate of each vertex $u \in L_2$ is chosen as the *barycenter* (average) of the x-coordinates of its neighbors. That is, we select $x_2(u)$ to be $avg(u)$ for all $u \in L_2$, where

$$avg(u) = \frac{1}{deg(u)} \sum_{v \in N_u} x_1(v),$$

where $deg(u)$ denotes the degree of u and N_u denotes the set of neighbors of u. If two vertices have the same barycenter, then we separate them arbitrarily by a small amount. The barycenter method can be implemented in linear time. The number of crossings output by the barycenter method is denoted by $avg(G, x_1)$.

The *median* method is similar to the barycenter method. Roughly speaking, the x-coordinate of each $u \in L_2$ is chosen to be a median of the x-coordinates of the neighbors of u. This rough definition needs refinement to achieve good performance. First, we need a precise definition of median. If the neighbors of u are $v_1, v_2, \ldots, v_j$, with $x_1(v_1) < x_1(v_2) < \ldots < x_1(v_j)$, then we define $med(u) = x_1(v_{\lfloor j/2 \rfloor})$. If u has no neighbors, then we choose $med(u) = 0$.

Next, we need to define how the values $med(u)$ are used to order the vertices in L_2. We sort L_2 on $med(u)$. We use the following criterion to break ties: if $med(u) = med(v)$ and one vertex has odd degree and the other even, then the odd degree vertex is placed on the left of the even degree vertex. If the parity of the degrees of u and v is the same, then we can choose the order of u and v arbitrarily. This rather curious method for breaking ties is necessary for one of the performance guarantees below.

For each vertex $u \in L_2$, $med(u)$ can be computed in time proportional to the degree of u, with a linear-time median finding algorithm (see, for example, [AHU83]), so that the drawing can be computed in linear time. The number of crossings in the output of the median method is denoted by $med(G, x_1)$.

It is easy to prove that both the barycenter and median methods give zero crossings when a zero-crossing layout is possible. We leave the proof of the following theorem as an exercise.

Theorem 9.1 *Suppose that $G = (L_1, L_2, E)$ is a two-layer digraph and x_1 is an ordering of L_1. If $opt(G, x_1) = 0$, then $avg(G, x_1) = med(G, x_1) = 0$.*

However, neither method gives an optimum solution. Figure 9.17 shows a pathological case for the barycenter method, and Figure 9.18 shows a pathological case for the median method. These examples imply the following lemma.

Lemma 9.2

1. *For each n there is a two-layered digraph $G = (L_1, L_2, E)$, with $|L_1| = n$, $|L_2| = 2$ and an ordering x_1 of L_1, for which $\frac{avg(G, x_1)}{opt(G, x_1)}$ is $\Omega(\sqrt{n})$.*

2. *For each n there is a two-layered digraph $G' = (L_1', L_2', E')$, with $|L_1'| = n$, $|L_2'| = 2$ and an ordering x_1 of L_1', for which $\frac{med(G', x_1)}{opt(G', x_1)} \geq 3 - O(\frac{1}{n})$.*

Proof: For the barycenter ordering, consider the digraph in Figure 9.17. Suppose that the vertices in L_1 are $w_1, w_2, \ldots, w_n$, from left to right, spaced one unit apart, where $n = k^2 + k - 1$. Let v be joined to w_{k^2}, and let u be joined to w_1, and $w_{k^2+1}, w_{k^2+2}, \ldots, w_{k^2+k-1}$. Then $avg(u) = k^2 - k/2 - 1/2 < k^2 = avg(v)$. Thus the barycenter method places u to the left of v, which creates $k - 1$ crossings. However, if v is to the left of u, then there is only one crossing. Since k is $O(\sqrt{n})$, the inequality follows.

A similar argument applies to the median method, using the digraph in Figure 9.18. $\square$

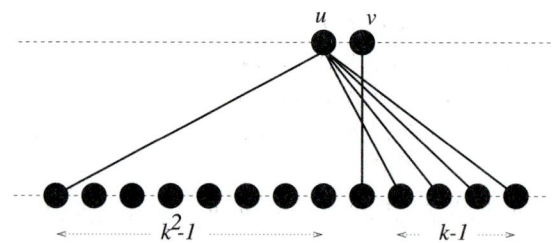

Figure 9.17: Worst case for the barycenter method. The barycenter method places u to the left of v and has $k - 1$ crossings; the optimal layout has only one crossing.

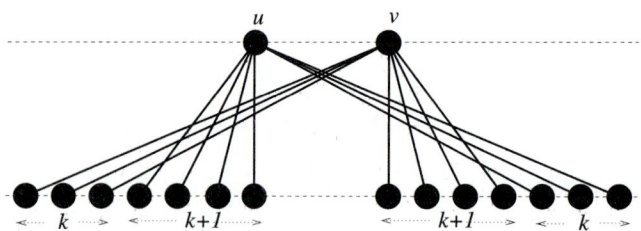

Figure 9.18: Worst case for the median method. The median method places u to the left of v and has $2k(k+1) + k^2$ crossings. The optimal layout has only $(k + 1)^2$ crossings.

Next, in Lemma 9.2, we give an upper bound that matches the lower bound for the median method.

Theorem 9.2 *For all two-layered digraphs $G = (L_1, L_2, E)$ and all vertex orderings x_1 of L_1, $med(G, x_1) \leq 3opt(G, x_1)$.*

Proof: Suppose that u and v are vertices in L_2 and the median method places u to the left of v. We define four groups of edges incident with u and

v as follows (see the schematic illustration of Figure 9.19.a and the example of Figure 9.20)

$$
\begin{aligned}
\alpha &= \{(u, w) \in E : x_1(w) < med(u)\} \\
\beta &= \{(v, w) \in E : x_1(w) > med(v)\} \\
\gamma &= \{(v, w) \in E : x_1(w) < med(v)\} \\
\delta &= \{(u, w) \in E : x_1(w) > med(u)\}.
\end{aligned}
$$

Note that u and v are both joined to a vertex at their respective medians. We denote these two edges by e_u and e_v respectively. These two edges are not included in any of the four groups.

Now let $a = |\alpha|$, $b = |\beta|$, $c = |\gamma|$, and $d = |\delta|$. We claim that

$$
c_{vu} \geq ab + a + b + \epsilon, \tag{9.3}
$$

where $\epsilon = 0$ if $med(u) = med(v)$, and $\epsilon = 1$ otherwise. To prove (9.3), suppose that v was placed to the left of u, as in Figure 9.19.b. Then all edges in α would be forced to cross e_v, as well as all edges in β, and edges in β would be forced to cross e_u. If $med(u) = med(v)$ then e_u does not cross e_v and $\epsilon = 0$. However, if $med(u) \neq med(v)$, then e_u would also cross e_v and $\epsilon = 1$. The lower bound (9.3) follows.

Further, we claim that

$$
c_{uv} \leq ac + cd + bd + c + d. \tag{9.4}
$$

The reason for this is that, if u is placed to the left of v, then edges in α cannot cross edges in β, and e_u cannot cross e_v.

Next, we note that a and d are closely related. If the degree of u is odd, then $a = d$; if the degree of u is even then $a + 1 = d$. Similarly, if the degree of v is odd, then $c = b$; if the degree of v is even then $c + 1 = b$. In any case, $d \leq a + 1$ and $c \leq b$. Using these inequalities in (9.4), we can deduce that

$$
c_{uv} \leq 3ab + a + 3b + 1. \tag{9.5}
$$

In order to prove that $med(G, x_1) \leq 3opt(G, x_1)$, we will show that $c_{uv} \leq 3c_{vu}$. Suppose, on the contrary, that $c_{uv} > 3c_{vu}$, that is

$$
c_{uv} - 3c_{vu} > 0. \tag{9.6}
$$

From (9.3) and (9.5), it follows that $2a + 3\epsilon - 1$ is negative. Since both a and ϵ are nonnegative integers, this implies that

$$
a = \epsilon = 0. \tag{9.7}
$$

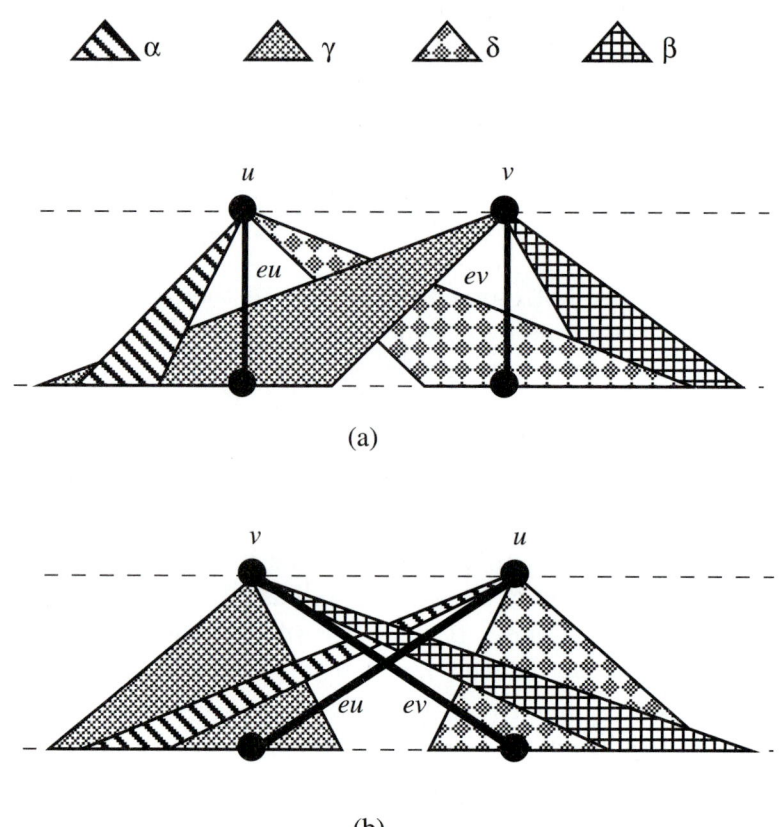

(a)

(b)

Figure 9.19: Schematic illustration of the four groups of edges α, β, γ, and δ.

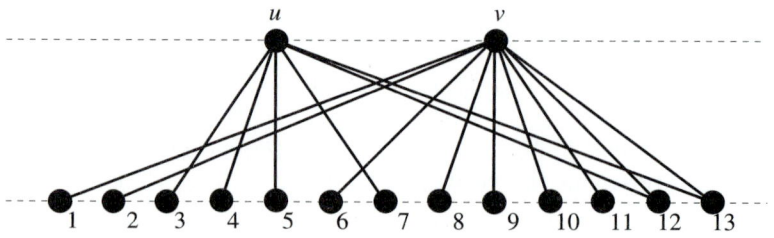

Figure 9.20: A digraph with groups of edges $\alpha = \{(u,3),(u,4)\}$, $\beta = \{(v,10),(v,11),(v,12),(v,13)\}$, $\gamma = \{(v,1),(v,2),(v,6),(v,8)\}$, and $\delta = \{(u,7),(u,12),(u,13)\}$.

This implies that α is empty, and thus u has degree at most two. It is easy to show that (9.6) is impossible when the degree of u is at most one, so we can deduce that the degree of u is precisely two; thus $d = 1$.

The definition of ϵ and (9.7) imply that $med(u) = med(v)$. Recall that if two vertices u and v have the same median, the degree of u is even, and the degree of v is odd, then the median method places v to the left of u. Thus we can deduce that the degree of v is even. It follows that $c = b - 1$. Using these values for $\epsilon, a, b, c,$ and d in (9.3) and (9.4), we can show that $c_{uv} = 3b - 1$ and $c_{vu} = b$. This contradicts the assumption (9.6).

Therefore $c_{uv} \le 3c_{vu}$. This holds for every pair $u, v \in L_2$. To complete the proof of the theorem, note that this implies that

$$c_{uv} \le 3\min(c_{uv}, c_{vu}).$$

By summing the above inequality over all pairs u, v with $x_2(u) < x_2(v)$, using both parts of Lemma 9.1, we conclude that

$$cross(G, x_1, x_2) \le 3opt(G, x_1).$$

$\square$

A more refined argument can be applied to digraphs with low degree and can be used for some tighter bounds. For instance, a case-by-case argument gives the following result.

Theorem 9.3 *Suppose that $G = (L_1, L_2, E)$ is a two-layered digraph and every vertex in L_2 has degree at most three. Then for all orderings x_1 of L_1, $med(G, x_1) \le 2opt(G, x_1)$.*

The proof of this theorem is left as an exercise.

9.2.4 Integer Programming Methods

An integer programming approach may be used for the two-layer crossing problem. For a two-layer digraph $G = (L_1, L_2, E)$, we define a binary vector $x \in \{0, 1\}^{\binom{|L_2|}{2}}$, with entries x_{uv} for $u < v$ and $x_{uv} = 1$, if u is to the left of v, and $x_{uv} = 0$ otherwise. From Lemma 9.1, we can deduce that

$$
\begin{aligned}
cross(G, x_1, x_2) &= \sum_{u<v\in L_2} (c_{uv}x_{uv} + c_{vu}(1 - x_{uv})) \\
&= \sum_{u<v\in L_2} (c_{uv} - c_{vu})x_{uv} + \sum_{u<v\in L_2} c_{vu}. \quad (9.8)
\end{aligned}
$$

Noting that $\sum_{u<v\in L_2} c_{vu}$ is a constant, we can restate the two-layer crossing problem as follows:

Minimize $z = \sum_{u < v \in L_2}(c_{uv} - c_{vu})x_{uv}$ subject to:

1. $0 \leq x_{uv} + x_{vw} - x_{uw} \leq 1$ for all triples $u < v < w$ of distinct vertices in L_2.

2. $x_{uv} \in \{0,1\}$ for all pairs $u < v$ of distinct vertices in L_2.

The first constraint above ensures that the vector x indeed defines a total order on the vertices in L_2. Note that the optimum value z^* of the cost function is not quite the same as the minimum number of crossings. From (9.8), the minimum number of crossings is $z^* + \sum_{u < v \in L_2} c_{vu}$.

Solving integer programs requires, in general, relatively sophisticated techniques. A *branch and cut approach* [JM97] can be used to obtain an optimal solution for digraphs of limited size. This begins by relaxing the second set of constraints to

$0 \leq x_{uv} \leq 1$ for all pairs $u < v$ of distinct vertices in L_2.

This can be solved using standard linear programming techniques. However, the first set of constraints is large ($O(|L_2|^3)$). Therefore, a cutting plane approach is used. The algorithm starts using only the above inequalities, then the elements of the first set are iteratively used to "cut" the solution space. If this finds an integral solution, then the procedure stops; otherwise, a variable x_{uv} is chosen, and two problems are spawned, one with $x_{uv} = 0$, the other with $x_{uv} = 1$. These problems are solved recursively. For more details, see [JM97].

The main advantage of the integer programming approach over the methods mentioned previously is that it is guaranteed to find the optimum solution. While there is no guarantee that it will terminate in polynomial time, it seems to be quite successful for small to medium sized digraphs.

9.2.5 The Two-Layer Crossing Problem on Dense Digraphs

In this section, we show that for dense digraphs, $cross(G, x_1, x_2)$ is close to $opt(G, x_1)$ for any ordering of L_2. The basic intuition is that if u and v have many common neighbors, then both c_{uv} and c_{vu} are large. For each pair u, v of vertices, denote the number of common neighbors of u and v by χ_{uv}.

We begin with a simple lemma bounding c_{uv} in terms of χ_{uv}. Here $deg(w)$ denotes the degree of vertex w.

Lemma 9.3 *If u and v are in L_2 then:*

(a) $c_{uv} + c_{vu} + \chi_{uv} = deg(u)deg(v)$

(b) $c_{uv} \geq \begin{pmatrix} \chi_{uv} \\ 2 \end{pmatrix}$

(c) $c_{uv} \leq deg(u)deg(v) - \begin{pmatrix} \chi_{uv}+1 \\ 2 \end{pmatrix}$.

The following theorem states that, for dense digraphs, the *maximum* number of crossings is close to the minimum.

Theorem 9.4 *Suppose that* $G = (L_1, L_2, E)$ *is a two-layer digraph,* $|L_1| = |L_2| = n$, *and* $|E| = \epsilon n^2$. *Then*

$$\lim_{\epsilon \to 1} \frac{\max_{x_2} cross(G, x_1, x_2)}{opt(G, x_1)} = 1.$$

Proof: The basic intuition for this theorem is from Lemma 9.3(b)b. Since, $\chi_{uv} = \chi_{vu}$, both c_{uv} and c_{vu} are large.

From Lemma 9.1

$$cross(G, x_1, x_2) - opt(G, x_1) \leq \sum_{x_2(u)<x_2(v)} |c_{uv} - c_{vu}|.$$

Also, from Lemma 9.3

$$|c_{uv} - c_{vu}| \leq deg(u)deg(v) - \begin{pmatrix} \chi_{uv}+1 \\ 2 \end{pmatrix} - \begin{pmatrix} \chi_{uv} \\ 2 \end{pmatrix},$$

and since

$$\begin{pmatrix} \chi_{uv}+1 \\ 2 \end{pmatrix} + \begin{pmatrix} \chi_{uv} \\ 2 \end{pmatrix} = \chi_{uv}^2,$$

we have

$$\sum_{x_2(u)<x_2(v)} \left(deg(u)deg(v) - \chi_{uv}^2 \right) \geq cross(G, x_1, x_2) - opt(G, x_1). \quad (9.9)$$

An upper bound on the sum of the first terms on the left-hand side of (9.9) is easy to compute

$$\sum_{x_2(u)<x_2(v)} deg(u)deg(v) \leq \frac{|E|^2}{2} = \frac{\epsilon^2 n^4}{2}. \quad (9.10)$$

Next we compute a lower bound on the sum of the second term of the left-hand side of (9.9). Note that

$$\sum_{x_2(u)<x_2(v)} \chi_{uv} = \sum_{w\in L_1} \binom{deg(w)}{2} \qquad (9.11)$$

and

$$\sum_{w\in L_1} deg(w) = |E| = \epsilon n^2.$$

It follows that

$$\sum_{w\in L_1} \binom{deg(w)}{2} \geq n\binom{\epsilon n}{2}. \qquad (9.12)$$

From (9.11) and (9.12), we can deduce that

$$\sum_{x_2(u)<x_2(v)} \chi_{uv}^2 \geq \binom{n}{2}\left(\frac{n\binom{\epsilon n}{2}}{\binom{n}{2}}\right)^2 = \frac{\epsilon^2 n^3(\epsilon n - 1)^2}{2(n-1)}. \qquad (9.13)$$

Thus from (9.9), (9.10), and (9.13), we obtain

$$cross(G, x_1, x_2) - opt(G, x_1) \leq \frac{\epsilon^2 n^4}{2} - \frac{\epsilon^2 n^3(\epsilon n - 1)^2}{2(n-1)},$$

that is

$$cross(G, x_1, x_2) - opt(G, x_1) = \epsilon^2 n^2 \left(\epsilon n - \frac{1}{2}\right). \qquad (9.14)$$

Using a similar argument, we can show that

$$opt(G, x_1) \geq \frac{\epsilon^2 n^4}{2} - o(n^3). \qquad (9.15)$$

From (9.14) and (9.15) we can deduce that $\frac{cross(G,x_1,x_2)-opt(G,x_1)}{opt(G,x_1)}$ is $O(\frac{\epsilon}{n})$ and the theorem follows. $\qquad\qquad\square$

9.2.6   Remarks on the Two-Layer Crossing Problem

From a theoretical point of view, the median method (Theorem 9.2) seems very attractive. It is guaranteed to construct an ordering within a constant factor of the optimal, and it runs in polynomial time. However, in practice, the effectiveness of a method must be verified by extensive testing. Many authors have performed comparative tests on pseudo-random digraphs [EK86, Mak88a, JM97] and on "real-world" digraphs [GKNV93]. Unfortunately, no clear single winner arises from these tests. The best advice seems to be to use a hybrid approach:

1. Use the median method to determine an initial ordering. If two vertices u and v have equal median values, then they are sorted on their barycenter values.

2. Use an adjacent exchange method (Algorithm 9.2 *Adjacent Exchange*) to refine the output of the first step.

Success with a hybrid method along these lines is reported in [GKNV93].

9.3   Horizontal Coordinate Assignment

Bends in edges occur at the dummy vertices introduced in the layer assignment step to replace edges of span greater than one. We want to reduce the angle of such bends by choosing an x-coordinate for each vertex, without perturbing the ordering established in the crossing reduction step.

We can state this problem as an optimization problem as follows. Consider the directed path $p = (v_1, v_2, \ldots, v_k)$, where $v_2, v_3, \ldots, v_{k-1}$ are dummy vertices. If this path was drawn straight, then for $2 \leq i \leq k-1$, the x-coordinate of v_i, $x(v_i)$, would satisfy

$$x(v_i) - x(v_1) = \frac{i-1}{k-1}(x(v_k) - x(v_1)). \tag{9.16}$$

Thus for each such path p corresponding to an edge (v_1, v_k) of the digraph before the introduction of dummy vertices, we define

$$g(p) = \sum_{i=2}^{k-1}(x(v_i) - a_i)^2,$$

where $a_i = \frac{i-1}{k-1}(x(v_k) - x(v_1)) + x(v_1)$, by rewriting (9.16). To make the edges as straight as possible, we minimize the global sum

$$\sum_p g(p)$$

over all paths p of dummy vertices subject to the constraints

$$x(w) - x(z) \geq \delta \tag{9.17}$$

for all pairs w, z of vertices in the same layer with w to the right of z. The constraints (9.17) ensure that the ordering within each layer (as computed at the crossing reduction step) is preserved. Further, they enforce a minimal horizontal distance δ between vertices in the same layer.

Note that it is possible that the solution to this optimization problem can affect the width of the drawing. In fact, using the same technique as in Section 11.1, we can show that some layered drawings require exponential area if edges are represented with straight lines. If the width of the drawing is of concern, then further constraints can be added to force the x-coordinates of each vertex to lie within specified boundaries.

We can attempt to draw edges as close to vertical lines as possible, subject to the ordering constraints. In this case, the objective function is slightly different. We want to minimize

$$\sum_{(u,v) \in E} (x(u) - x(v))^2,$$

subject to the constraints (9.17) above.

Either of these quadratic programming problems can be solved by standard methods. Note, however, that the solution requires considerable computational resources.

9.4   Cycle Removal

As discussed above, a good drawing of a digraph helps the viewer follow the direction of flow. This can be achieved if most of the edges follow the same general direction, say from top to bottom.

The previous three sections described techniques for drawing acyclic digraphs. Though in many applications, such as dependency graphs, the input digraph is acyclic, in other applications the input graph may contain cycles. Typically, we first obtain an acyclic digraph by reversing some edges. Next, we draw the acyclic digraph using the aforementioned techniques. Finally, we render the digraph with the reversed edges pointing in their original directions.

Each cycle of a digraph must have at least one edge pointing "against the flow." We need to keep the number of edges appearing "against the flow" small, to preserve the general downward flow of the diagram.

If $G = (V, E)$ is a digraph and $R \subseteq E$, then we denote the digraph obtained by reversing all the edges of R by $G_{rev(R)}$. To remove cycles, we choose a set R, such that the digraph $G_{rev(R)}$ is acyclic. The main problem is how to choose R so that $|R|$ is small. The rest of this section presents techniques to solve this problem.

A set R of edges of a digraph $G = (V, E)$ is a *feedback set*, if $G_{rev(R)}$ is acyclic (see Figure 9.21).

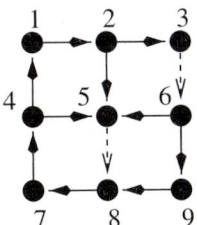

Figure 9.21: Feedback set of a digraph shown with dashed lines.

The feedback set is closely related to the well-known *feedback arc set*, which is defined as a set of edges whose *removal* makes the digraph acyclic. This is not the same as our definition. For instance, removing *all* the edges of a a cycle makes it acyclic, but reversing all the edges merely reverses the cycle. However, a minimal set in one sense is a minimal set in the other sense, which implies that if we reverse the direction of the edges in a minimal feedback arc set, the new digraph contains no cycles. In fact, the problem of finding a minimum cardinality feedback edge set of a given digraph is equivalent to the well-known *feedback arc set problem*. Unfortunately this problem is NP-complete [GJ79]. Thus effective heuristics are needed.

We state the problem in a slightly different form. Suppose that we choose an ordering $S = (v_1, v_2, \ldots, v_n)$ of the vertices of a digraph G. We say that S is a *vertex sequence* for G. An edge (v_i, v_j) with $i > j$ is called an *leftward edge* (with respect to S). In other words, if the vertices are drawn on a horizontal line in the left to right order as they appear in S, then the leftward edges point to the left. Figure 9.22 shows the same graph as in Figure 9.21, with the feedback arcs pointing to the left.

The set of leftward edges for a vertex sequence forms a feedback set. Conversely, if R is a feedback set, then by computing a topological ordering of the digraph obtained by reversing all edges in R; we obtain a vertex sequence, such that R contains every leftward edge. Thus the feedback set problem is equivalent to finding a vertex sequence with as few leftward edges as possible.

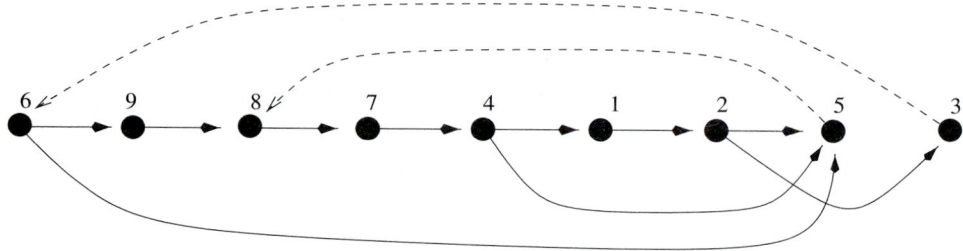

Figure 9.22: Leftward edges shown with dashed lines.

A simple technique to find a feedback set R is to perform a depth first search on the given digraph, and place all back edges in R. However, in the worst case, this may reverse $|E| - |V| - 1$ edges. The performance of this simple method is quite poor for all but the sparsest of digraphs. A better, but even simpler, approach is to start with an arbitrary ordering of the vertices of G and count the number of leftward edges. If it is larger than half, then we can choose the opposite order. This guarantees that at most half of the edges will be reversed.

The remainder of this section presents a greedy algorithm, called *Greedy-Cycle-Removal*, which computes a vertex sequence inducing a small set of leftward edges. The algorithm is quite simple, it runs in linear time, and it has a better guarantee on performance. We assume that the input digraph G is connected; if not, we deal with each connected component individually. The algorithm successively removes vertices from G, and adds each in turn, to one of two lists S_l and S_r. The vertices are added either to the end of S_l or to the beginning of S_r. When G has been reduced to an empty digraph by successive removals, the output vertex sequence S is the concatenation of S_l and S_r. This process is illustrated in Figure 9.23.

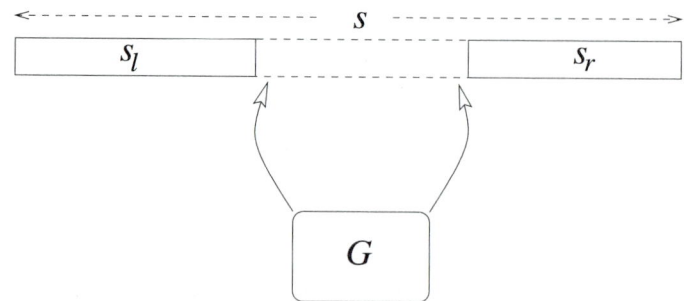

Figure 9.23: Visualization of Algorithm 9.4 *Greedy-Cycle-Removal*.

The algorithm is greedy in its choice of the vertex to be removed from G and the choice of the list (either S_l or S_r) to which it is added. All sinks should be added to S_r, and all sources of G should be added to S_l, since this procedure will prevent their incident edges from becoming leftward edges. Note that an isolated vertex is both a sink and a source. In our algorithm, we regard it as a sink and add it to S_r. After dealing with all sinks and sources, we choose a vertex u for which $outdeg(u) - indeg(u)$ is maximized. Vertex u is removed and added to S_l. The thought here is that this choice locally maximizes the number of "rightward" edges for a given number of leftward edges.

Algorithm 9.4 *Greedy-Cycle-Removal*
    Input: digraph G
    Output: vertex sequence S for G

1. Initialize both S_l and S_r to be empty lists.

2. **while** G is not empty **do**

   (a) **while** G contains a sink **do**

       Choose a sink u, remove it from G, and prepend it to S_r. (Note: isolated vertices are removed from G and prepended to S_r at this stage.)

   (b) **while** G contains a source **do**

       Choose a source v, remove it from G, and append it to S_l.

   (c) **if** G is not empty **then**

       Choose a vertex u, such that the difference $outdeg(u) - indeg(u)$ is maximum, remove it from G, and append it to S_l.

3. Concatenate S_l with S_r to form S. □

A two-cycle of a digraph is a directed cycle consisting of two edges (u, v) and (v, u). Digraphs with many two-cycles do not have small feedback sets, because every feedback set must contain at least one of the two edges of each two-cycle. In practice, we should delete all two-cycles before applying Algorithm 9.4 *Greedy-Cycle-Removal*. For digraphs without two-cycles, however, we can guarantee the performance of the algorithm.

Theorem 9.5 *Suppose that G is a connected digraph with n vertices and m edges, and no two-cycles. Then Algorithm 9.4* Greedy-Cycle-Removal *computes a vertex sequence S of G G, with at most $m/2 - n/6$ leftward edges.*

Proof: We say that a vertex is *isolated* if it has no incident edges. The vertex set V of G may be partitioned into five sets V_1, V_2, V_3, V_4, V_5, according to the indegrees and outdegrees of the vertices at the time that they were removed by one of Steps 2(a), (b), or (c) of Algorithm 9.4 *Greedy-Cycle-Removal*, as follows:

- V_1 consists of nonisolated sink vertices u removed from G at Step 2(a)

- V_2 consists of isolated vertices removed from G at Step 2(a).

- V_3 consists of vertices removed at Step 2(b) (that is, they were sources with positive outdegree at the time of removal).

- V_4 consists of vertices u removed at Step 2(c) with indegree equal to outdegree.

- V_5 consists of vertices u removed at Step 2(c) with indegree less than outdegree.

Note that these sets partition V. In particular, there is no vertex u with indegree greater than outdegree removed at Step 2(c), since the existence of such a vertex would imply the existence of a vertex v with indegree less than outdegree.

For $1 \leq i \leq 5$, let $n_i = |V_i|$ and let m_i denote the number of edges removed from G as a result of the removal of the vertices of V_i. Note that $n = \sum_{i=1}^{5} n_i$, $m = \sum_{i=1}^{5} m_i$, and $m_2 = 0$.

First, we compute a bound on the number n_2 of vertices that were isolated at the time of removal from G. Since G is connected, there is initially no isolated vertex. Suppose that removal of a vertex u at Step 2(c) creates an isolated vertex v. Then vertex v is isolated because of the removal of either (u, v) or (v, u), but not both (since G has no two-cycles). Hence, v was either a sink before the removal of (u, v) or a source before the removal of (v, u). In either case, v would already have been removed at either Step 2(a) or Step 2(b), and so the removal of u cannot give rise to a vertex $v \in V_2$. A similar argument shows that removal of a vertex $u \in V_3$ cannot create an isolated vertex v, and we then see that v can only be created by the prior removal of a sink u and an incident edge (v, u). In other words, isolated vertices are only created by the removal of vertices in V_1. Thus

$$n_2 \leq m_1. \tag{9.18}$$

Next we show that, after the removal of a vertex in V_4, vertices exist in G, for which indegree is not equal to outdegree. When Algorithm 9.4 *Greedy-Cycle-Removal* is ready to remove a vertex in V_4, all vertices have indegree equal to outdegree. Thus, after such a vertex is removed, the resulting digraph contains at least one vertex whose outdegree is not equal to its indegree. As we have seen, since the resulting digraph contains no isolated vertex, it follows that the next vertex to be removed is in $V_1 \cup V_3 \cup V_5$. That is

$$n_4 \leq n_1 + n_3 + n_5,$$

which, by substitution for n_4, becomes

$$\begin{aligned} n & \leq 2n_1 + n_2 + 2n_3 + 2n_5 \\ & \leq 2n_1 + n_2 + 3n_3 + 3n_5, \end{aligned}$$

so that, applying (9.18) and observing that $n_1 \leq m_1$, we find that

$$n \leq 3(m_1 + n_3 + n_5). \tag{9.19}$$

Finally, we count leftward edges. Adding a vertex to either S_l or S_r at Steps 2(a) and 2(b) does not contribute any leftward edges. Consider the number of leftward edges created by placing a vertex u into S_l at Step 2(c). If $u \in V_4$, then the number of leftward edges created by inserting u into S_l is exactly half of its degree. If $u \in V_5$, then the number of leftward edges created by inserting u into S_l is at most $(deg(u) - 1)/2$, where $deg(u)$ denotes the degree of u. It follows that the total number of leftward edges is at most

$$\begin{aligned} m_4/2 + (m_5 - n_5)/2 & = m/2 - (m_1 + m_3 + n_5)/2 \\ & \leq m/2 - (m_1 + n_3 + n_5)/2, \end{aligned}$$

since $n_3 \leq m_3$. Applying (9.19), we obtain the desired result. $\qquad\square$

Theorem 9.6 *There is an implementation of Algorithm 9.4* Greedy-Cycle-Removal *that runs in linear time and space.*

Proof: We maintain the vertex set of G in $2n - 3$ buckets B_i, for $-n + 2 \leq i \leq n - 2$, as follows. Isolated vertices and sinks are stored in B_{-n+2}, sources are stored in B_{n-2}, and for $-n + 2 < i < n - 2$, bucket B_i contains vertices for which the outdegree minus the indegree equals i. It is clear that every vertex $u \in V$ is stored in exactly one bucket. The buckets can be initialized in linear time. The removal of a vertex u moves all the neighbors of u from one bucket to another. Using an adjacency list, these vertices can be identified and moved in time proportional to the degree of u. The other operations are trivial.   □

The main attractions of Algorithm 9.4 *Greedy-Cycle-Removal* are its simplicity and its speed. Algorithms with better worst-case performance are presented in [BS90]. These algorithms are more complex and require $O(mn)$ time. Further, since most digraphs that need to be drawn are sparse, the performance bound in Theorem 9.5 is relatively good. For sparse digraphs, we can strengthen the result of Theorem 9.5 as follows [EL95]:

Theorem 9.7 *Suppose that G is a connected digraph with n vertices and m edges, and no two-cycles. Suppose that each vertex of G has total degree (sum of the indegree and outdegree) at most three. Then Algorithm 9.4 Greedy-Cycle-Removal computes a vertex sequence of G with at most $m/3$ leftward edges.*

Finally, note that an approximation algorithm for the feedback edge set problem, with a guarantee that the resulting feedback set is close in size to the minimum sized feedback set, is unlikely to exist (see [PY91]).

9.5   Exercises

1. Show how to adjust the Coffman-Graham algorithm to account for dummy vertices of nonzero size.

2. Complete the proof that there is an integer solution to the linear program in Section 9.1.3, for finding a layering with a minimum number of dummy vertices. (Hint: You need to find an appropriate ordering for the vertices with nonintegral values $y(u)$.)

3. Prove Theorem 9.1.

4. Prove Theorem 9.3.

5. Consider the following simplification of the median method. Order vertices in L_2 first on $med(u)$ and then on $avg(u)$. If two vertices have the same median and the same barycenter, then separate them arbitrarily. Does this method have a performance guarantee such as the median method (as in Theorem 9.2)?

6. Prove Lemma 9.3.

7. Show that a set of edges of a digraph is a minimum feedback set if and only if it is a minimum feedback arc set.

8. Prove Theorem 9.7.

Chapter 10

Force-Directed Methods

Force-directed algorithms use a physical analogy to draw graphs. We view a graph as a system of bodies with forces acting between the bodies. The algorithm seeks a configuration of the bodies with locally minimal energy, that is, a position for each body, such that the sum of the forces on each body is zero. For example, Figure 10.1.a shows a graph where vertices have been replaced with electrically charged particles that repel each other, and edges have been replaced with springs that connect the particles. An *equilibrium configuration*, where the sum of the forces on each particle is zero, is illustrated in Figure 10.1.b. This configuration can be interpreted as a straight-line drawing of the graph, as in Figure 10.1.c..

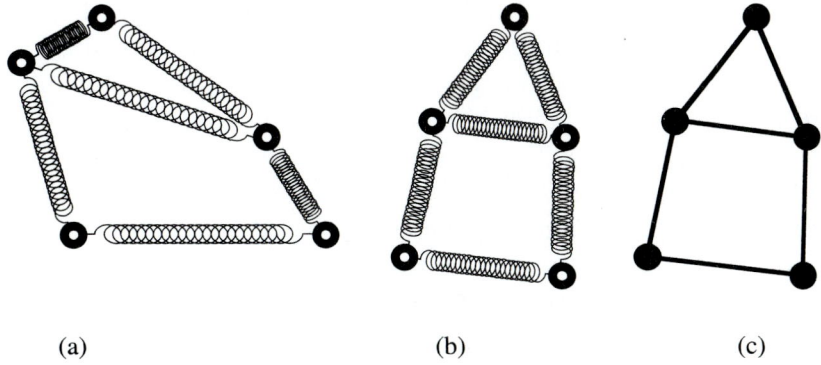

(a)   (b)   (c)

Figure 10.1: A spring algorithm.

There are many force-directed methods, and some are described below. In general, they have two parts:

The *model*: A *force system* defined by the vertices and edges, which provides a physical model for the graph.

The *algorithm*: This is a technique for finding an equilibrium state of the force system, that is, a position for each vertex, such that the total force on every vertex is zero. This state defines a drawing of the graph.

In a sense, the model encodes the aesthetic criteria. The forces are defined so that an equilibrium configuration is a pleasing drawing.

The model may be defined as an *energy system* rather than a force system. In this case, the algorithm may be viewed as a technique for finding a configuration with locally minimal energy. For example, the spring model above may be viewed as assigning potential energy (based on springs and electrical energy) to a drawing. The algorithm searches for a drawing in which the energy is locally minimal.

Force-directed algorithms are very popular for two reasons:

- The physical analogy makes them easy to understand and relatively simple to code.

- The results can be good.

Force-directed methods were in use before applications in graph visualization, for pure mathematics ([Tut60, Tut63]; see also [LW88]) and layout of printed circuit boards [FCW67, QB79]. More recently, many force-directed algorithms have been proposed and tested [Ead84, KK89, FR91, FLM95, BH87a, Tun92, CBHH87, LES95, ELMS91, CT96, MRS96, DH96, KM91, Men92, Men94, Ros97, FLM95, BF96, Bra96, MdNdS96, EK97, BBS97]. These differ, both in the force or energy model used, and in the method used to find an equilibrium or minimal energy configuration. Some examples of drawings from force-directed methods are in Figures 10.2–10.7.

This chapter describes a few of the best known force-directed methods. In Section 10.1 we introduce a simple model based on springs and electrical forces. In Section 10.2, we describe the famous algorithm of Tutte [Tut60, Tut63], called the *barycenter* method. Section 10.3 presents a more complex method, which attempts to draw graphs so that the Euclidean distance between two vertices is near to the number of edges on the shortest graph-theoretic path between the vertices. Section 10.4 introduces a global force field; magnetic forces act on edges. Extensions of the previously described energy functions are introduced in Section 10.5, most notably the simulated annealing method of Davidson and Harel [DH96]. Finally, Section 10.7 discusses further issues of force-directed methods.

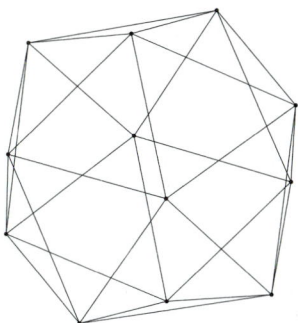

Figure 10.2: Icosahedron drawn using the `GEM` algorithm. (Courtesy of A. Frick and A. Ludwig.)

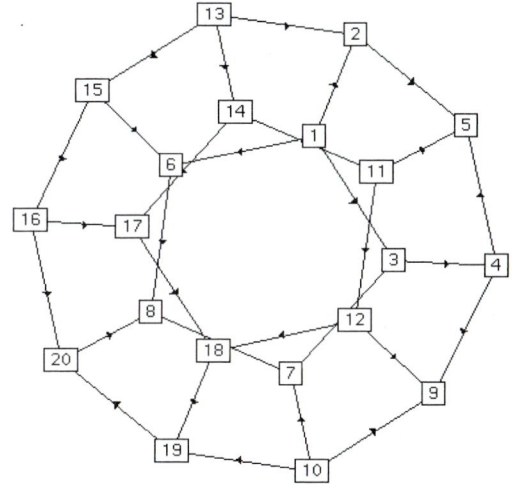

Figure 10.3: Dodecahedron drawn using a force-directed algorithm (Courtesy of U. Erlingsson and M. Krishnamoorthy.)

10.1 Springs and Electrical Forces

The simplest force-directed method uses a combination of *spring* and *electrical* forces mentioned above. Edges are modeled as springs, and vertices are equally charged particles which repel each other. More precisely, the

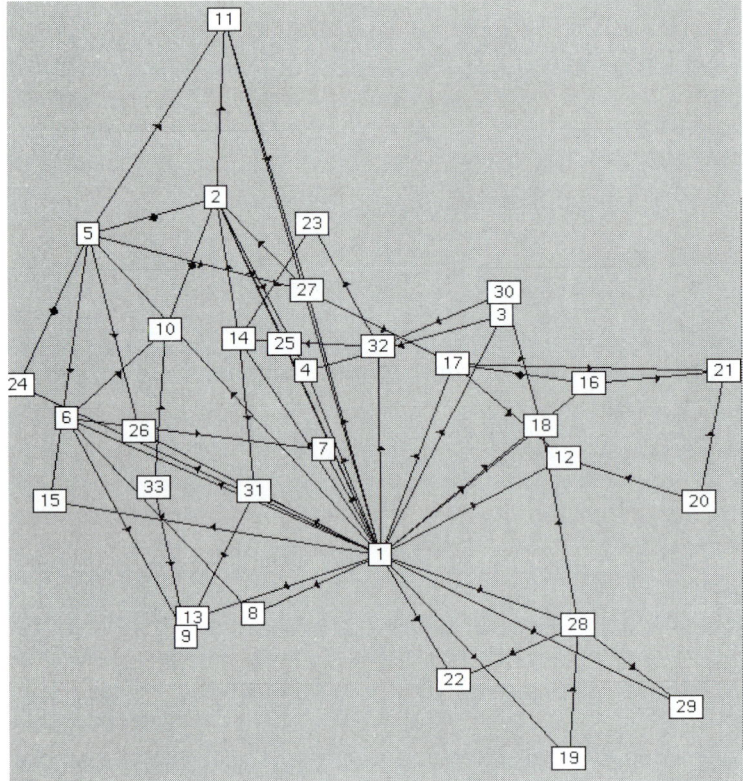

Figure 10.4: Graph of internet traffic drawn using a simple spring algorithm. (Courtesy of J. Fenwick, D. Thompson and R. Stacey.)

force on vertex v is

$$F(v) = \sum_{(u,v)\in E} f_{uv} + \sum_{(u,v)\in V\times V} g_{uv}, \qquad (10.1)$$

where f_{uv} is the force exerted on v by the spring between u and v, and g_{uv} is the electrical repulsion exerted on v by the vertex u. The force f_{uv} follows Hooke's law, that is, f_{uv} is proportional to the difference between the distance between u and v and the zero-energy length of the spring. The electrical force g_{uv} follows an inverse square law.

Let us denote the Euclidean distance between points p and q by $d(p,q)$, and suppose that the position of vertex v is denoted by $p_v = (x_v, y_v)$. Thus,

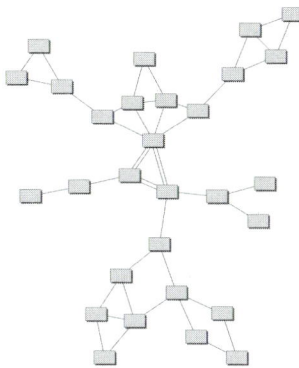

Figure 10.5: Graph drawn using a simple spring algorithm. (Courtesy of Tom Sawyer Software.)

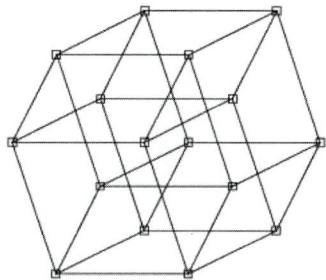

Figure 10.6: A hypercube drawn with the method of Tunkelang. (Courtesy of D. Tunkelang.)

from equation (10.1), the x component of the force $F(v)$ on v is

$$\sum_{(u,v)\in E} k_{uv}^{(1)} (d(p_u,p_v) - \ell_{uv}) \frac{x_v - x_u}{d(p_u,p_v)} + \sum_{(u,v)\in V\times V} \frac{k_{uv}^{(2)}}{(d(p_u,p_v))^2} \frac{x_v - x_u}{d(p_u,p_v)}. \quad (10.2)$$

The y component of $F(v)$ has a similar expression. The parameters ℓ_{uv}, $k_{uv}^{(1)}$, and $k_{uv}^{(2)}$ are independent of the positions of the vertices, and may be interpreted as follows:

- The natural (zero energy) length of the spring between u and v is ℓ_{uv}.

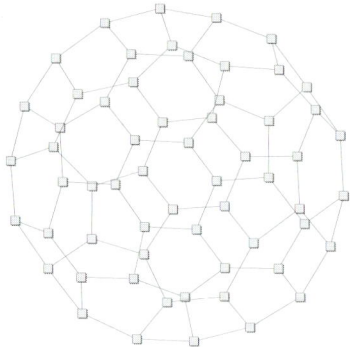

Figure 10.7: Graph drawn with an experimental force-directed algorithm from Tom Sawyer Software. (Courtesy of A. Frick.)

If the spring has length ℓ_{uv} (that is, $d(p_u, p_v) = \ell_{uv}$), then no force is exerted by (u, v).

- The *stiffness* of the spring between u and v is expressed with $k_{uv}^{(1)}$. The larger the value of $k_{uv}^{(1)}$, the more the tendency for the distance between u and v to be close to ℓ_{uv}.

- The strength of the electrical repulsion between u and v depends on $k_{uv}^{(2)}$.

This model directly aims to satisfy two important aesthetics:

- The spring force between adjacent vertices is aimed to ensure that the distance between adjacent vertices u and v is approximately equal to ℓ_{uv}.

- The electrical force aims to ensure that vertices should not be close together.

Further, experience with this model has shown an indirect benefit. Under certain assumptions, the drawing tends to be symmetric (see [EL97]).

It is possible to use *logarithmic* springs [Ead84] rather than Hooke's law springs, that is, the x component of f_{uv} in equation (10.1) becomes

$$k_{uv}^{(1)} \log \left(\frac{d(p_u, p_v)}{\ell_{uv}} \right) \frac{x_v - x_u}{d(p_u, p_v)}.$$

However, experience has shown that it is difficult to justify the extra computational effort by the quality of the resulting drawings.

In specific applications, one may choose the parameters ℓ_{uv}, $k_{uv}^{(1)}$, and $k_{uv}^{(2)}$ in order to customize the appearance of the drawing, or to express semantic features of the graph. For example, ℓ_{uv} represents the desirable distance between u and v. If the relationship expressed by the edge between u and v is strong, then ℓ_{uv} should be small. Thus the distance between u and v will tend to be smaller for stronger relationships.

The algorithm seeks an equilibrium configuration of these forces, that is, a drawing in which the total force $F(v)$ for each vertex v is zero. Equivalently, the algorithm seeks to find a drawing in which the energy is locally minimal with respect to the vertex positions.

A variety of numerical techniques can be used to find an equilibrium configuration. A simple "follow your nose" algorithm works as follows. Vertices are initially placed at random locations. At each iteration, the force $F(v)$ on each vertex is computed, and each vertex v is moved in the direction of $F(v)$ by a small amount proportional to the magnitude of $F(v)$.

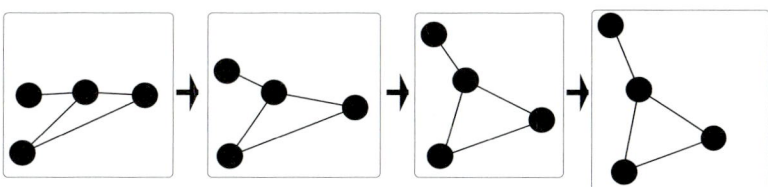

Figure 10.8: Frames in an animation of a spring algorithm.

This simple algorithm is not the fastest way to find an equilibrium. However, it allows an intuitive and smooth animation of the transformation from random locations to an equilibrium configuration. A sequence of frames from such an animation is shown in Figure 10.8.

10.2   The Barycenter Method

One of the earliest graph drawing methods, due to Tutte [Tut60, Tut63], can be described as a variation on the method presented in the previous section. The Tutte model uses springs with $\ell_{uv} = 0$, that is, the force exerted on vertex v by the edge (u, v) is proportional to $d(p_u, p_v)$. The stiffness parameter $k_{uv}^{(1)}$ is set to one for each edge (u, v), and there are no electrical forces. Thus force $F(v)$ can be simply expressed as

$$F(v) = \sum_{(u,v) \in E} (p_u - p_v). \tag{10.3}$$

Of course, equilibrium for the set of forces given by equation (10.3) implies the trivial solution $p_v = 0$ for all v. Indeed, this is not a good drawing! To avoid the trivial solution, the vertex set V is partitioned into two sets, a set of at least three *fixed* vertices, and a set of *free* vertices. The fixed vertices are "nailed down" so that the spring forces do not affect them. Normally, they are "nailed" at the vertices of a strictly convex polygon.

Positions for the free vertices are chosen according to forces defined in equation (10.3). That is, we choose p_v so that $F(v) = 0$ for each free vertex v. Thus

$$\sum_{(u,v) \in E} (x_u - x_v) = 0, \tag{10.4}$$

and

$$\sum_{(u,v) \in E} (y_u - y_v) = 0, \tag{10.5}$$

where $p_v = (x_v, y_v)$ for each vertex v. Suppose that the sets of fixed and free neighbors of v are denoted by $N_0(v)$ and $N_1(v)$, respectively. Rewriting equations (10.4) and (10.5) yields

$$deg(v)x_v - \sum_{u \in N_1(v)} x_u = \sum_{w \in N_0(v)} x_w^* \tag{10.6}$$

and

$$deg(v)y_v - \sum_{u \in N_1(v)} y_u = \sum_{w \in N_0(v)} y_w^*, \tag{10.7}$$

where the (fixed) position of a fixed vertex w is (x_w^*, y_w^*), and $deg(v)$ denotes the degree of v. Observe that equations (10.6) and (10.7) are linear, and the number of equations and the number of unknowns are both equal to the number of free vertices. Solving them amounts to placing each free vertex at the barycenter of its neighbors. Thus this technique is called the *barycenter method*.

The matrix resulting from the above system of equations is diagonally dominant and in practice, a simple Newton-Raphson iteration (Algorithm 10.1 *Barycenter-Draw*) converges quickly. Note that for planar graphs, the matrix is sparse and it is possible to solve the equations in $O(n^{1.5})$ time [LRT79].

Algorithm 10.1 *Barycenter-Draw*

    Input: graph $G = (V, E)$; a partition $V = V_0 \cup V_1$ of
               V into a set V_0 of at least three *fixed* vertices
               and a set V_1 of *free* vertices; a strictly convex
               polygon P with $|V_0|$ vertices
    Output: a position p_v for each vertex of V, such that
               the fixed vertices form a convex polygon P

1. Place each fixed vertex $u \in V_0$ at a vertex of P, and each free vertex at the origin.

2. **repeat**

        foreach free vertex v **do**

$$x_v = \frac{1}{deg(v)} \sum_{(u,v) \in E} x_u$$
$$y_v = \frac{1}{deg(v)} \sum_{(u,v) \in E} y_u$$

    until x_v and y_v converge for all free vertices v.

                                                      □

One of the main attractions of the barycenter method is that if the input graph is triconnected and planar, then the output drawing is planar and convex (that is, each face is a convex polygon).

Theorem 10.1 *Suppose that G is a triconnected planar graph, f is a face in a planar embedding of G, and P is a strictly convex planar drawing of f. Then applying the barycenter algorithm, with the vertices of f fixed and positioned according to P, yields a convex planar drawing of G.*

The proof of the above theorem can be found in [Tut60, Tut63].

A planar graph drawn with the barycenter method appears in Figure 10.9. Note that the resolution is poor. This is a characteristic of the barycenter method. In fact, for every $n > 1$ there is a graph G, such that the barycenter method outputs a drawing exponential area for any resolution rule [EG96].

Theorem 10.1 can be generalized to drawings obtained with a more complex energy function. For Algorithm 10.1 *Barycenter-Draw*, the energy of

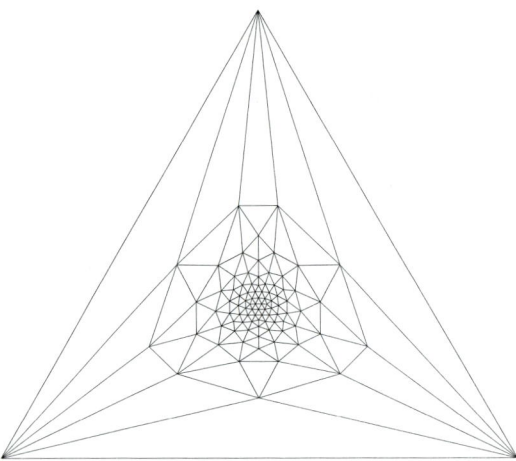

Figure 10.9: A large planar graph drawn with the barycenter method. (Courtesy of P. Garvan.)

a drawing is the sum of the squares of the lengths of the edges. More generally, we can define the energy of a drawing as the sum of the pth powers of the edge lengths. For these energy functions, a theorem analogous to Theorem 10.1 holds [BH87b, BO87].

10.3   Forces Simulating Graph Theoretic Distances

In this section, we describe a method that attempts to model graph theoretic distance with Euclidean distance. The model was pioneered in [KS80] and independently developed in [KK89]. If $G = (V, E)$ is a connected graph and $u, v \in V$, then the *graph theoretic distance*, denoted by $\delta(u, v)$, is the number of edges on a shortest path between u and v. The aim of this method is to find a drawing in which, for each pair u, v of vertices, the Euclidean distance $d(p_u, p_v)$ between u and v is approximately proportional to $\delta(u, v)$ between all pairs u and v of G. Thus the system has a force proportional to $d(p_u, p_v) - \delta(u, v)$ between vertices u and v.

Kamada and Kawai ([KK89]; see also [Kam89b]) take an energy view of this intuition. The potential energy in the "spring" between u and v is the integral of the force that the spring exerts, that is

$$\frac{1}{2}k_{uv}\left(d(p_u, p_v) - \delta(u, v)\right)^2.$$

Kamada chooses the *stiffness* parameter k_{uv} so that springs between vertices that have small graph theoretic distance are stronger. More precisely, $k_{uv} = k/\delta(u,v)^2$ for a constant k. Thus the energy in (u,v) is

$$\eta = \frac{k}{2}\left(\frac{d(p_u, p_v)}{\delta(u,v)} - 1\right)^2.$$

The energy η in the whole drawing is the sum of these individual energies, that is

$$\eta = \frac{k}{2}\sum_{u \neq v \in V}\left(\frac{d(p_u, p_v)}{\delta(u,v)} - 1\right)^2.$$

The algorithm seeks a position $p_v = (x_v, y_v)$, for each vertex v, to minimize η. Minima occur when the partial derivatives of η, with respect to each variable x_v and y_v, are zero. This gives a set of $2|V|$ equations

$$\frac{\partial \eta}{\partial x_v} = 0,\ \ \frac{\partial \eta}{\partial y_v} = 0,\ \ v \in V.$$

Unfortunately these equations are nonlinear. However, an iterative approach may be used to solve them. At each step, a vertex is moved to a position that minimizes energy, while all other vertices remain fixed. The vertex to be moved is chosen as the one that has the largest force acting on it, that is, the one for which

$$\sqrt{\left(\frac{\partial \eta}{\partial x_v}\right)^2 + \left(\frac{\partial \eta}{\partial y_v}\right)^2}$$

is maximized over all $v \in V$.

10.4   Magnetic Fields

Sugiyama and Misue [SM95a, SM95b] proposed a model in which some or all of the springs are magnetized, and there is a global magnetic field that acts on the springs. The magnetic field can be used to control the orientation of the edges and thus the model can handle a broader class of aesthetic criteria than the methods of previous sections.

There are three basic types of magnetic field, shown in Figure 10.10:

- *Parallel*: All magnetic forces operate in the same direction.

- *Radial*: The forces operate radially outward from a point.

- *Concentric*: The forces operate in concentric circles.

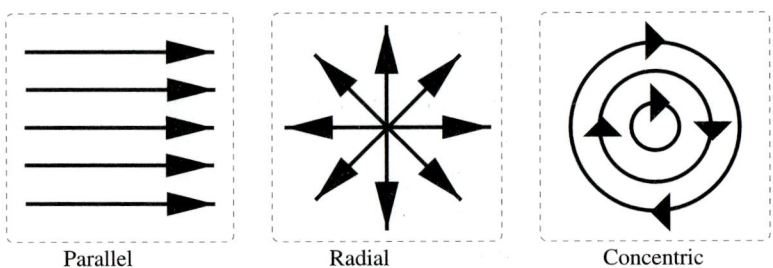

Figure 10.10: Types of magnetic field.

The three basic fields can be combined. For example, we can encourage orthogonal edges with a combination of parallel forces in the horizontal and vertical directions.

The springs can be magnetized in two ways:

- *Unidirectional*: The spring tends to align with the direction of the magnetic field.

- *Bidirectional*: The spring tends to align with the magnetic field, but in either direction.

Further, a spring may not be magnetized at all.

The magnetic field induces a torsion, or rotational force, on the magnetized springs. For a unidirectionally magnetized spring representing the edge (u, v), the force is proportional to $d(p_u, p_v)^\alpha \theta^\beta$, where $d(p_u, p_v)$ is the Euclidean distance between p_u and p_v, θ is the angle between the magnetic field and the line from p_u to p_v, and α and β are constants. This is illustrated in Figure 10.11. Forces on bidirectional springs are similar.

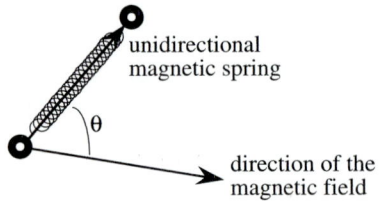

Figure 10.11: Magnetic spring.

The magnetic forces are combined with the spring and electrical forces described in Section 10.1.

Algorithms for finding an equilibrium configuration use the same "follow your nose" approach as in Section 10.1. In other words, vertices are placed initially at random locations, and, at each iteration, the vertices move to positions with a lower energy.

Unlike methods of the previous sections, the magnetic spring model is able to handle directed graphs. Unidirectional springs, combined with one of the fields in Figure 10.10, can give drawings in which most of the arcs point downward (in a downward parallel field), outward (in a radial field), or counterclockwise (in an counterclockwise concentric field).

The method has also been applied with some success to orthogonal drawings (using a combined vertical and horizontal field, with bidirectional springs) and *mixed graphs*, that is, graphs with both directed and undirected edges.

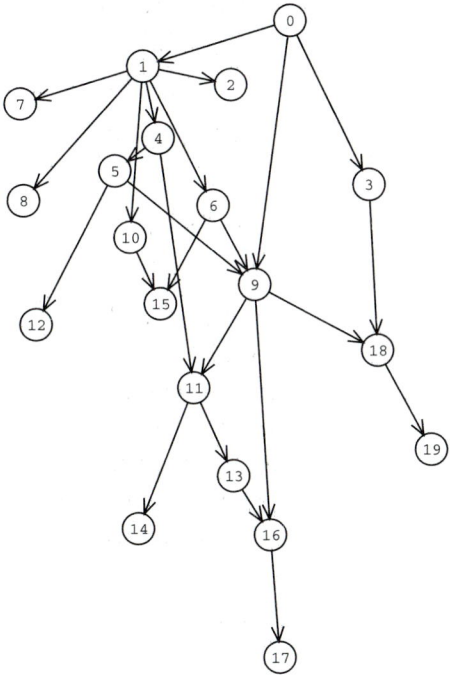

Figure 10.12: Magnetic spring drawing using a vertical magnetic field and unidirectional magnetic springs.

Some sample drawings are given in Figures 10.12 and 10.13. The drawing in Figure 10.12 uses a parallel magnetic field and unidirectional magnetic springs, and thus the edges tend to point downward. The drawing in Figure 10.13 uses two parallel magnetic fields, one horizontal and one vertical, as well as unidirectional magnetic springs. This ensures that the drawing has a tendency to be orthogonal, and the result is close to an hv-drawing (see Section 3.1.4).

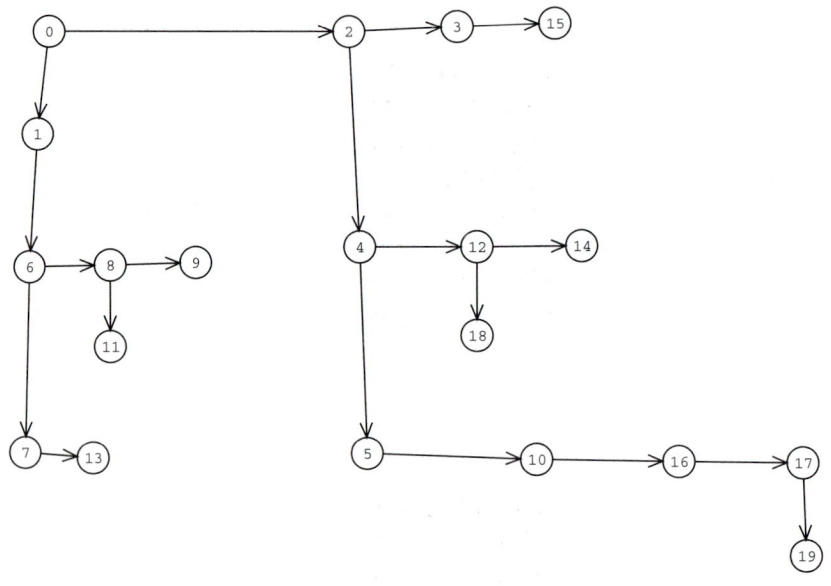

Figure 10.13: Magnetic spring drawing using a combination of horizontal and vertical magnetic fields and unidirectional magnetic springs.

10.5   General Energy Functions

In each of the methods discussed above, the energy function η is a simple and continuous function of the locations of the vertices. However, many of the important aesthetic criteria, such as the minimization of the number of edge crossings, are not continuous. By including discrete energy functions, we can broaden the class of aesthetic criteria.

For example, for each drawing, we can define

- The number of crossings

- The number of horizontal and vertical edges

- The number of bends in edges,

as well as the continuous measures described in the previous sections.

Also, recall from Section 2.2 that aesthetics conflict with each other, that is, in general, we cannot expect to optimize several criteria simultaneously. We can use an energy function that linearly combines a number of measures

$$\eta = \lambda_1 \eta_1 + \lambda_2 \eta_2 + \ldots + \lambda_k \eta_k, \qquad (10.8)$$

where, for $i = 1, 2, \ldots, k$, η_i is a measure for an aesthetic criterion and λ_i is a constant. The functions η_i may include spring energy, electrical energy, and magnetic energy, as well as discrete functions such as those mentioned above. In this way, the energy η measures the "ugliness" of the drawing and a drawing of minimum energy has maximum beauty.

As an example of this approach, Davidson and Harel [DH96] use the following energy function for straight-line drawings

$$\eta = \lambda_1 \eta_1 + \lambda_2 \eta_2 + \lambda_3 \eta_3 + \lambda_4 \eta_4, \qquad (10.9)$$

where

$\eta_1 = \sum_{u,v \in V} (1/d(p_u, p_v)^2)$: This is similar to the electrical repulsion used in Section 10.1. This term aims to ensure that vertices do not come too close together.

$\eta_2 = \sum_{u \in V} \left((1/r_u^2) + (1/\ell_u^2) + (1/t_u^2) + (1/b_u^2) \right)$, where $r_u, \ell_u, t_u,$ and b_u are the Euclidean distances between vertex u and the four sidelines (right, left, top, and bottom) of the rectangular frame in which the graph is drawn. This term ensures that vertices do not come too close to the borders of the screen.

$\eta_3 = \sum_{(u,v) \in E} d(p_u, p_v)^2$ ensures that edges do not become too long.

η_4 is the number of edge crossings in the drawing.

The flexibility of general energy function methods allows a variety of aesthetics to be used by adjusting the coeficients λ_i. For example, consider Figures 10.14 and 10.15, which are both pictures of the nonplanar graph $K_{3,3}$. These are both output from a general energy system from [BBS97]. Figure 10.14 has fewer edges that cross, and Figure 10.15 has more symmetry. The user of the system of [BBS97] can choose to emphasize either crossing minimization or symmetry, by simply adjusting system parameters.

In general, with a model of the form in equation (10.8), the user can adjust the weights $\lambda_1, \lambda_2, \ldots, \lambda_k$ to suit the aesthetics of a particular application or a particular user. A large value for λ_i indicates that the ith

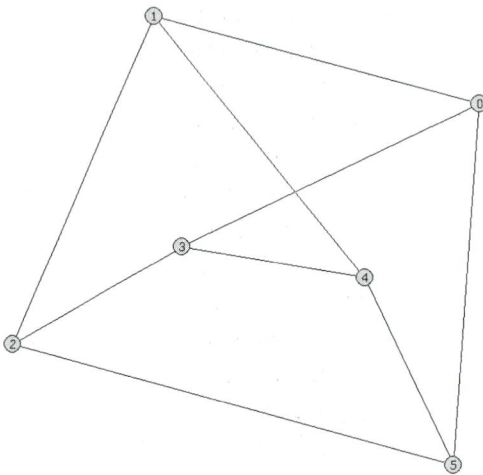

Figure 10.14: A drawing of $K_{3,3}$ with only two edges crossing.

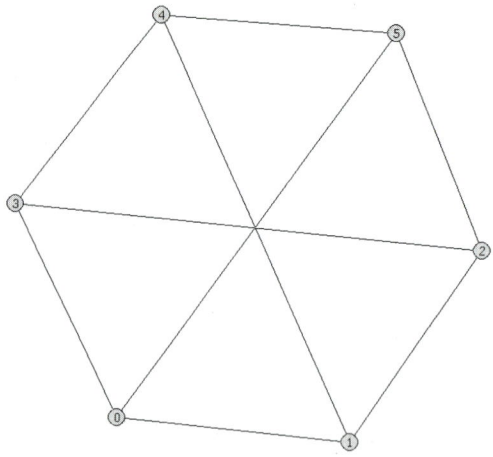

Figure 10.15: A drawing of $K_{3,3}$ with three edges crossing, but with a high degree of symmetry.

aesthetic criterion is important. Mendonca [Men94] shows how these co-efficients can be automatically adjusted to the user's preferences without explicit user intervention.

Figure 10.16 illustrates the successes and failures of techniques such as those described above. The first picture (a) shows an excellent drawing of a 12-vertex planar graph. It is symmetric and planar. Unfortunately, the method of [DH96] was not able to produce this drawing. The reason is that the planarity and high degree of symmetry depend on highly nonuniform edge lengths. It is an interesting problem to create a force-directed algorithm which can automatically adjust the strengths of the springs to obtain better drawings. However, the algorithm of [DH96] produced Figure 10.16.b–d, all of which are very good drawings. Figure 10.16(b) is planar, but the edge lengths are not uniform and it has no symmetry. This drawing used a version of the algorithm with a fairly large value of λ_4. When λ_4 was decreased, the drawings in Figure 10.16.c and d were obtained. These have crossings, but display symmetry and have a pleasing three-dimensional appearance. Note that Figure 10.16.d has fairly uniform edge lengths.

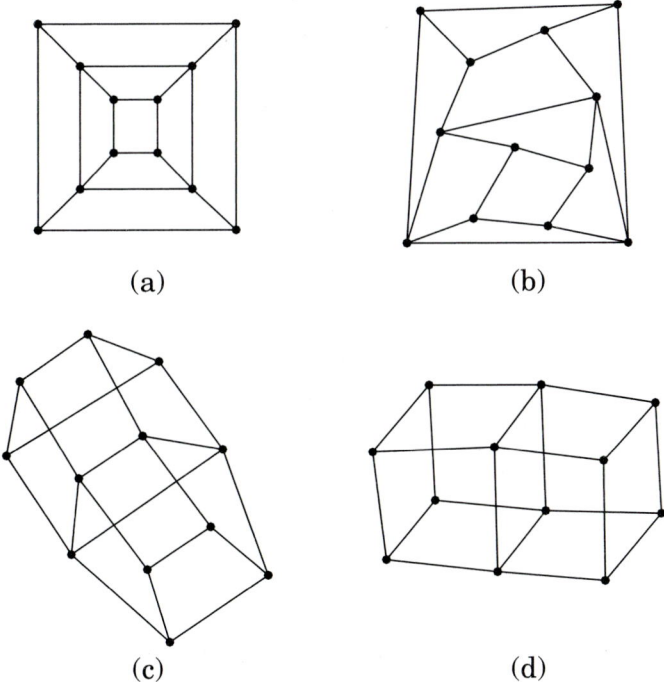

(a)   (b)

(c)   (d)

Figure 10.16: Drawings of a 12-vertex graph: (a) is an excellent drawing, not obtained by simluated annealing; (b), (c), and (d) were obtained using a general energy function, with various coefficients. The minimum energy state was found by a simulated annealing method. (Courtesy of David Harel.)

The main problem with using general energy functions is that it may be computationally expensive to find a minimum energy state. Since the cost function is general and discrete, we must resort to very general optimization methods such as simulated annealing [DH96, CT96, MRS96, Men94, CP96] and genetic algorithms [KM91, Bra96, Ros97, BBS97]. These methods are characteristically computationally intensive and are not suitable for interactive systems.

Despite the computational difficulties, the flexibility of such methods has ensured their popularity. For example, Figure 10.17 shows a social network. The layout was computed by `KrackPlot` [KBM94, Kra98], using a simulated annealing method.

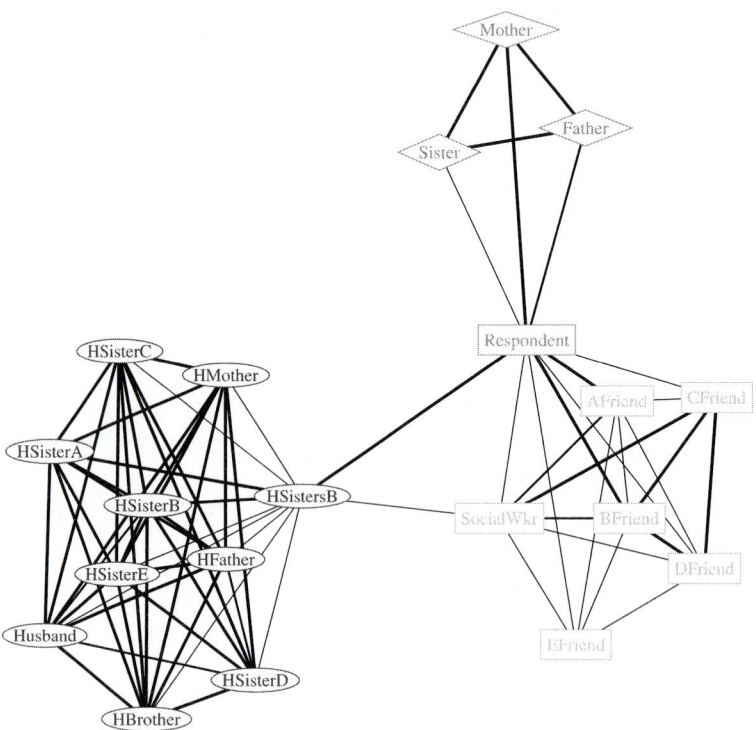

Figure 10.17: Drawings of a social network, computed by `KrackPlot`, using a simulated annealing method. (Courtesy of D. Krackhardt, J. Blythe, and C. McGrath.)

10.6 Constraints

The force-directed approach has been extended to support several types of constraints [Kam88, Kam89a, Ost96, DFM93, HM97, KKR96, RMS97, SM95a]. For example, force-directed methods can handle:

- Position constraints

- Fixed-subgraph constraints

- Constraints that can be expressed by forces or energy functions.

A position constraint assigns to a vertex a topologically connected region where the vertex should remain. Examples of prescribed regions include:

1. A single point, which allows a vertex to be to "nailed down" at a specific location.

2. A horizontal line, which allows a group of vertices to be arranged on a layer.

3. A circle, which allows a set of vertices to be restricted to a distinct region.

The numerical techniques that are used for unconstrained force-directed algorithms can be easily adjusted for constraints that involve restricting vertices to any region with a smooth boundary. Iterative methods, for example, can confine the movement of vertices to the prescribed region at each iteration. At the boundary of a constraining region, the vertices move along the boundary in a frictionless way. An analysis of the physical and numerical aspects of constraining vertices to curves (and to surfaces in three dimensions) is given by Ostry [Ost96].

A fixed-subgraph constraint assigns a prescribed subdrawing to a subgraph, which may appear translated or rotated, but not otherwise deformed, in the overall drawing of the graph. It can be supported by considering the subgraph as a rigid body. This body is translated and rotated at each simulation step according to the overall force and torque applied to it as a result of the individual forces applied to its vertices.

As an example, the barycenter method of Section 10.2 may be seen as a force-directed method that constrains a set of vertices to a polygonal shape.

Constraints that can be expressed by forces include:

- Orientation of directed edges in a given direction, for example, horizontal and vertical.

- Geometric clustering of specified sets vertices.

- Alignment of vertices.

The magnetic spring model in Section 10.4 allows the orientation of a user-specified set of edges in a specific direction by a choice of magnetizations of the springs and a choice global magnetic field.

Clustering can be achieved as follows (see Figure 10.18):

1. For each set C of vertices which need to be clustered, add to the graph a dummy "attractor" vertex v_C.

2. Add attractive forces between an attractor v_C and each vertex in C.

3. Add repulsive forces between pairs of attractors and between attractors and vertices not in any cluster.

This method has been used [ECH97] in web navigation systems to ensure clustering around nodes representing hypertext documents.

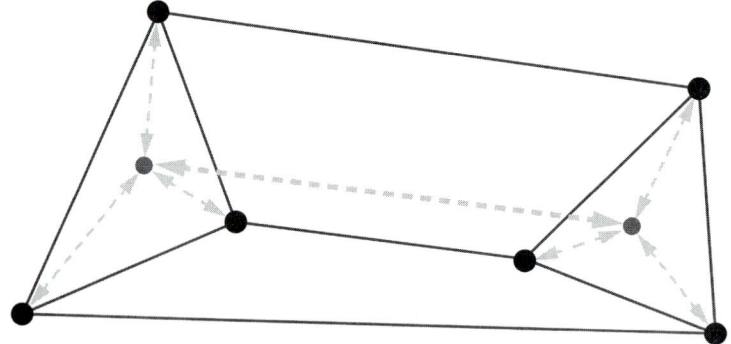

Figure 10.18: Example of clustering constraints realized by means of forces. The two shaded vertices represent the dummy attractors of the two clusters. The attractive forces between cluster vertices and attractors, and the repulsive force between attractors are shown with dashed double-arrows.

10.7   Remarks

Force-directed methods are notorious for using considerable computational resources, and several attempts have been made to improve their efficiency. These include:

- The use of force functions that are more amenable to efficient algorithms for finding local minimal [FR91].

- Methods which use some randomization in the style of simulated annealing [FLM95, Tun92].

- The use of sophisticated methods from numerical analysis to solve the equations that arise from the various models. An interesting point made by Ostry [Ost96] is that the equations describing the minimal energy states are *stiff* for some graphs of low connectivity. This means that classical numerical techniques can be very slow. However, special methods have been developed to deal with stiff equations and can speed up force-directed methods considerably.

- The use of combinatorial preprocessing methods. Harel and Sardas [HS95] give a variety of *ad hoc* combinatorial heuristics, which give a good initial layout of a graph. This layout can be used as a starting point for the method of Davidson and Harel described above.

  Ostry [Ost96] shows that replacing the cliques of a graph by stars can improve the speed of some spring algorithms (Section 10.1) for dense graphs.

Force-directed algorithms are heuristics which are best analyzed empirically. Brandenburg, Himsolt, and Rohrer [BHR96] performed an extensive empirical analysis of the following methods:

- The method of Fruchterman and Reingold [FR91]. This is similar to that described in Section 10.1.

- The method of Kamada and Kawai [KK89, Kam89b], as described in Section 10.3.

- The simulated annealing method of Davidson and Harel [DH96] as described in Section 10.5. A version of this method with a low value of λ_4 (that is, a version which ignores edge crossings) was also tested.

- The method of Tunkelang [Tun92]. This method uses the same cost function as Davidson and Harel, but has a method for finding a local minimum.

- The GEM method of Frick, Ludwig, and Mehldau [FLM95], which is one of the few methods that can handle graphs with more than 100 vertices.

They conclude that there is no universal winner among these methods, and their overall recommendation is to try several methods and choose the best.

An interesting conclusion from their experiments is that the drawings resulting from many of the algorithms (including the Davidson-Harel method with a low λ_4) are remarkably similar. They also note that algorithms from [FLM95] and [Kam89b] are relatively fast, and that the algorithm from [FR91] is fast on small graphs (less than about 60 vertices). If time is not important, then we can adjust the parameters of the algorithms from [Tun92] and [DH96] to obtain pleasing drawings.

10.8   Exercises

1. Show that the resolution of the output from the barycenter algorithm may be poor. More specifically, show that for each n there is a triconnected planar graph G with $O(n)$ vertices, such that if the the barycenter algorithm draws G inside the unit square, then at least two vertices have distance $O(\frac{1}{2^n})$.

2. Prove that the barycenter algorithm gives symmetric drawings of graphs (when the graph has appropriate automorphisms).

3. Consider the following force model algorithm for directed acyclic graphs. Each source (vertex of indegree zero) is fixed in a position at the top of the page. Every other vertex is subject to spring and electrical forces as in Section 10.1, as well as a linear attraction to the bottom of the page.

   Implement and evaluate a force-directed algorithm based on this model.

4. The discussion of force-directed algorithms in this chapter assumes that vertices have zero area. What adjustments are needed if the vertices are circles of nontrivial size? What about rectangles?

5. A straight-line drawing of a connected graph is *path-tension-free*, if for every pair u, v of vertices, the Euclidean distance between u and v is the number of edges on the shortest path between u and v. Describe the class of graphs which admit a path-tension-free drawing.

6. A straight-line drawing of a graph is *edge-tension-free*, if for every edge (u, v), the Euclidean distance between u and v is one. For each

of the following classes of graphs, describe the subclass which admits an edge-tension-free drawing.

(a) Trees.

(b) Biconnected graphs.

(c) Triconnected planar graphs.

Repeat the same exercise for drawings in three dimensions.

Chapter 11

Proving Lower Bounds

In this chapter, we present techniques for proving lower bounds on graph drawing problems. In Section 11.1, we give an example of a general method for proving lower bounds on the area of planar drawings, based on constructing a family of planar graphs with recursively nested subgraphs, and on expressing the area of the drawing with a recurrence relation. In particular, we show that there is a family of planar digraphs that require exponential area in any upward planar straight-line drawing.

In Section 11.2, we present a general paradigm for NP-completeness proofs related to graph drawing, based on a a mechanical device, called "logic engine." This device simulates well-known NP-complete problems.

11.1 A Technique for Proving Exponential Area Lower Bounds

In this section, we present a general technique for proving existential area lower bounds. We illustrate this technique by showing that there is a class of planar acyclic digraphs that requires exponential area in any planar straight-line upward drawing (see also [DTT92a]). This technique has also been used to prove lower bounds on the area of planar straight-line drawings of series-parallel digraphs [BCD+94], planar layered digraphs [LE97], planar clustered graphs [FCE95], and planar graphs with bounded angular resolution [GT94, MP94].

Let us define the following class of digraphs (see Figure 11.1). Digraph G_1, shown in Figure 11.1.a, consists of vertices s_0, s_1, t_0, and t_1, and edges (s_0, t_0), (s_1, s_0), (t_0, t_1), (s_1, t_0), and (s_0, t_1). For $n \geq 2$, digraph G_n is constructed from G_{n-1} by adding vertices s_n and t_n, and edges (s_n, s_{n-1}),

(t_{n-1}, t_n), (s_{n-2}, t_n), (s_n, t_{n-2}), (s_n, t_{n-1}), and (s_{n-1}, t_n), as shown in Figure 11.1.b.

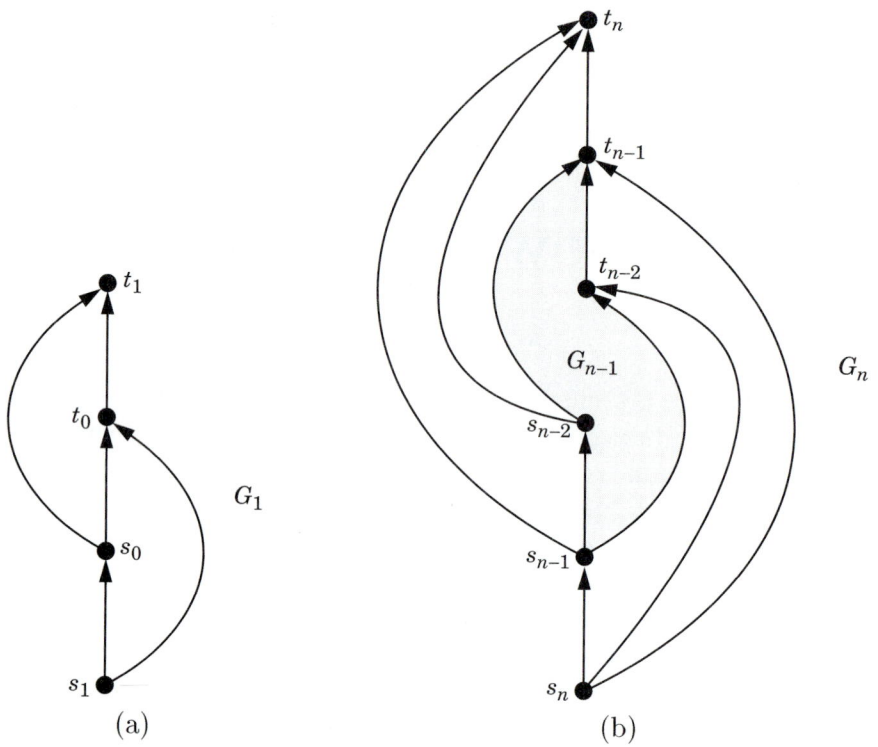

(a)   (b)

Figure 11.1: A class of digraphs that require exponential area: (a) digraph G_1; (b) digraph G_n.

It is easy to verify that G_n is a planar $s_n t_n$-graph (see Section 4.2) with $2n+2$ vertices and $6n+1$ edges. Also, G_n is triconnected for $n \geq 2$, and thus has a unique embedding. We show that the minimum area of a straight-line drawing of G_n is $\Omega(2^n)$ for every possible resolution rule.

Theorem 11.1 *Given any resolution rule, a planar straight-line upward drawing of digraph G_n (with $2n + 2$ vertices) has area $\Omega(2^n)$.*

Proof: Let A_n be the minimum area of a planar straight-line upward drawing of G_n. We use induction to prove that $A_n \geq 4 \cdot A_{n-2}$. Since $A_1 \geq c$, for some constant c depending on the resolution rule, this implies the claimed result.

Let Γ_n be a straight-line drawing of G_n with minimum area A_n. By removing vertices s_n and t_n and their incident edges from Γ_n, we obtain a straight-line drawing Γ_{n-1} of G_{n-1}. Also, by removing vertices s_{n-1} and t_{n-1} and their incident edges from Γ_{n-1}, we obtain a straight-line drawing Γ_{n-2} of G_{n-2}. Let σ and τ be horizontal lines through vertices s_{n-2} and t_{n-2}, respectively. Define θ_1 as the angle formed by edge (t_{n-3}, t_{n-2}) and the x-axis. Also, define θ_2 as the angle formed by edge (s_{n-2}, s_{n-3}) and the x-axis. We distinguish two cases:

Case 1: $\theta_1 \geq \theta_2$ (see Figure 11.2).

Let ρ_1 be the line extending edge (t_{n-3}, t_{n-2}), and λ_1 be the line parallel to ρ_1 through vertex s_{n-2}. Also, let λ_2 be either the line extending edge (s_{n-2}, s_{n-3}) (Figure 11.2.a), or the line through vertices s_{n-2} and t_{n-2} (Figure 11.2.b), whichever forms the largest angle with the x-axis. Vertex s_{n-1} must lie in the region S_{n-1} below σ and to the right of ρ_1, since it is connected to vertices s_{n-2} and t_{n-2} from the right. Similarly, vertex t_{n-1} must lie in the region T_{n-1} above τ and to the left of λ_2. With respect to vertices s_n and t_n, s_n must lie in the region $S_n = S_{n-1}$, since it is connected to t_{n-2} and t_{n-1} from the right, and t_n must lie in the region T_n above τ and to the left of λ_1, since it is connected to s_{n-1} from the left. (Actually, s_n and t_n must lie in proper subregions of S_{n-1} and T_{n-1}.)

Let P be the parallelogram delimited by lines σ, τ, λ_1, and ρ_1. Since s_{n-3} is vertically below t_{n-3}, the area of P is at least two times the area of Γ_{n-2}. Also, the area of Γ_{n-2} is greater than or equal to A_{n-2}, the minimum area required for drawing G_{n-2}. Hence,

$$Area(P) \geq 2 \cdot Area(\Gamma_{n-2}) \geq 2 \cdot A_{n-2}.$$

Now, consider the triangle delimited by lines τ, ρ_1, and the line δ parallel to edge (s_{n-1}, t_n) through vertex s_{n-2} (see Figure 11.3). Clearly, Γ_n must contain this triangle. Let Δ_1 be the triangle delimited by σ, ρ_1, and δ, and let Δ_2 be the triangle delimited by τ, λ_1, and δ. It follows that

$$A_n = Area(\Gamma_n) \geq Area(P) + Area(\Delta_1) + Area(\Delta_2).$$

Since Δ_1 and Δ_2 are similar, the minimum of $Area(\Delta_1) + Area(\Delta_2)$ is equal to $Area(P)$. Hence, we have

$$A_n \geq 2 \cdot Area(P) \geq 4 \cdot Area(\Gamma_{n-2}) = 4 \cdot A_{n-2}.$$

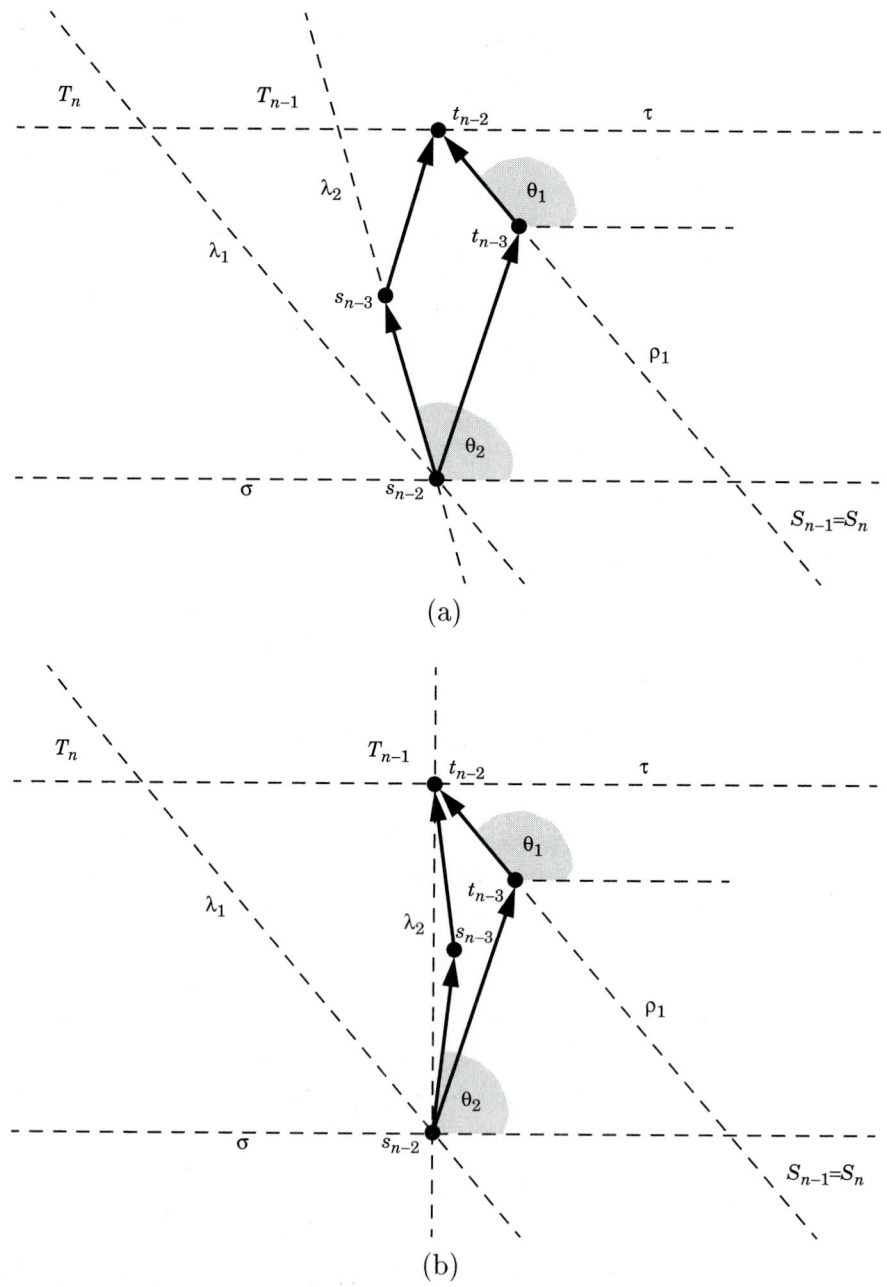

Figure 11.2: Illustration of the proof of Theorem 11.1 for $\theta_1 \geq \theta_2$.

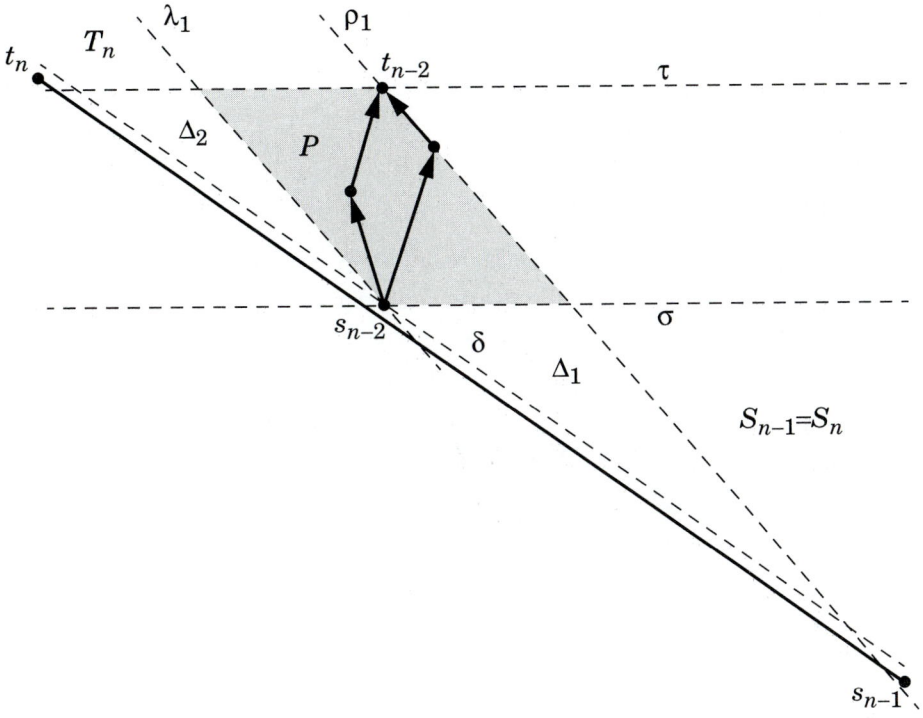

Figure 11.3: Regions P, Δ_1, and Δ_2.

Case 2: $\theta_1 < \theta_2$.

The proof for this case is symmetric to the one for the previous case and is left as an exercise.

$\square$

11.2 The Logic Engine: a Paradigm for NP-Hardness Proofs

In this section, we describe a powerful paradigm for proving NP-hardness of graph drawing problems. The technique was introduced by Bhatt and Cosmadakis [BC87] and later applied widely [EW96b, Idi90, Bra88, EW96a]. The paradigm uses a mechanical device called a "logic engine," illustrated in Figure 11.4. This device mechanically simulates the following well-known NP-complete problem:

Not-All-Equal-3-Sat (NAE3SAT)

Instance: A set C of clauses, each containing three literals from a set of boolean variables.

Question: Can truth values be assigned to the variables so that each clause contains at least one true literal and at least one false literal?

The following section describes the logic engine, and Section 11.2.2 illustrates its application to a specific graph drawing problem. In Section 11.2.3, we list several other graph drawing problems whose NP-hardness has been established using the logic engine paradigm.

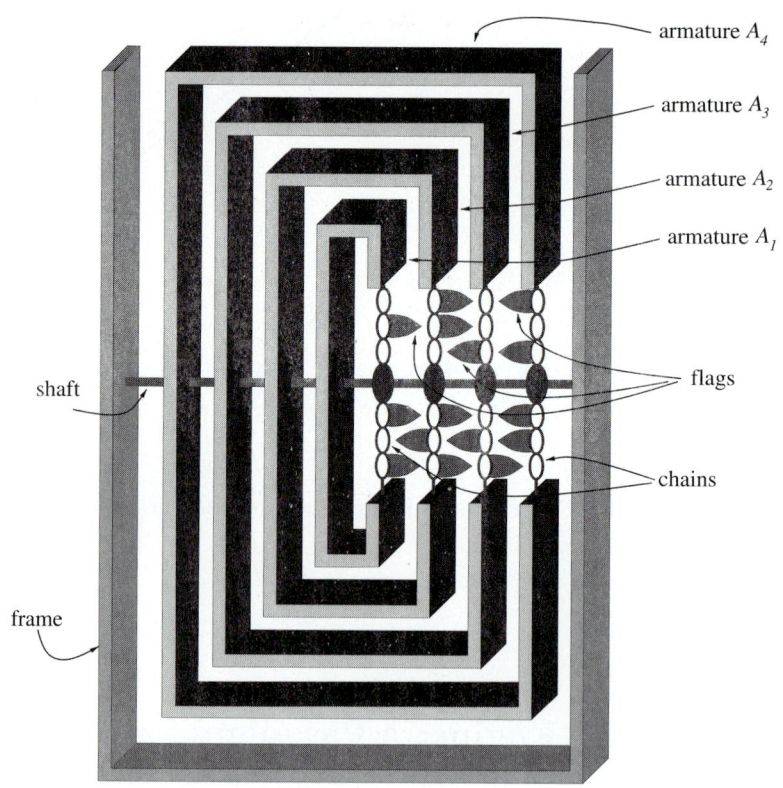

Figure 11.4: A logic engine.

11.2.1   The Logic Engine

First, we describe the *universal* part of the engine, that is, the part which depends only on the number of clauses and the number of variables. Then we show how to *customize* the engine to encode a particular instance of NAE3SAT.

The logic engine is illustrated in Figure 11.4. It consists of several parts, as follows:

- The engine has a *rigid frame*, which supports a *shaft*.

- A nested sequence of n *armatures* A_j, $1 \leq j \leq n$, where n is the number of variables, is mounted to the shaft. Each armature can rotate about the shaft, but its position on the shaft is fixed: It cannot slide back and forth along the shaft. The spacing between armatures is designed to ensure that the armatures can rotate independently of one another.

- Each armature A_j holds two *chains* a_j and $\bar{a}_j$ of equal-length *links*. One stretches from one end of the armature to the shaft, the other stretches from the other end of the armature to the shaft. Each of the chains holds m links, where m is the number of clauses.

Note that the sides of the frame extend on either side of the shaft, at least as far as the chains.

Each armature A_j corresponds to a variable x_j of an instance of NAE3SAT. The chain a_j corresponds to the literal x_j, and the chain $\bar{a}_j$ corresponds to its complement $\bar{x}_j$. If the engine lies flat (so that the frame, each chain, and each armature all lie in the same plane) then the armature A_j can be in one of two positions, either a_j or $\bar{a}_j$ can be above the shaft. These two positions correspond to the truth assignments $x_j = 1$ and $x_j = 0$, respectively.

Each of the clauses $c_1, c_2, \ldots, c_m$ in an instance of NAE3SAT corresponds to a set of links, as described below. The links of each chain are numbered $1, 2, \ldots, m$, outwards from the shaft, as illustrated in Figure 11.5. Clause c_k corresponds to the set consisting of all links numbered k. Note that if the engine lies flat, then the links numbered k form two rows, one on either side of the shaft.

The logic engine is customized by attaching *flags* to the links, as in Figure 11.6. Each flag can rotate freely about the chain, and thus has two possible positions when the logic engine is placed flat in the plane. It can point toward the front (that is, the right-hand side of Figure 11.4), or it can be "flipped" to point toward the rear (that is, the left). However, the flags are designed so that, when the logic engine is placed in the plane, a *collision* involving flags can occur under the following conditions.

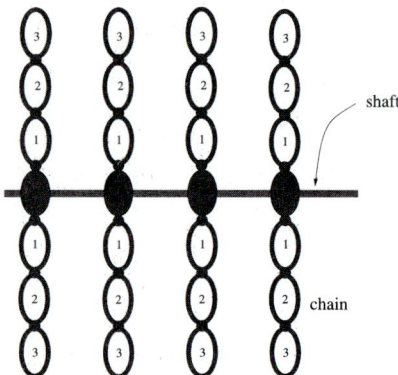

Figure 11.5: Numbering the links of each chain.

- Two flags that lie in the same row and that are attached to chains of adjacent armatures collide with each other if and only if they are flipped so that they point toward each other.

- Any flag attached to the chain of the outermost armature A_n collides with the frame if it points toward the front edge of the frame, and any flag attached to the chain of the innermost armature A_1 collides with that armature if it points toward the rear.

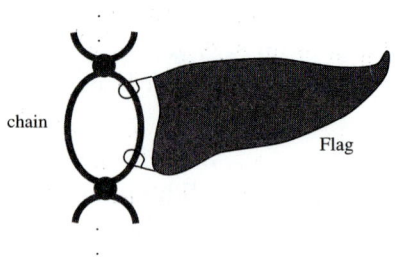

Figure 11.6: A flag on a link.

Flags are attached to specific links according to the clause-literal incidence relation. We attach a flag to every link i of every chain a_j and $\bar{a}_j$, except:

1. If the literal x_j appears in clause c_i then link i of a_j is unflagged

2. If the literal $\bar{x}_j$ appears in clause c_i then link i of $\bar{a}_j$ is unflagged.

The relationship between the logic engine and NAE3SAT is expressed in the following theorem.

Theorem 11.2 *An instance of NAE3SAT is a "yes" instance if and only if the corresponding logic engine has a flat collision-free configuration.*

Proof: Suppose that we have a "yes" instance of NAE3SAT, and the truth assignment t gives at least one true and at least one false literal for each clause. The armatures may be rotated to simulate the truth assignment t as follows. If $t(x_j) = 1$, then place a_j at the top and $\bar{a}_j$ at the bottom. If $t(x_j) = 0$, then place $\bar{a}_j$ at the top and a_j at the bottom. With this configuration of armatures, since each clause c_i contains at least one literal y with $t(y) = 1$ and at least one literal z with $t(z) = 0$, there is at least one unflagged link in each horizontal row of links. We can orient the flags in each row to point toward the unflagged link. This avoids collisions.

On the other hand, suppose that we have a flat collision-free configuration of the logic engine. This implies that there is at least one unflagged link in each row. Thus, with the truth assignment defined by the positions of the armatures, there is at least one true and at least one false literal in each clause. □

11.2.2 Logic Engine and a Graph Drawing Problem

In this section, we illustrate the use of the logic engine by showing that the following problem is NP-hard.

> **Unit Length Planar Straight-line Drawing (ULPGD)**
> *Instance:* A planar graph G.
> *Question:* Is there a straight-line planar drawing of G, such that every edge has length one?

Theorem 11.3 *ULPGD is NP-hard.*

Theorem 11.3 was proved in [EW90] using a complex flow approach. The proof below, using the logic engine, is much simpler.

Roughly speaking, the transformation proceeds as follows. Given an instance of NAE3SAT, we define a *logic graph*, which is an instance of ULPGD. We design the logic graph to simulate a logic engine. It follows from Theorem 11.2, that the logic graph has a unit length planar drawing if and only if the NAE3SAT instance is a "yes" instance.

First, we show how to construct the universal part of the logic graph. The critical property of this graph is that it has a limited number of unit length planar drawings. These drawings correspond to flat configurations of the logic engine. We say that a graph G is *uniquely drawable* if all the unit length planar drawings of G can be obtained from each other by rotations, reflections, translations, and changes of scale.

Figure 11.7 gives a unit length planar drawing of a *link graph*. The link graph is clearly uniquely drawable.

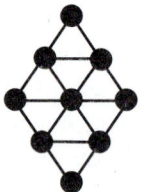

Figure 11.7: A link graph.

A *frame* and *armatures* for the logic graph are composed of link graphs, as shown in Figure 11.8. These are uniquely drawable as well.

Figure 11.8: The universal part of a logic graph.

A *chain* graph is a sequence of link graphs, joined together as shown in Figure 11.8. The *shaft* is a simple path.

As Figure 11.8 shows, the universal part of the logic graph has a unit length planar drawing. It is not difficult to show that the frame and armatures are uniquely drawable. We need to show that the shaft is taut, and thus unique. The maximum Euclidean distance between the extremal endpoints to the shaft is equal to the number of edges in the shaft, and this can be achieved only if the vertices are stretched out along a line. Thus the uniqueness of the drawing of the frame forces the shaft to be drawn as a straight line as shown. This argument can be extended to show the uniqueness of the chains when they are attached to the armatures.

The set of points in the plane occupied by the vertices in any unit length planar drawing of the universal part of the logic graph is unique up to rotations, translations, reflections, and changes of scale. However, the *labeled* logic graph has many unit length planar drawings. Each armature can be turned about the shaft so that either side of the armature can be placed on the outside face. Further, on each chain, each link except the center link can be turned independently of the other links, so that either one of the two degree three vertices of the link lies in the face defined by that particular armature and its chain. These possible motions of the logic graph correspond to the allowable motions of the logic engine.

Next, we show how to customize the logic graph. A link graph may be extended to a *flagged link graph* by the addition of three new vertices, as shown in Figure 11.9. Note that a flagged link graph has a unique drawing.

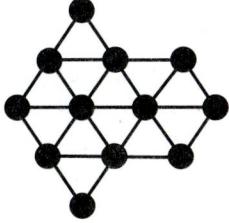

Figure 11.9: A link with a flag.

The customization of a logic graph (to simulate a specific instance of NAE3SAT) consists of replacing link graphs with flagged link graphs according to the incidence between literals and clauses, in the same way as the customization of the logic engine described above. A customized logic graph is shown in Figure 11.10.

Figure 11.10: A logic graph.

The proof that the logic graph has a unit length planar drawing if and only if the NAE3SAT instance is a "yes" instance follows the same argument as the logic engine. Note that the logic graph corresponding to an instance of NAE3SAT with n variables and m clauses has $O((m + n)^2)$ vertices and edges, and the time taken to construct the logic graph is linear in the size of the graph. Theorem 11.3 follows.

11.2.3   Other Problems which Simulate the Logic Engine

The logic engine approach was originally used by Bhatt and Cosmadakis [BC87] to prove that the following problem is NP-hard.

> **Unit Grid Drawings of Trees**
> *Instance*: A tree T.
> *Question*: Is there a grid drawing of T, such that each edge has length one?
> *Remarks*: See [BC87]. The problem remains NP-complete when restricted to binary trees [Gre89].

The technique used by Bhatt and Cosmadakis does not use the armatures, basically because the grid requirement makes them unnecessary. However, an extended frame is needed. Brandenburg [Bra88] showed that the basic ideas could be extended to prove NP-completeness of several related problems for grid drawings of trees, including the following.

Minimum Area Grid Drawings of Trees
Instance: A tree T and an integer K.
Question: Is there a grid drawing of T of area at most K?

Idicula [Idi90] extends these results to a variety of grids, including triangular and hexagonal grids.

The logic engine approach has been used [EW96b] to show that the problem of drawing a tree as a minimum spanning tree is NP-hard:

Euclidean Minimum Spanning Tree Realization
Instance: A tree T.
Question: Is there a drawing of T, such that T is a minimum spanning tree of the vertex locations?

A proof, similar to that in the previous section, has been used [EW96a] to show that *nearest neighbor graph realization* problems are NP-hard. In general, these problems ask for a drawing of a graph G, such that G is the nearest neighbor graph of the locations of its vertices. There are several definitions of "nearest neighbor graph." For example, a *mutual nearest neighbor graph* on a set of points P in the plane has a vertex v_p for each $p \in P$, and an edge (v_p, v_q) whenever p is a nearest neighbor of q and q is a nearest neighbor of p.

Mutual Nearest Neighbor Graph Realization
Instance: A graph G.
Question: Is there a drawing of G, such that G is the mutual nearest neighbor graph of the vertex locations?

The following problem was proved NP-hard in [BK98]. It is possible to adjust the proof in the previous section to provide another proof.

Unit Disk Touching
Instance: A graph G.
Question: Is there a drawing of G such that vertices are represented by unit disks, and there is an edge between u and v if and only if the disks representing u and v touch?

11.3   Exercises

1. Prove that embedded series-parallel digraphs exist, such that any upward straight-line drawing that preserves the embedding requires exponential area.

2. Prove that layered upward planar digraphs exist, such that any planar straight-line drawing that preserves the layering requires exponential area.

3. Use the logic engine to explore the complexity of the problems listed in Subsection 11.2.3.

Appendix A

Bounds

There are mathematical limits on the performance of graph drawing methods. These limits can be in terms of the aesthetic criteria which algorithms try to achieve, or in terms of computational resources required by the algorithms. In many cases, there are trade-offs between various aesthetic criteria, or between aesthetic criteria and computational resources. Designers of graph drawing algorithms need an appreciation of these limits and trade-offs in order to create effective techniques. In this chapter, we summarize upper and lower bounds on properties of various drawings of graphs, and discuss trade-offs between them.

For various classes of graphs and drawing types, many universal/existential upper and lower bounds have been discovered for specific drawing properties. Such bounds typically exhibit trade-offs between drawing properties. A universal bound applies to all the graphs of a given class. An existential bound applies to an infinite number of graphs of a class, that is, there is an infinite family of graphs that exhibit the lower bound.

In Sections A.1, A.2, and A.3, we present bounds on the area, angular resolution, and number of bends, respectively. Trade-offs between area and aspect ratio, as well as between area and angular resolution, are covered in Sections A.4 and A.5. Time complexity issues are discussed in Section A.6.

Throughout this chapter, we denote the number of vertices and edges of the graph being considered by n and m, respectively.

A.1 Area Bounds

In Tables A.2–A.5, we summarize selected universal upper bounds and existential lower bounds on the area of drawings of trees, planar graphs, planar digraphs, and general graphs.

When we give bounds on the area, we assume that the drawing is constrained by some resolution rule that prevents it from being arbitrarily scaled down (for example, we require a grid drawing or a minimum unit distance between any two vertices).

When we say that the *area requirement* of a class of graphs is $O(f(n))$, we mean that both an $O(f(n))$ universal upper bound and an $\Omega(f(n))$ existential lower bound exist on the area.

The following general comments apply.

- Bends have two effects on the area requirement. On one hand, bends occupy space and, hence, negatively affect the area. On the other hand, bends may help in routing edges without using additional space.

- Linear, or almost-linear, bounds on the area can be achieved for trees, as shown in Table A.2. See Table A.8 for trade-offs between area and aspect ratio in drawings of trees.

- As shown in Table A.3, planar graphs admit planar drawings with quadratic area. However, the area requirement of planar straight-line drawings may be exponential, if high angular resolution is also desired. Almost linear area can be achieved through nonplanar drawings of planar graphs, which have applications to VLSI circuits.

- As shown in Table A.4, upward planar drawings provide an interesting trade-off between area and total number of bends. Indeed, unless the digraph is reduced (see Section 4.7.1), the area of a straight-line drawing is exponential in the worst case. A quadratic area bound is achieved only at the expense of a linear number of bends.

A.1.1   Area of Drawings of Trees

Tables A.1 and A.2 summarize selected universal upper bounds and existential lower bounds on the area of drawings of trees. All the bounds assume grid drawings.

Rooted trees are usually represented by downward planar straight-line drawings. Layered drawings (see Section 3.1.2) have quadratic area requirement. The drawing method of [CDP92, Shi76] (see Section 3.1.4) for general rooted trees (which constructs hv-drawings for binary trees) and the recursive winding method of [CGKT97] for binary trees (see Section 3.1.5) yield $O(n \log n)$ area. Linear-area drawing methods are known for AVL-trees (which include complete binary trees) and Fibonacci trees [CDP92,

Table A.1: Universal upper bounds and existential lower bounds on the area of downward drawings of rooted trees. We denote by a an arbitrary constant such that $0 \leq a < 1$.

Graph	Drawing	Area		§, Ref.
rooted tree	layered (strictly downward) planar grid straight-line embedding-preserving	$\Omega(n^2)$	$O(n^2)$	§3.1.2, [RT81]
rooted tree	downward planar grid straight-line	$\Omega(n)$	$O(n \log n)$	§3.1.4, [CDP92, Shi76]
degree-$O(1)$ rooted tree	downward planar grid straight-line	$\Omega(n)$	$O(n \log \log n)$	[SKC96]
binary tree	hv (downward planar grid straight-line orthogonal)	$\Omega(n)$	$O(n \log n)$	§3.1.4, [CDP92, Shi76]
binary tree	downward planar grid straight-line orthogonal	$\Omega(n)$	$O(n \log n)$	§3.1.5, [CGKT97]
complete, AVL, and Fibonacci tree	downward planar grid straight-line	$\Omega(n)$	$O(n)$	[CP95b, Tre96]
degree-$O(n^a)$ rooted tree	downward planar grid polyline	$\Omega(n)$	$O(n)$	[GGT96]
binary tree	downward planar grid orthogonal	$\Omega(n \log \log n)$	$O(n \log \log n)$	[GGT96]
rooted tree	strictly downward planar grid straight-line	$\Omega(n \log n)$	$O(n \log n)$	[CDP92]
rooted tree	downward embedding-preserving planar grid polyline	$\Omega(n \log n)$	$O(n \log n)$	[GGT96]

Table A.2: Universal upper bounds and existential lower bounds on the
area of drawings of trees.

Graph	Drawing	Area		§, Ref.
tree	planar straight-line grid	$\Omega(n)$	$O(n \log n)$	[CDP92, Shi76]
binary tree	planar straight-line orthogonal grid	$\Omega(n)$	$O(n \log \log n)$	[CGKT97]
degree-$O(n^a)$ tree	planar polyline grid	$\Omega(n)$	$O(n)$	[GGT96]
degree-four tree	planar orthogonal grid	$\Omega(n)$	$O(n)$	[Val81, Lei80]

CP95b, Tre96]. No nontrivial lower bounds on the area of downward planar
straight-line drawings are known.

Allowing bends in downward planar drawings reduces the area requirement. Indeed, for downward planar orthogonal drawings of binary trees, the
area requirement is $O(n \log \log n)$ [GGT96], and for downward planar polyline drawings of trees with maximum degree $O(n^a)$, where a is an arbitrary
constant such that $0 \leq a < 1$, the area requirement is $O(n)$ [GGT96].

All the above planar downward drawing methods have two limitations:

- Horizontal edges may be used. Hence, the drawings are not strictly
  downward.

- The embedding (i.e., order of the children of each node) is not preserved. For example, in the hv-drawing method of [CDP92] for binary
  trees (see Section 3.1.4), the larger subtree is always placed to the
  right of the smaller subtree.

We can convert an hv-drawing of a binary tree, with height h and width
w, into a strictly downward drawing with height $h+w$ and width w [CDP92].
Hence, binary trees admit strictly downward drawings with $O(n \log n)$ area.
Also, there is a family of binary trees that require $\Omega(n \log n)$ area in
any strictly downward planar drawing [CDP92]. The area requirement of
embedding-preserving downward planar polyline drawings of rooted trees is

$O(n \log n)$ [GGT96]. However, polyline drawings of trees are not aesthetically pleasing.

If we do not require downwardness (for example, because the tree is not rooted), better bounds can be achieved for orthogonal drawings. Namely, $O(n \log \log n)$ area can be achieved for planar straight-line orthogonal drawings of binary trees [CGKT97], and $O(n)$ area can be obtained for planar orthogonal drawings of trees with maximum degree four [Val81, Lei80].

Note that the polyline drawing method of [GGT96] and the straight-line orthogonal drawing method of [CGKT97] construct drawings with a good aspect ratio (see Section A.4).

A.1.2 Area of Drawings of Planar Graphs

Table A.3 summarizes selected universal upper bounds and existential lower bounds on the area of drawings of planar graphs. All the bounds assume grid drawings.

There is an $O(n^2)$ existential lower bound on the area of planar grid drawings of planar graphs. Such a lower bound is achieved, for example, by a graph consisting of $n/3$ *nested triangles*. Inductively, adding one more triangle to the graph causes both the width and height of the drawing to increase by at least one unit.

Many techniques are available for constructing planar grid drawings with $O(n^2)$ area:

- Various methods based on orientations and numberings yield polyline drawings. See, for example, [DT88, DTT92a, Kan96] and Section 4.8.

- Orthogonal drawings can be constructed with methods based on orientations and numberings (see, for example, [BK94, Kan96, TT89a] and Section 4.9) and on network flow (see, for example, [DLV93, GT97b, Tam87] and Chapter 5).

- Several methods are available for straight-line drawings (see [CN95, CP95a, dFPP90, Kan96, Sch90]).

- An algorithm in [Kan96] constructs convex drawings, that is, straight-line drawings such that all the faces are convex polygons, for triconnected planar graphs.

Methods based on the planar separator theorem [LT80], originally developed for VLSI layout applications, construct (nonplanar) orthogonal grid

Table A.3: Universal upper bounds and existential lower bounds on the area of drawings of planar graphs.

Graph	Drawing	Area		§, Ref.
planar graph	tessellation representation with integer coordinates	$\Omega(n^2)$	$O(n^2)$	§4.3, [TT89b]
planar graph	visibility representation with integer coordinates	$\Omega(n^2)$	$O(n^2)$	§4.4, [RT86, TT86]
planar graph	embedding-preserving planar polyline grid	$\Omega(n^2)$	$O(n^2)$	§4.8, [DT88, DTT92a, Kan96]
planar graph	embedding-preserving planar grid straight-line	$\Omega(n^2)$	$O(n^2)$	[dFPP90, Sch90]
triconnected planar graph	embedding-preserving planar grid straight-line convex	$\Omega(n^2)$	$O(n^2)$	[Kan96]
planar graph	planar orthogonal grid	$\Omega(n^2)$	$O(n^2)$	§4.9 §5.5, [BK94, DLV93, GT97b, Kan96, Tam87, TT89a]
planar degree-four graph	(nonplanar) orthogonal grid	$\Omega(n \log n)$	$O(n \log^2 n)$	[Val81, Lei80, Lei84, BL84]

drawings with $O(n \log^2 n)$ area [Val81, Lei80, BL84]. An existential $\Omega(n \log n)$ lower bound on the area of (nonplanar) orthogonal grid drawings of planar graphs is also known [Lei84].

A.1.3 Area of Upward Planar Drawings of Planar Digraphs

Table A.4 summarizes selected universal upper bounds and existential lower bounds on the area of upward drawings of planar digraphs. All the upper bounds assume grid drawings.

Techniques based on orientations and numberings yield polyline drawings with $O(n^2)$ area. See, for example, [DT88, DTT92a] and Sections 4.6 and 4.7. As for planar polyline drawings of undirected graphs, quadratic area is also a lower bound.

For straight-line drawings, the area requirement is exponential [DTT92a, GT93] (see Section 11.1), even for embedding-preserving drawings of series-parallel digraphs [BCD$^+$94].

A.1.4 Area of Drawings of General Graphs

Table A.4 summarizes selected universal upper bounds and existential lower bounds on the area of drawings of general graphs. All the bounds assume grid drawings.

Techniques based on orientations yield $O(n^2)$ area orthogonal grid drawings for graphs of maximum degree four (see, for example, [BK94, PT95, Val81] and Chapter 8). A quadratic existential lower bound on the area also holds [Val81].

In order to draw a general graph, we can first planarize it, and then apply one of the planar drawing methods (see, for example, Section 2.3). This yields a drawing with $O((n + \chi)^2)$ area, where χ is the number of crossings of the drawing. Note that finding the minimum number of crossings is NP-hard (see Section A.6). A tighter $O(m^2)$ area bound is obtained with orientation techniques [Bie97, Pap96, PT97b] (see Section 8.3).

A.2 Bounds on the Angular Resolution

Table A.6 summarizes selected universal lower bounds and existential upper bounds on the angular resolution of drawings of graphs. Recall that it is desirable to maximize the angular resolution.

For general graphs, a trivial upper bound on the angular resolution is $2\pi/d$, where d is the maximum vertex degree of the graph. This fact im-

Table A.4: Universal upper bounds and existential lower bounds on the area of upward planar drawings of planar digraphs. We denote by b and c constants such that $1 < b < c$.

Class	Drawing Type	Area		§, Ref.
planar st-graph	tessellation representation with integer coordinates	$\Omega(n^2)$	$O(n^2)$	§4.3, [TT89b]
planar st-graph	visibility representation with integer coordinates	$\Omega(n^2)$	$O(n^2)$	§4.4, [RT86, TT86]
upward planar digraph	upward planar grid straight-line	$\Omega(b^n)$	$O(c^n)$	§11.1, [DTT92a, GT93]
reduced planar st-graph	dominance (upward) planar embedding-preserving grid straight-line	$\Omega(n^2)$	$O(n^2)$	§4.7, [DTT92a]
upward planar digraph	upward planar grid polyline	$O(n^2)$	$\Omega(n^2)$	§4.6 §4.7, [DT88, DTT92a]
series-parallel digraph	upward planar embedding-preserving grid straight-line	$\Omega(b^n)$	$O(c^n)$	[BCD+94, GT93]
series-parallel digraph	upward planar grid straight-line	$\Omega(n^2)$	$O(n^2)$	§3.2, [BCD+94]

Table A.5: Universal upper bounds and existential lower bounds on the area of drawings of general graphs. We denote the number of crossings in the drawing by χ.

Graph	Drawing	Area		§, Ref.
degree-four graph	orthogonal grid	$\Omega(n^2)$	$O(n^2)$	[Val81, Sch95]
degree-four graph	orthogonal grid	$\Omega(n^2)$	n^2	[BK94]
degree-four graph	orthogonal grid	$\Omega(n^2)$	$0.76n^2$	§8.1, §8.2, [PT97c, PT98]
general graph	orthogonal grid	$\Omega(n + \chi)$	$O(m^2)$	§8.3, [Bie97, Pap96, PT97b]

plies an existential $O(1/n)$ upper bound. By placing all the vertices of the graph at the vertices of a regular n-gon, we obtain a trivial $\Omega(1/n)$ universal lower bound. Existential upper bounds dependent only on d are known for straight-line drawings [FHH$^+$93] and for planar straight-line drawings [GT94].

A coloring technique [FHH$^+$93] can be used to prove the following universal lower bounds on the angular resolution of straight-line (nonplanar) drawings: $\Omega(1/d^2)$ for general graphs and $\Omega(1/d)$ for planar graphs.

For planar straight-line drawings, $\Omega(1/n^2)$ angular resolution is achieved by any planar straight-line grid drawing with $O(n)$ height and $O(n)$ width, such as those constructed by the algorithms of [dFPP90, Sch90]. On the other hand, the best known lower bound dependent only on d is $\Omega(1/c^d)$, where $c > 1$ is a constant. This is achieved using a circle packing method [MP94]. Note that there is a wide gap between the known upper and lower bounds on the angular resolution of planar straight-line drawings. They depend only on d.

Polyline drawings can optimally achieve an $\Omega(1/d)$ angular resolution. This is obtained through an orientation technique [Kan96]. Trade-offs between the area and the angular resolution are discussed in Section A.5.

Table A.6: Universal lower bounds and existential upper bounds on the angular resolution of drawings of graphs. We denote by d the maximum vertex degree of the graph, and by c a constant such that $c > 1$.

Class	Drawing Type	Angular Resolution		§, Ref.
general graph	straight-line	$\Omega(\frac{1}{n})$	$O(1/n)$	
general graph	straight-line	$\Omega(\frac{1}{d^2})$	$O(\frac{\log d}{d^2})$	[FHH$^+$93]
planar graph	straight-line	$\Omega(\frac{1}{d})$	$O(\frac{1}{d})$	[FHH$^+$93]
planar graph	planar straight-line	$\Omega(\frac{1}{c^d})$	$O(\sqrt{\frac{\log d}{d^3}})$	[GT94, MP94]
planar graph	planar straight-line	$\Omega(\frac{1}{n^2})$	$O(1/n)$	[dFPP90, Sch90]
planar graph	planar polyline	$\Omega(\frac{1}{d})$	$O(\frac{1}{d})$	[Kan96]

A.3   Bounds on the Number of Bends

Table A.7 summarizes selected universal upper bounds and existential lower bounds on the total and maximum number of bends in orthogonal drawings.

All the upper bounds are achieved by drawing algorithms based on orientations and numberings (see, for example, [Bie97, BK94, EG95, Kan96, LMS91, Pap96, PT95, PT97c, PT98, PT97b, TT89a], Section 4.9 and Chapter 8). Lower bounds are discussed in [TTV91b] and [Bie96b].

A.4   Trade-Off Between Area and Aspect-Ratio

A variety of trade-offs for the area and aspect ratio arise, even when drawing graphs with a simple structure, such as trees. Table A.8 summarizes selected universal bounds that can be simultaneously achieved on the area and the aspect ratio of various types of drawings of trees.

Downward planar drawings are the most natural way of visualizing rooted trees. Except for binary trees (see [CGKT97] and Section 3.1.5), the existing straight-line drawing techniques are unsatisfactory with respect to either the area requirement (see, for example, [RT81] and Section 3.1.2) or the as-

Table A.7: Universal upper bounds and existential lower bounds on the total number of bends and maximum number of bends per edge in orthogonal drawings. We consider only connected simple graphs. Some bounds hold only for n greater than a small constant. For example, in any planar orthogonal drawing of K_4, there is an edge with at least two bends. Similarly, the octohedron requires an edge with at least three bends.

Graph	Drawing	Bends			§, Ref.
		at least	at most	per edge	
graph	orthogonal		m	1	§8.3, [PT97b]
degree-four graph	orthogonal	$\frac{11}{6}n$	$2n+2$	2	§8.1, §8.2, [Bie96b, BK94, PT95, PT98]
degree-three graph	orthogonal		$\frac{1}{2}n$	1	[Bie96a, PT95, PT98]
planar degree-four graph	orthogonal planar	$2n-2$	$2n+2$	2	[BK94, TTV91b]
planar degree-four graph	orthogonal planar embedding-preserving	$2n-2$	$\frac{12}{5}n+2$	3	[EG95, LMS91, TT89a, TTV91b]
biconnected planar degree-four graph	orthogonal planar embedding-preserving	$2n-2$	$2n+2$	3	§4.9, [EG95, LMS91, TT89a, TTV91b]
triconnected planar degree-four graph	orthogonal planar embedding-preserving	$\frac{4}{3}(n-1)+2$	$\frac{3}{2}n+4$	2	[Kan96]
planar degree-three graph	orthogonal planar embedding-preserving	$\frac{1}{2}n+1$	$\frac{1}{2}n+1$	1	[Kan96, LMPS90]

Table A.8: Universal upper bounds that can be simultaneously achieved for the area and aspect ratio in drawings of trees. We denote by a an *arbitrary* constant such that $0 \leq a < 1$.

Class	Drawing Type	Area	Aspect-Ratio	§, Ref.
rooted tree	layered (upward planar straight-line) grid	$O(n^2)$	$O(1)$	[RT81]
rooted tree	upward planar straight-line grid	$O(n \log n)$	$O(n/\log n)$	[CDP92, Shi76]
binary tree	upward planar straight-line orthogonal grid	$O(n \log \log n)$	$O(1)$	[CGKT97]
rooted degree-$O(n^a)$ tree	upward planar polyline grid	$O(n)$	$O(n^a)$	[GGT96]
binary tree	upward planar orthogonal grid	$O(n \log \log n)$	$O(\frac{n \log \log n}{\log^2 n})$	[GGT96]
binary tree	planar straight-line orthogonal grid	$O(n \log n)$	$O(1)$	[CGKT97]
degree-four tree	planar orthogonal grid	$O(n)$	$O(1)$	[Val81, Lei80]

pect ratio (see, for example, [CDP92, Shi76] and Section 3.1.4). Linear area can be achieved for polyline drawings, even with a prescribed $O(n^a)$ aspect ratio, where a is an *arbitrary* constant such that $0 \leq a < 1$ (see [GGT96]).

For nonupward drawings of trees, $O(n \log \log n)$ area and $O(1)$ aspect ratio are achievable in planar straight-line orthogonal grid drawings of binary trees [CGKT97], and $O(n)$ area and $O(1)$ aspect ratio are possible for planar orthogonal drawings of degree-four trees [Val81, Lei80]. However, the latter method does not seem to yield aesthetically pleasing drawings, and is more suited for VLSI layout than for visualization applications.

A.5 Trade-Off Between Area and Angular Resolution

There are trade-offs between the area and the angular resolution. Table A.9 summarizes selected universal bounds that can be simultaneously achieved.

Table A.9: Asymptotic bounds for the area and angular resolution that can be simultaneously achieved in drawings of graphs. We denote by b and c constants such that $b > 1$ and $c > 1$.

Class	Drawing Type	Area	Angular Resol.	§, Ref.
planar graph	straight-line	$O(d^6 n)$	$\Omega(\frac{1}{d^2})$	[FHH$^+$93]
planar graph	straight-line	$O(d^3 n)$	$\Omega(\frac{1}{d})$	[FHH$^+$93]
planar graph	planar straight-line grid	$O(n^2)$	$\Omega(\frac{1}{n^2})$	[dFPP90, Sch90]
degree-$O(1)$ planar graph	planar straight-line	$\Omega(c^n)$	$\Omega(1)$	[GT94, MP94]
planar graph	planar straight-line	$\Omega(c^{\rho n})$	$\Omega(\rho)$	[GT94]
planar graph	planar straight-line	$O(b^n)$	$\Omega(\frac{1}{c^d})$	[MP94]
planar graph	planar polyline grid	$O(n^2)$	$\Omega(\frac{1}{d})$	[Kan96]

Good simultaneous bounds can be achieved only in nonplanar straight-line drawings [FHH$^+$93] and planar polyline drawings [Kan96]. Indeed, there is a class of degree-$O(1)$ planar graphs that require exponential area in any planar straight-line drawing with optimal $\Omega(1)$ angular resolution [GT94, MP94]. This result can be extended to a continuous trade-off between area and angular resolution in planar straight-line drawings [GT94].

A.6   Bounds on the Computational Complexity

Results on the computational complexity of planarity testing and embedding problems are summarized in Table A.10. It is interesting to observe that apparently similar problems exhibit very different time complexities. For example, while planarity testing can be done in linear time [BL76, CNAO85, ET76, dFR82, HT74, LEC67], upward planarity testing is NP-hard (see [GT95] and Section 6.6). Note that for restricted classes of digraphs, upward planarity testing can be performed in polynomial time (see [BDMT98, BDLM94, HL96, Pap95] and Sections 6.3–6.5).

Table A.10: Time complexity of selected graph drawing problems: planarity testing and embedding.

Class	Problem	Complexity	§, Ref.
general graph	minimize crossings	NP-hard	[GJ83]
two-layered graph with pre-assigned order on one layer	minimize crossings in a layered drawing	NP-hard	[EW94]
general graph	maximum planar subgraph	NP-hard	[GJ79]
general graph	planarity testing and computing a planar embedding	$\Theta(n)$	[BL76, CNAO85, ET76, dFR82, HT74, LEC67]
general graph	maximal planar subgraph	$\Theta(n+m)$	[DT89, CHT93, La 94, Dji95]
general digraph	upward planarity testing	NP-hard	[GT95]
embedded digraph	upward planarity testing	$\Omega(n), O(n^2)$	[BDLM94]
outerplanar digraph	upward planarity testing	$\Omega(n), O(n^2)$	[Pap95]
embedded outerplanar digraph	upward planarity testing	$\Theta(n)$	[Pap95]
single-source digraph	upward planarity testing	$\Theta(n)$	[BDMT98, HL96]

Table A.11: The time complexity of selected graph drawing problems: straight-line and polyline drawings of planar graphs.

Class	Problem	Complexity	§, Ref.
planar graph	planar straight- line drawing with prescribed edge lengths	NP-hard	§11.2.2, [EW90]
embedded planar graph	planar straight-line drawing with prescribed angles	NP-hard	[Gar95]
maximal planar graph	planar straight-line drawing with prescribed angles	$\Theta(n)$	[DV93]
planar graph	planar straight-line drawing with maximum angular resolution	NP-hard	[Gar95, Kan96]
planar graph	planar straight-line grid drawing with $O(n^2)$ area and $\Omega(1/n^2)$ angular resolution	$\Theta(n)$	[CP95a, dFPP90, Sch90]
planar graph	planar polyline grid drawing with $O(n^2)$ area, $O(n)$ bends, and $\Omega(1/d)$ angular resolution	$\Theta(n)$	[Kan96]
planar graph	visibility representation with $O(n^2)$ area	$\Theta(n)$	§4.4, §4.5, [DT88, DTT92b, Kan93, RT86, TT86]
triconnected planar graph	planar straight-line convex grid drawing with $O(n^2)$ area and $\Omega(1/n^2)$ angular resolution	$\Theta(n)$	[Kan96]
triconnected planar graph	planar straight-line strictly convex drawing	$\Theta(n)$	[CON85, Tut60, Tut63]
outerplanar graph	planar straight-line symmetric drawing	$\Theta(n)$	[MA92]
reduced planar st-graph	upward planar grid straight-line dominance drawing with minimum area	$\Theta(n)$	§4.7, [DTT92a]
upward planar digraph	upward planar polyline grid drawing witn $O(n^2)$ area and $O(n)$ bends	$\Theta(n)$	§4.6, §4.7, [DT88, DTT92a]

The technique for constructing orthogonal drawings of graphs presented in Chapter 8 yields algorithms that run in $O(n + m)$ time (see also [BK97, PT97b]). The computational complexity of other general techniques for drawings graphs (see Chapter 2) is difficult to summarize, because each of the steps of a given technique can be implemented with different algorithms. Detecting and displaying symmetries in drawings of general graphs is NP-hard [Man91].

Table A.11 summarizes the computational complexity of several problems arising in constructing straight-line and polyline drawings of planar graphs. It is NP-hard to construct planar straight-line drawings with prescribed edge lengths [EW90], prescribed angles [Gar95], or maximum angular resolution [Gar95, Kan96]. Linear time algorithms have been devised for the following problems:

- testing the existence of a planar straight-line drawing with prescribed angles for a maximal planar graph [DV93];

- constructing planar grid drawings with quadratic area [CP95a, dFPP90, Kan96, Sch90];

- constructing planar straight-line strictly convex drawings [CON85, Tut60, Tut63]; and

- constructing upward planar grid straight-line dominance and polyline drawings [DT88, DTT92a].

Constructing orthogonal grid drawings with $O(n^2)$ area and $O(n)$ bends can be done in $O(n)$ time for degree-four graphs (see Chapter 8 and [BK94, PT95, PT97c, PT98]). If the input graph is planar, planar orthogonal grid drawings with the same bounds on the area and number of bends, can be constructed in $O(n)$ time (see Section §4.9 and [BK94, Kan96, TT89a]. Minimizing the number of bends in planar orthogonal drawings is NP-hard [GT95]. However, the problem can be solved in polynomial time if the input graph has a prescribed embedding (see Chapter 5 and [GT97b, Tam87]) or has degree, at most, 3 [DLV93]. The above results are summarized in Table A.12.

A polynomial time algorithm, based on linear programming, minimizes the area of a planar straight-line upward layered drawing of a tree that displays symmetries and isomorphisms of subtrees [SR83]. Note that the drawing constructed by this algorithm is not, in general, a grid drawing. A polynomial time algorithm based, on dynamic programming, minimizes the area of hv-drawings of binary trees [ELL92]. Many other drawing optimization problems are NP-hard for trees, including area and edge-length minimization in planar grid drawings [BC87, Bra88, DLT85, Gre89, KvL85, Sto84, SR83]. Also, it is NP-hard to determine whether a tree can be drawn as the Euclidean minimum spanning tree of a set of points in the plane [EW96b]. Efficient drawing algorithms that guarantee good universal upper bounds on the area are known for rooted trees (see Section 3.1 and [CDP92, CGKT97, GGT93, RT81, Shi76]). The above results are summarized in Table A.13.

Table A.12: The time complexity of selected graph drawing problems: orthogonal drawings of graphs with degree, at most, four.

Class	Problem	Complexity	§, Ref.
degree-four graph	orthogonal grid drawing with $O(n^2)$ area and $O(n)$ bends	$\Theta(n)$	Chapter 8, [BK94, PT95, PT97c, PT98]
planar degree-four graph	planar orthogonal grid drawing with $O(n^2)$ area and $O(n)$ bends	$\Theta(n)$	§4.9, [BK94, Kan96, TT89a]
planar degree-four graph	planar orthogonal grid drawing with minimum number of bends	NP-hard	[GT95]
planar degree-three graph	planar orthogonal grid drawing with minimum number of bends and $O(n^2)$ area	$\Omega(n)$, $O(n^5 \log n)$	[DLV93]
embedded planar degree-four graph	planar orthogonal grid drawing with minimum number of bends and $O(n^2)$ area	$\Omega(n)$, $O(n^{7/4} \log n)$	Chapter 5, [GT97b, Tam87]

Table A.13: The time complexity of selected graph drawing problems: trees. We denote by k a constant such that $k \geq 1$.

Class	Problem	Complexity	§, Ref.
tree	draw as the Euclidean minimum spanning tree of a set of points in the plane	NP-hard	[EW96b]
degree-four tree	minimize area in planar orthogonal grid drawing	NP-hard	[Bra88, DLT85, KvL85, Sto84]
degree-four tree	minimize total/maximum edge length in planar orthogonal grid drawing	NP-hard	[BC87, Bra88, Gre89]
rooted tree	minimize area in a planar straight-line upward layered grid drawing that displays symmetries and isomorphisms of subtrees	NP-hard	[SR83]
rooted tree	minimize area in a planar straight-line upward layered drawing that displays symmetries and isomorphisms of subtrees	$\Omega(n)$, $O(n^k)$	[SR83]
binary tree	minimize area in hv-drawing	$\Omega(n)$, $O(n\sqrt{n\log n})$	[ELL92]
rooted tree	planar straight-line upward layered grid drawing with $O(n^2)$ area	$\Theta(n)$	§3.1.2, [RT81]
rooted tree	planar polyline upward grid drawing with $O(n)$ area	$\Theta(n)$	[GGT93]
rooted tree	planar straight-line upward grid drawing with $O(n\log n)$ area	$\Theta(n)$	§3.1.4, §3.1.5, [CDP92, Shi76, CGKT97]

Bibliography

[AHU74]   A. V. Aho, J. E. Hopcroft and J. D. Ullman, *The Design and Analysis of Computer Algorithms*. Addison-Wesley, Reading, MA, 1974.

[AHU83]   A. V. Aho, J. E. Hopcroft and J. D. Ullman, *Data Structures and Algorithms*. Addison-Wesley, Reading, MA, 1983.

[AMO93]   R. K. Ahuja, T. L. Magnanti and J. B. Orlin, *Network Flows: Theory, Algorithms, and Applications*. Prentice Hall, Englewood Cliffs, NJ, 1993.

[And92]   T. Andreae, *Some Results on Visibility Graphs*, Discrete Appl. Math., 40, 5–17, 1992.

[AP61]   L. Auslander and S. V. Parter, *On Imbedding Graphs in the Plane*, J. Math. and Mech., 10, 517–523, 1961.

[BBDL91]   M. Beccaria, P. Bertolazzi, G. Di Battista and G. Liotta, *A Tailorable and Extensible Automatic Layout Facility*, In Proc. IEEE Workshop on Visual Languages, pp. 68–73, 1991.

[BBS97]   J. Branke, F. Bucher and H. Schmeck, *Using genetic algorithms for drawing undirected graphs*, In J. T. Alander, editor, Proceedings of the Third Nordic Workshop on Genetic Algorithms and their Applications (3NWGA), pp. 193 – 205, 1997.

[BC87]   S. Bhatt and S. Cosmadakis, *The Complexity of Minimizing Wire Lengths in VLSI Layouts*, Inform. Process. Lett., 25, 263–267, 1987.

[BCD+94]   P. Bertolazzi, R. F. Cohen, G. Di Battista, R. Tamassia and I. G. Tollis, *How to Draw a Series-Parallel Digraph*, Internat. J. Comput. Geom. Appl., 4, 385–402, 1994.

[BD91]   P. Bertolazzi and G. Di Battista, *On upward drawing testing of triconnected digraphs*, In Proc. 7th Annu. ACM Sympos. Comput. Geom., pp. 272–280, 1991.

[BDL95]   P. Bertolazzi, G. Di Battista and G. Liotta, *Parametric Graph Drawing*, IEEE Trans. Softw. Eng., 21, no. 8, 662–673, 1995.

[BDLM94]   P. Bertolazzi, G. Di Battista, G. Liotta and C. Mannino, *Upward Drawings of Triconnected Digraphs*, Algorithmica, 6, no. 12, 476–497, 1994.

[BDMT98]   P. Bertolazzi, G. Di Battista, C. Mannino and R. Tamassia, *Optimal Upward Planarity Testing of Single-Source Digraphs*, SIAM J. Comput., 27, no. 1, 132–169, 1998.

[Ber81]   M. A. Bernard, *On the Automated Drawing of Graphs*, In Proc. 3rd Caribbean Conf. on Combinatorics and Computing, pp. 43–55, 1981.

[BF96]   I. Bruß and A. Frick, *Fast Interactive 3-D Graph Visualization*, In F. J. Brandenburg, editor, Graph Drawing (Proc. GD '95), vol. 1027 of *Lecture Notes Comput. Sci.*, pp. 99–110. Springer-Verlag, 1996.

[BFN85]   C. Batini, L. Furlani and E. Nardelli, *What is a Good Diagram? A Pragmatic Approach*, In Proc. 4th Internat. Conf. on the Entity Relationship Approach, 1985.

[BFR71]   K. A. Baker, P. Fishburn and F. S. Roberts, *Partial orders of dimension 2*, Networks, 2, 11–28, 1971.

[BGT97]   S. Bridgeman, A. Garg and R. Tamassia, *A Graph Drawing and Translation Service on the WWW*, In S. C. North, editor, Graph Drawing (Proc. GD '96), Lecture Notes Comput. Sci. Springer-Verlag, 1997.

[BH87a]   B. Becker and G. Hotz, *On The Optimal Layout of Planar Graphs with Fixed Boundary*, SIAM J. Comput., 16, no. 5, 946–972, 1987.

[BH87b]   B. Becker and G. Hotz, *On The Optimal Layout of Planar Graphs with Fixed Boundary*, SIAM J. Computing, 16, no. 5, 946–972, 1987.

[BHR96]   F. J. Brandenburg, M. Himsolt and C. Rohrer, *An Experimental Comparison of Force-Directed and Randomized Graph Drawing Algorithms*, In F. J. Brandenburg, editor, Graph Drawing (Proc. GD '95), vol. 1027 of *Lecture Notes Comput. Sci.*, pp. 76–87. Springer-Verlag, 1996.

[Bie96a]   T. Biedl, *Improved orthogonal drawings of 3-graphs*, In Proc. 8th Canad. Conf. Comput. Geom., pp. 295–299, 1996.

[Bie96b]   T. Biedl, *New Lower Bounds for Orthogonal Graph Drawings*, In F. J. Brandenburg, editor, Graph Drawing (Proc. GD '95), vol. 1027 of *Lecture Notes in Computer Science*, pp. 28–39. Springer-Verlag, 1996.

[Bie97]   T. C. Biedl, *Orthogonal Graph Visualization: The Three-Phase Method With Applications*, PhD thesis, RUTCOR, Rutgers University, May 1997.

[Bir67]   G. Birkhoff, *Lattice Theory*. American Mathematical Society, Providence, RI, 1967.

[BK94]   T. Biedl and G. Kant, *A Better Heuristic for Orthogonal Graph Drawings*, In Proc. 2nd Annu. European Sympos. Algorithms, vol. 855 of *Lecture Notes Comput. Sci.*, pp. 24–35. Springer-Verlag, 1994.

[BK97]   T. Biedl and M. Kaufmann, *Area-efficient static and incremental graph drawings*, In R. Burkard and G. Woeginger, editors, Proc. 5th Annu. European Sympos. Algorithms, vol. 1284 of *Lecture Notes Comput. Sci.*, pp. 37–52. Springer-Verlag, 1997.

[BK98]   H. Breu and D. G. Kirkpatrick, *Unit Disk Graph Recognition is NP-hard*, Comput. Geom. Theory Appl., 9, no. 1 – 2, 3 – 25, 1998.

[BL76]   K. Booth and G. Lueker, *Testing for the Consecutive Ones Property Interval Graphs and Graph Planarity Using PQ-Tree Algorithms*, J. Comput. Syst. Sci., 13, 335–379, 1976.

[BL84]   S. N. Bhatt and F. T. Leighton, *A framework for solving VLSI graph layout problems*, J. Comput. Syst. Sci., 28, 300–343, 1984.

[BLL96]   P. Bose, W. Lenhart and G. Liotta, *Characterizing Proximity Trees*, Algorithmica, 16, 83–110, 1996, (special issue on Graph Drawing, edited by G. Di Battista and R. Tamassia).

[BM76]   J. A. Bondy and U. S. R. Murty, *Graph Theory with Applications*. Macmillan, London, 1976. ISBN 0-333-17791-6.

[BNT86]   C. Batini, E. Nardelli and R. Tamassia, *A Layout Algorithm for Data-Flow Diagrams*, IEEE Trans. Softw. Eng., SE-12, no. 4, 538–546, 1986.

[BO87]   B. Becker and H. Osthof, *Layout with Wires of Balanced Length*, Information and Computation, 73, 45–58, 1987.

[BPCJ95]   S. Bhanji, H. C. Purchase, R. F. Cohen and M. James, *Validating Graph Drawing Aesthetics: A Pilot Study*, Technical Report 336, University of Queensland, Department of Computer Science, 1995.

[Bra88]   F. J. Brandenburg, *Nice Drawings of Graphs and Trees are Computationally Hard*, Technical Report MIP-8820, Fakultat fur Mathematik und Informatik, Univ. Passau, 1988.

[Bra95]   F. J. Brandenburg, *Designing Graph Drawings by Layout Graph Grammars*, In R. Tamassia and I. G. Tollis, editors, Graph Drawing (Proc. GD '94), vol. 894 of *Lecture Notes Comput. Sci.*, pp. 416–427. Springer-Verlag, 1995.

[Bra96]   J. Branke, *Drawing Graphs using Genetic Algorithms*, Manuscript, 1996.

[BS90]   B. Berger and P. Shor, *Approximation Algorithms for the Maximum Acyclic Subgraph Problem*, In Proc. 1st ACM-SIAM Sympos. Discrete Algorithms, pp. 236–243, 1990.

[Car80]   M. J. Carpano, *Automatic Display of Hierarchized Graphs for Computer Aided Decision Analysis*, IEEE Trans. Syst. Man Cybern., SMC-10, no. 11, 705–715, 1980.

[Cat88]   T. Catarci, *The Assignment Heuristic for Crossing Reduction in Bipartite Graphs*, In Proc. 26th Allerton Conf. Commun. Control Comput., 1988.

[CBHH87] J. E. Cuny, D. A. Bayley, J. W. Hagerman and A. A. Hough, *The Simple Simon Programming Environment: A Status Report*, Technical Report 87-22, Department of Computer and Information Science, University of Massachusetts, May 1987.

[CDP92]   P. Crescenzi, G. Di Battista and A. Piperno, *A Note on Optimal Area Algorithms for Upward Drawings of Binary Trees*, Comput. Geom. Theory Appl., 2, 187–200, 1992.

[CDTT95] R. F. Cohen, G. Di Battista, R. Tamassia and I. G. Tollis, *Dynamic Graph Drawings: Trees, Series-Parallel Digraphs, and Planar ST-Digraphs*, SIAM J. Comput., 24, no. 5, 970–1001, 1995.

[CELR95] R. F. Cohen, P. Eades, T. Lin and F. Ruskey, *Three-Dimensional Graph Drawing*, In R. Tamassia and I. G. Tollis, editors, Graph Drawing (Proc. GD '94), vol. 894 of *Lecture Notes Comput. Sci.*, pp. 1–11. Springer-Verlag, 1995.

[CG72]   E. G. Coffman and R. L. Graham, *Optimal scheduling for two processor systems*, Acta Informatica, 1, 200 – 213, 1972.

[CG95]   I. F. Cruz and A. Garg, *Drawing Graphs by Example Efficiently: Trees and Planar Acyclic Digraphs*, In R. Tamassia and I. G. Tollis, editors, Graph Drawing (Proc. GD '94), vol. 894 of *Lecture Notes Comput. Sci.*, pp. 404–415. Springer-Verlag, 1995.

[CGKT97] T. Chan, M. T. Goodrich, S. R. Kosaraju and R. Tamassia, *Optimizing Area and Aspect Ratio in Straight-Line Orthogonal Tree Drawings*, In S. North, editor, Graph Drawing (Proc. GD '96), vol. 1190 of *Lecture Notes Comput. Sci.*, pp. 63–75. Springer-Verlag, 1997.

[CGT96]   M. Chrobak, M. T. Goodrich and R. Tamassia, *Convex Drawings of Graphs in Two and Three Dimensions*, In Proc. 12th Annu. ACM Sympos. Comput. Geom., pp. 319–328, 1996.

[CHT93]   J. Cai, X. Han and R. E. Tarjan, *An $O(m \log n)$-time Algorithm for the Maximal Subgraph Problem*, SIAM J. Comput., 22, 1142–1162, 1993.

[CLR90]   T. H. Cormen, C. E. Leiserson and R. L. Rivest, *Introduction to Algorithms*. MIT Press, Cambridge, MA, 1990.

[CMS95]   J. Christensen, J. Marks and S. Shieber, *An empirical study of algorithms for point-feature label placement*, ACM Trans. Graph., 14, 202–232, 1995.

[CN95]   M. Chrobak and S. Nakano, *Minimum-Width Grid Drawings of Plane Graphs*, In R. Tamassia and I. G. Tollis, editors, Graph Drawing (Proc. GD '94), vol. 894 of *Lecture Notes Comput. Sci.*, pp. 104–110. Springer-Verlag, 1995.

[CNAO85] N. Chiba, T. Nishizeki, S. Abe and T. Ozawa, *A Linear Algorithm for Embedding Planar Graphs Using PQ-Trees*, J. Comput. Syst. Sci., 30, no. 1, 54–76, 1985.

[CNS79]   N. Chiba, I. Nishioka and I. Shirakawa, *An Algorithm of Maximal Planarization of Graphs*, In Proc. IEEE Internat. Sympos. on Circuits and Systems, pp. 649–652, 1979.

[CON85]   N. Chiba, K. Onoguchi and T. Nishizeki, *Drawing Planar Graphs Nicely*, Acta Inform., 22, 187–201, 1985.

[CP95a]   M. Chrobak and T. Payne, *A linear-time algorithm for drawing planar graphs*, Inform. Process. Lett., 54, 241–246, 1995.

[CP95b]   P. Crescenzi and A. Piperno, *Optimal-Area Upward Drawings of AVL Trees*, In R. Tamassia and I. G. Tollis, editors, Graph Drawing (Proc. GD '94), vol. 894 of *Lecture Notes Comput. Sci.*, pp. 307–317. Springer-Verlag, 1995.

[CP96]   M. K. Coleman and D. S. Parker, *Æsthetics-bases Graph Layout for Human Consumption*, Software Practice and Experience, 26, no. 12, 1415–1438, 1996.

[CT96]   I. F. Cruz and J. P. Twarog, *3D Graph Drawing with Simulated Annealing*, In F. J. Brandenburg, editor, Graph Drawing (Proc. GD '95), vol. 1027 of *Lecture Notes Comput. Sci.*, pp. 162–165. Springer-Verlag, 1996.

[DETT94] G. Di Battista, P. Eades, R. Tamassia and I. G. Tollis, *Algorithms for drawing graphs: an annotated bibliography*, Comput. Geom. Theory Appl., 4, 235–282, 1994.

[DFM93]   E. Dengler, M. Friedell and J. Marks, *Constraint-Driven Diagram Layout*, In Proc. IEEE Sympos. on Visual Languages, pp. 330–335, 1993.

[dFPP90]   H. de Fraysseix, J. Pach and R. Pollack, *How to Draw a Planar Graph on a Grid*, Combinatorica, 10, 41–51, 1990.

[dFR82]   H. de Fraysseix and P. Rosenstiehl, *A Depth-First-Search Characterization of Planarity*, Ann. Discrete Math., 13, 75–80, 1982.

[DGL⁺97a]   G. Di Battista, A. Garg, G. Liotta, A. Parise, R. Tamassia, E. Tassinari, F. Vargiu and L. Vismara, *Drawing Directed Graphs: an Experimental Study*, In S. North, editor, Graph Drawing (Proc. GD '96), Lecture Notes Comput. Sci. Springer-Verlag, 1997.

[DGL⁺97b]   G. Di Battista, A. Garg, G. Liotta, R. Tamassia, E. Tassinari and F. Vargiu, *An experimental comparison of four graph drawing algorithms*, Comput. Geom. Theory Appl., 7, 303–326, 1997.

[DGST90]   G. Di Battista, A. Giammarco, G. Santucci and R. Tamassia, *The Architecture of Diagram Server*, In Proc. IEEE Workshop on Visual Languages, pp. 60–65, 1990.

[DH96]   R. Davidson and D. Harel, *Drawing Graphics Nicely Using Simulated Annealing*, ACM Trans. Graph., 15, no. 4, 301–331, 1996.

[DHVM83]   P. Duchet, Y. Hamidoune, M. L. Vergnas and H. Meyniel, *Representing a Planar Graph by Vertical Lines Joining Different Levels*, Discrete Math., 46, 319–321, 1983.

[Dji95]   H. N. Djidjev, *A Linear Algorithm for the Maximal Planar Subgraph Problem*, In Proc. 4th Workshop Algorithms Data Struct., Lecture Notes Comput. Sci. Springer-Verlag, 1995.

[DLL95]   G. Di Battista, W. Lenhart and G. Liotta, *Proximity Drawability: a Survey*, In R. Tamassia and I. G. Tollis, editors, Graph Drawing (Proc. GD '94), vol. 894 of *Lecture Notes Comput. Sci.*, pp. 328–339. Springer-Verlag, 1995.

[DLR90]   G. Di Battista, W. P. Liu and I. Rival, *Bipartite Graphs Upward Drawings and Planarity*, Inform. Process. Lett., 36, 317–322, 1990.

[DLT85]   D. Dolev, F. T. Leighton and H. Trickey, *Planar Embedding of Planar Graphs*, In F. P. Preparata, editor, Adv. Comput. Res., vol. 2, pp. 147–161. JAI Press, Greenwich, Conn., 1985.

[DLV93]   G. Di Battista, G. Liotta and F. Vargiu, *Spirality of Orthogonal Representations and Optimal Drawings of Series-Parallel Graphs and 3-Planar Graphs*, In Proc. Workshop Algorithms Data Struct., vol. 709 of *Lecture Notes Comput. Sci.*, pp. 151–162. Springer-Verlag, 1993.

[DLV95]   G. Di Battista, G. Liotta and F. Vargiu, *Diagram Server*, J. Visual Lang. Comput., 6, no. 3, 275–298, 1995, (special issue on Graph Visualization, edited by I. F. Cruz and P. Eades).

[DS87]   P. F. Dietz and D. D. Sleator, *Two Algorithms for Maintaining Order in a List*, In Proc. 19th Annu. ACM Sympos. Theory Comput., pp. 365–372, 1987.

[DT88]   G. Di Battista and R. Tamassia, *Algorithms for Plane Representations of Acyclic Digraphs*, Theoret. Comput. Sci., 61, 175–198, 1988.

[DT89]   G. Di Battista and R. Tamassia, *Incremental Planarity Testing*, In Proc. 30th Annu. IEEE Sympos. Found. Comput. Sci., pp. 436–441, 1989.

[DT90]   G. Di Battista and R. Tamassia, *On-Line Graph Algorithms with SPQR-Trees*, In Automata, Languages and Programming (Proc. 17th ICALP), vol. 442 of *Lecture Notes Comput. Sci.*, pp. 598–611, 1990.

[DT96]   G. Di Battista and R. Tamassia, *On-Line Planarity Testing*, SIAM J. Comput., 25, 956–997, 1996.

[DTT92a]   G. Di Battista, R. Tamassia and I. G. Tollis, *Area Requirement and Symmetry Display of Planar Upward Drawings*, Discrete Comput. Geom., 7, 381–401, 1992.

[DTT92b]   G. Di Battista, R. Tamassia and I. G. Tollis, *Constrained Visibility Representations of Graphs*, Inform. Process. Lett., 41, 1–7, 1992.

[DV93]   G. Di Battista and L. Vismara, *Angles of Planar Triangular Graphs*, In Proc. 25th Annu. ACM Sympos. Theory Comput., pp. 431–437, 1993.

[Ead84]   P. Eades, *A Heuristic for Graph Drawing*, Congr. Numer., 42, 149–160, 1984.

[Ead88]   P. Eades, *Symmetry finding algorithms*, In G. T. Toussaint, editor, Computational Morphology, pp. 41–51. North-Holland, Amsterdam, Netherlands, 1988.

[Ead92]   P. D. Eades, *Drawing Free Trees*, Bulletin of the Institute for Combinatorics and its Applications, 5, 10–36, 1992.

[ECH97]   P. Eades, R. Cohen and M. Huang, *Online animated graph drawing for web navigation*, In G. DiBattista, editor, Graph Drawing 97, vol. 1353 of *Lecture Notes in Computer Science*, pp. 330 – 335. Springer-Verlag, 1997.

[EFG82]   P. Eades, L. Foulds and J. Giffin, *An Efficient Heuristic for Identifying a Maximal Weight Planar Subgraph*, In Combinatorial Mathematics IX, vol. 952 of *Lecture Notes Comput. Sci.*, pp. 239–251. Springer-Verlag, Berlin, West Germany, 1982.

[EFK88]   P. Eades, I. Fogg and D. Kelly, *SPREMB: a System for Developing Graph Algorithms*, Congr. Numer., 66, 123–140, 1988.

[EG95]   S. Even and G. Granot, *Grid Layouts of Block Diagrams — Bounding the Number of Bends in Each Connection*, In R. Tamassia and I. G. Tollis, editors, Graph Drawing (Proc. GD '94), vol. 894 of *Lecture Notes Comput. Sci.*, pp. 64–75. Springer-Verlag, 1995.

[EG96]   P. Eades and P. Garvan, *Drawing Stressed Planar Graphs in Three Dimensions*, In F. J. Brandenburg, editor, Graph Drawing (Proc. GD '95), vol. 1027 of *Lecture Notes Comput. Sci.* Springer-Verlag, 1996.

[EGHL+93]   H. El-Gindy, M. Houle, W. Lenhart, Miller, D. Rappaport and S. Whitesides, *Dominance drawings of bipartite graphs*, In Proc. 5th Canad. Conf. Comput. Geom., pp. 187–191, 1993.

[EK86]   P. Eades and D. Kelly, *Heuristics for Reducing Crossings in 2-Layered Networks*, Ars Combin., 21.A, 89–98, 1986.

[EK97]   U. Erlingsson and M. Krishnamoorthy, *Interactive graph drawing on the world wide web*, In Sixth World Wide Web Conference, 1997.

[EL95]   P. Eades and X. Lin, *A New Heuristic for the Feedback Arc Set Problem*, Australian Journal of Combinatorics, 12, 15 – 26, 1995.

[EL97]   P. Eades and X. Lin, *Spring Algorithms and Symmetry*, In Proceedings of COCOON 1997, vol. 1276 of *Lecture Notes in Computer Science*, pp. 109 – 112. Springer, 1997.

[ELL92]   P. Eades, T. Lin and X. Lin, *Minimum Size h-v Drawings*, In Proc. Advanced Visual Interfaces, vol. 36 of *World Scientific Series in Computer Science*, pp. 386–394, 1992.

[ELL93]   P. Eades, T. Lin and X. Lin, *Two Tree Drawing Conventions*, Internat. J. Comput. Geom. Appl., 3, 133–153, 1993.

[ELL$^+$95] H. ElGindy, G. Liotta, A. Lubiw, H. Meijer and S. H. Whitesides, *Recognizing Rectangle of Influence Drawable Graphs*, In R. Tamassia and I. G. Tollis, editors, Graph Drawing (Proc. GD '94), vol. 894 of *Lecture Notes Comput. Sci.*, pp. 352–363. Springer-Verlag, 1995.

[ELMS91]   P. Eades, W. Lai, K. Misue and K. Sugiyama, *Preserving the Mental Map of a Diagram*, In Proceedings of Compugraphics 91, pp. 24–33, 1991.

[ES91]   P. Eades and K. Sugiyama, *How to Draw a Directed Graph*, J. Inform. Process., 13, 424–437, 1991.

[Esp88]   C. Esposito, *Graph Graphics: Theory and Practice*, Comput. Math. Appl., 15, no. 4, 247–253, 1988.

[ESW96]   P. Eades, C. Stirk and S. Whitesides, *The Techniques of Kolmogorov and Bardzin for Three Dimensional Orthogonal Graph Drawings*, Information Processing Letters, 60, 97–103, 1996.

[ESW97]   P. Eades, A. Symvonis and S. Whitesides, *Two Algorithms for Three-Dimensional Orthogonal Graph Drawing*, In S. North, editor, Graph Drawing (Proc. GD '96), vol. 1190 of *Lecture Notes Comput. Sci.*, pp. 139–154. Springer-Verlag, 1997.

[ET76]   S. Even and R. E. Tarjan, *Computing an st-Numbering*, Theoret. Comput. Sci., 2, 339–344, 1976.

[Eve79]   S. Even, *Graph Algorithms*. Computer Science Press, Potomac, Maryland, 1979.

[EW90]   P. Eades and N. Wormald, *Fixed Edge Length Graph Drawing is NP-hard*, Discrete Appl. Math., 28, 111–134, 1990.

[EW94]   P. Eades and N. Wormald, *Edge Crossings in Drawings of Bipartite Graphs*, Algorithmica, 11, 379–403, 1994.

[EW96a]   P. Eades and S. Whitesides, *The logic engine and the realization problem for nearest neighbor graphs*, Theoretical Computer Science, 169, no. 1, 23 – 37, 1996.

[EW96b]   P. Eades and S. Whitesides, *The Realization Problem for Euclidean Minimum Spanning Trees is NP-hard*, Algorithmica, 16, 60–82, 1996, (special issue on Graph Drawing, edited by G. Di Battista and R. Tamassia).

[Far48]   I. Fary, *On Straight Lines Representation of Planar Graphs*, Acta Sci. Math. Szeged, 11, 229–233, 1948.

[FCE95]   Q.-W. Feng, R. F. Cohen and P. Eades, *How to Draw a Planar Clustered Graph*, In Proc. COCOON '9521–31, vol. 979 of *Lecture Notes in Computer Science*. Springer-Verlag, 1995.

[FCW67]   C. J. Fisk, D. L. Caskey and L. E. West, *ACCEL: Automated circuit card etching layout*, Proceedings of the IEEE, 55, no. 11, 1971–1982, November 1967.

[FHH⁺93]   M. Formann, T. Hagerup, J. Haralambides, M. Kaufmann, F. T. Leighton, A. Simvonis, E. Welzl and G. Woeginger, *Drawing Graphs in the Plane with High Resolution*, SIAM J. Comput., 22, 1035–1052, 1993.

[FK96]   U. Fößmeier and M. Kaufmann, *Drawing High Degree Graphs with Low Bend Numbers*, In F. J. Brandenburg, editor, Graph Drawing (Proc. GD '95), vol. 1027 of *Lecture Notes Comput. Sci.*, pp. 254–266. Springer-Verlag, 1996.

[FLM95]   A. Frick, A. Ludwig and H. Mehldau, *A Fast Adaptive Layout Algorithm for Undirected Graphs*, In R. Tamassia and I. G. Tollis, editors, Graph Drawing (Proc. GD '94), vol. 894 of *Lecture Notes Comput. Sci.*, pp. 388–403. Springer-Verlag, 1995.

[Föß97]   U. Fößmeier, *Interactive Orthogonal Graph Drawing: Algo-rithms and Bounds*, In G. Di Battista, editor, Graph Drawing (Proc. GD '97), Lecture Notes in Computer Science. Springer-Verlag, 1997.

[FR91]   T. Fruchterman and E. Reingold, *Graph Drawing by Force-Directed Placement*, Softw. – Pract. Exp., 21, no. 11, 1129–1164, 1991.

[FW95]   M. Fröhlich and M. Werner, *Demonstration of the Interactive Graph-Visualization System* daVinci, In R. Tamassia and I. G. Tollis, editors, Graph Drawing (Proc. GD '94), vol. 894 of *Lecture Notes Comput. Sci.*, pp. 266–269. Springer-Verlag, 1995.

[Gar95]   A. Garg, *On Drawing Angle Graphs*, In R. Tamassia and I. G. Tollis, editors, Graph Drawing (Proc. GD '94), vol. 894 of *Lecture Notes Comput. Sci.*, pp. 84–95. Springer-Verlag, 1995.

[GGT93]   A. Garg, M. T. Goodrich and R. Tamassia, *Area-efficient up-ward tree drawings*, In Proc. 9th Annu. ACM Sympos. Comput. Geom., pp. 359–368, 1993.

[GGT96]   A. Garg, M. T. Goodrich and R. Tamassia, *Planar upward tree drawings with optimal area*, Internat. J. Comput. Geom. Appl., 6, 333–356, 1996.

[Gib80]   A. Gibbons, *Algorithmic Graph Theory*. Cambridge University Press, Cambridge, 1980.

[GJ79]   M. R. Garey and D. S. Johnson, *Computers and Intractability: A Guide to the Theory of NP-Completeness*. W. H. Freeman, New York, NY, 1979.

[GJ83]   M. R. Garey and D. S. Johnson, *Crossing Number is NP-Complete*, SIAM J. Algebraic Discrete Methods, 4, no. 3, 312–316, 1983.

[GKNV93]   E. R. Gansner, E. Koutsofios, S. C. North and K. P. Vo, *A Technique for Drawing Directed Graphs*, IEEE Trans. Softw. Eng., 19, 214–230, 1993.

[GM89]   D. J. Gschwind and T. P. Murtagh, *A Recursive Algorithm for Drawing Hierarchical Directed Graphs*, Technical Report CS-89-02, Department of Computer Science, Williams College, 1989.

[GNV88]   E. R. Gansner, S. C. North and K. P. Vo, *DAG – A Program that Draws Directed Graphs*, Softw. – Pract. Exp., 18, no. 11, 1047–1062, 1988.

[Gol63]   A. J. Goldstein, *An efficient and constructive algorithm for testing whether a graph can be embedded in the plane*, In Graph and Combinatorics Conf., 1963.

[Gre89]   A. Gregori, *Unit Length Embedding of Binary Trees on a Square Grid*, Inform. Process. Lett., 31, 167–172, 1989.

[GT87]   J. L. Gross and T. W. Tucker, *Topological Graph Theory*. John Wiley & Sons, 1987.

[GT93]   A. Garg and R. Tamassia, *Efficient Computation of Planar Straight-Line Upward Drawings*, In Graph Drawing '93 (Proc. ALCOM Workshop on Graph Drawing), 1993.

[GT94]   A. Garg and R. Tamassia, *Planar Drawings and Angular Resolution: Algorithms and Bounds*, In Proc. 2nd Annu. European Sympos. Algorithms, vol. 855 of *Lecture Notes Comput. Sci.*, pp. 12–23. Springer-Verlag, 1994.

[GT95]   A. Garg and R. Tamassia, *On the Computational Complexity of Upward and Rectilinear Planarity Testing*, In R. Tamassia and I. G. Tollis, editors, Graph Drawing (Proc. GD '94), vol. 894 of *Lecture Notes Comput. Sci.*, pp. 286–297. Springer-Verlag, 1995.

[GT97a]   A. Garg and R. Tamassia, *GIOTTO3D: A System for Visualizing Hierarchical Structures in 3D*, In S. North, editor, Graph Drawing (Proc. GD '96), Lecture Notes Comput. Sci. Springer-Verlag, 1997, to appear.

[GT97b]   A. Garg and R. Tamassia, *A New Minimum Cost Flow Algorithm with Applications to Graph Drawing*, In S. C. North, editor, Graph Drawing (Proc. GD '96), Lecture Notes Comput. Sci. Springer-Verlag, 1997.

[GT98]   M. T. Goodrich and R. Tamassia, *Data Structures and Algorithms in Java*. Wiley, 1998.

[GTV96] A. Garg, R. Tamassia and P. Vocca, *Drawing with Colors*, In Proc. 4th Annu. European Sympos. Algorithms, vol. 1136 of *Lecture Notes Comput. Sci.*, pp. 12–26. Springer-Verlag, 1996.

[Har72] F. Harary, *Graph Theory*. Addison-Wesley, Reading, MA, 1972.

[Him95a] M. Himsolt, *Comparing and Evaluating Layout Algorithms within GraphEd*, J. Visual Lang. Comput., 6, no. 3, 255–273, 1995, (special issue on Graph Visualization, edited by I. F. Cruz and P. Eades).

[Him95b] M. Himsolt, *GraphEd: a Graphical Platform for the Implementation of Graph Algorithms*, In R. Tamassia and I. G. Tollis, editors, Graph Drawing (Proc. GD '94), vol. 894 of *Lecture Notes Comput. Sci.*, pp. 182–193. Springer-Verlag, 1995.

[HL96] M. D. Hutton and A. Lubiw, *Upward Planar Drawing of Single-Source Acyclic Digraphs*, SIAM J. Comput., 25, no. 2, 291–311, 1996.

[HM97] W. He and K. Marriott, *Constrained Graph Layout*, In S. North, editor, Graph Drawing (Proc. GD '96), vol. 1190 of *Lecture Notes Comput. Sci.*, pp. 217–232. Springer-Verlag, 1997.

[HR94] S. M. Hashemi and I. Rival, *Upward Drawings to Fit Surfaces*, In Proc. Workshop on Orders, Algorithms and Applications, vol. 831 of *Lecture Notes Comput. Sci.*, pp. 53–58. Springer-Verlag, 1994.

[HS95] D. Harel and M. Sardas, *Randomized Graph Drawing with Heavy-Duty Preprocessing*, J. Visual Lang. Comput., 6, no. 3, 1995, (special issue on Graph Visualization, edited by I. F. Cruz and P. Eades).

[HT73] J. Hopcroft and R. E. Tarjan, *Dividing a Graph into Triconnected Components*, SIAM J. Comput., 2, 135–158, 1973.

[HT74] J. Hopcroft and R. E. Tarjan, *Efficient Planarity Testing*, J. ACM, 21, no. 4, 549–568, 1974.

[Idi90] P. J. Idicula, *Drawing Trees in Grids*, Master's thesis, Department of Computer Science, University of Auckland, 1990.

[JEM+91]   S. Jones, P. Eades, A. Moran, N. Ward, G. Delott and R. Tamassia, *A Note on Planar Graph Drawing Algorithms*, Technical Report 216, Department of Computer Science, University of Queensland, 1991.

[JJ95]   T. Jéron and C. Jard, *3D Layout of Reachability Graphs of Communicating Processes*, In R. Tamassia and I. G. Tollis, editors, Graph Drawing (Proc. GD '94), vol. 894 of *Lecture Notes Comput. Sci.*, pp. 25–32. Springer-Verlag, 1995.

[JLM97]   M. Jünger, S. Leipert and P. Mutzel, *Pitfalls of using PQ-trees in automatic graph drawing*, In G. Di Battista, editor, Graph Drawing (Proc. GD '97), vol. 1353 of *Lecture Notes in Computer Science*, pp. 193–204. Springer-Verlag, 1997.

[JM96]   M. Jünger and P. Mutzel, *Maximum Planar Subgraphs and Nice Embeddings: Practical Layout Tools*, Algorithmica, 16, 33–59, 1996, (special issue on Graph Drawing, edited by G. Di Battista and R. Tamassia).

[JM97]   M. Jünger and P. Mutzel, *2-Layer Straightline Crossing Minimization: Performance of Exact and Heuristic Algorithms*, Journal of Graph Algorithms and Applications, 1, no. 1, 1–25, 1997.

[JTS86]   R. Jayakumar, K. Thulasiraman and M. N. S. Swamy, *An Optimal Algorithm for Maximal Planarization of Nonplanar Graphs*, In Proc. IEEE Internat. Sympos. on Circuits and Systems, pp. 1237–1240, 1986.

[JTS89]   R. Jayakumar, K. Thulasiraman and M. N. S. Swamy, $O(n^2)$ *Algorithms for Graph Planarization*, IEEE Trans. Comp.-Aided Design, 8, 257–267, 1989.

[Kam88]   T. Kamada, *On Visualization of Abstract Objects and Relations*, PhD thesis, Department of Information Science, University of Tokyo, 1988.

[Kam89a]   T. Kamada, *Symmetric Graph Drawing by a Spring Algorithm and its Applications to Radial Drawing*, Technical report, Department of Information Science, University of Tokyo, 1989.

[Kam89b]   T. Kamada, *Visualizing Abstract Objects and Relations*. World Scientific Series in Computer Science, 1989.

[Kan92a]   G. Kant, *Hexagonal grid drawings*, In Proc. 18th Internat. Workshop Graph-Theoret. Concepts Comput. Sci., 1992.

[Kan92b]   G. Kant, *An $O(n^2)$ Maximal Planarization Algorithm based on PQ-trees*, Technical Report RUU-CS-92-03, Dept. Comput. Sci., Utrecht Univ., Utrecht, Netherlands, 1992.

[Kan93]   G. Kant, *A More Compact Visibility Representation*, In Proc. 19th Internat. Workshop Graph-Theoret. Concepts Comput. Sci., 1993.

[Kan96]   G. Kant, *Drawing Planar Graphs Using the Canonical Ordering*, Algorithmica, 16, 4–32, 1996, (special issue on Graph Drawing, edited by G. Di Battista and R. Tamassia).

[KB91]   G. Kant and H. L. Bodlaender, *Planar Graph Augmentation Problems*, In Proc. 2nd Workshop Algorithms Data Struct., vol. 519 of *Lecture Notes Comput. Sci.*, pp. 286–298. Springer-Verlag, 1991.

[KB92]   G. Kant and H. L. Bodlaender, *Triangulating planar graphs while minimizing the maximum degree*, In Proc. 3rd Scand. Workshop Algorithm Theory, vol. 621 of *Lecture Notes Comput. Sci.*, pp. 258–271. Springer-Verlag, 1992.

[KBM94]   D. Krackhardt, J. Blythe and C. McGrath, *KrackPlot 3.0: An Improved Network Drawing Program*, Connections, 17, no. 2, 53 – 55, 1994.

[Kel87]   D. Kelly, *Fundamentals of Planar Ordered Sets*, Discrete Math., 63, 197–216, 1987.

[Kim95]   S. K. Kim, *Simple Algorithms for Orthogonal Upward Drawings of Binary and Ternary Trees*, In Proc. 7th Canad. Conf. Comput. Geom., pp. 115–120, 1995.

[Kim96]   S. K. Kim, *H-V Drawings of Binary Trees*, In Software Visualisation, vol. 7 of *Software Engineering and Knowledge Engineering*, pp. 101 – 116. 1996.

[KK89]   T. Kamada and S. Kawai, *An Algorithm for Drawing General Undirected Graphs*, Inform. Process. Lett., 31, 7–15, 1989.

[KKR96]   T. Kamps, J. Kleinz and J. Read, *Constraint-Based Spring-Model Algorithm for Graph Layout*, In F. J. Brandenburg, editor, Graph Drawing (Proc. GD '95), vol. 1027 of *Lecture Notes Comput. Sci.*, pp. 349–360. Springer-Verlag, 1996.

[KM91]   C. Kosak and J. Marks, *A Parallel Genetic Algorithm for Network-Diagram Layout*, In Proc. 4th Internat. Conf. on Genetic Algorithms, 1991.

[KM94]   J. Kratochvíl and J. Matoušek, *Intersection graphs of segments*, J. Combin. Theory Ser. B, 35, no. 2, 317–339, 1994.

[KMS94]   C. Kosak, J. Marks and S. Shieber, *Automating the Layout of Network Diagrams with Specified Visual Organization*, IEEE Trans. Syst. Man Cybern., 24, no. 3, 440–454, 1994.

[KN95]   E. Koutsofios and S. North, *Drawing Graphs with* dot, Technical report, AT&T Bell Laboratories, Murray Hill, NJ., 1995, Available from `http://www.research.bell-labs.com/dist/drawdag`.

[Knu63]   D. E. Knuth, *Computer Drawn Flowcharts*, Commun. ACM, 6, 1963.

[KPTV97]   G. Károlyi, J. Pach, G. Tóth and P. Valtr, *Ramsey-Type Theorems for Geometric Graphs*, In Proc. 13th Annu. ACM Sympos. Comput. Geom., pp. 94–103, 1997.

[KR75]   D. Kelly and I. Rival, *Planar Lattices*, Canad. J. Math., 27, no. 3, 636–665, 1975.

[Kra98]   D. Krackhardt, *KrackPlot: a social network visualization program*, 1998.

[KRRS94]   P. N. Klein, S. Rao, M. Rauch and S. Subramanian, *Faster shortest-path algorithms for planar graphs*, In Proc. ACM Symp. on Theory of Computing, 1994.

[KS80]   J. B. Kruskal and J. B. Seery, *Designing Network Diagrams*, In Proc. First General Conference on Social Graphics, pp. 22–50. U. S. Department of the Census, 1980.

[KT97]   K. G. Kakoulis and I. G. Tollis, *An algorithm for labeling edges of hierarchical drawings*, In G. DiBattista, editor, Graph Drawing 97, vol. 1353 of *Lecture Notes in Computer Science*, pp. 169–180. Springer-Verlag, 1997.

[KT98]   K. G. Kakoulis and I. G. Tollis, *A unified approach to labeling graphical features*, In Proc. 14th Annu. ACM Sympos. Comput. Geom., 1998.

[KvL85]   M. R. Kramer and J. van Leeuwen, *The Complexity of Wire-Routing and Finding Minimum Area Layouts for Arbitrary VLSI Circuits*, In F. P. Preparata, editor, Adv. Comput. Res., vol. 2, pp. 129–146. JAI Press, Greenwich, Conn., 1985.

[KW89]   D. G. Kirkpatrick and S. K. Wismath, *Weighted visibility graphs of bars and related flow problems*, In Proc. 1st Workshop Algorithms Data Struct., vol. 382 of *Lecture Notes Comput. Sci.*, pp. 325–334. Springer-Verlag, 1989.

[La 94]   J. A. La Poutré, *Alpha-algorithms for incremental planarity testing*, In Proc. 26th Annu. ACM Sympos. Theory Comput., pp. 706–715, 1994.

[LD95]   G. Liotta and G. Di Battista, *Computing Proximity Drawings of Trees in the 3-Dimensional Space*, In Proc. 4th Workshop Algorithms Data Struct., vol. 955 of *Lecture Notes Comput. Sci.*, pp. 239–250. Springer-Verlag, 1995.

[LE95]   T. Lin and P. Eades, *Integration of Declarative and Algorithmic Approaches for Layout Creation*, In R. Tamassia and I. G. Tollis, editors, Graph Drawing (Proc. GD '94), vol. 894 of *Lecture Notes Comput. Sci.*, pp. 376–387. Springer-Verlag, 1995.

[LE97]   X. Lin and P. Eades, *Area Requirements for Drawing Hierarchically Planar Graphs*, In G. Di Battista, editor, Graph Drawing (Proc. GD '97), Lecture Notes in Computer Science. Springer-Verlag, 1997.

[LEC67]   A. Lempel, S. Even and I. Cederbaum, *An Algorithm for Planarity Testing of Graphs*, In Theory of Graphs: Internat. Symposium (Rome 1966), pp. 215–232, New York, 1967. Gordon and Breach.

[Lei80]   C. E. Leiserson, *Area-efficient graph layouts (for VLSI)*, In Proc. 21st Annu. IEEE Sympos. Found. Comput. Sci., pp. 270–281, 1980.

[Lei84]   F. T. Leighton, *New lower bound techniques for VLSI*, Math. Syst. Theory, 17, 47–70, 1984.

[LES95]   P. Luders, R. Ernst and S. Stille, *An approach to automatic display layout using combinatorial optimization*, Software-Practice and Experience, 25, no. 11, 1183–1202, 1995.

[Lin92]   X. Lin, *Analysis of Algorithms for Drawing Graphs*, PhD thesis, Department of Computer Science, University of Queensland, 1992.

[LL97]   W. Lenhart and G. Liotta, *Proximity Drawings of Outerplanar Graphs*, In S. North, editor, Graph Drawing (Proc. GD '96), vol. 1190 of *Lecture Notes Comput. Sci.*, pp. 286–302. Springer-Verlag, 1997.

[LMPS90] Y. Liu, P. Marchioro, R. Petreschi and B. Simeone, *Theoretical Results on at Most 1-Bend Embeddability of Graphs*, Technical report, Dipartimento di Statistica, Univ. di Roma "La Sapienza", 1990.

[LMS91]   Y. Liu, A. Morgana and B. Simeone, *General Theoretical Results on Rectilinear Embeddability of Graphs*, Acta Math. Appl. Sinica, 7, 187–192, 1991.

[LMW87]   F. Luccio, S. Mazzone and C. Wong, *A Note on Visibility Graphs*, Discrete Math., 64, 209–219, 1987.

[LNS85]   R. J. Lipton, S. C. North and J. S. Sandberg, *A method for drawing graphs*, In Proc. 1st Annu. ACM Sympos. Comput. Geom., pp. 153–160, 1985.

[LRT79]   R. J. Lipton, D. J. Rose and R. E. Tarjan, *Generalized nested dissection*, SIAM J. Numer. Anal., 16, no. 2, 346–358, 1979.

[LS77]   S. Lam and R. Sethi, *Worst case analysis of two scheduling algorithms*, SIAM Journal on Computing, 6, no. 3, 518, Sept. 1977.

[LT80]   R. J. Lipton and R. E. Tarjan, *Applications of a planar separator theorem*, SIAM J. Comput., 9, 615–627, 1980.

[LTTV97]   G. Liotta, R. Tamassia, I. G. Tollis and P. Vocca, *Area Requirement of Gabriel Drawings*, In Algorithms and Complexity (Proc. CIAC' 97), vol. 1203 of *Lecture Notes Comput. Sci.*, pp. 135–146. Springer-Verlag, 1997.

[LW88]   N. L. L. Lovasz and A. Wigderson, *Rubber Bands, Convex Embeddings and Graph Connectivity*, Combinatorica, 8, 91–102, 1988.

[MA88]   J. Manning and M. J. Atallah, *Fast Detection and Display of Symmetry in Trees*, Congr. Numer., 64, 159–169, 1988.

[MA92]   J. Manning and M. J. Atallah, *Fast Detection and Display of Symmetry in Outerplanar Graphs*, Discrete Applied Mathematics, 39, 13–35, 1992.

[MAC⁺95]   J. Manning, M. Atallah, K. Cudjoe, J. Lozito and R. Pacheco, *A System for Drawing Graphs with Geometric Symmetry*, In R. Tamassia and I. G. Tollis, editors, Graph Drawing (Proc. GD '94), vol. 894 of *Lecture Notes Comput. Sci.*, pp. 262–265. Springer-Verlag, 1995.

[Mak88a]   E. Makinen, *Experiments of Drawing 2-Level Hierarchical Graphs*, Technical Report A-1988-1, Department of Computer Science, University of Tampere, Jan. 1988.

[Mak88b]   E. Makinen, *A Note on the Median Heuristic for Drawing Bipartite Graphs*, Technical Report A-1988-4, Department of Computer Science, University of Tampere, May 1988.

[Man91]   J. Manning, *Computational Complexity of Geometric Symmetry Detection in Graphs*, In Computing in the 90s, vol. 507 of *Lecture Notes Comput. Sci.*, pp. 1–7. Springer-Verlag, 1991.

[Mar91]   J. Marks, *A formal specification for network diagrams that facilitates automated design*, J. Visual Lang. Comput., 2, 395–414, 1991.

[MdNdS96]   C. F. X. Mendonca, H. A. D. do Nascimiento and P. S. de Souza, *An Asyncronous Team to Draw Directed Graphs*, Manuscript, University of Campinas, 1996.

[Meh84]   K. Mehlhorn, *Data Structures and Algorithms*. Springer-Verlag, 1984, Volumes 1–3.

[MELS95]   K. Misue, P. Eades, W. Lai and K. Sugiyama, *Layout Adjustment and the Mental Map*, J. Visual Lang. Comput., 6, no. 2, 183–210, 1995.

[Men92]   X. Mendonca, *Heuristics for Planarization by Vertex Splitting*, 1992.

[Men94]   X. Mendonca, *A System for Drawing Conceptual Scheme Diagrams*, PhD thesis, University of Queensland, 1994.

[Mes88]   E. B. Messinger, *Automatic Layout of Large Directed Graphs*, Technical Report 88-07-08, Department of Computer Science, University of Washington, 1988.

[MHT93]   K. Miriyala, S. W. Hornick and R. Tamassia, *An Incremental Approach to Aesthetic Graph Layout*, In Proc. Internat. Workshop on Computer-Aided Software Engineering, 1993.

[MM96]   K. Mehlhorn and P. Mutzel, *On the Embedding Phase of the Hopcroft and Tarjan Planarity Testing Algorithm*, Algorithmica, 16, 233–242, 1996.

[MNKF90]   S. Masuda, K. Nakajima, T. Kashiwabara and T. Fujisawa, *Crossing Minimization in Linear Embeddings of Graphs*, IEEE Transactions on Computers, 39, no. 1, 124 – 127, 1990.

[Moe90]   S. Moen, *Drawing Dynamic Trees*, IEEE Software, 7, 21–8, 1990.

[Moh93]   B. Mohar, *A polynomial time circle packing algorithm*, Discrete Math., 117, 257–263, 1993.

[MP94]   S. Malitz and A. Papakostas, *On the Angular Resolution of Planar Graphs*, SIAM J. Discrete Math., 7, 172–183, 1994.

[MR95]   B. Mohar and P. Rosenstiehl, *A Flow Approach to Upward Drawings of Toroidal Maps*, In R. Tamassia and I. G. Tollis, editors, Graph Drawing (Proc. GD '94), vol. 894 of *Lecture Notes Comput. Sci.*, pp. 33–39. Springer-Verlag, 1995.

[MRH91]   E. B. Messinger, L. A. Rowe and R. H. Henry, *A Divide-and-Conquer Algorithm for the Automatic Layout of Large Directed Graphs*, IEEE Trans. Syst. Man Cybern., SMC-21, no. 1, 1–12, 1991.

[MRS96]   B. Monien, F. Ramme and H. Salmen, *A Parallel Simulated Annealing Algorithm for Generating 3D Layouts of Undirected Graphs*, In F. J. Brandenburg, editor, Graph Drawing (Proc. GD '95), vol. 1027 of *Lecture Notes Comput. Sci.*, pp. 396–408. Springer-Verlag, 1996.

[MS78]   M. Marek-Sadowska, *Planarization Algorithms for Integrated Circuits Engineering*, In Proc. IEEE Internat. Sympos. on Circuits and Systems, pp. 919–923, 1978.

[MSG95]   C. McCreary, F.-S. Shieh and H. Gill, *CG: a Graph Drawing System Using Graph-Grammar Parsing*, In R. Tamassia and I. G. Tollis, editors, Graph Drawing (Proc. GD '94), vol. 894 of *Lecture Notes Comput. Sci.*, pp. 270–273. Springer-Verlag, 1995.

[NC88]   T. Nishizeki and N. Chiba, *Planar Graphs: Theory and Algorithms*, Ann. Discrete Math., 32, 1988.

[Nor96]   S. North, *Incremental Layout in DynaDAG*, In F. J. Brandenburg, editor, Graph Drawing (Proc. GD '95), vol. 1027 of *Lecture Notes Comput. Sci.*, pp. 409–418. Springer-Verlag, 1996.

[NT84]   E. Nardelli and M. Talamo, *A Fast Algorithm for Planarization of Sparse Diagrams*, Technical Report R.105, IASI-CNR, Rome, 1984.

[Ost96]   D. Ostry, *Drawing Graphs on Convex Surfaces*, Master's thesis, Dept. of Computer Science, University of Newcastle, 1996.

[OT81]   T. Ozawa and H. Takahashi, *A Graph-planarization Algorithm and its Applications to Random Graphs*, In Graph Theory and Algorithms, vol. 108 of *Lecture Notes Comput. Sci.*, pp. 95–107. Springer-Verlag, Berlin, Germany, 1981.

[OvW78]   R. H. J. M. Otten and J. G. van Wijk, *Graph Representations in Interactive Layout Design*, In Proc. IEEE Internat. Sympos. on Circuits and Systems, pp. 914–918, 1978.

[Pap95]   A. Papakostas, *Upward Planarity Testing of Outerplanar Dags*, In R. Tamassia and I. G. Tollis, editors, Graph Drawing (Proc. GD '94), vol. 894 of *Lecture Notes Comput. Sci.*, pp. 298–306. Springer-Verlag, 1995.

[Pap96]   A. Papakostas, *Information Visualization: Orthogonal Drawings of Graphs*, PhD thesis, Department of Computer Science, University of Texas at Dallas, November 1996.

[PCJ96]   H. C. Purchase, R. F. Cohen and M. James, *Validating Graph Drawing Aesthetics*, In F. J. Brandenburg, editor, Graph Drawing (Proc. GD '95), vol. 1027 of *Lecture Notes Comput. Sci.*, pp. 435–446. Springer-Verlag, 1996.

[Pla76]   C. Platt, *Planar Lattices and Planar Graphs*, J. Combin. Theory Ser. B, 21, 30–39, 1976.

[PS85]   F. P. Preparata and M. I. Shamos, *Computational Geometry: An Introduction*. Springer-Verlag, New York, NY, 1985.

[PSS96]   J. Pach, F. Shahrokhi and M. Szegedy, *Applications of the Crossing Number*, Algorithmica, 16, 111–117, 1996, (special issue on Graph Drawing, edited by G. Di Battista and R. Tamassia).

[PST97]   A. Papakostas, J. M. Six and I. G. Tollis, *Experimental and Theoretical Results in Interactive Graph Drawing*, In S. North, editor, Graph Drawing (Proc. GD '96), vol. 1190 of *Lecture Notes Comput. Sci.*, pp. 371–386. Springer-Verlag, 1997.

[PT]   A. Papakostas and I. G. Tollis, *Interactive Orthogonal Graph Drawing*, IEEE Trans. Computers, To appear.

[PT90]   F. N. Paulish and W. F. Tichy, *EDGE: An Extendible Graph Editor*, Softw. – Pract. Exp., 20, no. S1, 1/63–S1/88, 1990, also as Technical Report 8/88, Fakultat fur Informatik, Univ. of Karlsruhe, 1988.

[PT95]   A. Papakostas and I. G. Tollis, *Improved Algorithms and Bounds for Orthogonal Drawings*, In R. Tamassia and I. G. Tollis, editors, Graph Drawing (Proc. GD '94), vol. 894 of *Lecture Notes Comput. Sci.*, pp. 40–51. Springer-Verlag, 1995.

[PT96]   A. Papakostas and I. G. Tollis, *Issues in Interactive Orthogonal Graph Drawing*, In F. J. Brandenburg, editor, Graph Drawing (Proc. GD '95), vol. 1027 of *Lecture Notes in Computer Science*, pp. 419–430. Springer-Verlag, 1996.

[PT97a]   A. Papakostas and I. G. Tollis, *Incremental Orthogonal Graph Drawing in Three Dimensions*, In G. Di Battista, editor, Graph Drawing (Proc. GD '97), vol. 1353 of *Lecture Notes in Computer Science*, pp. 52–63. Springer-Verlag, 1997.

[PT97b]   A. Papakostas and I. G. Tollis, *Orthogonal Drawing of High Degree Graphs with Small Area and Few Bends*, In Proc. WADS '97, vol. 1272 of *Lecture Notes in Computer Science*, pp. 354–367. Springer-Verlag, 1997.

[PT97c]   A. Papakostas and I. G. Tollis, *A Pairing Technique for Area-Efficient Orthogonal Drawings*, In S. North, editor, Graph Drawing (Proc. GD '96), vol. 1190 of *Lecture Notes in Computer Science*, pp. 354–370. Springer-Verlag, 1997.

[PT98]   A. Papakostas and I. G. Tollis, *Algorithms for area-efficient orthogonal drawings*, Comput. Geom. Theory Appl., 9, no. 1 – 2, 83 – 110, 1998.

[Pur97]   H. Purchase, *Which aesthetic has greatest effect on human understanding*, In G. DiBattista, editor, Graph Drawing 97, vol. 1353 of *Lecture Notes in Computer Science*, pp. 248 – 259. Springer-Verlag, 1997.

[PV97]   M. Patrignani and F. Vargiu, *3DCube: a tool for three dimensional graph drawing*, In G. DiBattista, editor, Graph Drawing 97, vol. 1353 of *Lecture Notes in Computer Science*, pp. 284 – 290. Springer-Verlag, 1997.

[PY91]   C. Papadimitriou and M. Yannakakis, *Optimization, Approximization and Complexity Classes*, Journal of Computer and System Sciences, 43, 425–440, 1991.

[QB79]   N. R. Quinn, Jr. and M. A. Breuer, *A forced directed component placement procedure for printed circuit boards*, IEEE Transactions on Circuits and Systems, CAS-26, no. 6, 377–388, 1979.

[Rei95]   S. P. Reiss, *An Engine for the 3D Visualization of Program Information*, J. Visual Lang. Comput., 6, no. 3, 1995, (special issue on Graph Visualization, edited by I. F. Cruz and P. Eades).

[Riv93]   I. Rival, *Reading, Drawing, and Order*, In I. G. Rosenberg and G. Sabidussi, editors, Algebras and Orders, pp. 359–404. Kluwer Academic Publishers, 1993.

[RMC91]   G. G. Robertson, J. D. Mackinlay and S. K. Card, *Cone Trees: Animated 3D Visualizations of Hierarchical Information*, In Proc. ACM Conf. on Human Factors in Computing Systems, pp. 189–193, 1991.

[RMS97]   K. Ryall, J. Marks and S. Shieber, *An Interactive System for Drawing Graphs*, In S. North, editor, Graph Drawing (Proc. GD '96), vol. 1190 of *Lecture Notes Comput. Sci.*, pp. 387–393. Springer-Verlag, 1997.

[Ros97]   A. Rosete, *Drawing Graphs using Genetic Algorithms*, Manuscript, 1997.

[RT81]   E. Reingold and J. Tilford, *Tidier Drawing of Trees*, IEEE Trans. Softw. Eng., SE-7, no. 2, 223–228, 1981.

[RT86]   P. Rosenstiehl and R. E. Tarjan, *Rectilinear Planar Layouts and Bipolar Orientations of Planar Graphs*, Discrete Comput. Geom., 1, no. 4, 343–353, 1986.

[San95]   G. Sander, *Graph Layout through the VCG Tool*, In R. Tamassia and I. G. Tollis, editors, Graph Drawing (Proc. GD '94), vol. 894 of *Lecture Notes Comput. Sci.*, pp. 194–205. Springer-Verlag, 1995.

[Sch90]   W. Schnyder, *Embedding Planar Graphs on the Grid*, In Proc. 1st ACM-SIAM Sympos. Discrete Algorithms, pp. 138–148, 1990.

[Sch95]   M. Schäffter, *Drawing graphs on rectangular grids*, Discrete Appl. Math., 63, 75–89, 1995.

[Shi69]   R. W. Shirey, *Implementation and Analysis of Efficient Graph Planarity Testing Algorithms*, PhD thesis, Univ. of Wisconsin, Madison, 1969.

[Shi76]   Y. Shiloach, *Arrangements of Planar Graphs on the Planar Lat-
            tice*, PhD thesis, Weizmann Institute of Science, 1976.

[SKC96]   C.-S. Shin, S. K. Kim and K.-Y. Chwa, *Area-Efficient Algo-
            rithms for Upward Straight-Line Tree Drawings*, In Proc. 2nd
            International Computing and Combinatorics: COCOON'96,
            vol. 1090 of *Lecture Notes Comput. Sci.*, pp. 106–116. Springer-
            Verlag, 1996.

[SLM+84]   M. Schlag, F. Luccio, P. Maestrini, D. T. Lee and C. K.
            Wong, *A visibility problem in VLSI layout compaction*, In F. P.
            Preparata, editor, VLSI Theory, vol. 2 of *Adv. Comput. Res.*,
            pp. 259–282. JAI Press, London, England, 1984.

[SM95a]   K. Sugiyama and K. Misue, *Graph Drawing by Magnetic-Spring
            Model*, J. Visual Lang. Comput., 6, no. 3, 1995, (special issue
            on Graph Visualization, edited by I. F. Cruz and P. Eades).

[SM95b]   K. Sugiyama and K. Misue, *A Simple and Unified Method for
            Drawing Graphs: Magnetic-Spring Algorithm*, In R. Tamas-
            sia and I. G. Tollis, editors, Graph Drawing (Proc. GD '94),
            vol. 894 of *Lecture Notes Comput. Sci.*, pp. 364–375. Springer-
            Verlag, 1995.

[SR34]   E. Steinitz and H. Rademacher, *Vorlesungen über die Theorie
            der Polyeder*. Julius Springer, Berlin, Germany, 1934.

[SR83]   K. J. Supowit and E. M. Reingold, *The Complexity of Drawing
            Trees Nicely*, Acta Inform., 18, 377–392, 1983.

[SSV95]   F. Shahrokhi, L. A. Székely and I. Vrt'o, *Crossing Numbers of
            Graphs, Lower Bound Techniques and Algorithms: a Survey*,
            In R. Tamassia and I. G. Tollis, editors, Graph Drawing (Proc.
            GD '94), vol. 894 of *Lecture Notes Comput. Sci.*, pp. 131–142.
            Springer-Verlag, 1995.

[Ste51]   S. K. Stein, *Convex Maps*, Proc. Amer. Math. Soc., 2, 464–466,
            1951.

[Sto84]   J. A. Storer, *On minimal node-cost planar embeddings*, Net-
            works, 14, 181–212, 1984.

[STT81]   K. Sugiyama, S. Tagawa and M. Toda, *Methods for Visual Understanding of Hierarchical Systems*, IEEE Trans. Syst. Man Cybern., SMC-11, no. 2, 109–125, 1981.

[Tam85]   R. Tamassia, *New Layout Techniques for Entity-Relationship Diagrams*, In Proc. 4th Internat. Conf. on Entity-Relationship Approach, pp. 304–311, 1985.

[Tam87]   R. Tamassia, *On Embedding a Graph in the Grid with the Minimum Number of Bends*, SIAM J. Comput., 16, no. 3, 421–444, 1987.

[Tar83]   R. E. Tarjan, *Data Structures and Network Algorithms*, vol. 44 of *CBMS-NSF Regional Conference Series in Applied Mathematics*. Society for Industrial Applied Mathematics, 1983.

[TDB88]   R. Tamassia, G. Di Battista and C. Batini, *Automatic Graph Drawing and Readability of Diagrams*, IEEE Trans. Syst. Man Cybern., SMC-18, no. 1, 61–79, 1988.

[Tho84]   C. Thomassen, *Plane Representations of Graphs*, In J. A. Bondy and U. S. R. Murty, editors, Progress in Graph Theory, pp. 43–69. Academic Press, New York, NY, 1984.

[Tho89]   C. Thomassen, *Planar Acyclic Oriented Graphs*, Order, 5, no. 4, 349–361, 1989.

[Til81]   J. S. Tilford, *Tree Drawing Algorithms*, Technical Report UIUCDCS-R-81-1055, Department of Computer Science, University of Illinois at Urbana-Champaign, 1981.

[TP90]   R. Tamassia and F. P. Preparata, *Dynamic maintenance of planar digraphs, with applications*, Algorithmica, 5, 509–527, 1990.

[Tre96]   L. Trevisan, *A note on minimum-area upward drawing of complete and Fibonacci trees*, Inform. Process. Lett., 57, no. 5, 231–236, 1996.

[TT86]   R. Tamassia and I. G. Tollis, *A Unified Approach to Visibility Representations of Planar Graphs*, Discrete Comput. Geom., 1, no. 4, 321–341, 1986.

[TT87]   R. Tamassia and I. G. Tollis, *Efficient Embedding of Planar Graphs in Linear Time*, In Proc. IEEE Internat. Sympos. on Circuits and Systems, pp. 495–498, 1987.

[TT89a]   R. Tamassia and I. G. Tollis, *Planar Grid Embedding in Linear Time*, IEEE Trans. Circuits Syst., CAS-36, no. 9, 1230–1234, 1989.

[TT89b]   R. Tamassia and I. G. Tollis, *Tessellation Representations of Planar Graphs*, In Proc. 27th Allerton Conf. Commun. Control Comput., pp. 48–57, 1989.

[TT91]   R. Tamassia and I. G. Tollis, *Representations of Graphs on a Cylinder*, SIAM J. Discrete Math., 4, no. 1, 139–149, 1991.

[TTV91a]   R. Tamassia, I. G. Tollis and J. S. Vitter, *Lower Bounds and Parallel Algorithms for Planar Orthogonal Grid Drawings*, In Proc. IEEE Symposium on Parallel and Distributed Processing, pp. 386–393, 1991.

[TTV91b]   R. Tamassia, I. G. Tollis and J. S. Vitter, *Lower Bounds for Planar Orthogonal Drawings of Graphs*, Inform. Process. Lett., 39, 35–40, 1991.

[Tun92]   D. Tunkelang, *An Aesthetic Layout Algorithm for Undirected Graphs*, Master's thesis, MIT, 1992.

[Tut60]   W. T. Tutte, *Convex Representations of Graphs*, Proceedings London Mathematical Society, 10, no. 3, 304–320, 1960.

[Tut63]   W. T. Tutte, *How to Draw a Graph*, Proceedings London Mathematical Society, 13, no. 3, 743–768, 1963.

[Val81]   L. Valiant, *Universality Considerations in VLSI Circuits*, IEEE Trans. Comput., C-30, no. 2, 135–140, 1981.

[VTL82]   J. Valdes, R. E. Tarjan and E. L. Lawler, *The Recognition of Series-Parallel Digraphs*, SIAM J. Comput., 11, no. 2, 298–313, 1982.

[VW95]   F. Vogt and R. Wille, *TOSCANA — a Graphical Tool for Analyzing and Exploring Data*, In R. Tamassia and I. G. Tollis, editors, Graph Drawing (Proc. GD '94), vol. 894 of *Lecture Notes Comput. Sci.*, pp. 226–233. Springer-Verlag, 1995.

[Wag36] K. Wagner, *Bemerkungen zum Vierfarbenproblem*, Jahres-
bericht der Deutschen Mathematiker-Vereinigung, 46, 26–32,
1936.

[Wal90] J. Q. Walker II, *A Node-positioning Algorithm for General
Trees*, Softw. – Pract. Exp., 20, no. 7, 685–705, 1990.

[War77a] J. Warfield, *Crossing Theory and Hierarchy Mapping*, IEEE
Trans. Syst. Man Cybern., SMC-7, no. 7, 502–523, 1977.

[War77b] J. Warfield, *Crossing Theory and Hierarchy Mapping*, IEEE
Transactions on Systems, Man and Cybernetics, SMC-7, no. 7,
502–523, 1977.

[Wis85] S. K. Wismath, *Characterizing bar line-of-sight graphs*, In Proc.
1st Annu. ACM Sympos. Comput. Geom., pp. 147–152, 1985.

[YB61] I. M. Yaglom and V. G. Bolyanski, *Convex Figures*. English
Translation, Holt, Rinehart and Winston, New York, NY, 1961.

Index